Withdrawn

Second Edition

Instructor's Manual with Video Guide

Jane Boyd Thomas

Winthrop University

Marketing
Real People
Real Choices

Michael R. Solomon
Elnora W. Stuart

Prentice Hall
Upper Saddle River, NJ 07458

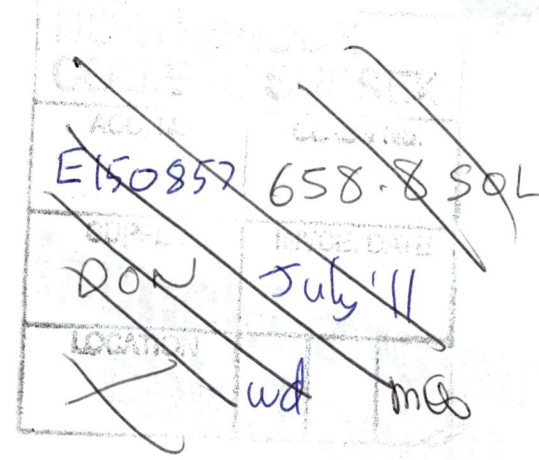
Acquisitions editor: *Leah Johnson*
Associate editor: *John Larkin*
Project editor: *Joseph F. Tomasso*
Manufacturer: *Technical Communication Services*
Formatter: *M&N Toscano*

©2000 by Prentice Hall, Inc.
Upper Saddle River, New Jersey 07458

Printed in the United States of America

10 9 8 7 6 5 4 3 2 1

ISBN 0-13-013610-7

Prentice-Hall International (UK) Limited, *London*
Prentice-Hall of Australia Pty. Limited, *Sydney*
Prentice-Hall Canada Inc., *Toronto*
Prentice-Hall Hispanoamericana, S.A., *Mexico*
Prentice-Hall of India Private Limited, *New Delhi*
Prentice-Hall of Japan, Inc., *Tokyo*
Prentice-Hall (Singapore) Pte Ltd
Editora Prentice-Hall do Brasil, L

Contents

PREFACE

Teaching a Principles of Marketing course should be an exciting teaching experience for the instructor and an exciting learning experience for the student. Each chapter outline contains a variety of items that are designed to enhance students' learning of marketing principles and to help create excitement in the classroom. Because so many suggested activities are provided for each chapter, instructors might want to read through each chapter outline and highlight the suggested items which they want to use. Below is a list of the items that are included for each chapter in the Instructor's Manual.

1. Chapter Overview
2. Chapter Objectives
3. Introduction activity and/or discussion
4. Discussion questions
5. References to all Tables and Figures in the textbook
6. A summary of each of the following segments:
   - Real People, Bad Choices?
   - Spotlight on Real People
   - Real People, Real Choices: How it worked out
7. Suggested placement for the following items:
   - Marketing in Action (end of chapter cases)
   - End of section cases
   - Marketing Practice: Applying What You've Learned
   - Marketing Mini-Project: Learning by Doing
   - Real People, Real Surfers: Exploring the Web
   - Video's
8. Complete answers for chapter review questions

Organization of the Instructors Manual

The major headings used in the Instructor's Manual are the same major headings that are used in the book. Every key term from the book is presented in the chapter outline along with the complete definition of the term. Key terms are printed in bold face type and the definition of the term is printed in italics.

Looking for an activity to use in class? Look for the asterisk. Asterisks are used to denote the suggested placement of all learning activities included in the textbook.

Need an idea to help encourage class discussion? Look for the boxes. Suggested class discussion questions are included in boxes.

Chapter Objectives

Learning objectives are provided for each chapter and the chapter outline denotes where each objective is covered. Instructors might want to try presenting these objectives at the beginning or at the end of each class and/or chapter. When used at the beginning of a lecture and/or chapter discussion, objectives provide students with an overview of the concepts that will be presented in the chapter. Another method is to use objectives at the end of a lecture and/or chapter. Chapter objectives used at the end of a chapter serve as review of the material and topics covered. You may also want to encourage students to refer to the chapter objectives when preparing for their tests.

Introduction Activity

Each chapter outline begins with a suggested introduction activity. The purpose of these activities is to provide students with an overview of the chapter or some important concept presented in the chapter. Instructors may want to modify these introduction activities as needed.

Real People, Bad Choices?

Each "Real People, Bad Choices?" segment presents an ethical situation faced by marketers. Suggested discussion questions and answers are provided for each segment. Instructors are encouraged to discuss some of these situations with students to help them see that often marketers have to make difficult choices.

Spotlight on Real People

This segment spotlights a real person within an organization and highlights some of the decisions made the individual and the organization. Many of the people highlighted are entrepreneurs.

Suggested discussion questions and answers are provided for each segment.

Real People, Real Choices: How It Worked Out

At the beginning of each chapter students are introduced to a marketing executive who had to make a decision. The options developed by the individual and the decisions made are summarized at the end of each chapter outline in the Instructor's Manual. Instructors are encouraged to discuss with students these *real people* and the *real choices* that they had to make.

Case Studies

There are two types of case studies included in the textbook: end of the chapter cases (referred to in the textbook as "Marketing in Action" and end of section cases. Suggested answers are provided in the Instructor's Manual for both types of cases.

All of the end of section cases focus on the company Computer Friendly Stuff (CFS). Instructors may want to use some or all of the cases from this series. The marketing plan for CFS is included in Appendix A of the textbook. Suggested discussion questions for the CFS cases and marketing plan are included in the chapter outline.

Marketing Practice: Applying What You've Learned

The "Marketing Practice: Applying What You've Learned" section is included in the textbook at the end of chapter under the heading Review Questions. These activities could be used to generate class discussion and/or as break out sessions in class. Suggested placement of where to use these activities is included in the Instructor's Manual. Instructors may want to try a variety of approaches for using these activities.

Marketing Mini-Projects: Learning By Doing

The philosophy behind the mini-projects is that students learn best through experiential exercises. Each chapter in the book contains one mini-project. At the end of each chapter in the Instructor's Manual two additional marketing mini-research projects are provided. Mini-projects are an excellent way to help students develop a better understanding of marketing principles and practices.

These projects can be used as individual, group, or in class assignments. Students should be encouraged to "think out of the box" when working on their assignment. Students can usually be very creative if challenged to go beyond the assignment. While each assignment contains a written exercise, an oral presentation for some, or all, of the exercises selected is suggested. Student presentation of these exercises provides an excellent opportunity for them to see marketing in action. Presentations also reinforce marketing principles and concepts which have been previously presented in class.

Before the semester begins, the instructor will probably want to read all of the assignments and select ones to be used during the course. Individual and/or group assignments will usually be made during the first few weeks of class. This will help to give the students time to properly complete their mini-project. The instructor may want to encourage use of the Internet, interviews with business managers, and primary research in completing these assignments. Instructors who are teaching in a multimedia classroom will usually want to encourage students to prepare presentations, which include a variety of media formats.

Real People Real Surfers: Exploring the Web

Each Internet exercise is tied to one or more of the major concepts presented in the chapter. Internet assignments provide another important learning activity for students. Most of these assignments work best when assigned as individual projects; however, there are a few exercises which could be used as a group assignment. Instructor's who are teaching in a multi-media classroom with Internet connections may want to use the Internet sites listed in these exercises as part of their lecture. Instructors may even wish to have students find a specific site in class and discuss their findings concerning this site. Once students have gained competence in using the Internet, they should be encouraged to use this information source for other marketing class assignments.

Videos

Each video segment depicts marketing decisions made by organizations. Interviews with executives and managers enhance the information contained in each video segment. Current information on these firms could be used to examine the outcomes of decisions made by the firms and/or new opportunities and threats facing these organizations. A grid indicating the recommended placement of these videos is provided in the manual.

Learning Through
Case Analysis

A case analysis method of study provides experiential education—learning by doing. Therefore, the amount of learning students receive from an individual case is directly related to the amount of work they put into it.

A major goal of the use of cases is to allow students to gain experience in problem solving (in marketing, in this case.) Cases help students learn to:

- develop an understanding of problems,
- learn how to dissect the various factors relevant to a problem,
- learn how to think creatively about solutions to a problem,
- learn to critically and thoroughly evaluate alternative solutions,
- learn how to make a final decision—one that you are willing to move forward with and one that you feel confident in supporting.

Through the use of cases, students learn that the most obvious solution is not always the best solution. The only way to discover a "best" solution is to consider all (the emphasis here is on the ALL) possible alternatives, to identify the potential positive and negative outcomes for all alternatives possible, and then to select what seems best. Students need to understand the basic factual and theoretical foundations for marketing management to make such decisions intelligently.

Students should understand from the outset that this outline for cases is one developed for this class. There are no universal rules for case analysis. Therefore, if students are in another case course, the format may be slightly different. No apologies. That's just the way life is.

Outline for Analysis of Cases

1. **Problem statement**
    This statement should state clearly, concisely—generally in one sentence—what problem is faced for which a solution/answer must be decided upon. It is not a discussion of all the ills of the world. After (or perhaps before) the problem is stated, you will probably wish to provide some explanatory material so your reader/listener will understand the causes, implications, etc., of the problem
    Note: a problem is *not* something that is "wrong;" it is a need. In most cases, your problem statement will be something like this:

    - "Mr. X needs to decide..."
    - "The marketing manager must develop...."
    - "XYZ Corporation has to determine..."

2. **Situation Analysis**
    (May include any or all of the following)
    a. Organizational assessment
        This section may include such items as
        - Mission of the organization
        - Present goals of the organization
        - Policies of the organization, i.e., marketing policies,
        - Financial policies, production/operations, research and development, human resources and organizational systems
    b. Internal environment assessment
        - Strengths or qualities of the organization
        - Weaknesses or problems of the organization

c.   External environmental assessment
- Competition/market conditions
- Economic/financial conditions
- Legal/political conditions
- Social/demographic conditions
- Technology/ research and development
- Constituencies/resources
- Opportunities
- Threats

3.   Alternatives

This section should list ALL possible alternative solutions to the problem and discuss the positive and negative outcomes for each. For example, one possible alternative for nearly every problem is to do nothing. What will happen if nothing is done? Will the company continue to face declining sales? Will a competitor or the government take legal action? Will the competition continue to erode our market share?

IMPORTANT NOTE: BE CREATIVE. BE CREATIVE. BE CREATIVE.

Try brainstorming with someone. Consider the alternatives, which appear a bit ridiculous. What would happen if you do that? I would much prefer our case discussions be filled with insane, laughable, incredible alternatives than with boring unimaginative ones. (This, of course, is not a license to ignore sensible alternatives.)

NOTE: YOU MUST INCLUDE EITHER IN THE ALTERNATIVES OR RECOMMENDATIONS SECTION OF THE CASE DISCUSSION A PRESENTATION OF QUANTITATIVE ANALYSES SUCH AS BREAK-EVEN WHEN APPROPRIATE.

4.   Recommendations

At this point you must make your decision–you are not allowed to sit on the fence (that is, if you want a positive evaluation by the instructor). You have to decide which of the alternatives you have considered you feel is best. And you must defend your decision.

In most cases, you should also discuss the specifics—strategies and action plans—for how the alternative plan will be implemented. This part of your case analysis will provide a rough but fairly complete blueprint of what the organization should do to solve the problem.

(As a check for yourself, go back and review your statement of the problem and your alternatives. Does this recommendation solve the problem as you stated it? Did you list this recommendation as one of your alternatives? If not, your statement of the problem, your alternatives section, or your recommendation needs more work.)

1

Welcome to the World of Marketing

*O*verview The primary goal of this first chapter is help dispel misconceptions that students have about what is marketing. Much time is devoted to helping the student understand what is marketing. In addition to providing the standard definition of marketing and the marketing concept, the terms and concepts which are used in these definitions are also examined. The evolution of the marketing concept and the role of marketing in society are also discussed. Levi Strauss is the focus of the real people, real choices segment.

Objectives

1.   Define the marketing concept.

2   Describe the marketing mix.

3.   Understand the basics of marketing planning.

4.   Describe the evolution of the marketing concept.

5.   Explain how marketing is important to both individual and business customers in the marketplace, in our daily lives, and in society.

6.   Explain marketing's role within an organization.

Chapter Outline and Suggested Activities

Introduction: The following exercise could be used at the beginning of class to help students understand what marketing is and the role that marketing activities have in their everyday life. Begin by asking students to answer a few questions about their activities for that day. For example, you might begin the discussion by asking students to think about their answers to the following questions:

- What did you have for breakfast and why did you eat that particular food? Or
- What brand(s) of bath soap or shampoo did you use this morning? And Why did you use that brand?

Student responses to these questions will of course vary, but if you probe and ask "why" did you eat Lucky Charms cereal or "why" did you use Dove body wash you will begin to find some aspects of the marketing concept and the marketing mix emerge.

Try to engage students in a discussion directed toward examining the 4 P's of the marketing mix. For example:

Product: Why do you eat Lucky Charms and not Special K? Try to probe and discuss the feature benefits of products and the use of brand names. You might want to also discuss the new cereal combos which are available from Kellogg where a milk box and cereal box are packaged together. You might also want to mention that some cereals, like Cheerio's for example, are now packaged in small single serving bags and are available at convenience stores. Discuss the importance of convenience and adapting packaging to meet the demands of a time pressured society.
Ask students if the product they mentioned satisfied a need or a want? See if students know the difference between a need and a want.

Place: Where did you buy the cereal? Discuss all of the possible places for purchasing cereal. Responses will probably be the grocery store or the store cafeteria, but be sure to discuss the importance of modifying where a product is sold and the channels of distribution used to deliver the product. Mention that groceries can even be purchased over the Internet and the role of the Internet in delivering goods.

Price: Was price a factor in your selection? For example did you buy a cereal that was on sale or that you had a coupon for? Price competition from private brands of cereal could also be explored.

Promotion: Ask students about any marketing messages they recall for the cereal. Discuss whether or not these messages had any impact on their selection and purchase of a cereal. Ask students if marketers create needs.

Ideally the above discussion will provide the class with an overview of marketing and the objectives for the first chapter.

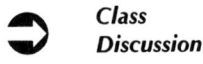

Class Discussion

Having completed the opening exercise, ask students to define marketing and then show them the definition of marketing and lead them through the terms found in the definition.

1. **What Is Marketing?**
Marketing: is the process of planning and executing the conception, pricing, promotion, and distribution of ideas, goods, and services to create exchanges that satisfy individual and organizational objectives.

Instructor's Resource Manual with Video Guide t/a Marketing: Real People, Real Choices 2/e

➥	*Class* *Discussion*	Refer students to the definition of marketing. Who are the individuals and organizations and what do they desire? Engage students in a discussion to examine who are the individuals and organizations referred to in the definition and what are their needs and wants.

a. Marketing Satisfies Needs

1). Marketing more than any other business function deals with people. The **consumer**, *the ultimate user of a good or service* is the focus all marketing activities.

2). The consumer can be individuals or organizations, whether a company (Levi), government (federal, state, local), sorority, or a charity.

3). The **Marketing Concept:** *A management orientation that focuses on identifying and satisfying consumer needs to ensure the organization's long term profitability objectives.*

    a). **Need:** *Recognition of any difference between a consumer's actual state and some ideal or desired state.*

    b). **Want:** *The desire to satisfy needs in specific ways that are culturally and socially influenced.*

    c). **Benefit:** *The outcome sought by a customer that motivates buying behavior.*

    d). **Demand:** *Customers' desire for products coupled with the resources to obtain them.*

➥	*Class* *Discussion*	What is the difference between a need and a want? Students will probably be quick to answer this question. If they are having trouble distinguishing between the two ask if any student has recently made a large purchase (i.e., car, stereo, computer, or even a diamond ring). Then ask what need was meet when you made the purchase? How was your want satisfied by the purchase? Discuss with students that needs can be satisfied in different ways that are culturally and socially influenced. If you have any international students in your class might ask to discuss how needs might be satisfied differently in their home country.
➥	*Class* *Discussion*	Have students comment on the growth of the cosmetic surgery market. Discuss how new procedures, like Botox injections and laser peels can be done during lunch hour and the individual can return to work immediately after the procedure is performed. Discuss the concepts of need, want, desire, and demand.

4). The **market** *is composed of all customers and potential customers who share a common need that can be satisfied by a specific product, who have the resources to exchange for it and are willing to make the exchange, and who have exchange authority.*

    a). **Marketplace:** *is any location or medium used to conduct an exchange.*

    b). Technology has greatly changed the meaning of "marketplace". Today exchanges occur via telephone, fax, and the Internet. These new technologies, coupled with the increased use of credit and debit cards, have changed where and how exchanges occur.

➥	*Class* *Discussion*	Involve students in a discussion of purchasing over the Internet. What types of products have they purchased and why did they choose to make the purchases via the Internet rather than through a retail store? What concerns do students have about Internet purchasing?

5). A recent movement in marketing is the **societal marketing concept:** an orientation that focuses on satisfying consumer needs while addressing the needs of a larger society.

➔ **Class Discussion**   In what ways might a firm practice the societal marketing concept? How does the consumer, society, and the firm benefit from these actions?

b.   Marketing is an Exchange of Value.
  1).   *Exchange: The process by which some transfer of value occurs between a buyer and a seller.* There are two requirements which must be meet for an exchange to occur:
    a).   Need two willing people or organizations.
    b).   Each must possess something that the other wants.
  2).   Electronic commerce systems are changing not only the place where the transaction occurs, but the role of money in the exchange process.
c.   (Almost) Anything Can Be Marketed
  1).   Consumer Goods and Services
    a).   *Product: A tangible good, a service, an idea, or some combination of these that through the exchange process satisfies consumer or business customer needs, a bundle of attributes, features, functions, benefits, and uses.*
    b).   Consumer goods are purchased by individuals for personal or family consumption.
    c).   *Services: Intangible products that are exchanged directly from the producer to the customer. Examples include a haircut or computer assistance.*
  2).   Business-to-Business Marketing
    a).   Businesses and organizations are also consumers of goods and services.
    b).   *Industrial Goods: Goods bought by individuals or organizations for further processing or for use in doing business.*

➔ **Class Discussion**   Consider a product that is purchased by both individual customers and organizations. For each group discuss the needs and benefits sought.

  3).   Not-For-Profit Marketing
  Marketing is not just for goods and services. Local school districts, churches, and the Red Cross are all examples of not-for-profit organizations which engage in marketing activities.
  4).   Idea, People, and Place Marketing
  Marketing activities can be used to convince consumers to change a behavior, change their attitude about a person, and to help consumers decide on a vacation location.

➔ **Class Discussion**   What behaviors have you changed as a result of idea marketing? Listed below are some slogans from recent advertisements. Have any of these had an impact on behaviors?

Just Say No to Drugs   Don't Drink and Drive
Get High, Get Aids, Die   Abuse hurts

People—How are the principles of marketing applied to people? Consider President Clinton, or Monica Lewinsky? Discuss candidates for public offices, how are marketing concepts used by these individuals? How do you market yourself? A resume and/or an interview are both examples of situations in which you market yourself.

Place: Places are also involved in marketing. For example, your school baseball team, the symphony, Disney World, New York City all rely heavily on the activities involved in marketing.

Spotlight on Real People at JobDirect

Summary: Rachel Bell and Sara Sutton, two 21 year olds, believed that the Internet was the answer to matching up student job seekers with employers. So Bell and Sutton put their last year of college on hold and started JobDirect, an Internet-based service that is now the largest database of entry-level student jobs on the Web (www.jobdirect.com).

Suggested Answers to Discussion Questions

1. **What is JobDirect's market?**

   JobDirect serves two markets, the consumer market and the business market. College students who are looking for jobs use the services of JobDirect and so do businesses who are searching for employees.

2. **What benefits does the service provide to customers?**

   For college students the service is free. Students can enter their resume directly into the database and they also have access to one of the largest databases of entry-level jobs on the Web. Although businesses pay a fee to access the resume database, they can search for resumes fitting specific criteria.

3. **How does the chapter's concept of people marketing fit here?**

   A resume is nothing more than a vehicle to market one's self. In a resume the product, in this case the person, is described. It is very important that the resume be professionally written and contain the appropriate information desired by firms in the area where employment is being sought. Thus, the resume is similar to product packaging. Consumers often examine a product's package when they are purchasing a new product. In the same way, employers examine resumes to help determine if an individual would be a good candidate for a position in their organization.

4. **If you were running this business, what advice might you give to Bell and Sutton about how to get even more students to register their resumes in the database?**

   Bell and Sutton need to be more aggressive about recruiting students. The bus tour of universities was successful, but now Bell and Sutton need to develop some new promotional activities. Below are some suggested promotional activities:
   a. Be a guest speaker on university campuses.
   b. Provide promotional give-aways which include the firms name. T-shirts and drink cup holders would be good promotional items.
   c. Spend time networking and calling on prospective businesses.

d. Marketing's Tools: The Marketing Mix
   ** Refer to Objective 2
   ** Use the video on Terra Chips
   ** Use Instructor's Manual Mini-Project 1-B
   ** Use Marketing in Action: Real Choices at Florida International Museum

** Use Figure 1.1

Class
Discussion

Begin this topic by referring to the opening exercise and the class discussion which followed. You might also want to use question one in Marketing Practice: Applying What You've Learned as part of a class discussion on the marketing mix.

Marketing Mix: *A combination of the product itself, the price of the product, the place where it is made available, and the activities that introduce it to consumers that creates a desired response among a set of pre-defined consumers.*

    1).   **Product:** Good, service, idea offered for exchange.

    2).   **Price:** The assignment of value to a product.

➔ **Class Discussion**   What is value? Students will probably provide a variety of definitions, but basically value is based on perception. Do consumer's definitions value change for different purchase situations? For example, would value be defined the same way for a purchase of a pair of jeans and dinner at a fine restaurant? Discuss the popularity and growth of value oriented retail formats like the Dollar Store where every item in the store costs only $1 dollar.

    3).   **Place:** The availability of the product to the customer at the desired time and location.

➔ **Class Discussion**   Discuss the channel of distribution used for Levi Jeans. How has the Internet changed channels of distribution?

    4).   **Promotion:** The coordination of efforts by a marketer to inform or persuade consumers or organizations about goods, services or ideas.

➔ **Class Discussion**   Many think that promotion is only advertising. Promotion includes the combination of advertising, sales promotion, and personal selling. Discuss the variety of promotional methods which might be used by Levi. If you are using the Computer Friendly Stuff (CFS) case series, refer to the Marketing Plan (Appendix A) for CFS and examine the promotional activities used by CFS

2.   **How is Marketing Done?**
    ** Refer to Objective 3
    a.   Marketing Planning: The first phase of marketing planning is analyzing the organization's current strengths and weaknesses. This analysis also examines threats and opportunities the organization might face in the marketplace.
    b.   Finding and Reaching a Target Market: Part of the marketing planning process is determining which customer groups should be reached and with which product. There are several strategies which can be used to find and reach the desired target market. Some products, like sugar, fresh fruit, and toilet paper have mass market appeal.
        1).   **Mass Market:** *All possible customers in a market, regardless of the differences in their specific needs and wants.* The mass market approach does not work for all goods. Consider a one-size fits-all jacket. Does this jacket fit all or just "fit–most"? The success of an organization's marketing plan is its ability to find, reach, and satisfy a market.
        2).   **The Market Segment** *is a distinct group of customers within a larger market who are similar to one another in some way and whose needs differ from other customers in the larger market.* For Levi, the market segment of interest is aging Baby Boomers.
        3).   The **Target Market** *is the market segment(s) on which an organization focuses it's marketing plan and toward which it directs its market efforts.*
        4)   Target marketing involves 3 steps:
            ■   Segmenting
            ■   Targeting
            ■   Positioning

| *Class* | Discuss the market segment(s) targeted by firms like Levi, Kellogg, and Saturn. |

Class
Discussion   Discuss the market segment(s) targeted by firms like Levi, Kellogg, and Saturn. Discuss the variables which were perhaps used to segment the market. How is the product positioned relative to competitors?

Class
Discussion   Discuss the Marketing Real People, Real Choices section on Levi. Use the questions about planning and developing marketing strategy listed on page 12 of the text for discussion. Following are some possible answers to these questions.

Suggested Answers to Discussion Questions on page 12

1. **What jeans styles will our core customers of young people be looking for in five years?**

   It is difficult to predict trends, especially fashion trends. The fashion industry uses a variety of predictors to help them forecast fashion trends. Levi might watch what celebrities and what band members are wearing to help predict what their core customer will want in 3–5 years. Levi might also watch trends in other areas and even examine historical fashion cycles. For example, the wide leg jeans style was the result of several influences like, rap singers, skateboarders, and a revival of 70's fashion.

2. **Which customer group that don't currently buy a lot of blue jeans might we target for Levi's products?**

   One of the largest growing students is adults over 45 years old. This group represents a great opportunity for Levi due to the number of people in this group and their familiarity with brand Levi. In targeting the over 45 group Levi would want to consider the specific style and fit needs to this segment.

3. **How will new developments in computerized production technologies affect the denim manufacturing process?**

   Some of the newest technologies in manufacturing apparel have occurred in the manufacturing of denim products. Because denim fabric is stiffer than many types of products, it can be used in an automated manufacturing process; although lasers are often used to cut all types of fabrics, denim is the only fabric which can be sewn by a totally automated process.

   Customized fit is also a new technology that has been tested by Levi. Customized fit involves the use of automated manufacturing, express delivery services, and kiosk which are located at select retailers. Customers input their measurements and style preference at the kiosk. The information is transferred to Levi, and in about two weeks, the customer has a perfect fitting pair of jeans at an average cost of $55.00.

4. **How will consumers growing awareness about the use of child labor in third world countries affect their attitudes toward manufacturers that locate plants overseas?**

   This is an ethical issue which Levi and other manufacturers must consider. Recently, brands like Nike and Liz Claiborne have received negative publicity and criticism because of the use of child labor and poor working conditions in the World Countries. Thus, it is important that Levi, and other firms closely monitor the manufacturing of their product in foreign countries.

5. **Will the current trend for many companies to institute "Casual Friday" where employees can wear jeans to work, affect long-term demand for Levi's products?**

   The "Casual Friday" trend is a blessing for Levi and other casual apparel manufacturers. This trend has enabled Levi to sell more denim and to develop other brands like Dockers.

3.   **When Did Marketing Begin? The Evolution of the Marketing Concept.**
** Refer to Objective 4
** Use Q #3 Marketing Practice: Applying What You've Learned
** Refer to Table 1.1
The discipline of marketing as we know it today has evolved over a period of 100 plus years. The evolution of marketing can be traced through four eras:

a.   ***Production Orientation****: during this era the efficient production and distribution of products was emphasized.*
   1).   Customers have to take whatever is available.
   2).   Marketing plays an insignificant role.

b.   ***Selling Orientation****: A managerial view of marketing as a sales function, or a way to move products of the warehouses to reduce inventory.*
   1).   Management views marketing as a sales function.
   2).   The selling orientation prevailed well into the 1950's.
      This emphasis on the "hard sell" gave marketing a bad image.
      This focus is used today to sell **unsought goods**; *products that people do not intend to buy. A good example would be cemetery plots, caskets, or even special features on a washing machine.*

c.   ***Customer Orientation****: A management philosophy that focuses on ways to satisfy customer's needs and wants.*
   1).   Relationship marketing and social marketing are outgrowths of this new era.
   2).   For example, fast food companies like McDonald's reduced the use of styrofoam containers in an effort to increase both economic and social profit.

d.   ***New Era Orientation****: In this era marketing means a devotion to excellence in designing and producing products that benefit the customer, plus, the firms employees, shareholders, and communities.*
   ** Use the Real People Real Surfers: Exploring the Web

4.   **Why is Marketing Important?**
** Use Objective 5

Class Discussion	Marketing is important to individuals, business and society. Refer to the opening exercise. What role does marketing play in our daily lives.

a.   Marketing creates ***utility****, the usefulness or benefit received by consumers from a product.* Marketing activities create four types of utility:
   1).   ***Form Utility:*** *The consumer benefit provided by organizations when they change raw materials into finished products desired by customers.*
   2).   ***Place Utility:*** *The consumer benefit provided when organizations make products available to consumers.*
   3).   ***Time Utility:*** *The consumer benefit provided by storing products until they are needed by buyers.*
   4).   ***Possession Utility:*** *The consumer benefits provided by an organization by allowing the consumer to own, use, and enjoy the product.*

b.   Marketing's Role In the Firm
   ** Use Marketing Mini- Project: Learning by Doing
   Marketers work with financial and accounting officers to determine which products are financially profitable to produce, to set marketing budgets, and to determine prices.
      Organizations function most efficiently when the marketing department interacts with the other functional areas of the organization. For example, marketing must work with R/D on the creation of new products and with manufacturing.

c.   Marketing's Role In Our Daily Lives: Opera To Oprah

→ *Class
  Discussion*   Refer students to the Introduction exercise (if used) for this chapter. How does
                 marketing daily impact out lives? You might also want to discuss with students how
                 popular culture and marketing myths impact our daily lives and the purchase
                 decisions we make.

1).   ***Popular Culture:*** *The music, movies, sports, books, celebrities, and other forms of
      entertainment consumed by the mass market.*
2).   ***Myths:*** Stories containing symbolic elements that express the shared emotions and ideals
      of culture.

d.   Marketing's Role In Society
      In business, just as in everyday life, conflicts often arise concerning ethical and moral behavior.
      1).   Ethical behavior is good business

→ *Class
  Discussion*   Firms which practice ethical behavior are usually better off in the long run. For
                 example, when a firm decides to recall a product which is defective, and might
                 even cause harm to individuals, the firm will most surely lose money in the short
                 term. However, the firm hopefully gains the respect of customers and society.

2).   Social and Ethical Criticisms of Marketing
      a).   Marketing creates artificial needs
      b).   Marketing teaches us to value people for what they own rather than who they
            are.

→ *Class
  Discussion*   Have students comment on the two social and ethical and criticisms of marketing.
                 Do they agree or disagree with these criticisms?

Real People, Bad Choices?

Summary: To promote an on-line game, Segasoft creates a fictional violent cult called the Cyber
Diversion Movement. The firm set up Web sites that were deigned to look like they were put up by
members of the cult.

Suggested Answer to Discussion Question

1.   **Is it appropriate to market a product that may encourage violence?**
      Hopefully many of your students will respond no to this question. Creating products which
      do not encourage violence is part of the ethical behavior and social responsibility of the
      firm. However, the US is still a free market economy where producers have the right to
      manufacture and sell the products demanded and desired by consumers. Other students may
      also comment that parents have a responsibility to monitor the video games and Internet
      usage of their children. However, what happens when your child is spending the night at a
      friends house and has the opportunity to play violent video games?

```
┌─────────────────────────────────────────────────────────────────────────────┐
│                      Real People, Real Choices:                              │
│                    How it worked out at Levi–Strauss                         │
│                                                                              │
│  The "How it worked out" section provides a good summary for chapter one. You │
│  may want to begin by reviewing with students the facts surrounding the       │
│  situation at Levi. Then review the three options developed by Steve          │
│  Goldstein. Ask students to comment on which option they would choose. Are    │
│  there any other options which should be considered?                          │
│                                                                              │
│  Summary: When Steve Goldstein saw sales figures decline, he realized that    │
│  there was a problem. The problem for Levi related to the issue of satisfying  │
│  the needs of a changing consumer market. Customers had to be given a reason  │
│  to buy yet another pair of Levi pants.                                        │
│        Which products to produce for which consumer groups was the issue      │
│  which Levi had to address. Listed below are the four issues which Levi had to │
│  consider.                                                                     │
│                                                                              │
│  ■   Aging Baby Boomers: This group grew up wearing Levi jeans. For some      │
│      members of this growth changes in body shape have made the traditional    │
│      fit Levi's less figure flattering.                                        │
│  ■   Growth of the Casual Apparel Market: The growth and popularity of casual  │
│      dress in the workplace is an opportunity for Levi. Levi specifically       │
│      developed the Docker's brand to meet the needs of this market.            │
│  ■   Closet full of Jeans: How do you convince a customer that she needs       │
│      another pair of jeans? One strategy used by Levi and others is to develop  │
│      new style features, such as a stone washed or loose fit and new colors,    │
│      like brown, black, and red.                                               │
│  ■   Growth of Fashion: Jeans had also seen a growth in popularity and         │
│      acceptance. Many restaurants and places of business consider "nice jeans"  │
│      to be acceptable. Changes in jean styles and consumer acceptance have     │
│      lead to this change.                                                      │
│                                                                              │
│        Three options were developed by Goldstein and his marketing team:      │
│                                                                              │
│  Option 1: Make looser fitting jeans under the Dockers label.                 │
│  Option 2: Forget it.—Do nothing                                              │
│  Option 3: Market a modified looser-fitting jean for the 18–34 year old.      │
│                                                                              │
│        Mr. Goldstein chose option 3. Levi's introduced "Loose Fitting Jeans"   │
│  and gave them the numbers 550 and 560. This proved to be a successful         │
│  strategy because it meet the needs and wants of a very loyal group of          │
│  customers. If Levi had not developed a pair of loose fitting jeans for this    │
│  segment one of their competitors would.                                       │
└─────────────────────────────────────────────────────────────────────────────┘
```

Potential Discussion Questions

** You might also want to include a discussion of the questions found on page 21 in the book. Answers to these questions were presented in section 2.

** Information from the Real People, Real Surfers: Exploring the Web exercise could also be used in a discussion of Levi jeans.

1.   Why is option 3 the best choice?

2.   Do you think Levi-Strauss is operating as a New Era firm?

Marketing Concepts: Testing Your Knowledge

1. **Briefly explain what marketing is.**
    Though marketing can be described in many ways, the best definition is that marketing is the process of planning and executing the conception, pricing promotion, and distribution of ideas, goods, and services to create exchanges that satisfy individual and organizational objectives.

2. **What is the marketing concept? How is it different from the social marketing concept?**
    The marketing concept is a management orientation that focuses on identifying and satisfying consumer needs to ensure the organization's long-term profitability objectives.

    The marketing concept differs from the societal marketing concept in that today many firms are moving toward a new interpretation of responsibility and orientation to the consumer that focuses on satisfying consumer needs while also addressing the needs of the larger society. The philosophy is an expansion of the marketing concept that focuses on making a profit but also on enhancing benefits to communities and society in general.

3. **How does marketing facilitate exchange?**
    Marketers facilitate exchange by creating marketing, communication, and information system. Marketing systems make it easier for buyers and sellers to come together. Information systems are used to collect and analyze data that help the organization find, reach, and satisfy consumers. Communication systems provide the means for informing, persuading, and influencing consumers.

4. **Define the terms consumer goods, services, and industrial products.**
    Consumer goods are products which are purchased by individual consumers for personal or family use. Some examples include food, health and beauty products, automobiles, and computers.

    Services are tangible products that we pay for and use, but we never own. Consider a haircut. When you go to the stylist you receive a service, a haircut; however, you cannot physically hold the service in your hand. You can collect hair trimmings of course, but that is not the service which you received, rather it is a product which is produced as a result of the service.

    Industrial goods are goods bought by individuals or organizations for further processing or for use in doing business. For example, an office may purchase some of the same office supplies which you, an individual consumer, purchase at Office Depot. The difference is that you are using these supplies for personal or family use and the organization is using the supplies in the operations of the firm.

5. **What are the elements of the marketing mix?**
    The marketing mix has been characterized as the marketers strategic tool box. Elements found in this tool box include product, price, place (or channel of distribution), and promotion.

6. **What are target markets? How do marketers select and reach target markets?**
    A target market is the market segment(s) on which an organization focuses its marketing plan and toward which it directs its marketing efforts. Marketers select and reach target markets by first slicing up the "marketing pie" (segmenting the market), targeting specific pieces of it (choosing a targeting strategy), and then developing specific products and design tactics which meet the segment's specific needs (positioning the product).

7. **Trace the evolution of the marketing concept.**
    Early in this century, companies followed a production orientation in which they focused on the most efficient ways to produce and distribute products. Beginning in the 1930's some firms adopted a sales orientation that encouraged sales people to push products aggressively on consumers. In 1950's organizations began to adopt a consumer orientation that focused on customer satisfaction and that led to the widespread adoption of the marketing concept. The future of the concept's application seems to be in

the direction of quality improvement, concern for society's welfare, appreciation of the environment through stewardship, and a commitment to a long–term relationship with the consumer. **New Era** marketing means a devotion to excellence in designing and producing products that benefit the customer, plus, the firms employees, shareholders, and communities.

8. **What is utility? How does marketing create different forms of utility?**
Utility is the usefulness or benefit received by consumers from a product. Marketing creates several forms of utility: form utility—raw materials are changed into finished products; place utility—the organization makes products available where consumers want them; time utility—products are stored until they are needed by the consumer; and, possession utility—the organization allows the consumer to own, use, and/or enjoy the product.

9. **How is marketing related to popular culture?**
Marketing influences popular culture (such as movies, sports, music, etc.) by producing products that are an expression of the popular culture and people's ideas. Many popular cultural myths come from marketing organizations such as McDonald's, Betty Crocker, and Ivory Snow. Our nation's culture and the products produced by that culture are very closely tied.

10. **What are some of the criticisms of marketing?**
Some of the criticisms of marketing include: 1) marketers create artificial needs; 2) marketing teaches us to value people for what they own rather than who they are; 3) marketers promise miracles.

Marketing Concepts: Discussing Choices and Issues

1. **The marketing concept focuses on the ability of marketing to satisfy customer needs. As a typical college student, how does marketing satisfy your needs? What areas of your life are affected by marketing? What areas of your life (if any) are not affected by marketing?**
In answering this question the student should be encouraged to examine their life personally and relate marketing to their daily activities and events. Areas that should be mentioned in this discussion are consumer purchases (such as buying food, clothes, supplies at the bookstore, and major purchases such as computers or cars), advertising's impact on their learning processes (such as learning about new products, how to do things, and contemporary trends), interactions with groups (such as learning about new products, how to do things, and contemporary trends), interactions with groups (such as the role that reference groups plays in their purchase processes and how others might be affected by marketing practice), and career plans and aspirations (since most of these students will be business student they should understand how to pursue job opportunities and market themselves). There are obviously other areas that the students might mention (such as the international environment, the environment itself, and the legal environment). Each area mentioned should be examined and justified. Most students will find that there will be few (if any) activities that they pursue in their daily lives that are not touched by marketing. One way to stimulate discussion in this area is to relate your own (the instructor's) personal daily experiences with marketing.

2. **Do you think students should study marketing even if they are not planning a career in marketing or business? Explain your reasoning.**
This question is one of judgment and could be defended in either direction. Those students that have carefully read Chapter One will understand that knowledge of marketing (just like knowledge of consumer activities) will aid the individual in making decisions in their daily lives. From the standpoint of business, knowledge of marketing is essential if the business person is to fully appreciate the various functions (accounting, finance, computer science, manufacturing, information processing, economics, and management) and be able to integrate them into and overall business plan or strategy. It has often been said that "nothing happens until someone sells something." This phrase might be used to stimulate the students thinking in the above area. The answer to this question is not as important as is the justification.

3.   **In this chapter a number of criticisms of marketing were discussed. Have you heard these criticisms? What other criticisms of marketing have you heard? Do you agree or disagree with these criticisms and why?**

The criticisms cited in the text were: *1) Marketers create artificial needs; 2) Marketing teaches us to value people for what they own rather that who they are; and, 3) Marketers promise miracles.*

Students will probably not have heard the above criticisms in those exact words but they will most certainly have heard criticisms of marketing and marketers. This would be an interesting side discussion—are the primary criticisms by consumers with marketing (as a field, function, or practice) or are criticisms more likely associated with marketers themselves (individuals, retailers, wholesalers, or manufacturers)? The answer to this question might indicate what the true consumer's criticisms might be. For instance, if a person feels that they have been cheated or deceived, what is the source of that fraud or deception? Is it the field or marketing or the marketer?

Other criticisms that are commonly cited that might be discussed are that marketing is deceptive (promises are false), marketers really don't care about your needs or solving your problems, marketers only care about money, marketers will say anything to make a sale, marketers don't care about the environment, marketers show too much sex and sexual innuendo, and marketers don't care about social reform or the welfare of society.

Be sure to ask students to generalize their specific complaints about marketing so they can be discussed in a broader context. Once the students have voiced their complaints, press them for solutions.

4.   **In this chapter we talked about how marketing communicates myths. What exactly is a myth? What are popular myths depicted in marketing? Does marketing create some of these myths?**

Myths are stories containing symbolic elements that express the shared emotions and ideals of culture. At McDonald's the basic struggles of good versus evil are played out in the fantasy world of advertising when Ronald McDonald confounds the Hamburgler. Jimmy Buffett created a fantasy tropical paradise in his hit song Margaritaville. In the case of McDonald's marketing has helped to create the myth. However, fans of Jimmy Buffett helped to immortalized this fantasy place called Margaritaville.

Real People, Real Surfers: Exploring the Web

This exercise could be used when discussing New Era firms and/or market segmentation. Students should enjoy searching the Web for information on jeans. Encourage students to identify other jean manufacturers on the Web. Responses to questions 3, 4 , and 5 might be very interesting to use for class discussion.

Marketing In Action: Real Choices at Florida International Museum

Summary: Florida International Museum had suffered several disastrous years which had resulted in a $10 million debt. Management reorganization occurred and a new in-house marketing team led by Wayne Atherholt was established. Atherholt knew that marketing was not just for laundry detergents and that marketing planning needed to take place in order for the museum to be financially successful.

Suggested Answers to Case Questions

1. **What is the problem facing Florida International Museum?**
   There are many problems which students might discuss, but the primary problem is the need for a marketing plan.

2. **What factors are causing the problem?**
   The following factors are important to understanding the above problem.
   a. The museum is $10 million in debt and needs to make a profit.
   b. Putting on an exhibit, like Titanic would be very expensive.
   c. In the past local hotels and travel agents had been ignored. These organizations should have been used to help market the museum.
   d. The museum suffered from a lack of awareness in the community.
   e. The atmosphere of the museum was not comfortable or relaxed.
   f. The outside of the building looked liked a department store.
   g. Nothing was done to encourage repeat visits to the museum.

3. **What are the alternatives?**
   a. The museum could decide to have the Titanic exhibit in hopes this exhibit would help to increase museum traffic.
   b. Attempt to develop relationships with local hotels and travel agencies.
   c. Give the interior and the exterior of the building a facelift.
   d. Develop a web site for the museum.
   e. Develop a season pass program for museum patrons.
   f. Create new signage for the museum.

4. **What are your recommendations for solving the problem?**
   Students may have developed other alternatives and recommendations will be tied to those alternatives. Florida International Museum should consider all of the above alternatives in the development of a marketing plan. Try to help student's understand that implementing only one of the above alternatives would only represent a "short-term fix" and would not solve the big problem facing the museum.

5. **What are some ways to implement your recommendations?**
   Wayne Atherholt should begin by examining each element of the marketing mix (product, price, place, and promotion). Some amount of research may be necessary to determine what customers and potential customers actually desire. After the marketing plan has been developed and approved, Wayne needs to prioritize the marketing tactics and decide which actions need to be taken first.
   Yes. New Era firms are devoted to excellence in designing and producing products that benefit the customer and society. Not only did Levi design a new line of jeans for the 18–34 year old group, but they also practiced social marketing by using natural dyes which were less harmful to the environment. Finally, by meeting the needs of an important group of consumers, Levi was practicing relationship marketing. In other words, Levi did not abandon their loyal customers just because their waist lines began to expand.

Mini-Project 1-A
Examining a New Era Organization

Purpose: To learn about the ways in which New Era organizations seek and earn both economic and social profit.

1. With two or three others in your class, first identify one or two firms which may be classified as having a New Era Orientation. If possible, find firms which are located in your area. You may find the following useful in identifying such firms:

    - Newspaper articles on firms that have been recognized for their service to the community
    - Recommendations from one or more of your instructors for firms which qualify as New Era organizations
    - Firms which have been Baldridge Award winners
    - Library resources such as corporate annual reports
    - Recommendations of business leaders in your community
    - Information about businesses provided at internet sites

2. Learn as much as you can about one particular firm. If possible visit the firm and talk with the firm's employees. Interview other business people to find out what they think about the firm.

3. Prepare a report which includes the following:
    a. Describe the firm's business and its marketing management structure.
    b. Tell about the firm's commitment to quality.
    c. Describe the ways the firm practices environmental stewardship?
    d. Explain the ways the form works to earn social profit?
    e. Describe efforts the firm has made to promote consumers' health, safety, and social well-being?
    f. How does the firm rate on its efforts to encourage cultural diversity and ethical business practices?
    g. Your recommendations for ways in which the firm could make improvements in its New Era focus.

4. Present your findings to your class.

Mini-Project 1-B
The 4 Ps for Different Organizations

Purpose: To better understand how different types of organizations implement product, price, place, and promotion.

The American Marketing Association has formulated the following as its definition of marketing:

> "The process of planning and executing the conception, pricing, promotion and distribution of ideas, goods, and services to create exchanges that satisfy individual and organizational objectives."

For each of the organizations and other marketing opportunities listed, identify the following:
- a. The product which is marketed
- b. Individual or organizational consumer of the product
- c. The need satisfied by the product
- d. The price or value exchanged in return for the product
- e. The channels of distribution used to make the product available to the customer
- f. The promotional activities used by the marketer to inform or persuade customers

Opportunity	Product	Customer	Consumer Need	Price/value exchanged	Distribution channels	Promotional activities
1. A candidate for governor						
2. A new up-and-coming country and western singer						
3. A new prescription medicine which will cure teenage acne in a matter of a few weeks.						
4. A local church, synagogue or other place of worship						
5. A new process which turns radioactive waste into glass pellets which can be safely stored indefinitely.						
6. A campaign to get people to wear seat belts						
7. A new line of sexy swimwear.						
8. Swish, a new non-cola soft drink.						
9. The Peace Corps						

Opportunity	Product	Customer	Consumer Need	Price/value exchanged	Distribution channels	Promotional activities
10. The American Red Cross's blood drives						
11. Your college teams' basketball games						
12. The medical practice of a group of family physicians						

2

Strategic Planning: Making Choices in a Dynamic Environment

*O*verview   There is an old saying which states "failing to plan is planning to fail." Although some firms without formal plans appear to be successful, these firms are probably not reaching their full potential. In this chapter the strategic planning process and the activities involved in developing, executing, and evaluating the plan are discussed. The marketing planning process and the stages in that process that lead to the development and implementation of a marketing plan are also presented. One important aspect of strategic planning that students should learn is that business planning is an integrated activity.

Harley-Davidson is the focus of the Real People, Real Choices segment. Students will enjoy learning how this famous motorcycle company transformed their image and profitability.

Objectives

1.   Explain the strategic planning process.

2.   Tell how firms gain a competitive advantage and describe the factors that influence marketing objectives.

3.   Describe the steps in the marketing planning process.

4.   Explain the factors involved in the implementation and control of the marketing plan.

Chapter Outline and Suggested Activities

Introduction: The following exercise could be used at the beginning of class to help students understand the changes which have taken place at Harley-Davidson. Find a picture of a Harley-Davidson motorcycle owner/rider. If possible, find a picture of a rough looking motorcycle gang member. Ask students to comment on the picture and bike rider.

Next find a picture of a "RUB" (rich urban rider). Again ask students to comment on the picture.

Briefly discuss the problems/issues faced by Harley-Davidson (i.e. brand image, capacity, and quality issues). Discuss what the future might hold for Harley-Davidson.

1. **Plan Well And Prosper**
   ** Refer to Objective 1
   ** Use Nike video
   a. ***Strategic planning** is the managerial decision process that matches an organization's resources and capabilities to its market opportunities for long-term growth and survival.*
   b. Strategic Planning is used by both large and small firms and is an ongoing process.
   c. Business Planning occurs at three levels
   ** Refer to Figure 2.1
   1). The ***Strategic plan** is usually developed by top management by examining how the firm should respond to changes and opportunities in the environment.*
   2). ***Tactical planning** is a decision process that concentrates on developing detailed plans for strategies and tactics for the short term that support an organization's long-term strategic plan.* This type of planning is performed by middle level managers and includes both the five-year and annual plan.
   3). ***Operational Planning** is a decision process that focuses on developing detailed plans for day-to-day activities that carry out an organization's tactical plans.*
   4). All business planning is an integrated activity.

2. **Strategic Planning: Guiding The Business**

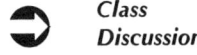 *Class Discussion* — What other functional areas in the organization did Harley-Davidson marketing managers have to work with in developing a strategic plan? Why is cross-functional planning critical to the success of the tactical plan?

Following is a discussion of each level of the strategic plan. Figure 2.1 can be used as a guide when presenting this information.

**Refer to Objectives 1 and 2
**Use Q#1 Marketing Practice: Applying What You've Learned

   a. There are four stages in top-level strategic planing
   1). Define the ***Mission Statement:** A formal statement in an organization's strategic plan that describes the overall purpose of the organization and what it intends to achieve in terms of its customers, products, and resources.*

Class Discussion — Provide students with several examples of mission statements. Ask students to determine the name of the organization and what type of business they operate. Be sure to remove any identifying cues from each mission statement. Use the mission statement of your college or university. Are any of the mission statement myopic?

2). Evaluating the Environment: SWOT Analysis

    a). *SWOT analysis is used to assess an organization's internal and external environments. A SWOT analysis seeks to identify strengths(s) weaknesses(w) opportunities (o) and threats (t)*

    b). *Internal environment—all of the controllable elements inside an organization that influence how an organization operates.*
Examples: employees, technologies, patents, physical facilities, and relationships with suppliers.

    c). *External environment consists of those uncontrollable elements outside of the organization that may affect it either positively or negatively.*
Examples: consumers, government regulations

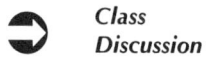

Class Discussion

Have students conduct a SWOT analysis for a local restaurant or fast food chain. You might also want to continue any discussions which your class has had regarding Harley-Davidson and conduct a SWOT analysis for Harley-Davidson.

    Be sure to have student's comment on the internal and external environmental factors which may impact the firms strategies.

Real People Bad Choices

Summary: Former Staples Inc. chairmen Thomas G. Sternberg had his wife apply for a job with rival Office Deport in order to confirm rumors that Office Depot was starting its own delivery service?

Suggested Answers to Discussion Questions

1. **How far should a company be allowed to go to learn about its competitors?**
Trying to learn what your competitor is doing is part of doing business. But should a firm be dishonest in their pursuit of competitive information? The answer is no!

2. **Was it unethical for Sternberg to have his wife apply for a job with rival Office Depot in order to confirm rumors that Office Depot was starting its own delivery service?**
Yes it was wrong. Sternberg's purpose in having his wife go to work at Office Depot was so that she could eavesdrop and learn about the organizations strategic plans.

---

3). **Setting Organizational Objectives.** *Objectives are the specific accomplishments or outcomes that an organization hopes to achieve by a specific time.*

    a). Objectives are a direct out growth of the mission statement

    b). Objectives may be related to revenue/sales, profitability, market share, ROI, etc.

    c). Well written objectives are measurable and state the time frame for completing the task.

4). Planning for Growth: The Business Portfolio
**Use Q #2 Marketing Practice: Applying What You've Learned

    a). In small firms that offer a single product/service business strategy is simple. Larger firms however offer multiple products/brands; thus, these organizations have multiple SBU's. *SBU's (strategic business unit) are individual units within the firm, each having its own mission, business objectives, resources, managers, and competitors.*
**Refer to Figure 2.3

    b). *Business portfolio is the different products, or brands owned by an organization and characterized by different income-generating and growth capabilities.*

There are two models for assessing the portfolio
Boston Consulting Group Matrix
**Refer to Figure 2.4
**Use Instructor's Manual Marketing Mini-Project 2-B
Product Growth Matrix
**Refer to Figure 2.5

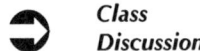

Class
Discussion

1. Select a product category and discuss the four different fundamental marketing strategies presented in the Product Growth Matrix.

2. Discuss how many firms relay on more than one of these strategies to achieve growth. What strategies were used by Harley-Davidson?

Spotlight On Real People: Aliah, Inc.

Summary: Aly Abuullei develops strategic planning software that captures emotions. The software planning program breaks every issue down into a series of questions, each with only two alternatives. Managers have to choose an option and indicate how strongly they feel about their choice. In 1996, IBM and other firms like Boeing and Lubrizol adopted the software as a planning tool. Plans are being made to take Aliah public by 2002.

Suggested Answers to Discussion Questions

1. **How does Aliah help managers in the strategic planning process?**
   The software planning program helps managers break down issues into a series of questions: Each question has only two alternatives. Thus, managers are forced to focus on the issue.

2. **What role should emotions or intuition versus rational, objective analysis play in this process?**
   This unique approach of incorporating feelings into strategic planning may seem like "fluff" to some, but can provide very useful information. For example, if a manager feels very strongly about an alternative they will be more likely to work hard to have the alternative implemented. Emotions and intuition should not totally replace the rational and objective process. However, emotions and "gut feelings" can be very useful when combined with more rational and objective analysis.

3. **How can Aliah best convey its different approach so that the company can increase its own market share among products and services used to facilitate strategic planning? Are there other potential customers besides corporate planners who might be convinced to use the software?**
   Aliah needs to collect testimonials from its satisfied customers. These testimonials would help to convey the message that this different approach to planning works. Organizations like churches and other non-profit groups are potential customers.

---

3. **The Marketing Planning Process**
   **Refer to Objective 3
   **Use Instructor's Manual Marketing Mini-Project: Learning by Doing
   a. A *competitive advantage is the ability of a firm to outperform the competition providing customers with a benefit the competitor can't.*
   b. It is because of a competitive advantage that consumers choose one product over another.
      **Use Q#5 Marketing Practice: Applying What You've Learned
      **Use Instructor's Manual Marketing Mini-project 2-A

c. Steps in creating a competitive advantage
   1). *Distinctive Competency*—*a superior capability of a firm in comparison to its direct competitors.*
   2). Turn a distinctive competency into a *differential benefit*—*set products apart from competitors' products by providing something unique that customers want.*
   **Use Q#4 Marketing Practice: Applying What You've Learned

➡ *Class Discussion*

Have students comment on this statement:

"Effective product benefits must be both different from the competition and wanted by customers."

d. Setting Marketing Objectives
   1). Once objectives have been written, decisions regarding the marketing function needed to accomplish the objectives must be made.
   2). Some examples of objectives include:
      a). Sales objectives
      b). Product-oriented objectives
      c). Market objectives
e. Developing *marketing mix strategies:*
   1). In this stage decisions about what activities must be accomplished to reach objectives are made.
   2). The two most important areas for decisions are:
      a). Selecting a target market
      b). Developing marketing mix program
   **Use Real People, Real Surfers: Exploring the Web

3. **Preparing A Marketing Plan**
   **Refer to the plan for Computer Friendly Stuff
   **Refer to Objective #3
   a. This is the final stage in the marketing plan process.
   b. The *marketing plan* is a document that describes the marketing environment, outlines the marketing objectives and strategy and identifies who will be responsible for carrying out each part of the marketing strategy.

4. **Implementation And Control Of The Marketing Plan**
   **Refer to Objective 4
   ** Refer to the Marketing Plan for Computer Friendly Stuff (CFS) (Appendix A)
   a. *Implementation is the stage of the strategic planning process in which strategies are put into action on a day-to-day basis.*
   b. There are two key factors in the successful implementation of marketing plans.
      1). Marketing Budget
      2). Organization of the marketing function.
   c. Controlling the marketing plan involves measuring actual performance, comparing it to planned performance, and making necessary changes in plans and implementation.
   d. A *marketing audit is a comprehensive review of a firm's marketing function- the audit is used to help determine if a firm can improve its marketing programs.*
      **Refer to Table 2-1
      ** Use Marketing in Action: Real Choices at McDonald's

Real People, Real Choices: How it Worked Out at Harley-Davidson

Summary: The major problem faced by Harley-Davidson's marketing team was how to keep with demand. The company needed to spend $300 million to build manufacturing capacity to meet the current demand. Was this increase in demand a fad? This dilemma highlighted the need for careful strategic planning. Frank Cimermancic, Director of Business Planning, and the Harley team identified three alternative courses of action.

Option 1: Invest $300 million in new manufacturing capacity
Option 2: Do nothing and see if demand continues to grow
Option 3: Contract out manufacturing to other producers who would actually make the bikes and put the Harley name on them.

Harley chose option 1. They invested $300 million in order to increase manufacturing capacity by 60 percent. Results (1994) 17% increase in orders shipped, (1995)—reached production objective a year ahead of schedule—increase (30%) in exports to foreign countries.

Potential Discussion Questions

1. Use the decisions made by Harley-Davidson to explore the role of strategic planning.

2. Have students look up the Harley-Davidson homepage. What is the mission of Harley Davidson? What customers does it want to serve?

3. What new market can it develop? Should they target the twenty-something generation? Can this group afford a Harley or should Harley produce a new less expensive product for this group?

Marketing Concepts: Testing Your Knowledge

1. **What are strategic, tactical, and operational planning? What is cross-functional planning?**

   Strategic planning is the managerial decision process that matches an organization's resources and capabilities to its market opportunities for long-term growth and survival. *Tactical planning* is a decision process that concentrates on developing detailed plans for strategies and tactics for the short-term that support an organization's long-term strategic plan. *Operational planning* is a decision process that focuses on developing detailed plans for day-to-day activities that carry out an organization's tactical plans.

   Similarities include the fact that planning decisions made at each level in the firm are interrelated. All of the planning forms may include instructions to the various functional components of the organization even though the functional managers generally develop their own plans. See Figure 2.1 for additional information.

   Differences primarily focus on the planning horizon (time frame) and scope of the plan (general organizational objectives versus specific functional objectives). In addition, the level of manager would also change as we move from one planning level to another (corporate manager to mid-level to lower-level manager) as we move down the planning scale.

   Many forms of planning are important to the firm. One of the most important forms of planning is marketing planning. Marketing plans provide mechanisms to produce the firm's products at a price consumers are willing to pay, the means to get that product to the place consumers want it, or a way to promote the product to the right consumers. Without this form of planning, few firms would be able to exist.

   Cross-functional planning is an approach to planning in which managers work together in developing tactical plans for each functional area in the firm, so that each plan considers the objectives of the other areas.

   Cross-functional planning helps the firm to achieve its marketing objective by integrating all other functional plans into a unified effort. Since marketing planning is one of the most important of the planning processes, coordination of all plans makes the attainment of objectives more realistic.

2. **What is a mission statement? Why is a mission statement important to an organization?**

   A *mission statement* is a formal statement in an organization's strategic plan that describes the overall purpose of the organization and what it intends to achieve in terms of its customers, products, and resources. The mission statement is important to an organization because it defines the scope of the firm's activities and identifies its strategic focus. When the mission statement has been constructed correctly it not only spells out the organization's scope and focus but it sets the direction for everyone's efforts.

   Normally, a statement of business mission usually covers four basic areas:

   a. The group of individuals or firms—the *customer segment*—the firm will serve.
   b. The nature of the *benefits* the firm will attempt to supply.
   c. The *stage in the value-added process* in which the firm will compete.
   d. The *competencies* the firm will develop.

3. **What is a SWOT analysis? What role does it play in the planning process?**

   The first step in developing a strategic marketing direction and specific marketing plan is to identify marketing opportunities by evaluating the internal and external environments of the organization. The evaluation of these business environments is often referred to as *SWOT analysis* because it seeks meaningful *strengths (S)* and *weaknesses (W)* inside the organization and *opportunities (O)* and *threats (T)* coming from outside.

   Information about a firm's external and internal environments helps managers keep their balance in a constantly shifting marketplace. Firms that regularly or continuously monitor what is going on both inside and outside their own four walls are able to capitalize on opportunities and minimize threats because they are able to develop strategies (and make plans) that successfully match business strengths to market opportunities.

4. **What is a business portfolio? Why do firms develop SBUs? Describe the planning tools firms use to plan and assess its portfolio of SBUs and to develop growth strategies?**

    A *business portfolio* is the group of different businesses, products, or brands owned by an organization and characterized by different income-generating capabilities. Firms develop SBUs so separate strategic focus can be developed for the multifaceted firm. A *strategic business unit* (*SBUs*) is an individual unit within the firm that operates like a separate business, each having its own mission, business and marketing objectives, resources, managers, and competitors.

    There are two tools that may be used to plan and assess the organization's portfolio of SBUs:
    a.   The *Boston Consulting Group Matrix* (see Figure 2.4).
    b.   The *Product-Market Growth Matrix* (see Figure 2.5).

5. **Why is marketing planning important to a firm?**

    Many forms of planning are important to the firm. One of the most important forms of planning is marketing planning. Marketing plans provide mechanisms to produce the firm's products at a price consumers are willing to pay, the means to get that product to the place consumers want it, and a way to promote the product to the right consumers. Without this form of planning, few firms would be able to exist.

6. **What does it mean for a firm to have a competitive advantage? What gives a firm a competitive advantage?**

    A *competitive advantage* is an advantage over competitors that an organization gains through its superior capabilities and unique product benefits that provide greater value in the minds of consumers. In other words, the firm must develop some reason why consumers will perceive its products to be of greater value than competing products. The focus is on *why* consumers choose products.

    Two independent elements affect competitive advantage. First, *distinctive competency* where there is a superior capability of a firm in comparison to its direct competitors. Second, *differential benefits* provide values that customers obtain from using, experiencing, or possessing a firm's products that are superior to those of competing products. When the firm focuses its strategy on developing both of these elements (and also understanding these elements as presented by the competition), competitive advantage can be developed and increased.

7. **What are marketing objectives? What types of marketing objectives do firms normally include in marketing planning?**

    Most firms have sales objectives. These sales objectives (usually stated in terms of dollars or unit sales) are really forecasts of demand in the total market and the level of sales the firm can be expected to make in the market during a specific time period. Reliable sales predictions are at the heart of successful planning. The objectives affect marketing budgets and the marketing mix allocation.

    By choosing goals or objectives that are related to product development (new or improved products for customers), the firm has chosen product-oriented objectives. If the firm decided to pursue an objective of developing existing products for sale to new customers, then they are committed to market-oriented objectives. One method focuses on the product and the other focuses on the market or the consumer.

8. **What are some of the factors that firms consider when developing product strategies? What are some of the influences on pricing strategies? What are some of issues involved in developing promotion strategies? What do firms consider when developing distribution strategies?**

    Factors considered in developing product strategies include which product to market, unique characteristics of the products (as matched to the target market), the best design for the product (including packaging decisions), what services might accompany the product, how the product will be positioned, and whether or not variations of the product will be offered.

    Factors considered in developing pricing strategies include customers' perception of the product's value, competing product's prices, and return that the company expects from the product that might be applied to the company's revenue desires.

    Factors considered in developing promotion strategies include communication of product benefits and features, how to work with price to communicate a consistent image, the desired message or theme, how the message is to be delivered, how to mix the elements of the promotional mix (advertising, sales promotion, and personal selling) together, and how to integrate communication strategy into the fabric of the firm.

Factors considered in developing distribution strategies include whether the product will be sold directly to the final customer or whether the distribution channel will include retailers and wholesalers, which middlemen might be used, what type of store should be considered as a distribution outlet (specialty to discount for example), and how will the product be physically distributed and transported to the final customer.

9.   What are the elements of a formal marketing plan?

A *marketing plan* is a document that identifies where the organization is now, where it wants to go, how it plans to get there, and who will be responsible for carrying out each part of the marketing strategy. Therefore, the plan outlines the activities included in the planning process.

Elements of the plan include a description of the firm's current situation (a Business Review—which includes the results of SWOTs analysis), after reviewing the current situation marketing problems and opportunities are outlined, target markets are selected, identified and explained, marketing objectives are stated and justified, presentation positioning strategy, presentation and elaboration of specific strategies and action plans (or tactics) for the elements of the marketing mix, and how the plan will be implemented and controlled (including budgets and timing). See Appendix II for an example of a plan.

10.   What are the important elements of the implementation and control of marketing plans?

Implementation means putting plans into action. The implementation sections of a marketing plan contains a marketing budget, development of specific action plans, and the assignment of major areas of responsibility to individuals or teams.

Control means measuring actual performance, comparing it to planned performance, and making necessary changes in plans and implementation. Important elements include trend analysis, marketing research (customer complaint feedback, posttransaction surveys, customer focus group interviews, mystery shoppers, market surveys, and employee surveys), and the marketing audit.

Marketing Concepts: Discussing Choices and Issues

1.   The Boston Consulting Group matrix identifies products as stars, cash cows, question marks, and dogs. Do you think this is a useful way for organizations to examine their businesses? What are some examples of products that fit in each category?

The reason for the rather simplistic titles used in the description of the Boston Consulting Group matrix was to make the cells simple to remember and to be somewhat reflective of slang language used to describe companies that might be associated with the different cell areas (losers are often referred to as "dogs" for example). The axis descriptions (market growth rate and relative market share) are useful measures of performance.

Examples that might fit into the Boston Consulting Group categories can be found in the text description of the matrix (see the text illustration of Proctor and Gamble products). The students should be encourage to cite examples from areas that they are familiar with such as computers and associated software, music appliances and/or groups, fashion clothing, automobiles, or snack foods/cereals. Be sure to ask the students why they placed a particular product into the matrix category. To get a better response to this question, try photocopying a blank BCG matrix and ask the students to fill in the cells before class in a chosen area (computer software for example).

2.   Do you agree with the idea that marketing is a firm's most essential functional areas, or do you think a firm's success depends equally on all of its functional areas? Explain your reasoning.

Most students will probably state that a firm's success depends more on all of the functional areas instead of just marketing. One would expect a marketing text to state that marketing is the most important function. However, since Principles of Marketing classes are usually composed of students from various backgrounds, each will believe that their chosen field is important. To illustrate the importance of the marketing function (and its role in cross-functional planning), the instructor might wish to talk about how the various functions within a firm are in independent and dependent at the same time. In addition, ask students to name an organization that does not use marketing. Most examples (usually from the service sector) can be shown to have a marketing component. Next, relate how that planning is what makes the organization successful. One illustration that might be tried is to show how churches use internal (member participation) and external (new member development) marketing to achieve stability and growth.

3. **Do you think firms should concentrate on developing products that are better in some way than competitor's products, or should each firm focus on making the best product it can without regard to competing products? As a consumer, which approach is more likely to produce products that satisfy you most?**
    To respond to this question, students should consider two basic issues. First, how do firms develop distinctive competencies and differential benefits? Second, what is the firm's view towards product-oriented objectives versus market-oriented objectives? Firms may relate themselves primarily to competition with competitors or to pleasing consumers. Some would say that the question is just opposite sides of the same coin.
    It would be very difficult to be an effective marketer without paying some attention to competitors. However, if one does not listen to the customer the business will not have a long-term future. A mixture of the two approaches is probably what occurs most often. Listening to customers is very important (it is the basis of the marketing concept) but careful assessment of the competitive environment is essential to effect planning and strategy development. Fight competition by pleasing customers and please customers by always striving to better than the competition is probably the safest strategy to follow.

4. **Most planning, whether by businesses or not-for-profit organizations involves strategies for growth. But is growth always the right direction? Can you think of some organizations that should have contraction rather than expansion as their goal? Do you know of any organizations that have planned to get smaller rather than larger in order to be successful?**
    Begin by asking students if growth is always the right direction. Have students consider the cost associated with growth. These costs might include the costs of manufacturing, distribution, and marketing.
    Organizations which have contraction rather than expansion as their goal might include a small specialty retailer or a manufacturer of specialty equipment. In an effort to maintain a high level of quality, service contraction is often desired Expansion might be the goal when demand for the product or service is not being served by the firm or its competitors.

Real People, Real Surfers: Exploring the Web

This exercise will help students to learn more about businesses and their customers. In addition to searching the Web sites for the businesses listed in Figure 2.2, instructors might want to have student's search other businesses. A team approach would work well for this exercise. You could assign each team a different company to examine and then each team could present his findings to the class. Although students would benefit from answering all of the questions listed for this exercise, the instructor might want to focus class discussion on responses to question four. Responses to this question should produce some interesting class discussion.

Marketing in Action: Real Choices at McDonald's

Summary: Ray Kroc opened the first McDonald's in 1937 and over the next several decades dominated the fast food industry. McDonald's strategy of new products to meet the changing food wants of customers helped to give the firm a competitive advantage.

Soon however there was fierce competition for rival firms like Burger King and Wendy's. McDonald's began to confuse customers with a series of failed new products, like pizza and the Arche Deluxe, and a series of discounting strategies.

McDonald's market share was still strong (42 percent), but sales were below projections. Between 1987 and 1997, McDonald's share of the market dropped to 16.2 percent even though the restaurants had increased by 50 percent. Per-store profits had decreased by 20 percent.

Members of the McDonald's marketing team suggested that the company needed a product development strategy or new menu items. Another idea was diversification and to sell a line of kids toys. Continued expansion into international markets was also considered

None of these strategies would solve the problem—food quality. In a survey consumers ranked taste and quality as very important factors in restaurant choice while convenience and speed were much lower-rated.

Suggested Answers to Case Questions

1. **What is the problem facing McDonald's?**
   The major problem facing McDonald's is how to grow the chain. The fast-food industry is very competitive and chains such as Wendy's and Burger King were taking away McDonald's market share.

2. **What factors are important to understanding the problem?**
   a. McDonald's was penetrating the market by adding more units, yet sales were still declining. Between 1987–1997 McDonald's increased the number of restaurants by 50 percent, but per-store profits still decreased 20 percent.
   b. Changing consumer tastes and concerns over fat intake lead McDonald's to make changes in their menu. New products like pizza, veggie burgers, and the Arche Deluxe were all introduced—and all failed. It appeared that McDonald's was moving away from their cash cows (burgers, fried, and shakes) and were developing to many dogs (pizza, veggie burgers, and the Arche Deluxe). Consumers were confused and McDonald's was losing profits and market share.
   c. Poor food quality—In a national survey, McDonald's food quality was rated poorly by consumers
   d. International markets—New international market opportunities included Japan and Russia.

3. **What are the alternatives?**
   Below are some possible alternatives. Students and the instructor may have other alternatives.
   a. Do nothing—McDonald's is a strong brand and will once again be strong.
   b. Install new cookers which allow the hamburgers to be flame broiled like Burger King.
   c. Development of new operational procedures for food preparation.
   d. Focus on improving food quality for one or two menu items.
   e. Build on McDonald's brand value and sell a line of toys.
   f. Expand into the more difficult international markets like Japan and Germany.

4. **What are your recommendations for solving the problem?**
   To help grow the business McDonald's should consider alternatives c, d, and f. Implementing these combined alternatives may help McDonald's to improve their profitability and market share.

5. **What are some ways to implement your recommendations?**
   Before McDonald's spends the money to update their equipment, training of employees needs to be conducted. Franchise owners, all the way down to line workers, need to understand why these changes in equipment, food preparation, and procedures are being made. These training sessions would also be a good time to conduct customer service training. It is well known that part of satisfaction from the dining experience is not just food quality but also service. If the service is poor, the perception will be that the food tastes bad.

Marketing in Action: Real Choices at McDonald's (Continued)

McDonald's needs to implement a promotional campaign to inform customers of the improvements which have been made in food quality. Perhaps an "800" food quality/service hotline could be installed. This hotline number could be posted in restaurants, on advertisements, and on register receipts. Customers would be encouraged to call and comment about the food quality of their recent meal and even make suggestions for improvements.

Rewards should also be offered to individual restaurant units and employees. An incentive program which rewards the preparation and delivery of consistent good quality food and service should be developed. This program would encourage all workers to do their best and would reward outstanding efforts.

Research needs to be conducted prior to expanding into Germany and/or Japan. Information in the case stated that these two countries represented profitable expansion opportunities for McDonald's but expansion into these two countries would be difficult.

Mini-Project 2-A
Creating Competitive Advantages

Purpose: To learn how different firms identify distinctive competencies for providing differential benefits to customers.

When firms provide products with differential benefits, customers are willing to pay a premium for those products. Furthermore, those customers become brand loyal. Differential benefits result from the firm's distinctive competencies.

1. Conduct a brief informal survey of some of your fellow students. Ask them to tell you the names of some products which they 1) are willing to pay more for and/or 2) are brand loyal to, that is, they will do without rather than buy a substitute brand.

2. Based on the results of the survey, select one or more brands to study.

3. For each of these brands, identify the differential benefit(s) provided to customers. Is the physical good or service different? Does it contain a different ingredient? Is the service-after-the-sale superior? Does it provide a better warranty? Does the brand or company image create a differential benefit in the minds of customers?

4. Next, identify the customer need which is satisfied better because of the differential benefit. In other words, why is this differential benefit important to customers?

5. Identify the firm's distinctive competency which results in the differential benefit. Does the firm have superior manufacturing facilities, better channels of distribution, a better communications or advertising program, or better research and development capabilities? Does the size of the firm allow them to take advantage of economies of scale which lead to a lower-priced product than that of the competition?

6. Develop a report of your findings and present it to your class.

Mini-Project 2-B
Using the BCG Growth-Market Share Matrix

Purpose: To gain an understanding of the usefulness of portfolio analysis for organizations.

It is easy to see how organizations "sell" a wide range of intangible products—services, ideas, people, etc. It may be less clear how strategic planning works for these intangible products. In this project, you are to practice making strategic marketing decisions based on the Boston Consulting Group Matrix. You are to do this using the different units within your university.

1.   First, identify the different SBUs of your university. These will probably be the different academic units on your campus although you may also have some other distinct units such as a Continuing Education Department.

2.   Find out as much as you can about the market for the "product." Is the market for graduates with this major growing or declining? Is the need for knowledge or skills in the area increasing or becoming less important? You can probably find help with this in the periodicals area of you library, from faculty, from business people in your area, and from your school's career services office.

3.   Make an estimate of your university's relative market share for each SBU. That is, for the geographic market which your university serves, is the unit a major or a minor supplier of graduates or training in this area?

4.   Using the BCG Matrix provided below, classify each SBU as a Star, a Cash Cow, a Question Mark or a Dog.

5.   Finally develop your recommendations for each SBU. Should your university increase, decrease, or leave funding the same for the unit? Are there units which your university might consider phasing out? Are there units which might be combined?

Market
Growth
Rate

High

Low

High   Low

Relative Market Share

Recommendations

Stars

_____

_____

_____

_____

_____

Cash Cows

_____

_____

_____

_____

_____

Question Marks

_____

_____

_____

_____

_____

Dogs

_____

_____

_____

_____

_____

3

Decision Making in the New Era of Marketing: Enriching the Marketing Environment

*O*verview Chapter 3 is one of the most important chapters in this text book. The concept of social profit and its net benefit to economic profit and society are explored. New Era firms, those who do business right and do it well are highlighted. The meaning of quality and why quality products and services are critical to the firm is discussed. Finally, the elements of a firm's internal and external environments are examined.

Interface Americas is highlighted in the Real People, Real Choices section. Interface had to decide whether or not they wanted to be a New Era firm. Students should enjoy debating about which is best, economic profit or social profit.

Objectives

1. Explain why organizations have adopted a New Era marketing orientation focus on ethics and social responsibility.

2. Describe the New Era emphasis on quality.

3. Discuss some of the important aspects of an organization's internal environment.

4. Explain why marketers scan an organization's external business environment.

Chapter Outline and Suggested Activities

Introduction: Begin class by having students identify ethical and unethical practices of business. One strategy would be to have students identify organizations which have the following:

1. Removed a product from distribution because of health or safety reasons.

2. Organizations which have removed their endorsements.

3. Organizations which have removed their advertising from television shows or magazines

4. Organizations which have changed their advertisements because of pressure from consumers

5. Organizations which have donated a portion of their profits to charitable causes.

1. **Welcome To The New Era Of Marketing**
    **Refer to Objective 1
    **Use Figure 3.1
    **Use Marketing in Action: Real Choices at Nickelodeon
    a. Marketing managers are concerned with the "bottomline", but many marketing managers today must also consider social profit
    b. ***Social Profit** is the net benefit an organization and society receive from its ethical practices, community service, efforts to promote cultural diversity, and concern for the natural environment.*
        **Use Q #2 Marketing Concepts: Discussing Choices and Issues
    c. The New Era of Marketing is concerned with efforts to do business right and do it well.
    d. Doing it Right. The first step toward creating social profit is to do it right.
        **Use Q#1 Marketing Practice: Applying What You've Learned
        1). ***Business ethics**, rules of conduct for an organization.*
        2). Business ethics are the basic values that guide a firm's behavior. Many firms today are realizing that ethical production, distribution, pricing, and promotional standards and behaviors are necessary in order to develop relationships with customers.

Class Discussion

Note: If the introduction exercise for this chapter was used, you may want to refer back to students' comments for this discussion.

Ask students to identify ways in which organizations behave in an ethical manner. Discuss whether or not business ethics is important. The instructor may want to "play the devils advocate" in this discussion.

    e. Notions of what is right and wrong differ among organizations and cultures.
    f. ***Codes of ethics**: written standards of behavior to which everyone in the organization must subscribe.*
        1). Codes of ethics help to eliminate confusion about what the firm considers to be ethically acceptable behavior for employees
        2). Refer to Figure 3-2, the AMA Code of Ethics

Spotlight on Real People: Daydream Software

Summary: Daydream Software was formed by a group of five young people in Sweden who wanted to offer alternative video games to the gore and violence videos. Daydream games reward players who think strategically—no machine guns!

Have students visit the web site, www.daydream.se/. Discuss these questions with your class.

1. **What is the ethical problem facing a game software company?**
    Game software companies have to decide if it is ethical to produce violent software and whether or not they are contributing to violent behaviors in youth.

2. **Are game software companies being wrongly accused of contributing to violence in society?**
    Game software companies should be responsible in the material that they produce. However, parents are ultimately responsible for monitoring the computer games that their children play.

3. **Why is Daydream a New Era company?**
    Daydream is a New Era company because they are concerned with social profit. Members of this organization obviously are concerned with the violence in computer games and have developed fun and challenging computer games for kids.

Class Discussion   If you have students from other countries in your class ask them to comment on business practices which are considered ethical and unethical in their home country. Discuss how each culture has its own set of values, beliefs, and customs which impact behavior.

g.   The high costs of unethical marketplace behavior.
    1).   Unethical behavior can cost the firm financially and its reputation.
    2).   Consumers need to behave ethically in their dealings with organizations.

Class Discussion   Discuss the Olympic scandal where members of the Salt Lake City recruiting team were accused of taking bribes. Some believe that giving gifts is ok, after all, it is "just business". Comment.

    3).   ***Retail borrowing**—when a consumer purchases an item such as a party dress, wears it for a special occasion and returns it the next day as if it had not been worn.*

Class Discussion   Are students aware of any incidents of retail borrowing. Why is retail borrowing wrong and who pays the price for this unethical behavior? What are some examples of policies and/or procedures that could be used to deter retail borrowing?

h.   ***Consumerism** is a social movement directed toward protecting consumers from harmful business practices*
    1).   The ***Consumer Bill of Rights*** *outlines the rights of consumers to be protected by the federal government.*
    2).   The ***Consumer Bill of Rights includes***:
        a).   Right to be safe

b).   Right to be informed

c).   Right to be heard

d).   Right to choose freely

**Use Instructor's Manual Marketing Mini-Project 3-A

**Use Real People, Real Surfers: Exploring the Web

i.   Ethics in the Marketing mix—marketing managers are responsible for determining the most ethical way to price, package, promote, and distribute their offerings.

**Refer to the introduction exercise (if used) for a discussion on ethics

Below are marketing mix decisions which must be made

1).   How to make the product safe

2).   How to price the product fairly

     a).   *Price fixing: an illegal business practice in which firms decide in advance on a common price for their product.*

     b).   New Era firms price their products fairly

3).   How to promote the product ethically

     a).   Federal Trade Commission (FTC)

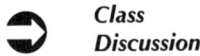

Class Discussion

During the 1998 Hurricane season Lowe's added to their web site "stormwatch '98". This sight contained information about how to protect your home and/or business from damage caused by hurricanes. Storms could also be tracked by logging onto the web site. Comment on Lowe's strategy. Where they behaving like a New Era firm?

     b).   *Puffery: claims made in advertising of product superiority that cannot be proven true or untrue.*

     c).   The FTC fines firms for deceptive advertising and has the power to require them to run corrective advertising: advertising that clarifies or qualifies previous deceptive advertising claims.

4).   Getting the product where it belongs

     a).   channels of distribution can create ethical dilemmas.

     b).   *slotting allowances: a fee paid by a manufacturer to a retailer in exchange for agreeing to place products on the retailers' shelves.*

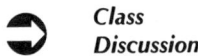

Class Discussion

Are slotting allowances unfair to smaller manufacturers? If possible, discuss the practice of slotting allowances with a retailer and a manufacturer. Do the two agree or disagree on the use and benefit of slotting allowances?

Real People, Bad Choices?

Summary: A California life insurance company encouraged its agents to scan newspapers for stories of crime. Then agents were to call on households in affected neighborhoods.

Suggested Answer to Discussion Question

1.   **Is this ethical?**

     No—the agents were taking advantage of emotions and were using fear tactics to sell insurance. Others may feel that the insurance company behaved ethically.—After all, people want to do something to make them feel safe and protected.

2.   **Doing It Right: A Focus On Social Responsibility**
       **Refer to Objective 1
       **Use Q #2 Marketing Practice: Applying What You've Learned
       a.   The second part of social profit is social responsibility
       b.   *Social responsibility: is a management practice in which organizations seek to engage in activities that have a positive effect on society and promote the public good.*
       c.   *Environmental stewardship: A position taken by an organization to protect or enhance the natural environment as it conducts its business activities.*
              1).   *Green marketing: A marketing strategy that supports environmental stewardship by creating an environmental founded differential benefit in the minds of consumers.*

Class   Do New Era firms practice environmental stewardship because they're "good" or
Discussion   because they will benefit financially? The answer is a little of both.

       d.   *Cause Marketing: A marketing strategy in which an organization serves its community by promoting and supporting a worthy cause or by allying itself with non-profit organization to tackle a social problem.*
              1).   Today many firms make a long-term commitment to tackle social problems.
              2).   Examples: Avon's support to Breast Cancer Awareness; Target's contributions to local schools

Class   Does cause marketing encourage consumers to be more loyal? Does it help to
Discussion   create a positive image of the company?

       e.   Serving the Community: Promoting Cultural Diversity
              1).   *Cultural diversity: A management practice that actively seeks to include people of different sexes, races, ethnic groups, and religions in an organization's employees, customers, suppliers, and distribution channels.*

Class   Discuss the cultural diversity of your university or college. You might also ask
Discussion   students to comment on any cultural diversity policies of the organizations in
                 which they are employed.
                          Are cultural diversity statements and polices necessary or are they just
                 another example of political correctness?

3.   **Doing It Well: A Focus On Quality**
       **Refer to Objective 2
       **Use Q #5 Marketing Practice: Applying What You've Learned
       a.   *Quality: the level of performance, reliability, features, safety, cost or other product characteristics that consumers expect to satisfy their needs and wants.*
       b.   Quality is important for firms competing in a global marketplace.
       c.   *Total Quality Management (TQM): a management philosophy that focuses on satisfying customers through empowering employees to be an active part of continuous quality improvement.*
              1).   The Malcolm Baldrige National Quality Award established by U.S. Congress in 1987 to recognize quality excellence
              2).   *ISO 9000: criteria developed by International Standards Organizations to regulate product quality in Europe.*
                    a).   Geneva—based organization

b).　　U.S. companies must comply with these standards to be competitive in the global market.

 **Class Discussion**　　Have students look up the web sites of current Baldrige winners.

　　　　1.　　What did each organization do to earn this award?
　　　　2.　　Are these recipients New Era firms?

d.　　Adding a dose of quality to the marketing mix
　　1).　　New Era firms seek to improve product, place, price and promotion.

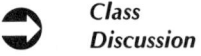 **Class Discussion**　　Discuss how quality concerns impacted the alternatives developed and the solution selected by Interface Americas (refer to the Real People, Real Choices: How it Worked Out at Interface Americas). Specifically examine how quality concerns impacted each element of the marketing mix.

4.　　**The Internal Business Environment**
　　**Refer to Objective 3
　　**Refer to Figure 3.1
　　a.　　Corporate Resources and competencies:
　　　　1).　　***Resources include*** *money, people, reputation, brand image, and physical resources.*
　　　　2).　　***Competencies*** *refer to what an organization does well.*
　　b.　　***Corporate Culture:*** *The set of values, norms, and beliefs held by an organization's managers and that influence the behavior of everyone in that organization.*
　　　　The New Era mission includes a concern for employees and shareholders.

Class Discussion　　Have students who are involved in internships or other career training jobs discuss the corporate resources and competencies of their firms. Ask students to also comment on the culture of their firms. How are corporate values, norms, and beliefs communicated to employees and shareholders?
　　　　Another strategy would be to answer the above questions for the firms examined in the Real People, Real Surfers: Exploring the Web exercise for this chapter.

　　c.　　Relationship with Publics
　　　　1).　　***Publics:*** *groups of people—including suppliers, channel intermediaries, customers, employees, shareholders, financial institutions, government, the media and public interest groups—that have an interest in the organization.*
　　　　2).　　Developing good relationships with suppliers and intermediaries are critical to the manufacturing of quality products.
　　d.　　Relationship with Competitors
　　　　1).　　Firms often band together for legislation that affects an entire industry.
　　　　2).　　Insurance companies often form political action groups in order to help support their mutual business interests.

5.　　**Scanning The External Environment**
　　**Refer to Objective 4
　　**Use Q#3 Marketing Practice: Applying What You've Learned
　　**Use Instructor's Manual Marketing Mini-Project 3-B
　　**Refer to Figure 3.1

a. Figure 3.1 shows the major elements of the external business environment

b. Economic Environment

  1). ***Business Cycles:*** *the overall pattern of changes or fluctuations of an economy*

  2). *All economies go through cycles.*

    a). ***Prosperity:*** *high levels of demand, employment and income.*

    b). ***Recession:*** *falling demand, employment, and income.*

    c). ***Recovery:*** *gradual improvement.*

    d). ***Depression:*** *a severe recession in which prices fall, but there is little demand.*

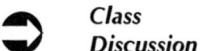

Class Discussion

1. Have students discuss their predictions for the economic environment. What economic indicators are used for making economic forecasts?

2. What are some ways marketers respond to each of the various business cycles.

  3). ***Consumer Confidence:*** *an indicator of future spending patterns are measured by the extent to which people are optimistic or pessimistic about the state of the economy.*

c. Competitive Environment

  1). ***Competitive Intelligence (CI):*** *the process of gathering and analyzing publicly available information about rivals.*

  2). Before a firm can develop strategies that will create a competitive advantage , they must understand what their competitors are doing.

  3). Marketers need to understand the competitive marketplace (MircoEnvironment).

    a). ***Discretionary income:*** *the amount of money left after paying for necessities.*

    b). ***Product competition:*** *when firms offer very different product compete to satisfy the same consumer needs and wants.*

    c). ***Brand competition:*** *when firms offering similar products or services compete based on their brand's reputation or perceived benefits.*

  4). Competition in the Macro Environment

    a). Marketers need to understand the overall structure of their industry.

    b). ***Monopoly:*** *a market situation in which one firm, the only supplier of a particular product, is able to control the price, quality, and supply of that product.*

    c). ***Oligopoly:*** *a market structure in which a relatively small number of sellers, each holding a substantial share of the market, compete in a market with many buyers.*

    d). ***Monopolistic competition:*** *a market structure in which many firms, each having slightly different products, offer consumer unique benefits.*

    e). ***Perfect competition:*** *a market structure in which many small sellers, all of whom offer similar products, are unable to have an impact on the quality, price, or supply of a product.*

d. The technological environment

  1). Technology is an investment in the future.

  2). Changes in technology can transform an industry.

  3). ***Patent:*** *legal documentation granting an individual or firm exclusive right to produce and sell a particular invention.*

Class Discussion

How has technology changed our daily lives in the past five years? How have recent technological innovations changed marketing activities?

e.   *Legal environment: the local, state, national and global laws and regulations that affect businesses.*

   1).   Laws governing businesses have two purposes
      a).   Make sure that businesses compete fairly—for example Sherman Antitrust Act
      b).   Make sure that businesses do not take advantage of consumers—for example, the Food and Drug Act
      **Refer to Table 3.1 for an overview of the legal environment
   2).   *Regulatory agencies: governmental bodies that monitor business activities and enforce laws.*
      **Use Real People, Real Surfers: Exploring the Web
      ■   Food and Drug Administration (FDA)
      ■   Federal Trade Commission (FTC)
      ■   Federal Communications Commission (FCC)
      ■   Consumer Product Safety Commission (CPSC)
      ■   Environmental Protection Agency (EPA)
f.   Sociocultural environment refers to the characteristics of society
   1).   *Demographics: statistics that measure observable aspects of a population, including size, age, gender, ethnic group, income, education, occupation, and family structure.*
   2).   An important part of examining the sociocultural environment is understanding consumer values and beliefs.

Real People, Real Choices: How it Worked Out at Interface Americas

Summary: Joyce LaValle, the Chief Innovations Officer for Interface Americas, is responsible for the marketing, environmental and educational initiatives of the Interface Americas Companies. Interface is one of the world's leading producers of carpet, fabrics, and other interior finishes for the commercial market. The Prince Street division of Interface, makes floor coverings exclusively for the commercial market and at one time was regarded as a market leader for innovative designs and colors. Ms. LaValle's task was to re-engineer the company from top to bottom—manufacturing, product design, workplace cultures, and customer relations

Interface places a high priority on social responsibility, this resulted in a strong push to update practices in the Prince Street division to ensure that minimum environmental damage occurred during manufacturing. Unfortunately, luxurious carpets require the use of more raw materials and create a great deal of waste. Ms. LaValle developed three options.

Option 1: Develop and introduce a new line of lower-priced carpeting under the Prince Street name with a lower face weight that would produce less waste.
Option 2: Create an entirely new carpet line that is less expensive and more earth-friendly, but as opposed to option #1 market it separately from the existing line
Option 3: Continue to manufacture Prince Street carpets as before and target these products to the high-end designer market.

Ms. LaValle choose option 2. Prince Street developed a separate line of commercial carpeting called the Post Script (PS) Series target to the lower price market.

Potential Discussion Questions

1.   Why is option 2 the best choice?

2.   Should PS be expanded beyond the present product mix? What internal and external factors should Interface consider when examining the issue of expansion of the PS line?

Chapter Review

Marketing Concepts: Testing Your Knowledge

1. **What is meant by the New Era of Marketing? What are business ethics? What are some ways that marketers practice ethical behavior in the marketing mix?**
    New Era marketers have come to realize that decisions and strategies designed to satisfy consumer needs and wants must not only be economically sound, they must have a strong ethical foundation and be socially responsible.

    In the New Era of marketing, we are witnessing greater concern about the consequences of business decisions based on short-term profits instead of long-term benefits. "Business as usual" is not necessarily the best business philosophy. Business ethics are rules of conduct for an organization that are standards against which most people in its environments judge what is right and what is wrong. It has become profitable for firms to engage in business practices that are both morally defensible and beneficial to the community in which the firm operates.

2. **What is consumerism? What is the Consumer Bill of Rights?**
    Consumerism is a social movement directed toward protecting consumers from harmful business practices. Like other social movements, consumerism activities include the use of economic, moral, and legal pressure to force businesses to make ethical decisions and treat their customers fairly.

    In 1962 President John F. Kennedy, in his inaugural speech, outlined the rights of consumers to be protected by the federal government. These rights, which have come to be called the "*Consumer Bill of Rights*" include:

    - *The right to be safe.*
    - *The right to be informed.*
    - *The right to be heard.*
    - *The right to choose freely.*

3. **What is social responsibility? What is cause marketing? How do marketers promote cultural diversity?**
    Social responsibility means that New Era firms act in ways that benefit the public, the community, and the natural environment. New Era marketers assume social responsibility through environmental stewardship (the actions of the firm improves or at least maintains the natural environment). Cause marketing focuses on marketing strategies that promote the public good, such as Target's support of local school's. In addition, New Era marketing organizations promote cultural diversity by including people from different sexes, races, ethnic groups, and religions as customers, suppliers, employees, and distribution channel members.

4. **What is Total Quality Management? How do marketers add quality to the marketing mix?**
    Quality refers to the level of performance, dependability, and cost that customers expect in products that satisfy their needs and wants. Quality focused firms in the New Era of marketing strive to provide goods and services that go beyond customer expectations about the relationship between cost and value.

    Total quality management (TQM) is a management philosophy that focuses on satisfying customers and reducing production costs through such programs as continuous quality improvements, total quality assurance programs, benchmarking, employee empowerment, participatory management programs, and a team approach (quality circles) that involves employees in all levels of the organization in cross-functional planning and task-related activities.

5. **What is "corporate culture"? What are some ways that the corporate culture of one organization might differ from that of another? How does corporate culture affect decision making? How are relationships with a firm's publics an important part of an organization's internal environment?**
    Corporate culture is the set of values, norms, beliefs, and practices held by an organization's managers.

New Era firms tend to be more people-centered and concerned with the welfare of employees. Some corporate cultures are more inclined to take risk than others. Though many large firms have lost their sense of entrepreneurship, others are trying to regain this cultural spirit by encouraging intrapreneurship (seeking new solutions to old problems). Profit-centered firms still abound, however, New Era firms and their approach seem to having more success.

Corporate culture affects decision making by establishing the environment (rules) in which the decisions are made. The culture interprets and establishes the decision making process. For example, does the organization encourage risk, long-term strategic thinking, new idea development, short-term profit taking, or risk avoidance?

It is also important that an organization develop good relationships with its publics. These publics include the firms' employees, shareholders, and communities. Employees should be valued members of the team. Employees should understand how they contribute to the overall mission and objectives of the firm. Shareholders also need to know and understand the mission of the firm and how they benefit when the firms' mission is fulfilled. Finally, the firm needs to develop good relationships with the community. Relationships with the community can be fostered through the giving of monetary contributions and/or in-kind gifts.

6. **Describe the business cycle. What is consumer confidence? How do consumer expectations affect the business cycle?**
    The *business cycle* is the overall pattern of change in the economy—including periods of prosperity, recession, depression, and recovery—that affect consumer and business purchasing power.

    Consumer confidence is an indicator of future spending patterns as measured by the extent to which people are optimistic or pessimistic about the state of the economy.

    Many economists suggest that changes in the economy are primarily a "self-fulfilling prophecy": When consumers feel that the economy is going to get better, they spend money to buy goods and services, industry flourishes, and lo and behold, the economy improves! Similarly the reverse also happens if the consumers fear a recession.

7. **What different types of competition do marketers face? What is competitive intelligence?**
    Competition may be characterized as:

    Brand competition where there is a marketing situation in which firms offering similar products or services compete for consumers based on their brand's reputation or perceived benefits.

    Product competition where there is a marketing situation in which competitors offering very different products compete to satisfy the same consumer needs and wants.

    General competition within a specific industry where competition is determined by whether the industry is a monopoly, an oligopoly, or an example of perfect competition or "imperfect" monopolistic competition.

    Competitive intelligence is the process of gathering and analyzing publicly available information about rivals.

8. **What are some ways that technological advances have affected marketing?**
    Forward thinking managers see technology as the key to the future, even if it means a risky investment at the expense of short-term profits. Changes in technology can dramatically transform an industry. Some examples of technological advances that have affected marketing include:

    - Toll-free numbers
    - Data processing
    - UPC codes and scanners
    - Customer databases
    - Home shopping network
    - Next day delivery

9. **Describe the important elements in marketing's legal environment?**

The legal environment affects production, product development, pricing, distribution, and advertising activities. Many businesspeople see laws and regulations as hindrances to business, but others look to the benefits of laws that protect competition in a free market and help business. Laws and regulations tend to level the playing field and encourage fair competition. As long as there are domestic and international forces that would choose to play the game of competition unfairly, watchdog agencies are needed.

10. **What is the sociocultural environment? What are demographics?**

The sociocultural environment consists primarily of those demographic and lifestyle variables that affect the consumer and their decision making process. Consumer demographics for example segment a population according to such characteristics as age, gender, family structure, social class, race, and geography, while consumer values and lifestyles indicate the way people conduct their lives.

Marketing Concepts: Discussing Choices and Issues

1. **When New Era firms seek to create social profit, they practice environmental stewardship. Environmental stewardship may mean taking some products off the market and changing other products. What are some products that have a good chance of being removed from the market? What are some products which are likely to be positively affected by environmental stewardship? What are some ideas for new products that would be in tune with these trends?**

Products that might be negatively impacted by the trend towards environmentalism and a return to value might be oil based products, fur coats, skins from endangered species (for clothing and shoes), medical research animals, throw away products and packages, products that are not biodegradable, products that have controversial health side effects (cigarettes and alcohol), and red meat based foods.

Some examples of products that might be positively affected by the trend towards environmentalism and a return to value might be solar and electric powered appliances, homes, and cars, natural fiber clothing (cotton), natural fiber foods (whole grain cereal), recyclable products and packages, simple but high quality products that don't wear out or break easily, and products that replaceable components that prevent the master product from being scrapped (circuit panels in computers).

Some ideas for new products that are in keeping with these trends might be electric cars, urban bicycles (acceptable for adult transportation), a VCR that has easily replaceable parts, refill containers for laundry products, non-polluting dyes for clothing, and recycled packaging.

2. **Taking a firm's perspective, what do you think are the positive and negative aspects of social profit?**

Social profit is the benefit an organization and society receive from its ethical practices, community service, efforts to promote cultural diversity, and concern for the natural environment.

History has shown that those firms that give back to society are generally rewarded by society. The rewards might be in increased business, less legislative control, more freedom to operate their businesses, more forgiveness when problems occur (such as an environmental problem), and a true sense of community team spirit. However, social profit does have its costs. Many firms that have invested heavily in communities are criticized when the funds are withdrawn because of poor economic conditions or performance. It is easier to be socially responsible when business is good. It is very difficult to "give back" when downsizing is occurring. Some argue that moneys spent in social causes are really just public relations gimmicks and the money should be going to R&D or shareholders. After all, a shareholder invested in a company not in a community. These ideas should cause interesting discussion on the part of the students.

3. **The U.S. government has been both criticized and praised for its efforts to regulate and control business practices. What is your stand on this issue as a consumer?**

Most students may very easily have no opinion on the subject. However, those that have been harmed by a manufacturer or retailer will no doubt think that regulation and control are good. Though protection does seem wise, the instructor might raise the issue of cost. How many employees do firms have that do nothing but monitor compliance with regulations? What are the students feelings about the cost of regulation being passed on to them in the way of increased prices? These questions might stimulate discussion.

4. **This chapter pointed out that business ethics needs to be a two-way street, that consumers as well as businesses must behave ethically in the marketplace? What are some examples of unethical consumer behavior? What should businesses do about these types of behavior?**

    The first thing to do with question is to get the students to define what might be meant by public spaces. Next, ask them to cite instances when they feel their rights were violated by advertisers. There is currently a movement to sell sponsorships to fund our National Parks. Ask the students to imagine what it would be like to go to the Nike Grand Canyon. Under what circumstances would that be OK? One favorite question is to ask is "Would it be OK to put a billboard on the moon"? Coca-Cola has thought about funding such a project.

Real People, Real Surfers: Exploring the Web

The purpose of this exercise is to gain information about not-for-profit organizations and government agencies that are important in a firm's legal and ethical environment.

Web sites for the following organizations are investigated: Better Business Bureau (BBB), American Marketing Association (AMA), Federal Trade Commission (FTC) and The Federal Communications Commission (FCC). Instructors might want to use student responses to questions 1 and 2 for class discussion. One good method for answering question one would be to develop a grid. A suggested format for this grid is provided below.

	Purpose	**Service**
BBB	To promote and foster ethical relationships between businesses, organizations and the public	Consumer alerts, online complaints, business report databases
AMA	A resource for marketing professionals	career assistance publications research
FTC	To ensure that the nation's marketing function competitively	educational information advocate for consumers and businesses
FCC	To encourage competition in all communications market and to protect the public interest	educational information advocate and industry watchdog

Marketing in Action: Real Choices at Nickelodeon

Teaching Suggestions: This case works well with helping students to understand the broad scope of a New Era marketing orientation. If students have not seen one of the kids shows on Nickelodeon suggest that they do so. Another option would be to play a portion of one of the popular programs on Nickelodeon, such as Blue's Clues or Gullah Gullah Island in class. Finally have students visit the Nickelodeon web site www.nickjr.com. What evidence is there that Nickelodeon is a New Era firm?

   If you are teaching in a multimedia classroom that has Internet access you could download some of the games and sound bites from the Nickjr web site and play them in class.

Summary: Nickelodeon is a cable network for kids and those who are "young at heart." Nickelodeon has adopted the New Era marketing orientation in its business practices. Network executives believe that their long-term success has been closely tied to the company's emphasis on ethical behavior and social responsibility toward kids.

Suggested Answers to Discussion Questions

1. **What is the problem facing Nickelodeon?**
   Broadly put, the primary problem facing Nickelodeon is how to transpose a strategy designed to foster and encourage cultural diversity and minority programming into reality in light of cost constraints and existing program format limitations.

2. **What factors are important in understanding this problem?**
   The following factors are important to understanding the above problem:
   a. Advertising revenue is what keeps the network operating.
   b. There is a trend in the social and business environment that is moving toward the appreciation of and desire for cultural diversity and minority programming.
   c. Existing programming does not really suit this trend.
   d. New programming is expensive and cannot rely on old re-runs.
   e. Cultural diversity issues and minority characters cannot just be automatically plugged into existing program format structures.
   f. New program formats are expensive and there is a difficulty in finding producers who can develop such programs.
   g. How much air time to give to the new programs is an unknown.

3. **What alternatives might Nickelodeon consider?**
   Students should be encouraged to be creative in response to this question. Several suggestions that might stimulate that discussion are:
   a. Develop focus groups from the cultural and minority areas to determine what they would like to see in programming. Let the kids design the programs (as they have done in the past for Nickelodeon).
   b. Create joint ventures with existing minority networks (such as BET—Black Entertainment network—or Spanish TV).
   c. Poll advertisers to determine what forms of programming would match their products (sports matching sports products for example).
   d. Review existing programs to see which ones could be converted to a more culturally diverse cast of characters.
   e. Examine programming that is not culturally sensitive (such as nature shows) to be used in filler situations.
   f. Create scholarships for minority producers and directors to encourage program development.

4. **What are your recommendations for solving the problem?**
   The answer to this question is based on the breadth of alternatives generated in Question #3 above. Given the alternatives listed above solutions a, b, and c would seem to be the most practical in the short run.

Marketing in Action: Real Choices at Nickelodeon (*Continued*)

5. **What are some ways to implement your recommendations?**
    The organization might choose to ask advertisers to aid in the development of new programming by sponsoring innovative programming. Advertisers could also be of help in formulating joint ventures between networks (if advertisers would support the networks equally). Advertisers (or their agencies) are also equipped to conduct focus groups to determine program format desires. In conclusion, the involvement of the market or the advertiser is probably one of the secrets to the success of this venture. The involvement gives true meaning to consumer involvement and is the foundation of the New Era marketer.

Mini-project 3-A
Consumer Social Responsibility

Purpose: to help you better appreciate the ethical and social responsibilities of consumers in the marketing process.

For this mini-project, you will work with several of your classmates in studying attitudes toward consumer ethics.

1.   First you will need to identify the types of unethical consumer behavior which marketers face. Some are listed in your text. You may want to discuss the problems of consumer ethics with a local retailer.

2.   Next, design and conduct a research study with students on your campus about the types of unethical behaviors you have found to be a problem. You might want to find out some of the following:
     a.   Do the students think such behavior is OK or is unethical?
     b.   Do the students recognize that the costs incurred by retailers are passed on to them as customers?.
     c.   What ideas do students have about solutions to the problem?

3.   Based on your research, develop a report which outlines
     a.   The unethical behavior(s) you have examined
     b.   The perspective of the retailer
     c.   The perspective of the consumer
     d.   Several original recommendations for improving the problem

4.   Present your findings and your recommendations to your class.

Mini-project 3-B
Environmental Scanning

Purpose: To better understand how organizations scan their external environments in order to identify opportunities and threats.

As we know all types of organizations engage in marketing planning. One of the first steps in that planning is to scan the external environment searching for factors beyond direct control that create opportunities and threats. In this project, you are to examine the different environments of an organization.

1.   First, select a real or imaginary organization such as one of the following
    a.   Your university
    b.   A new restaurant in your community
    c.   An existing business in your community

2.   Identify the important factors and trends in each of the environments listed below.

3.   Determine what opportunities and threats the environmental factors present for the organization.

Important environmental factors	Opportunities	Threats
Economic Environment		
Competitive Environment		

Natural Environment		
Technological Environment		
Legal/Regulatory Environment		

Sociocultural Environment		

4

Think Globally and Act Locally: Marketing in a Multinational Environment

*O*verview We are all aware that the world is getting smaller. Advances in transportation and communication have contributed to the feeling that the world is getting smaller. In this chapter the "big picture" of international marketing is explored. The interrelationships among countries and regions as well as environmental factors a marketer must consider before venturing to another country are presented. Methods for entering foreign markets and decisions regarding the marketing mix are also discussed.

MTV Europe is the focus of the Real People, Real Choices segment. Most students are probably aware of MTV and should enjoy reading and discussing this segment. The video segment on MTV could also be used to introduce this chapter or you could play a few minutes of an actual MTV show or music video.

The first case in the Computer Friendly Stuff (CFS) case series ("It's a small market after all") is presented in the book at the end of chapter 4. This case could be used to discuss international marketing and/or the marketing concepts learned in chapters 1–4.

Objectives

1. Explain how complex relationships among firms, countries, and regions influence world trade.

2. Understand how political, legal, and cultural issues influence global marketing strategies and outcomes.

3. Explain the strategies a firm can choose to enter global markets.

4. Understand the arguments for standardization versus localization of marketing strategies in global markets, and understand how elements of the marketing mix apply in foreign countries.

Chapter Outline and Suggested Activities

Introduction: Have student(s) and/or a faculty member from another country come to class and discuss marketing activities in their country. Students typically enjoy this type of presentation and are often surprised that there are more marketing similarities than differences.

1. **Let's Get Small**
    **Refer to Objective 1
    **Use MTV video segment
    ** Use the Real People, Real Choices at MTV
    **Refer to Figure 4.1

    a. Marketers need to think globally by seeing the world as their market, but act locally by being willing to adopt its businesses practices when necessary.

    b. How "worldly" can a company be? There are four types of firms which define international marketing.
        1). Domestic firm: confines its sales and marketing efforts to its home market.
        2). Exporting firm: expands sales by offering its products for sale in other countries.
        3). Multinational firm: operates in many foreign markets, and modifies the product it sells accordingly.
        4). Global firm: views the world as its market, and tends to operate the same way in many countries, adapting its basic strategy when necessary to conform to local conditions.

    Class Discussion Have students provide examples of each type of firm listed above. Is it possible for an organization to begin conducting business at the global level?

    c. *Countertrade: Type of trade in which goods are paid for with other items instead of with cash.*
        1). Countertrade accounts for about 25% of all world trade

    Class Discussion Students have probably used countertrade. For example, Joe might assist Tom with his calculus and in return Tom helps Joe write his English paper. Why is countertrade used?

    d. *Trade flow: the pattern of economic interdependence among countries or regions.*
        1). World trade is increasing steadily year by year.
        2). The most significant U.S. exports are foods, industrial supplies, and services including tourism and entertainment

    e. Competitive Advantage: the factors working in a company's favor making it easier for it to compete in both domestic and foreign markets.
        1). Firms need to capitalize on their home country's assets
        2). Firms should avoid competing in areas where they are at a disadvantage

    Class Discussion During the past 20 years more and more of the sewing component of apparel manufacturing has been performed in small less developed countries. American workers complain about job losses while apparel manufacturers say that they must go off-shore in order to remain competitive. Consider the issue of a competitive advantage. What is the U.S.'s competitive advantage? Is it sewing? Consider the skill level required of workers in an apparel sewing factory and the type of equipment needed to sew a garment. What would you do if you were a designer? Would you manufacture your garments in another country? Consider Michael Porter's model in your discussion.

3).   Michael Porter's model describes four keys to a nation's competitive advantage
   a).   Demand conditions
   b).   Related and supporting industries
   c).   Factor conditions
   d).   Company strategy, structure, and rivalry
f.   Borders, Roadblocks, and Communities
   1).   Company's efforts to expand into foreign markets are often hindered by roadblocks. Consider the following types of roadblocks which are designed to favor local businesses over outsiders.
   2).   Protected trade—*Protectionism: a policy adopted by a government to give domestic companies an advantage*

Class Discussion   Are you in favor of protectionism? Should the U.S. support and protect industries which are weak or in their infancy in hopes that the industries will grow strong?

   3).   **Import quotas:** limitations set by government on the amount of a product allowed to enter a country
   4).   **Embargo:** a quota completely prohibiting specified goods from entering or leaving a country

Class Discussion   Do embargoes work? Embargoes are often used as a political weapon to punish countries who are behaving in a manner which the U.S. opposes. Who is the loser when there is an embargo?

   5).   *Tariffs: Taxes on imported goods*
      a).   *The General Agreement on Tariffs and Trade (GATT) works to encourage and reduce import tax levels and trade restrictions among the member nations.*
   6).   *World Trade Organization (WTO): formed to mediate trade disputes between nations and to deal with cases in which unfair protectionism by one country is claimed by another.*
   7).   *Economic Communities: groups of countries that band together to promote trade amongst themselves and to make it easier for member nations to compete elsewhere.*
      a).   *European Union (EU): Economic Community that now includes most of Western Europe.*

Class Discussion   If you have any students from Europe in your class ask them to comment on any changes that have occurred since the formation of the EU. Do they think that consumers will benefit by the EU and if yes—in what ways?

      b).   *North American Free Trade Agreement (NAFTA) The world's largest economic community composed of the Unites States, Canada, and Mexico.*

2.   **The Global Marketing Environment**
   **Refer to Objective 2
   **Refer to Figure 4.2
   **Use Q#2 Marketing Practice: Applying What You've Learned
   **Use Real People, Real Surfers: Exploring the Web

**Use Marketing in Action: Real Choices for Major League Baseball International Partners
Environmental scanning is very important when considering foreign markets. Firms need to consider the economic, political, and cultural factors of each country or region they are considering entering.

a.   The economic environment

    1).   Indicators of economic health

        a).   ***Standard of living:*** *an indicator of the average quality and quantity of goods and services consumed in a country.*

        b).   ***Gross domestic product:*** *the total dollar value of goods and services produced by a nation in a year.*

        c).   ***Economic infrastructure:*** *the quality of a country's distribution, financial, and communications systems.*

    2).   Level of economic development
        **Use Instructor's Manual Mini-Project 4-B
        Economists describe three levels of development

        a).   ***Less developed country* (LDC):** *a country at the lowest stage of economic development*

        b).   ***Developing country:*** *countries in which the economy is shifting its emphasis from agriculture to industry.*

        c).   ***Developed Country:*** *a country that boasts sophisticated marketing systems , strong private enterprise, and bountiful market potential for many goods and services.*

b.   The Political and Legal Environment

    1).   Political Issues

        a).   ***Economic sanctions:*** *trade prohibitions imposed by one country against another.*

        b).   ***Nationalization:*** *a domestic government's takeover of a foreign company for its assets with some reimbursement, though often not for the full value.*

        c).   ***Expropriation:*** *a domestic government's seizure of a foreign company's assets without any compensation.*

    2).   Regulatory Issues

        a).   ***Local content rules:*** *a form of protectionism stipulating that a certain proportion of a product must consist of components supplied by industries in the host country.*

        b).   Many nations impose quotas on foreign TV programming, television networks may also be state-controlled.

    3).   Human Rights Issues

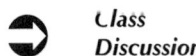

Class Discussion   Consider the recent negative media coverage received by Nike regarding working conditions in their foreign factories. Should poor working conditions concern Nike customers?

Real People, Bad Choices?

Summary: Kathie Lee Gifford drew heat for promoting a line of Wal-Mart clothing made in overseas sweatshops. She didn't know about the conditions in the foreign factories! Gifford turned around and became a spokesperson for human rights.

1.   **Should a spokesperson be responsible for the quality of the product she endorses or whether it is manufactured under acceptable conditions?**
    This issue is critical to endorsers, especially if an endorser wants to maintain his integrity; because people "look up" to well known celebrities like Gifford, it is important that they be knowledgeable about the product and the conditions of the manufacturing facility. Kathie Lee Gifford had to work hard to help restore her credibility after the Wal-Mart incident.

c.   The Cultural Environment
    1).   Values
        a).   ***Cultural values:*** *a society's deeply-held beliefs about right and wrong ways to live.*
        b).   ***Collectivist culture:*** *culture in which people subordinate their personal goals to those of a stable community.*
        c).   ***Individualist culture:*** *culture in which people tend to attach more importance to personal goals than to those of the larger community.*
    2).   Norms and Customs
        a).   ***Norms:*** *specific rules dictating what is right or wrong, acceptable or unacceptable.*
        b).   ***Customs:*** *a norm handed down from the past that controls basic behaviors.*
        c).   ***More:*** *a custom with a strong moral over.*
        d).   ***Conventions:*** *norms regarding everyday life.*

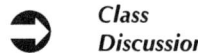 ***Class Discussion***   Have students from different parts of the U.S. and the world share some of their interesting norms and customs. Why is the understanding of regional norms and customs critical to marketing success?

    3).   Symbols and Superstitions
        a).   The meanings we assign symbols are influenced by culture.
        b).   ***Semiotics:*** *field of study that examines how meanings are assigned to symbols.*
        c).   Marketers need to also be concerned about taboos and superstitions.
    4).   Language
        a).   Language barriers can be a big obstacle.
        b).   Language barriers affect product labeling and usage instructions, advertising, and personal selling.

Spotlight on Real People: Getting Through Customs, Inc.

Summary: Getting through customs was established in 1990 by Terri Morrison and Wayne Conaway to help clients understand and adapt to cultural differences. The owners train executives to do business abroad by schooling them in local customs.
    Web site, www.getcustoms.com

Suggested Answers to Discussion Questions

1.   **What benefits does getting through customs offer its clients?**
    Clients learn about the local culture and customs. This information and training is very helpful in preventing costly mistakes.

2.   **What are the norms and customs highlighted in this summary?**
    In Colombia
    ■   Take time to greet everyone formally
    ■   Men shake hands with men and women
    ■   Women shake hands with other women or clasp each other forearms
    ■   Friends are expected to hug and exchange kisses on the cheeks

3.   **How can the two partners try to expand their own business to foreign markets?**
    Terri Morrison and Wayne Conaway, the two partners, might begin by focusing on a region in which they want to conduct business. Hopefully the American firms which they have assisted will offer them leads and networking assistance.

---

5).   ***Ethnocentrism:*** *the tendency to prefer products or people of one's own culture.*

➲ ***Class***
Discussion   Ask students about their level of agreement with the following statements. Probe to identify why/how these attitudes were formed.

■   Purchasing foreign-made products is un-American.
■   Restrictions should be put on all imports.
■   American consumers who purchase products made in other countries are responsible for putting their fellow Americans out of work.

➲ ***Class***
Discussion   What factors must be considered when developing a distribution system in a foreign country?

3.   **How Global Should a Global Marketing Strategy Be?**
        **Refer to Objective 3
        **Use Figure 4.4
        **Use Q#4 Marketing Practice: Applying What You've Learned
        a.   There are four market entry strategies representing increased levels of involvement:
                1).   Exporting
                        a).   Exporting involves the least amount of risk.
                        b).   Firms that decide to export must determine whether they will attempt to sell their products on their own, or rely on some type of intermediary.
                        c).   ***Export merchant:*** *an intermediary used by a firm to represent it in another country.*

➲ ***Class***
Discussion   How do firms decide when to use or not to use an export merchant? What factors should be considered when making this decision?

                2).   Contractual Agreements: There are two common types:
                        a).   ***Licensing:*** *agreement where one firm gives another firm the right to produce and market its product in a specified location in return for royalties.*
                        b).   ***Franchising:*** *A form of licensing involving the right to adopt an entire system of doing business.*

➲ ***Class***
Discussion   Discuss with students the differences between licensing and franchising. What are some potential problems that may occur with contractual agreements?

                3).   ***Strategic Alliances:*** relationship developed between a firm seeking a deeper commitment to a foreign market and a domestic firm in the target country.
                        a).   ***Joint Venture:*** *a strategic alliance in which a new entity owned by two or more firms is created to allow the partners to pool their resources for common goals.*

> **Class Discussion**
>
> In some ways a strategic alliance is like a marriage. Two companies come together as one. Like married partners, these two firms have to share secrets and adapt to new ways of doing things.
>
> Discuss some of the potential problems which may incur when a strategic alliance is formed. What could be done by both firms to help avoid some of these conflicts or problems.

    4).   Direct Investment: the most common way a firm expands internationally is to buy a business in the host country. Ownership gives a firm maximum freedom and control.

> **Class Discussion**
>
> Discuss the advantages and disadvantage of direct investment.

4.   Product Level Decisions: Choosing a Marketing Mix Strategy
**Refer to Objective 4
**Use Q#3 Marketing Practice: Applying What You've Learned
**Use Real People, Real Choices at MTV
**Real People, Real Surfers: Exploring the Web

> **Class Discussion**
>
> Marketers who operate in two or more countries have a crucial decision to make. How necessary is it to develop a customized marketing mix for each country?
>
> Discuss the decisions made by MTV regarding standardization versus localization. What types of products are best suited for standardization strategies? What types of products typically need to be altered to meet the needs and wants of the target country?

After an entry strategy is made, decisions regarding the marketing mix are made.

    a.   Standardization versus localization
           **Use Instructor's Manual Marketing Mini-project 4-A
    b.   Product decisions – three choices
        1).   Straight extension strategy retains the same product for domestic and foreign market
        2).   Product adaptation strategy recognizes that in some cultures people do have strong and different product preferences
        3).   Product invention strategy means that a company develops a new product as it expands to foreign markets.
    c.   Promotion decisions
        1).   Marketers must decide whether it is necessary to change product promotions in a foreign market.
        2).   Decisions regarding when and how to change the message are typically based on the firm's overall global strategy and cultural differences

> **Class Discussion**
>
> What are some examples of concepts which are universal in appeal? (i.e., love, romance, etc.)? Ask your international students to comment on how promotion messages are different in their home country.

    d.   Price decisions
    1).   Costs associated with transportation tariffs and currency fluctuations often make the product too expensive for the targeted country.

2).   Free trade zones ease the problems by providing areas where foreign companies can warehouse goods without paying taxes or custom duties until the goods are moved into the marketplace.

3).   Two basic problems occur when the price becomes too high in the foreign country.

    a).   ***Gray market:*** *when an unauthorized party imports products and then sells them for a fraction of the price.*

    b).   ***Dumping:*** *when a company tries to get a toehold in a foreign market by pricing its product lower than they are offered at home.*

e.   Distribution decisions

Establishing a reliable distribution system is essential if the marketer is to succeed in a foreign market. A reliable system can be especially difficult to establish in developing countries where the infrastructure is under developed.

Class Discussion

Consider the following situation. After extensive research on international market opportunities, a manufacturer of toothpaste has learned that Ethiopia might be a good market. One of the unresolved issues is the development of a distribution system. Discuss some of the potential problems that the manufacturer might encounter when developing a distribution system in Ethiopia.

Note: The above situation is only an example. You could use any country and/or product for this discussion. If you are using the Real People, Real Surfers exercise you might want to discuss one of the countries and/or regions that the students are researching. Finally, if you have any students from developing or less developed countries in your class you might ask them to comment on the complexity of distribution decisions in their home country.

Real People, Real Choices: How it Worked out at MTV Europe

Summary: Peter Einstein is the Director of Marketing and Network Development for MTV Europe. Founded in 1987, MTV Europe transmits music-based programs for young adults across the continent. All of its shows are broadcast in English.

Marketing research revealed that the European teen audience was less homogeneous than MTV presumed. The result, local competition competitors tailored their programming to individual markets rather than an entire continent.

Peter Einstein faced a critical marketing mix decision: Should MTV continue its pan-European strategy, or develop regional products? Mr. Einstein considered three options:

Option 1: Stay with the pan-European strategy.
Option 2: Create different regional channels to compete head-to-head with local alternatives.
Option 3: Maintain the pan-European entity, but devote a few parts of the channel to certain regions.

MTV Europe chose option 3. This allowed some limited customization, including local advertising for these countries while still retaining most of the international programming and positioning.

Potential Discussion Questions

1.   Why do you think option 3 was selected?

2.   To what other countries or regions should MTV consider expanding?

Marketing Concepts: Testing Your Knowledge

1. **What are domestic firms, exporting firms, multinational firms, and global firms?**
A *domestic firm* confines its sales to and marketing efforts to its home market. A **multinational firm** operates in many foreign markets, and it modifies the product it sells accordingly. A **global firm** views the world as its market and it tends to operate the same way in many countries, adapting its basic strategy when necessary to conform to local conditions.

2. **Describe the market conditions that influence a firm's decision to enter foreign markets?**
The decision to expand globally typically depends on the company's goals for growth and management's assessment of the business environment at home. Reasons to enter the global marketplace include a leveling of domestic demand (which can reduce a firm's profitability and prohibit its growth), comparative advantage (where superiority of production exists), and comparative market potential (whether demand is high for the company's products and opportunities in sales abound relative to other markets).

3. **How do governments develop policies and regulations that protect home companies? How have GATT and the WTO reduced protectionism?**
Protectionism is a policy adopted by a government give domestic firms an advantage. These polices help to shield firms from foreign competitors. *GATT* (General Agreement on Tariffs and Trade) and the *WTO* (World Trade Organization) accords have helped to reduce the problems protectionism created. GATT's position is to reduce import tax levels and trade restrictions. The WTO was formed to mediate trade disputes between nations and to deal with cases in which unfair protectionism by one country is claimed by another.

4. **What are economic communities? How have they changed global marketing opportunities?**
An economic community is a group of countries that have agreed to work together in regulation of international trade for the good of all member nations.
    For global marketers, economic communities have the positive effect of eliminating the need for a firm to adapt its actions to the specific policies of each country. On the other hand, opportunities might be adversely affected because these same agreements tend to favor the home industries of member countries.

5. **How are countries classified according to their level of economic development? What marketing opportunities are afforded by countries in each stage of economic development?**
There are three classifications of countries according to their level of economic development:
    a. *Less developed country*—a country at the lowest stage of economic development, characterized by low standards of living, little or no technology, extremely low per capita GNP, and limited market potential.
    b. *Developing country*—a country at the middle stage of economic development, characterized by rising standards of living, some use of technology, a relatively low GNP, high market potential for many goods, and a potentially attractive labor supply.
    c. *Developed country*—a country at the highest level of economic development, characterized by high standards of living, extensive use of modern technology, a high per capita GNP, and a high market potential for limitless goods and services.
Opportunities that are afforded by these country descriptions are:
    a. Less developed country—usually limited to staples and inexpensive discretionary items.
    b. Developing country—the rising middle class creates great demand for basic consumer goods.
    c. Developed country—has a highly sophisticated marketing system and offers almost limitless marketing opportunities for goods and services.

6. **What aspects of the political and legal environment influence a firm's decision to a enter a foreign market?**

A firm assesses the political risks of entering a foreign market by considering such factors as economic sanctions imposed by the country to prohibit trade with another country for political reasons, as well as political upheaval within the country that creates the potential for confiscation of foreign business interests. Policies of economic sanctions, expropriation, or nationalization can all be harmful to business interests. In addition, political factors can result in numerous conditions a firm must meet just to enter the global market or lead to excessive controls that inhibit a firm's ability to do business.

In the legal environment, global marketers find that some countries have protectionist trade policies that protect domestic industries by erecting barriers to entry in the form of import quotas, tariffs, and embargoes. In addition, the global marketer faces other concerns such as local content laws, rights violations, bribery practices, and advertising regulations

7. **What cultural factors in a country influence a foreign firm's ability to succeed there?**

The cultural environment embraces all of the factors that make people unique, including their language, beliefs, and customs. A country's demographic characteristics, for example, play an extremely important role in determining the products and services that are likely to succeed in that environment. Language affects everything from product labeling and usage instructions to advertising and personal selling and can be a huge problem. Customs and beliefs affect business practices, the relationship between men and women, the role of the family, importance of career, and consumers' basic responses to products and services.

8. **How is a firm's level of commitment related to its level of control in a foreign market? Describe.**

Different foreign market entry strategies represent varying levels of commitment for a firm, each accompanied by varying levels of control by the firm. This commitment can range from a casual involvement to a full-scale "marriage." Generally, the more a firm becomes involved in a global relationship, the more control it will have over how its products are treated in the international marketplace. But increased control has a price. The more that a firm is involved, the more that it has to lose.

When firms seek greater involvement (and usually profit) in the international market, they negotiate contractual agreements with foreign middlemen. The firm that seeks to manufacture its products in the foreign country needs to find partners with which to license, franchise, or subcontract (outsource). *Licensing* is a contractual arrangement that assigns the limited right to produce and market a firm's goods to another in exchange for a fee or royalties on sales. *Franchising* is a contractual arrangement that assigns limited rights to an entire business to another in exchange for a fee or royalties on sales. *Subcontracting (outsourcing)* is a contractual arrangement in which a firm purchases custom components or production services from another firm on a permanent or temporary basis.

A *strategic alliance* is a formal partnership agreement between two firms to pool their resources in order to achieve common goals. Forms might include a joint production and marketing agreement where a synergy is created (could be vertical or horizontal) or a *strategic equity alliance* (each firm has an equity or financial stake in the partnership). A special version of the equity alliance is a *joint venture* (a strategic equity alliance that usually results in a jointly run corporate entity).

9. **What are the arguments for standardization of marketing strategies in the global marketplace? What are the arguments for localization?**

Standardization is an international marketing perspective in which the same marketing mix strategies are used in all global situations. *Localization* is an international marketing perspective in which marketing mix strategies are adapted for different global markets.

Proponents of the standardization perspective focus on commonalties across countries. In reality many of the world's industrialization nations have become surprisingly similar in the age of communication and rapidly expanding technology. By focusing on standardization, producers are able to produce truly strong global brands that have consistent images from country to country.

Advocates of localization, on the other hand, seek to adapt to the national character of each country. These marketers believe that each country has its own set of value systems, conventions, and regulations (in many instances a company has no choice but to adopt this philosophy). Cost is usually a drawback to this strategy.

Marketing Concepts: Discussing Choices and Issues

1. **Do you think U.S. firms should be allowed to use bribes to compete in countries where bribery is an accepted and legal form of doing business? Why or why not?**

   Under the *Foreign Corrupt Practices Act of 1977*, U.S. firms are barred from paying bribes to products overseas. The rest of the world sees this issue differently from the United States. In fact in Italy and Germany, bribes can even be deducted as a business expense. Students will have to examine their own ethical beliefs to answer this question. It is suggested that the instructor appoint students to argue the pro and con viewpoint. Give the assignment in advance so the students will have the opportunity to prepare in advance. Rationale for comments can come from historical precedence and tradition, biblical reference, common practice, and what is legal.

   The issue of quasi-bribery should also be discussed. An example would be taking a client to lunch, providing entertainment, providing recreation (such as hunting, fishing, skiing, etc.), or contributing to the client's favorite causes (charities for example). What do the students see as the primary differences between these practices?

2. **Some countries have been critical of the exporting of American culture by U.S. businesses. Do you think this attitude is reasonable? Explain your thinking.**

   National pride versus practical marketing sense is a difficult subject in many countries around the world. Students should be encouraged to examine the phenomenon and comment on the French view (where even certain American expressions have been banned). This anti-American sentiment is supposedly one of the reasons for the poor performance of EuroDisney outside of Paris. Similar problems also exist between the United States and bilingual Canada. Many countries fear that as they accept American products (such as music, movies, magazines, news, and styles of dress) that there own culture is adversely affected and sometimes changed or destroyed. "Is this good or bad?"—only time will tell.

   For another interesting discussion, reverse the question and ask if we are being changed by the Japanese and their flood of products? What would the students say is different about the two situations? Is fear of foreigners and their culture a global concern?

3. **Trade regulations and protectionism are important political issues in the United States. Do economic communities increase or decrease protectionism? What do you think are the positive and negative aspects of protectionist policies for the U.S. firms?**

   Protectionism is the government policy that erects trade barriers to protect a country's domestic industries. Generally, it is how a government becomes selfish and puts self interest ahead of free trade. One's view toward protectionism tends to be supported by the philosophy of "don't do as I do, but do as I say."

   Government officials decry the Japanese product invasion (and erect trade barriers) in the United States and then complain when American products run up against trade barriers in the Japanese market.

   These issues (especially, when associated with loss of domestic jobs) are always popular political issues. Positive aspects might be home industries (and their jobs) are protected against foreign competitors, barriers reduce the effect of "dumping", and no one gets an unfair advantage in the host domestic environment. Negative aspects might be that trade is reduced, costs go up, artificial barriers limit progress, and nations distrust one another.

4. **Every society has its own unique cultural environment. People in developed countries where it is legal for children to work long hours in factories that abound with health and safety hazards and where the rights of women and minorities are not protected. Do firms that wish to do business in these countries need to accept all such cultural differences without question or should they work to change the culture or should firms in the U.S. and other developed countries totally avoid markets where there are such human rights violations? What are the pros and cons of entering such markets?**

   When discussing this issue you might want to refer back to the "Real People, Bad Choices?" segment which discussed child labor in foreign countries.

   Not only is more manufacturing done offshore, but thanks to the Internet and fax machines communication with foreign factories is involving fewer face-to-face interactions. This means that a firm who has hired a foreign company to manufacturer their product may or may not be aware of the working conditions in the foreign factory.

Ask students to discuss what they would do if faced with deciding between cheaper labor, no labor unions and higher profits; versus, expensive labor, labor unions, and lower profit margins. Student opinions will vary, but try to get students to understand that this is an example of one of the decisions faced by firms manufacturing their products in foreign countries. Firm must decide which is more important, people, or economic profit. (You might want to remind students about your discussion in chapter 3 of the New Era of marketing and social responsibility).

There are those who would argue that US firms who manufacture their products in foreign countries are actually helping to improve the living conditions of people in these countries by providing job opportunities. Industry can also bring to a foreign country improvements in the infrastructure, for example, clean water and electricity.

One negative aspect of knowingly or unknowingly entering markets which have what the US considers to be poor an inhumane working conditions is a tarnished image. Kathie Lee Gifford and Nike are good examples of tarnished images that resulted when their products where manufactured in countries which used child labor and had poor working conditions for employees.

Real People, Real Surfers: Exploring the Web

In this exercise students are instructed to identify a foreign country where they could sell their product. The Internet is used to gather specific information about the country and the people who live in that country. This exercise is more involved and time consuming than some of the other web exercises; however, the experience of completing this exercise can be very beneficial to students.

If you have any international students in your class you might want to use their home country as the focus of this exercise. Not only would these students have greater insight into the country being researched, but the American students in your class would benefit from learning more about the counties which some of their classmates call home.

Marketing in Action: Real Choices for Major League Baseball International Partners

Summary: The Major League Baseball International Partners want to make baseball popular and profitable in Europe. The motivation for making baseball a global sport is to expand and increase the sales of league-licensed merchandise. The high level of disposable income and an intense liking for sports make Europe an attractive market.

Many cultural factors however are working against the success of baseball as a profitable sport in Europe. The popularity of soccer and lack of no "history" of baseball make Europe a difficult market for success.

Suggested Answers to Case Questions:

1. **What is the problem facing the Major League Baseball International Partners?**
   The basic problem facing MLBIP is how to expand the sport of baseball internationally (specifically to Europe) and capitalize on the lucrative league-licensed merchandise business.

   A secondary (but related problem) is how to change the image of the sport to fit the needs and expectations of the European sports fan.

2. **What factors are important in understanding this problem?**
   First, it would be wise to appreciate the history of the sport in the United States and in Europe. Second, a careful examination of the two different sports fans will be necessary. Third, an exploration of competitive sports (such as soccer) should be undertaken. Fourth, analyze the sports fan's desire for league sponsored merchandise. And fifth, analyze the appeal of the American lifestyle in Europe. In each instance, expectations and desires and knowledge must carefully be appreciated. This is not unlike the problem of introducing competitive soccer into the United States. Since that movement is on the upswing, it might be analyzed.

3. **What are the alternatives?**
   The following alternatives might be discussed (students should be encouraged to build on these ideas):
   a. Do nothing—it's a bad idea.
   b. Secure sponsorship from U.S. corporations to start amateur leagues and develop them over a five year period.
   c. Secure U.S. college coaching assistance in the summer for amateur leagues.
   d. Encourage MLB scouts to observe players in Europe.
   e. Have MLB players tour Europe to boost recognition and sales of licensed merchandise.
   f. Begin developmental work on playing a few Spring games in Europe (similar to what is done in Japan and Mexico)
   h. Begin the process of securing investors.

4. **What are your recommendations for solving this problem?**
   The answer to this question is dependent on what creative ideas that the student is able to generate from the list of recommendations supplied above. At this point (given the data in the case), the group should still do more investigation. However, items b, c, and e would seem feasible at this point. The group can also carefully study the attempts of the National Basketball Association at securing European participation. That attempt seems to be several years ahead of any now being considered by MLIP.

Marketing in Action: Real Choices for Major League Baseball International Partners
(Continued)

5.   **What are some ways to implement your recommendations?**
Recommendations (b, c, or e) can be implemented by first examining regions where facilities might be conducive to amateur leagues (stadiums left over from Olympic games, adaptable soccer stadiums, etc.). Next, the group should contact U.S. colleges to determine a list of acceptable and available coaches, teachers, and players that can be brought to Europe during the summer to begin to train players (ex-MLB players might also be considered). And third, MLB agents should be contacted to determine the availability and interest on the part of MLB players for doing a promotion tour in Europe. Since one of the real drawbacks is cost of equipment (to start the proposed amateur leagues), the group should move quickly to contact colleges, MLB farm teams, MLB, and equipment manufacturers to secure commitment for supplying start up equipment.

Mini-Project 4-A
Standardize or Individualize

Purpose: to learn more about the opportunities and problems with standardization of marketing for international markets.

1.   First, with two or three members of your class, select several magazine ads for products which college students normally purchase and which would be used in many different countries. You might find ads for such products as

- shampoo or other hair care products
- cleaning supplies
- frozen foods
- fast food
- athletic shoes
- soft drinks

2.   Place the ads in protective covers in a notebook to create a portfolio of ads.

3.   Show the ads to students or others in your community who are from different countries. Ask them to assume that the ad were in a magazine in their country. They should also assume that the headline and copy of the ad would be translated into the language of that country but that everything else would be the same.

4.   Next ask them to respond to each ad.

- How would people in their home country feel about the ad?
- Would they understand the message?
- Would they understand the visual?
- Would they like the product?
- Would they be likely to purchase the product?

5.   Develop a report based on your research. Present your report to your class.

Mini-Project 4-B
Global Differences

Purpose: to learn how the elements of the marketing mix differ around the globe

It is sometimes almost impossible to imagine how life is in another part of the world. For the American who drives to school on a super highway, it is probably unimaginable that in some countries there are only a few miles of paved roads—anywhere. For a student who comes to the United States from Kenya or Tanzania or even Romania to study, choosing a bottle of shampoo from among the dozens of brands on a drug store shelf can be a Herculean task.

For this mini-project you need to select three countries to learn about—one less developed country, one developing country, and one developed country.

If possible find an individual—a fellow student or a member of your community—who has recently lived in each of the countries. Talk with them about the marketing activities that exist in that country and about the infrastructure that is available to support marketing. If you are not able to find people to help you with the information, you may be able to learn much from the library or even from sources on the Internet. Describe what you learn about the 4 Ps in the space below.

Less-developed countries—many of the countries in Africa and in Southeast Asia

Country_____

Advertising and other forms of promotion

_____

_____

_____

_____

Pricing

_____

_____

_____

_____

Products including laws, patents, packaging, etc.

_____

_____

_____

_____

_____

Distribution

_____

_____

_____

_____

_____

Developing countries—many of the countries in Eastern Europe, Latin America, and the Pacific Rim

Country_____

Advertising and other forms of promotion

_____

_____

_____

_____

_____

Pricing

_____

_____

_____

_____

_____

Products including laws, patents, packaging, etc.

_____

_____

_____

_____

_____

Distribution

_____

_____

_____

_____

_____

Developed countries such as the United Kingdom, Canada, France, Italy, Germany and Japan

Country_____

Advertising and other forms of promotion

_____

_____

_____

_____

_____

Pricing

_____

_____

_____

_____

_____

Products including laws, patents, packaging, etc.

_____

_____

_____

_____

_____

Distribution

_____

_____

_____

_____

_____

5

Marketing Information and Research: Analyzing the Business Environment

*O*verview   The topic of marketing research probably sounds boring to most college students. Students probably have images of computer printouts and annoying telemarketers when they think of marketing research.

In chapter 5 students will learn of the extremely important role marketing information and marketing research have on marketing decisions. The marketing research process is presented and discussed. Lambesis is the focus of the Real People, Real Choices section. Lambesis is the advertising firm which publishes the L Report. This report contains information on teen trends and provides forecasts of emerging cool products and styles.

Objectives

1.   Describe the marketing research process.

2.   Understand the differences among exploratory, problem-solving, and causal research, and describe the variety of research techniques available to marketers.

3.   Understand the issues involved in making sense of research results.

4.   Discuss how marketers implement research results.

Chapter Outline and Suggested Activities

Introduction: Ask students "What is marketing research?" You will probably get responses referring to surveys and telephone interviews. Next ask whether or not research is important. Finally, attempt to lead the discussion into examining the definition for research. Help students to understand that marketing research is not just about collecting information.

1. **Information Is Cool**
   **Use Objective 1
   **Use Real People, Real Surfers: Exploring the Web
   a. Firms succeed by knowing what customers want, when they want it, and where they want it.
   b. Firms also need to know what the competition is doing.
   c. **Marketing research:** *the process of collecting, analyzing, and interpreting data about customers, competitors, and the business environment, in order to improve marketing effectiveness.*
   d. Three types of information a firm may collect
      1). Ongoing information: Information collected on a regular basis. Examples, daily or weekly sales data
      2). Monitored intelligence: Information about a firm's external environment.
         a). **Marketing intelligence:** *Information about a firm's external environment which allows marketers to monitor conditions that affect demand for existing products or create demand for new products.*
      3). Specific information: Specific information related to a brands performance.

2. **The Steps In Marketing Research**
   **Refer to Objective 1
   **Use Figure 5.1
   a. Marketing research is an ongoing process
   b. Refer to Figure 5.1 for the steps involved in the marketing research process.
   c. Defining the problem—Step 1
      1). An accurate definition of the problem is the first and most crucial step in the marketing research process.
      2). Failure to properly define the problem and the research objectives can lead to meaningless data collection and analysis.

➡ *Class Discussion* Have students read the Real People, Real Choices on Lambesis segment before class. In class discuss the three components of defining the problem as it relates to Lambesis.
1. Specifying the research objectives
2. Identifying the consumer population of interest.
3 Placing the problem in an environmental context.

3. **Determining The Research Technique—Step 2**
   **Refer to Objective 2
   **Use Figure 5.2
   a. After the problem has correctly been identified the second step in the research process involves developing the research design.
   b. **Research design:** *A plan that specifies what information will be collected and what type of study will be done.*
      Following are types of research techniques
   c. **Exploratory research:** *Technique used by marketers to generate insights for future, more rigorous studies.*

1). Exploratory research provides qualitative data
2). There are many forms of exploratory research
    a). *Consumer interviews: One-on-One discussions between a consumer and a researcher*
    b). *Focus group: A product oriented discussion among a small group of consumers led by a trained moderator*
    c). *Projective techniques: Tests used by marketers to explore peoples underlying feelings about a product*
    d). *Case study: A comprehensive examination of a particular firm or organization*
    e). *Ethnography: A detailed report based on observations of people in their own homes or communities.*

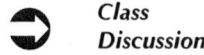

Class Discussion

Most students are probably familiar with consumer interviews and focus groups. They may have even participated in an interview or focus group. Ask students to comment on their experiences.

If time permits develop three or four projective techniques for use in class. (You could even have the students develop these exercises.) Divide the class into groups and assign each group a projective technique to complete. Have each group share their responses with the class.

Spotlight on Real People: Growing Healthy, Inc.

Summary: Growing Healthy, Inc. is a frozen baby food company. Company founder Julia Knight, regularly hangs out in the aisles of local supermarkets and observes parents shopping for baby food.

1. **The chapter describes several ways to conduct marketing research. How would you classify the research technique use by mystery shoppers?**
Exploratory research is being used by Julia Knight. Specifically, she is using observational research in order to observe how parents shop for baby food.

2. **What are the advantages of mystery shopping over other forms of marketing research?**
Mystery shopping gives marketers a "birds-eye-view" of how shoppers behave in the retail environment. It also allows marketers the ability to examine factors which influence purchase decisions which consumers may not have mentioned in an interview or on a survey. For example, parents may not have mentioned the problems with the frozen-food section being too cold for children and marketers may not have known to ask about this problem.

3. **Mystery shopping can give the researcher a "birds-eye-view" of the sales floor. Why should a company be cautious about making decisions based on the reports of mystery shoppers?**
These reports are very subjective and contain information which may be biased. Remember, a mystery shopper has to observe the environment and then make notes on her observations. Thus, there is great potential for error. Proper training of mystery shoppers can help to reduce the amount of error.

Finally, observations made by mystery shoppers may or may not be representative of the population.

---

    d. *Descriptive research: Tools used by marketers that probe more systematically into the problem and bases its conclusions on larger numbers of observations.*
       1). In descriptive research quantitative data is usually collected.
       2). A *cross-sectional design* is used most often in descriptive research and is a one-shot technique. *Cross-sectional is a type of descriptive technique used by marketers which involves the systematic collection of quantitative information.*

3). *Longitudinal design: Technique used by market researchers which tracks the responses of the same sample of respondents overtime.*

4). Types of interactive instruments
   **Use Q#3 Marketing Practice: Applying What You've Learned
   a). A *survey, a questionnaire used by market researchers which asks participants about their beliefs or behaviors* is the most common type of interactive instrument used in descriptive research.
   b). Mail surveys
   c). Face-face surveys
   d). On-line surveys
   e). Personal Observation

e. Causal Research
   1). Causal research helps to answer the question why?
   2). *Causal research: Techniques that attempt to understand cause-and-effect relationships.*
   3). *Experiments: Techniques used by researchers which test pre-specified relationships among variables in a controlled environment, are used in causal research*

4. **Gathering Data—Step 3**
   **Refer to Objective 1
   **Use Real People, Real Surfers: Exploring the Web
   a. Once the problem has been determined and the research design has been developed, the next step in the research process is to gather the data
   b. Existing data, secondary data, or primary data, data for the specific purpose of the study, may be gathered by researchers
      **Use Instructor's Manual Marketing Mini-Projects 5-B
   c. *Single-source data: Information that is integrated from multiple sources such as in-store coupon redemptions, sales data, and household data, to monitor the impact of marketing communications on a particular customer group overtime.*
      1). checkout scanners in stores enable researchers to collect specific information on consumer purchasers
      2). 90% of apparel, electronics, and grocery purchases in the U.S. are scanned
   d. *Data mining: Sophisticated analysis techniques used by firms to take advantage of the massive amount of transaction information now available.*
      1). Data mining is used to help marketers better understand shopping patterns and to aid in the development of marketing strategies aimed at increasing sales.
      2). Data mining has four important applications for marketers.
         a). Customer acquisition
         b). Customer retention
         c). Customer abandonment
         d). Market basket analysis

5. **Ensuring the Quality of the Research: Garbage In, Garbage Out**
   **Refer to Objective 3
   a. A research project is only as good as the information it collects.
   b. Typically three factors influence the quality of research results.
      1). *Validity: The extent to which research actually measures what it was intended to measure*
      2). *Reliability: The extent to which research measurement techniques are free of errors*
      3). *Representativeness: The extent to which consumers in a study are similar to a larger group in which the organization has an interest*
   c. Firms can seldom afford to ask everybody in a market segment their reactions. Thus, samples from the population of interest are taken.

```
┌─────────────────────────────────────────────────────────────────────┐
│                     Real People, Bad Choices?                        │
│                                                                       │
│  Summary: One goal of data mining is customer abandonment by weeding  │
│  out customers who don't contribute very much to the bottom line.     │
│                                                                       │
│                    Suggested Answer to Discussion Question            │
│                                                                       │
│  1.    Is it appropriate for a bank to serve only its more profitable │
│        customers and ignore the others?                               │
│        No one knows the financial wealth or prestige which a young     │
│        college student or any person, may acquire during his          │
│        lifetime. In terms of the bottom-line, it makes good business  │
│        sense to target and encourage customers who make large         │
│        deposits and purchase many financial services from the bank.   │
│        However, a firm operating under the New Era philosophy would   │
│        probably not exclude or discourage customers with smaller      │
│        financial abilities.                                           │
│                                                                       │
│  ** A discussion of this situation could also be used with question 5 │
│  in the Marketing Concepts: Discussing Choices and Issues.            │
│                                                                       │
└─────────────────────────────────────────────────────────────────────┘
```

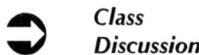 *Class Discussion* What is a random sample? Explain one technique that could be used to collect a random sample?

Many students will give incorrect answers for these questions. Show students the definition for a random sample and discuss correct methods for collecting a random sample.

d.   *Sampling: The process of selecting the respondents who statistically represent a larger population of interest.*
There are a variety of sampling techniques
1).   Random sampling
2).   Quota sample
3).   Convenience sample

6.   **Implementing the Research Results—Step 4**
**Refer to Objective #4
**Use Marketing in Action: Real Choices at General Motors
**Refer to the Marketing Plan for Computer Friendly Stuff (CFS) (Appendix A)
a.   The final step in the marketing research process is to prepare the research report and to integrate the results into long-term planning.

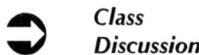 *Class Discussion* Use information from Marketing in Action: Real Choices at General Motors to answer the following questions.

1.   What was the problem being studied?
2.   What were the limitations of the study?
3.   What are the important findings?

b.   Integrating feedback into long-term planning.
1).   Marketing research is an ongoing process and firms need to continuously gather and analyze information.
2).   *Marketing information system (MIS): Technique developed by a firm to continuously gather, sort, analyze, store, and distribute relevant and timely marketing information to mangers*

c.   Predicting the future
  1).   Long-term planning attempts to anticipate future marketplace conditions
  2).   ***Scenarios:*** *Possible future situations used by futurists to access the likely impact.*

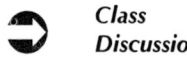

***Class
Discussion***

It is the year 2010; describe the following:

- ■   Yourself
- ■   Your friends
- ■   How you shop for groceries
- ■   What will be your greatest success?
- ■   What will be your greatest failure?

Discuss how a marketer of packaged foods could use the information for long-term planning.

Real People, Real Choices: How it Worked Out at Lambesis

Summary: Dee Dee Gorden is the creator of the L Report, a publication that tracks trends in youth culture. In 1995 the California—based advertising agency Lambesis decided to publish the L Report four times a year. Today Dee Dee is head of the Research Department at Lambesis and provides advice on emerging trends in fashion, sporting events, music, and technology to several Fortune 500 companies.

In 1996, the Cosmar division of Renaissance Cosmetics, Inc. launched a product called Nail Fetish, a small collection of colored artificial nails and decals targeted to teenage girls. A fragrance named Fetish was soon developed for the same audience. The company retained Lambesis to help it research the best way to capture the hearts and pocketbooks of this young audience.

Dee Dee saw an opportunity to create a new, mass market fragrance targeted to teenage girls. A set of eight package concepts were developed and focus groups among girls ages 14–17 were conducted. Based on their responses, the company narrowed its package choice down to three options (see photos of three bottle designs on page 133).

The decision was made to merge the strongest features of options one and two.

Potential Discussion Questions

1.   Which option would you choose?

2.   What factors do you think might have contributed to the success of Fetish?

3.   Other than focus groups, what other technique(s) could be used to gather the information needed for the development of Fetish?

4.   Have students look for this product in your area. What do they think of the product and the packaging? (Some Sears stores carry Fetish.)

Marketing Concepts: Testing Your Knowledge

1. **Describe the types of information marketers need to make smart decisions.**
    There are three types of information needed to make smart decisions:
    a. Ongoing Information, for example daily or weekly sales data.
    b. Monitored Information, for example information about the external environment.
    c. Specific Information, for example information to identify opportunities for new products.

2. **What are the phases in the marketing research process? Why is defining the problem to be researched so important?**
    The marketing research process has six distinct phases. They are:
    a. Define the Research Problem.
    b. Determine the Type of Research to Use.
    c. Choose a Technique for Gathering Data.
    d. Analyze the Data and Draw Conclusions.
    e. Prepare a Research Report.
    f. Integrate Findings and Recommendations with Other Data in the Firm's MIS.
    The first phase (defining the research problem) is critical to the research project. Defining the research issue as precisely as possible allows researchers to set objectives that will result in the right answers to the right questions. It also ensures that the questions are asked of the right consumers and are focusing on the right factors in the problem solution.

3. **What is the goal of exploratory research? What techniques are used to gather data in exploratory research?**
    Exploratory research is a type of marketing research designed to investigate or explore a marketing issue or problem that is not well defined by gathering qualitative descriptive information from a small group of consumers. Most of this research is relatively flexible and unstructured to allow researchers to follow up on each consumer's unique responses in depth.
    Exploratory research seeks qualitative data through such techniques as individual interviews, focus groups, projective techniques, and observational techniques such as ethnography. Since the researchers are not concerned that the findings of exploratory research is actionable or generalizable, a wide variety of the techniques illustrated above can be used.

4. **What is problem-solving research? What techniques are used in problem-solving research?**
    Problem-solving or descriptive research is a type of problem solving research that seeks to describe a specific issue or problem without looking for the reason or cause of the phenomenon.
    Descriptive studies can attempt to describe an issue or problem at one point in time (cross-sectional design) or over time (longitudinal design). In descriptive studies data are most frequently gathered through mail, phone, Internet, or personal interview surveys or can come from personal or mechanical observation techniques.

5. **What ethical problems are associated with marketing research? What problems does a researcher encounter when conducting marketing research in global markets?**
    The text discusses several that might be ethically sensitive. Students should be encouraged to express their own opinions. Several points that might be used to begin the discussion include the abuse of trust in the relationship between marketer and consumer (salespeople pretending to be researchers when they are really attempting to sell products), privacy of the consumer (asking consumers to divulge personal information and then using it for some other purpose than originally requested—such as selling database information to another marketer), unethical practices concerning gathering intelligence on competition, and unsupervised research on children. Any of these topics should generate student discussion.

Problems encountered when attempting to do marketing research abroad can be numerous. Several problems encountered when going abroad include the quantity and quality of the data available, differences in local conditions and customs, distrust of those asking questions, lack of sophisticated technology (even telephones or mail service), legal differences, communication and transportation differences, lack of the ability to use high-tech equipment, language and symbol differences, and lack of sophistication among marketing professionals. Any of these areas can be used to enhance discussion.

6. **What are single-source data? What are some ways that marketers use single-source data?**
Single-source data is data gathered by research services that use technologies to monitor a particular consumer group's exposure to marketing communications and to track purchases made by the group over time. Marketers use single-source data to determine a profile of who is purchasing their product, to identify heavy users, or to provide insight about the magazines most likely to be read by the loyal customers so that advertising can be placed there.

7. **What is meant by reliability, validity, and representativeness of research results?**
Reliability is an evaluation criterion that indicates the extent to which marketing research techniques are dependable and consistent and will give the same results time after time.
   Validity is an evaluation criterion that indicates the extent to which marketing research actually measures what it was intended to measure.
   Representiveness is an evaluation criterion for marketing research that indicates the extent to which data collected from respondents can be generalized to the larger customer group.

8. **What is a marketing information system (MIS)? What types of information are included in an MIS? What are some of the sources data in the MIS?**
A *marketing information system (MIS)* is a system for gathering, sorting, analyzing, storing, and distributing relevant marketing informational to managers in a timely manner. There are three primary reasons that a firm needs a MIS. First, marketers generally require ongoing information (which is in the form of company records and reports added to the MIS on an ongoing basis). Second, the firm needs to monitor information (which is comes from regular scanning of the important marketing environments). And third, marketers use a MIS to handle requested information (which is not available in the MIS and must be obtained through customized research studies).

Marketing Concepts: Discussing Choices and Issues

1. **Some marketers attempt to disguise themselves as marketing researchers when their real intent is to sell something to the consumer. What is the impact of this practice on legitimate researchers? What do you think might be done about this practice?**
The practice of "sugging" has been decried by honest marketing researchers. The impact of the practice (since consumers do not react well to this practice) has been to "poison the well" for real researchers who try to contact the victims of these procedures later on.
   Students may have a variety of opinions about what to do about the practice. Some suggestions to begin the discussion might include the spectrum of ideas below:
   a.   Do nothing—most consumers can recognize honest research.
   b.   Ask for legislation that would curb this deceptive practice under state or Federal law.
   c.   Encourage a code of ethics that would prohibit the practice.
   d.   Have honest marketing researchers join an organization that would give validity to honest research (such as saying a dental product is endorsed by the American Dental Association).
   e.   Educate consumers about what to look for in honest and fake marketing research.

2. **Do you think marketers should be allowed to conduct marketing research with young children? Why or why not?**
Unlike the United States, many countries in Europe restrict marketers from interviewing children. Researchers are not really sure that they should consider children as valid research subjects because kids tend to make undependable reporters of their own behavior, they have poor recall, and they often do not understand abstract questions. However, most marketers like to research "the consumers of the future."

Students should be encouraged to list the types of research that would be permissible (playing with toys) and that would not be permissible (tobacco and alcohol research). What should be the role of the parent in testing (should they be present to monitor the process or should the research take place at school) and their participation responsibility? How valid are "kid's questionnaires"? Have any of the students ever been researched? Be sure to examine the supporting arguments for the student's why or why not answers.

3. **Are you willing to divulge personal information to marketing research? How much are you willing to tell, or where would you draw the line?**
    The answer to this question is a matter of student opinion and preference. The best way to generate response is to give the students a list of potential question areas and ask would they be willing to answer questions about these subjects. A list to begin the discussion would be:
    a.   Clothing (formal, casual, underwear, footwear).
    b.   Food preference (types of food, where to eat, likes and dislikes, taste tests).
    c.   Personal hygiene products (dental care, cosmetics, hair care, sanitary care).
    d.   Transportation (cars, bicycles, recreational vehicles).
    e.   Entertainment preferences.
    f.   Dating or sexual behavior
    g.   Lifestyle measures (entertainment, attitudes, beliefs about social issues, biases).

4. **What is your overall attitude toward marketing research? Do you think it is a beneficial activity from a consumer's perspective? Or do you think it merely gives marketers new insights on how to convince consumers to buy something they really don't want or need?**
    As students may determine, the answer to this question is on of how the marketing environment is viewed (Is the glass half full or half empty?). Those students that believe that marketing performs a useful function in business and society will probably see marketing research as a mechanism by which the marketer can learn how to better serve (extend the marketing concept) the consumer. Those that think that marketing "rips off" consumers will probably see marketing research as a form of sinister intelligence gathering. Dependent on which answer is given, the instructor might ask "Under what circumstances would your opinion change?" If most of the students respond negatively to the question, the instructor might want to make a special appeal on the behalf of good productive research (use some of the illustrations in the text as examples of how good research can provide useful answers).

5. **Sometimes firms use data mining to identify and abandon customers who are not profitable because they do not spend enough to justify the service needed or because they return a large portion of the items they buy. What do you think of such practices? Is it ethical for firms to prune out these customers?**
    Refer to the "Real People, Bad Choices?" segment which discussed how some banks abandon customers who are not as financially profitable as others.

Real People, Real Surfers: Exploring the Web

This exercise exposes students to the vast amount of statistical information available on the web. To help make this exercise more exciting, instructors may want to assign students a city and develop a marketing scenario about why this information is being sought.

Marketing in Action: Real Choices at General Motors

Summary: In the early 1990's General Motors (GM) faced several potentially disastrous situations. The Oldsmobile division was fighting for its life, and GM was only beginning to recover from embarrassing stumbles in small and mid-size cars, mini-vans, and sport-utility vehicles

Suggested Answers to Case Questions:

1. **What is the problem facing GM?**
   There are many problems facing GM, but the key issue is "How to put the customer first?" In other words, what does GM need to do in order to survive?

2. **What factors are important in understanding this problem?**
   In the past GM has over-differentiated its product line and has been more concerned with engineering capabilities than consumer needs. In addition, they are not necessarily sure how to interpret consumer needs since many of the consumer expressions are not necessarily backed up with sales results. In reality the car market is fickle and ever changing in its desires. GM is currently under pressure to shore up sagging sales in its Oldsmobile line.

3. **What are the alternatives?**
   a.   Ride it out and do nothing.
   b.   Develop a new car.
   c.   Redesign one or more of the existing brands to better meet customers demands.
   d.   Try to lure drivers of other luxury cars to the Oldsmobile
   e.   Conduct more research

4. **What are your recommendations for solving the problem?**
   Following the rationale of listening to the desires of the consumer (based on needs assessment) the company should probably redesign the Lumina or the Grand Prix to better meet the needs of the market as expressed in the research (alternative c). This would especially be true if all trends were pointing in this direction (which they seemed to be).

5. **What some ways to implement your recommendation?**
   Implementation will depend on the recommendation. If the recommendation offered above is accepted, then the company should begin to immediately design a car that has great styling and room for passengers but did not have the pretense of a "big car" or its sticker price. The company should carefully match up consumers (in the targeted needs assessment areas) with the various models produced by the company and observe if there were any positions that were overfull or under utilized. Lastly, an accurate assessment of demand must be undertaken to make sure that the trend shift is long-term and there are an adequate amount of consumers in the category to warrant the production of a new model to meet their needs.

Mini-Project 5-A
More Than that One Way to Solve a Problem

Purpose: to understand the strengths and weaknesses of different research techniques for obtaining marketing information.

1.　With a group of your classmates, select a topic or question which is of interest to you and which would be typical of that faced by marketing managers. Some examples might be
   a.　Which brand of cola (or hamburger or ketchup or shoes) do certain consumers prefer and why?
   b.　What are the most important attributes that certain consumers want in an automobile (or a computer or a college or a product of your choice)?
   c.　What information do consumers want and need when they are purchasing an automobile (or a computer, etc.)? Where is the best place for them to obtain that information?

2.　Decide on three different research techniques that can be used to obtain the information.
   Research techniques which you might use include:
   a.　Focus group discussions
   b.　Field experiments
   c.　Laboratory experiments
   d.　Self-administered (pencil and paper) surveys
   e.　Telephone surveys
   f.　Personal observation
   g.　Personal interviews

3.　Design and conduct research using each of the three techniques.

4.　Present your research and your findings to your class.

Mini-Project 5-B
Secondary Research for Business and Industry

Purpose: to familiarize you with some of the information on business and industry widely available to marketers.
**The Internet could also be used for completing this mini-project.

Select a manufacturing industry of interest to you and provide the following information

1.   Use the *North American Industry Classification System* to find the following:

NAICS sector   _____

NAICS subsector   _____

NAICS Industry group   _____

NAICS Industry (five digit)   _____

Based on the NAICS manual, what types of products are or are not included in this industry?

_____

_____

_____

2.   The following questions should be answered using *Standard and Poor's Industry Surveys*:

a.   What was the total dollar sales for the industry by U.S. manufacturers in the latest year reported?

_____

b.   What is an important concern of firms in this industry that affects their planning for the coming years?

_____

_____

3.   Several publications including *Ward's Business Directory* and *Manufacturing USA* provide useful industry-specific information. Use one of these sources to answer the following questions:
        What are the names and addresses of the top four **public** companies in the industry and their sales revenues?

	Company Name	Company address	Sales revenue
1.			
2.			
3.			
4.			

4.   The U.S. Census Bureau publishes a number of economic censuses irregularly in different years. These include

-    *Census of Retail Trade*
-    *Census of Wholesale Trade*
-    *Census of Service Industries*
-    *Census of Transportation*
-    *Census of Manufactures*
-    *Census of Mineral Industries*
-    *Census of Construction Industries*

Using the *Census of Manufactures*, answer the following questions:
(Note the *Census of Manufactures* is also available on the internet at the following address: http:\\www.access.gpo.gov\sudocs\sale\sb-146.html)
What is the value of shipments for each of the last five years reported in the *Census of Manufacturers* for your industry?

Year	Value of shipments

5.   To appreciate the changes in an industry, it is necessary that you understand the economy and the forces which shape the industry. One measure of economic trends is the Gross Domestic Product (GDP). There are a number of good sources of the GDP and other measures of economic activity including the Information Please Almanac and Yearbook and a monthly government publication Survey of Current Business. Use one of these to find the GDP for the years you have listed in number 4 above.

Year	GDP

6.   Use the data found in questions 4 and 5 to answer the following:
   a.   Calculate the annual growth rate for the industry shipments and for the GDP.

Year	Industry Shipments	Annual Growth	GDP	Annual Growth
		/////////////		/////////////

   b.   Describe the growth for industry shipments and for GDP during these five years. How does the growth rate of the two compare, that is, have the growth rates been the same or has industry shipments increased faster or more slowly than the GDP? What are the implications of this relationship to your industry?

_____

_____

_____

_____

6

Why People Buy: Consumer Behavior

*O*verview   Understanding why and how people buy products is part of the focus of the marketing concept. The process used by individuals in selecting, purchasing, and using goods and services is of great importance to marketers. It is through an understanding of this process, called consumer behavior, that marketers are better able to meet the needs and wants of consumers.

The American Sheep Industry Association (ASI) is the focus of the Real People, Real Choices segment. Options related to "How can American wool compete in the Chinese market?" are presented and discussed.

Objectives

1.   Explain why understanding consumer behavior is important to organizations.

2.   Describe how internal factors influence consumers' decision-making processes.

3.   Understand how situational factors can influence consumer behavior.

4.   Describe how consumers' social relationships influence their decision-making processes.

5.   Explain the prepurchase, purchase, and postpurchase activities consumers engage in when making decisions.

Chapter Outline and Suggested Activities

Introduction: Begin by dividing the class into groups of two or three students. Have each group discuss the following questions regarding a recent purchase.

1. What did you purchase?
2. Why did you purchase this product or service?
3. What factor(s) influenced you to purchase this particular type of brand of product or service?
4. What sources of information, if any, were used in making your purchase decision?
5. How long did it take you to evaluate your alternatives and make a purchase decision?
6. Were you satisfied or dissatisfied with your purchase?

The above set of questions basically leads the students through the consumer decision making process which is summarized in Figure 6.1 after students have discussed these questions (this usually takes about 5–10 minutes) bring the class back together and ask for volunteers to discuss their findings with the class. Try to find a variety of product/or service purchases, including small and large purchase decisions.

Student responses and discussion of these questions can also be used to discuss the following topics: habitual, limited, and extended problem solving, involvement, and influences on consumer decisions.

1. **Decisions, Decisions**
   **Refer to Objectives 1 and 5
   **Use Figure 6.1
   a. The focus of the marketing concept is satisfying consumers' needs and wants. To satisfy these needs and wants marketers must understand the behavior which drives consumers to purchase one product over another.
   b. ***Consumer behavior:*** *The process involved when individuals or groups select, purchase, use, and dispose of goods, services, ideas, or exercises to satisfy needs and desires*
   c. Decision making is a continuum that ranges from simple to complex. There are three levels of decision making:
      1). Habitual decision making: such as the purchase of a soft drink
      2). Extended decision making: such as the purchase of a car
      3). Limited problem solving: such as the purchase of a pair of jeans.
   d. Involvement determines the extent of effort a person puts into deciding what to buy.
      1). ***Involvement:*** *The relative importance of perceived consequences of the purchase to a consumer*
      2). In general, we are more involved in the decision-making process for products that we perceive are risky.

➡️ ***Class Discussion***

Discuss the various levels of involvement students have for the purchase of a car, a pair of jeans, and a soft drink.

      3). ***Perceived risk:*** *The belief that use of a product has potentially negative consequences, either financial, physical, or social*
         a). When perceived risk is low, the consumer feels low involvement.
         b). When perceived risk is high, the consumer feels high involvement.
   e. Problem Recognition
      **Use Q#4 Marketing Practice: Applying What You've Learned

Problem recognition: *the process that occurs whenever the consumer sees a significant difference between his or her current state of affairs and some desired ideal state; this recognition initiates the decision-making process.*

Class Discussion   Refer to the introduction activity. Ask students what "triggered" their need or want for a specific product or service?

f.   **Information search:** *The process whereby a consumer searches for appropriate information to make a reasonable decision*
     1).   Consumers use a variety of sources to collect the information needed to aid decision-making.
     2).   Information may be from a simple source—like memory, or from a more complex source like consumer reports.

Class Discussion   Ask students what source(s) of information they would use when making the following purchase decisions.

- Car
- Computer
- Dinner for you and your date
- Running shoes

Discuss the reliability of the various sources cited by students.

g.   Evaluation of Alternatives
     **Use Instructor's Manual Marketing Mini-project 6-A
     1).   Once the alternatives are identified the next step is to decide which alternatives are favorable.
     2).   **Evaluate criteria:** *The dimensions used by consumers to compare competing products' alternatives.*
         a).   For each purchase, consumers develop a set of evaluative criteria
         b).   The importance of each criteria is highly variable.

Class Discussion   Refer students back to either the introduction activity or another previous discussion on decision-making.

- Discuss the evaluative criteria selected for a particular purchase decision.
- Why were these criteria selected?
- How important is it that the selected product possess all of the dimensions listed?
- What was the role of brand in the decision?
- Were any heuristics used to help simplify the decision process?

h.   Product Choice
     1).   After the product choices have been evaluated, the consumer selects the product which they feel best meets his/her needs and wants.
     2).   The product choice process is complicated.
     3).   Guidelines, called heuristics, are often used when selecting the product choice
         a).   **Heuristics:** *A mental rule-of-thumb that leads to a speedy decision by simplifying the process.*

b). Two common heuristics 1) ***Brand loyalty:*** A pattern of repeat product purchases, accompanied by an underlying positive attitude toward the brand, that is based on the belief that the brand makes products superior to its competition. 2) country-of-origin

i. Postpurchase Evaluation

1). This is the last stage of the decision making process.

2). In this stage the consumer evaluates how good a choice was.

3). The evaluation results in either ***consumer satisfaction/dissatisfaction (CS/D).*** *The overall feelings or attitude a person has about a product after it has been purchased.*

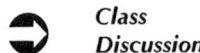

Class Discussion

Ask students to recall a time when they were dissatisfied with a product.

■ What factor(s) influenced this dissatisfaction?

■ What actions could have been made by the firm to help lesson or alleviate your dissatisfaction?

2. **Internal Influences On Consumer Decisions**

**Refer to Objective 2

**Use Figure 6.2

a. There are several internal factors which relate to the way people absorb and interpret marketing information.

b. ***Perception:*** *is the process by which people select, organize, and interpret information from the outside world.*

1). Information is received in the form of sensations on our sensory receptors

2). Perception process has important implications for marketers. Marketers want to work to ensure that the meaning they assign to products is correctly received and interpreted by the consumer.

3). Marketers need to understand three issues related to perception.

a). Exposure

b). Perceptual selection

c). Interpretation

c. ***Motivation:*** *is an internal state that drives us to satisfy needs by activating goal-oriented behavior.*

**Use Instructor's Manual Marketing Mini-project 6-B

1). Figure 6.3 shows Maslow's hierarchy of needs.

2). ***Hierarchy of needs:*** *an approach that categorizes motives according to five levels of importance, the more basic needs being on the bottom of the hierarchy and the higher needs at the top.*

3). Marketers need to understand the particular level of needs relevant to a consumer group so that they can tailor their products and messages to point out how these needs can be satisfied.

d. ***Learning:*** *a relatively permanent change in behavior caused by acquired information or experience*

1). There are many theories on how people learn. Since marketers want to "teach" consumers to prefer their product, it is very important that they understand the basic theories how people learn.

2). There are two theories of behavioral learning.

Behavioral learning theories: *focus on how consumer behavior is changed by external events or stimuli*

a). ***Classical conditioning:*** The learning that occurs when a stimulus eliciting a response is paired with another stimulus that initially does not elicit a response on its own but will cause a similar response over time because of its association with the first stimulus.

b). **Operant learning:** Learning that occurs as the result of reward and punishment.

3). Learned associations often transfer to other similar stimuli in the process called stimulus generalization. In **stimulus generation:** *behavior caused by a reaction to one stimulus occurs in the presence of other, similar stimuli.*

4). **Cognitive learning theory:** *Theories of learning that stress the importance of internal mental processes and that view people as problem solvers who actively use information from the world around them to master their environment.*

    a). **Observational learning** is one type of cognitive learning

    b). *In observational learning, people learn by watching the actions of others.*

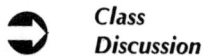 **Class Discussion**   Ask students to think of something they have learned in life. How did they learn this information? See if the class can identify what type of learning theory was involved.

e. **Attitudes:** *A learned predisposition to respond favorably or unfavorably to stimuli, based on relatively enduring evaluations of people, objects, and issues.*

1). Attitudes have three components

    a). Affect

    b). Behavior

    c). Cognition

2). The dominant influence these components have on forming attitudes varies.

f. **Personality:** *The psychological characteristics that consistently influence the way a person respond to situations in his or her environment.*

1). Personality should be considered when developing marketing strategies.

2). Three personality traits relevant to marketing strategies:

    a). Innovativeness

    b). Self confidence

    c). Sociability

3). Brand personalities are created for products so that the product will appeal to different types of consumers.

Class Discussion   Discuss the brand personality created by marketers for the following brands.

    ■ Nike

    ■ Marlboro cigarettes

    ■ Jeep

4). Another important aspect of an individual's personality is their self-concept. **Self-concept:** *an individual's self-image that is composed of a mixture of beliefs, observations, and feelings about personal attributes.*

g. **Age Group**

1). Age is an important determinant of needs and wants

2). Products and services often appeal to a specific age group

3). Purchase preferences depend upon our stage in the family life-cycle. The **family life cycle:** *A means of characterizing consumers within a family structure based on different stages through which people pass as they grow older.*

Class Discussion   How do consumers needs change in each stage of the family life cycle?

h. *Lifestyles: The pattern of living that determines how people choose to spend their time, money, and energy and that reflects their values, tastes, and preferences.*
    1). Demographics characteristics help marketers understand what people will buy
    2). *Psychographics help marketers to understand why people buy by examining individual activities, interests, and opinions (AIO).*
    3). *Psychographics the use of psychological, sociological, and anthropological factors to construct market segments.*

3.   Situational Influences On Consumer Behavior
**Refer to Objective #3
**Use Instructor's Manual Mini project: Learning By Doing
a.   The physical environment
   **Use Q#1 Marketing Practice: Applying What You've Learned
    1). Physical surroundings strongly influence moods and behaviors
    2). Examples of how the physical environment can be altered to encourage positive feelings (i.e., arousal and pleasure) from consumers.
       a). Shopping as entertainment
       b). Use of music, color, and odors
       c). In-store display

Class Discussion   Have students describe the physical environment of Victoria's Secret. How does the physical environment of the store encourage shoppers, both men and women, to purchase?

b.   Time
    1). How much time one has to make a decision is an important factor in purchase decisions.
    2). The sense of time poverty felt by many consumers has lead to many innovations such as one-hour photo processing and drive-thru pharmacies.

4.   Social Influences On Consumer Decisions
**Refer to Objective #4
**Use Marketing in Action: Real Choices at Playboy Enterprises, Inc.
**Use Q#2 Marketing Practice: Applying What You've Learned
a.   *Culture: The values, beliefs, customs, and tastes valued by a group of people*
b.   *Subcultures: A group within a society whose members share a distinctive set of beliefs, characteristics, or common experiences.*
    1). Racial groups
    2). Ethnic groups

Spotlight on Real People: Nantucket Nectars

Summary: Nantucket Nectars is an alternative natural beverage which is made from homemade fruit juice. The product was developed by two twenty something college graduates around Nantucket Island in Massachusetts.

Suggested Answers to Discussion Questions

1. **How does Nantucket Nectar utilize lifestyle marketing to sell its juice products?**
    Nantucket focuses on the carefully-cultivated image of a drink for the bohemian, young lifestyle group. The image of two young guys who created and market this drink is also very attractive to the core customer group, college students.

2. **What are the steps in the decision process that buyers of the juice probably undergo?**
    (Refer to Figure 6.1)

    - *Problem recognition:* Thirst
    - *Information search:* Limited; Consumers might look at the package or recall comments from friends about the product
    - *Evaluation of alternatives:* For college students this would probably focus on price, taste, nutrition.
    - Product decision: Which flavor of Nantucket Nectar to purchase
    - Postpurchase evaluation: Hopefully, this will be satisfaction

3. **How are situational factors used to encourage juice purchases?**
    Major situational influences might include the physical environment (in-store displays), culture, status symbols, and group behavior

4. **What are some other strategies the partners might use to further expand the market for Nantucket Nectars?**

    - Sponsorship of college athletic activities
    - Give-away drinks and/or sponsorship of community activities like festivals or a 5 k run.

Real People, Bad Choices?

Summary: Supermodel Claudia Schiffer and the House of Chanel designer Karl Lagerfeld offended many with a dress that included Arabic letters that spelled out a verse from the Koran. Both the designer and the model received death threats.

Potential Discussion Question

1. **Is it acceptable for a product to "borrow" words and images from other cultures to make a fashion statement?**
    The organization needs to determine why the words and/or image are being used. Is it for "shock" effect? This was the situation for the Karl Lagerfeld dress. Secondly, the organization needs to consider how customers and *the public* will view the use of a selected cultural word and/or image. Generally, it is believed to be offensive, even if only to a few people, the organization would be wise not to use the "borrowed" word and/or image.

c. *Social class:* The overall rank or social standing of groups of people within a society according to the value assigned to such factors as family background, education, occupation, and income.

    1). *Status symbols:* products that are purchased and displayed to signal membership in a desirable social class.

d. Group Behavior

    1). *Reference group:* an actual or imaginary individual or group that has a significant effect on an individual's evaluations, aspirations, or behavior.

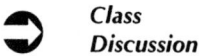

Class Discussion

What are netizens? Answer: Members of virtual communities. Explore some of the virtual communities listed in the text on page 166.

    2). *Opinion Leaders:* A person who is frequently able to influence others' attitudes or behaviors by virtue of his or her active interest and expertise in one or more product categories.

Real People, Real Choices: How It Worked Out at American Sheep Industry Council

Summary: Richard Wertheimer is the director of business development for the American Sheep Industry (ASI). ASI is the promotion and marketing organization for the U.S. lamb and wool industry. Along with cotton, wool is one of the most important natural fibers produced worldwide.

    The majority of developing countries have built the basis of their economies on the textile business. China and Hong Kong together account for 40 percent of world imports of wool yarn and 22 percent of imports of wool fabrics. A strong presence in China and Hong Kong (the hub of the textiles business in the Pacific Rim) is essential to gain access to all Asian markets. How can the US gain a foothold in this difficult market? Wertheimer considered three options:

Option 1: Do nothing

Option 2: Stimulate exports of U.S wool textiles by creating greater awareness of their advantages among Chinese garment manufacturers.

Option 3: Build demand at the consumer level by positioning U.S. wool as better suited to modern lifestyles than wool textiles from other countries.

    Richard Wertheimer chose option 2.

Potential Discussion Questions

1. Why is option 2 the best solution?

2. Discuss the advantages of option 3.

Marketing Concepts: Testing Your Knowledge

1. **What is consumer behavior? Why is it important for marketers to understand consumer behavior?**
    Consumer behavior is the process involved when individual or groups select, purchase, use, and dispose of goods, services, ideas, or experiences to satisfy their needs and desires. It is important that marketers understand consumer behavior because wants and needs are satisfied best when marketers understand the behaviors of consumers.

2. **How does the decision process differ under conditions of high involvement and low involvement? What are the steps in the decision process, and what activities occur in each?**
    Involvement is the relative importance of the perceived consequences of the purchase to a consumer. The degree to which consumers commit themselves to the decision process is determined by the perceived risks (their involvement) with the purchase and the relative importance of the perceived consequences to the consumer. Under conditions of high involvement, the consumer carefully goes through the entire decision making process and searches for unique solutions to their problem. Under conditions of low involvement, the consumer will follow habits or will not put much time or energy into solving the problem. Simplifying the process is a common strategy.
    The steps in the decision making process include (See Figure 6.4 for a more detailed description):
    a. *Problem recognition* occurs whenever the consumer sees a significant difference between his or her current state of affairs and some desired or ideal state. Problems are recognized in this stage.
    b. *Information Search* is the process in which the consumer checks his or her memory and/or surveys his or her environment to collect data required to make a reasonable decision. The consumer looks for solutions to their problem.
    c. *Evaluation of Alternatives* includes two steps. First, the consumer identifies alternatives based on the results of the information search. Second, the consumer evaluates and decides whether and how to choose from among those identified alternatives in order to solve their problem. The consumer will evaluate products from their evoked set by means of evaluative criteria and make picks using choice heuristics (see the next step below).
    d. *Product Choice* is made based upon evaluations of existing product data and choice heuristics. Brand loyalty may be a factor.
    e. *Postpurchase Evaluation* or consumer satisfaction/dissatisfaction is determined by the overall feelings or attitudes of the person once that the product has been purchased. It is very important that the marketer works hard to have a satisfied customer so repeat sales may occur.

3. **What is perception? For marketers, what are the implications of each component of the perceptual process?**
    Below are some examples that can be used to help begin a discussion for this question.
    Housing: As the number of senior adults grows so does the need for housing. Housing which allows senior adults to live independently while providing needed services is in great demand.
    Health Care: The health care system in the United States is undergoing many types of pains. The complex battle between HMO's, insurance providers, doctors, and hospitals is increasing. What will health care be like in the year 2010?
    Newspapers: Will the newspaper continue to be delivered in paper form or will it be delivered electronically over the Internet?
    Textbooks: In the future students might pay an access fee and log onto the textbook publishers Web site and download the chapters and information which they need for class.
    Travel and Tourism: The Internet has already begun to change the way travel plans are made. By visiting the Web site of an airline and/or hotel, travelers can easily compare prices and make reservations. Many cities and towns have also developed Web sites to market their area.

4. **How are consumers motivated to buy certain products over others? How has Maslow's hierarchy of needs contributed to an understanding of consumer behavior?**

    Motivation is an internal state that activates goal-directed behavior on the part of consumers in order to satisfy some need. The specific products people want to satisfy a need are influenced by their unique sets of experiences and backgrounds, and the degree to which a consumer is willing to expend energy to satisfy a need depends on the underlying motivation. People are driven to purchase certain products to satisfy basic needs, utilitarian needs, or hedonic needs.

    Freud's theory of motivation and Maslow's hierarchy of needs provide insights into why consumers are motivated to buy certain types of products. Some consumers engage in compulsive consumption because they are compelled to shop, not because they are motivated to satisfy a need. People may do things subconsciously that they are not even aware of. Maslow's hierarchy probably has more practical value. Satisfying the needs of lower-order needs then progressing to higher-order needs seems to fit more consumption decisions than the Freudian approach (See Figure 6.3 for a more detailed description of the needs hierarchy).

5. **What behavioral and cognitive learning theories are important to marketers? How do these perspectives differ when applied to consumer behavior?**

    Learning is a relatively permanent change in consumer behavior that is caused by experience or acquired information. *Behavioral learning theories* are those theories of learning that focus on how consumer behavior is changed by external events, or stimuli. *Cognitive theories* are those theories that stress the importance of internal mental processes and that view people as problem solvers who actively use information from the world around them to master their environment.

    The more important of these theories (for the marketer) are classical conditioning, operant conditioning, reinforcement, repetition, and stimulus generalization in the behavioral learning area. Cognitive theory components that are of interest are observational learning and modeling.

    By observing the different views (external or internal orientation), the marketer can explore different paths to reach the consumer and influence his behavior.

6. **How do the three components of attitudes account for consumer decision making and purchasing behavior?**

    An *attitude* is a learned predisposition to respond favorably or unfavorably to stimuli, based on relatively enduring evaluations of people, objects, and issues. The *ABC model of attitudes* is a behavioral theory suggesting that an attitude has three components—affect, behavior, and cognition—and emphasizing the interrelationships among knowing, feeling, and doing. Depending on the nature of the product, one of these three components—knowing, feeling, or doing—will be the dominant influence in creating an attitude toward a product.

7. **What is personality? How is consumer behavior influenced by an individual's personality and self-concept?**

    The unique psychological characteristics that consistently influence the way a person responds to situations make up his or her personality. Several theories attempt to explain consumptive differences based on personality. Trait theory focuses on identifiable personality characteristics, such as innovativeness, self-confidence, and sociability, which influence many purchase decisions. Studies have linked these characteristics, as well as a person's self-concept, to buying behavior in which people seek products that enhance or minimize their personal attributes.

8. **Why is self-concept such an important personal influence on purchasing behavior? How do age and the family life cycle influence consumers? What is the significance of lifestyles in understanding consumer behavior and purchasing decisions?**

    A person's *self-concept* is his or her attitude toward the self. The self-concept is a complex mixture of belief's about one's abilities, observations of one's own behavior, and feelings about one's personal attributes such as body type of facial features.

    Age and the family life cycle both influence consumers. Age is an important determinant of needs and wants. Where a family is in the family life cycle also influences needs and wants. For example young families with children have different needs and wants for goods and services than families whose kids are in college.

A *lifestyle* is the pattern if living that determines how people choose to spend their time, money, and energy and that reflects values, tastes, and preferences. Lifestyle marketing is a strategy that recognizes that people can be grouped into common market segments based on similarities in lifestyle preferences.

9. **Why is an understanding of social influences such as culture and subculture important to marketers? What is the significance of social class to marketers? What are reference groups, and how do they influence consumers?**

Culture is the learned values and patterns of behavior that stem from the shared meanings, rituals, and traditions among the members of a society and that influence their attitudes, beliefs, preferences, and priorities towards abstract ideas, activities, and products. *Subculture* is a group within a society whose members share a distinctive set of beliefs, characteristics, or common experiences. The consumer's overall priorities for products and activities are significantly influenced by cultural values. Therefore, the marketer must be keenly aware of these influences if they are too market and communicate with these sometimes diverse groups.

Social class is the overall rank or social standing of groups of people within a society according to the value assigned to such factors as family background, education, occupation, and income. For marketers, social class identifies large groups of people with much in common. It is also an important determinant of how much money a consumer spends, and it influences how it is spent.

Reference groups are a set of people that a consumer is motivated to please or imitate and that influences consumer purchasing to the extent that the purchase is conspicuous to others.

10. **What are situational influences on consumer purchasing behavior? How does each affect purchasing decisions?**

Situational influences are events and conditions—such as the shopping environment, the consumer's mood, and the time of day as well as time available—that affect how products are evaluated and chosen at the time of purchase.

Time (or the lack of it) influences the which products and brands are selected because of the importance of time to the individual consumer in our society. For many products, their sole function is to save us time (microwave cooking for example). It is one of the consumer's most limited resources. Time pressure can sometimes be intense and lead to mistakes or poor choices.

A person's mood can also affect purchases. Pleasure and arousal may dictate whether the consumer will be favorably disposed to the product or not. Marketers would hope to give the consumer a pleasant shopping experience

The shopping environment—such as store layout, store fixtures, colors, lighting, smells, and music—can interact with or affect moods and the shopping experience. The above mentioned features are especially important in stressful shopping trips such as grocery shopping. The consumer is more likely to impulse buy when they enter into a pleasant shopping environment.

Marketing Concepts: Discussing Choices and Issues

1. **Some consumer advocates have criticized marketing messages that link products to idealized people and situations and encourage the belief that the products will change consumers' lives in the portrayed direction. Tell whether you agree and explain why or why not.**

Each of us is constantly confronted with the activities of marketers competing for our attention and our money. Wherever we turn we are bombarded by marketing communications intended to influence our purchase decisions or even the decision to purchase something at all. Our identities as consumers are intimately related to other people with whom we identify. We are all individuals, but rarely do the same products or services appeal to people who differ in age, educational background, income, and so on.

The students should determine if having an idealized self is bad. Is bad in relationship to products and product purchase? The more intimately that we know consumers the more likely that we will pursue idealized desires. Be sure to ask students to explain their choice response to this question. Are their circumstances under which they can agree with the other direction of choice? What might they be?

2. **This chapter raised the question, "Do we buy what we are?" What answer would you give based on your experience? Provide examples that support your opinion.**

It has often been said that marketing provides a mirror image of our society—be it good or be it bad. Consumption is the reaction that the consumer exhibits to communications from the producers and distributors of goods and services. To help the student formulate an answer to this question ask them about purchasing a car, fashion clothing, a stereo, entertainment, an education at a university. What type of products are they most involved with?

One interesting project for the students is to ask them to list five to eight products (by specific brand name) that they buy that best illustrates who they are, pass them around (no names on the papers), and see if the class can guess who the students are based on their product purchases or at least what type of person might purchase the indicated items.

3. **A number of current demographic or cultural trends are important to marketers. What are some important trends that may affect marketing of the following products:**
    a. housing
    b. health care
    c. newspapers
    d. textbooks
    e. travel and tourism

First, the older that the consumer is, the more likely that more extended and involved decision making will probably be. Reasons for this might be the amount of experience in life and consumption, the experience in searching for alternatives, or the more rational decision making mode used.

Second, income is difficult to trace. However, the more discretionary income available the more likely that person will extend their problem solving skills and widen their choice alternatives. Since income is of great importance to marketers, many focus their strategies on this variable. The less the income level, the more the concentration on satisfying the basic needs. The higher the income level, the more likely that the higher order needs will be satisfied.

Third, family status involves the consumer in an unusual sequence of purchasing activities, since more than one person may be involved in the decision making and purchase task. Problem searches tend to be extended when more than one person is involved in the decision making.

Fourth, lifestyle dictates the choice of goods and services based how one chooses to live one's life. This is a mixture of internal and external factors. It is not clear that lifestyle alters the actual decision making model or whether some of the factors that affect lifestyle itself alter the model.

4. **The ABC model of attitudes identifies three components that can be used by marketers to shape people's attitudes about products. Identify the product categories you think are most likely to be affected by each component, and discuss the merits of trying to change people's attitudes about them.**

The three components of the ABC model are *affect (feeling)*, *behavior (doing)*, and *cognition (knowing)*. First, those products that are sensory in nature (such as perfume) are associated with *affect (feeling)* components of attitudes. Second, those products that are based on experiences (such as everyday products like chewing gum) are associated with *behavior (doing)* components of attitudes. And third, those products that are important or complex products (such as computers) are more associated with *cognition (knowing)* components of attitudes.

Attitudes can be changed. However, it is usually easier to establish new attitudes. If change is the objective, it usually easier to associate the attitude change with an established attitude. An example would be to ask a smoker to quit by emphasizing the positive health benefits of the change in habit and attitude.

5. **Culture is not static—it continues to change. What changes in the values, beliefs and customs of your culture do you see changing? How are these changes affecting marketing? What product will be affected more by these changes?**

An interesting way to discuss this question would be to have students assist you in listing ways that values, beliefs, and customs have changed in the past 20 years. For assistance in answering this question you might want to explore the characters and situations used in old television shows. Next, ask students to predict what changes in culture will occur by the year 2010. What should be the response of marketing for these predicted changes?

6.   **Consumers often buy products because they feel pressure from reference groups to conform. Does conformity exert a positive or negative influence on consumers? How do consumer demographics, psychographics and lifestyle affect their readiness to conform? With what types of products is conformity more likely to occur?**

Most students will probably be reluctant to admit that they have at some time made a purchase because of peer pressure. But we all have! Ask the students to think back to some of the clothes they wore in 7th and 8th grades. Did their peers influence what they wore? When did their peers begin to have less influence on their purchase decisions?

Conformity can be positive or negative. For example, some public elementary schools have established school uniform policies in order to help students focus on learning rather than what they are wearing. Some forms of peer pressure are also lessened when everyone is dressed the same. Conformity can be negative when individuals choose to participate in activities which they believe are morally wrong or when they purchase products which they cannot afford.

The need to conform often seems to lessen as we become older and more mature. However, there are adults who still feel pressure to conform. The availability of credit has made it easy for individuals to purchase products and services which they may not be able to afford. This type of conformity is most likely to occur for products which are highly visible to others.

 **Real People, Real Surfers: Exploring the Web**

In this exercise students are instructed to visit the Web site for the American Sheep Industry (ASI) and the American Wool Council. You might want to focus class discussion on student responses' to questions 3 and 4. This discussion could also be used when discussing the "How it Worked Out at ASI" segment.

Marketing in Action: Real Choices at Playboy Enterprises, Inc.

Summary: Playboy Enterprises must develop strategies that will assure success in a changing consumer environment.

Suggested Answers to Case Questions:

1. **What are the problems facing Playboy Enterprises, Inc.?**
    Playboy Enterprises (though still successful by many standards) has seen a decline the popularity of their Playboy clubs and their "cash cow" Playboy Magazine in the 1990s.

2. **What factors are important in understanding these problems?**
    Playboy Enterprises, Inc is one of the best known companies in America. In the 1960s and 1970s circulation of the magazine surged and the Playboy Club was "hot". Things have changed and the once successful magazine and nightclubs are not as popular as they once were. In an era where morally offensive and sexually degrading enterprises are on the wane, Playboy has failed to accept the reality of a need to change. In addition, there are many more avenues available to men (competition) who seek this form of entertainment and fantasy.

3. **What are the alternatives?**
    Playboy has chosen to refocus its efforts in the direction of updating its entertainment function. It has decided not to pursue men's contemporary tastes (such as health and fitness) and has decided to pursue entertainment through several options. The options are:
    a. Focus on producing popular home videos and promoting Playboy-branded videos of popular vintage movies.
    b. Pursue experiments in producing Playboy interviews on CD-ROM and building a home page on the Web to offset magazine losses and to carve out a niche for the future.

4. **What are your recommendations for solving the problems?**
    The students should see that "the times they are a changing" and that Playboy Enterprises should consider seeking new ventures that address the needs of adult men and women. Health, physical fitness, investment planning, luxury product purchases, medical advice, political comment, lifestyle expression, and freedom of speech should all be considered as viable alternative mixes for new products and entertainment ventures or the organization will have great difficulty competing in the next century.

5. **What are some ways to implement your recommendations?**
    The students might recommend new ventures (even if under a different name than Playboy Enterprises) in magazines, entertainment centers (health clubs for singles), programming production, cable TV (using the existing Playboy channel), and exploration on the Web. The first step would be to design an extensive research project to understand the changing tastes and preferences of men and women as they reach their middle adult years. The organization might also determine if it is possible to attract younger consumers that seem to have avoided the Playboy philosophy and organization.

Mini-Project 6-A
Understanding Evaluative Criteria in the Decision Process

Purpose: By conducting a simple experiment you will better understand how consumers make decisions and how marketers use this information to develop marketing strategies.

1.   With a few of your classmates, first select a product category that interests you. You might consider

- automobiles
- a man's dress suit
- a university
- an apartment
- a new stereo
- some other product of your choice

2.   Next, select 6 to 10 product attributes which you feel are important to consumers in choosing among different brands of the product. Also select 6 to 8 brands or models of the product which someone might consider. Then determine how each brand would be rated on each of the attributes.

3.   Use this information to build an information display board. This board can be made of cardboard or wood or some other material. List the attributes down the left side of the board and the brands across the top. Then fill in the ratings for each brand as suggested below. Construct your board so that the ratings can be covered up. (You might use Post-It notes to cover each of the rating blocks on the board.)

Auto Attributes	Ford Mustang	Jeep Wrangler	Pontiac Grand Am	Chevrolet Cavalier	Ford Explorer
Roominess/ Size	Small	Small	Average	Small	Large
Comfort	Average	Poor			
Gas economy					

4.   Conduct research with your board by asking student research subjects (only one at a time) to imagine they are buying a car and to uncover the information they want in the same way that they would go about gathering information about a new car purchase. (Some subjects may look at all of the information about the first car, then all about the second car, etc. Others may look at the gas economy of all the cars first and so on.)

5.   Observe and record the subjects' selections. Then use that information to develop recommendations for marketing strategies (any or all of the 4 Ps) for one of the brands.

6.   Present your findings to your class.

Mini-Project 6-B
Maslow's Hierarchy in Ads

Purpose: to understand how advertisers appeal to different consumer needs.

Maslow's hierarchy of needs categorizes motives according to five levels.

1. Physiological
2. Safety
3. Belongingness
4. Ego
5. Self-Actualization

The hierarchy implies that needs at a certain level must be at least partially satisfied before consumers will seek to satisfy needs at a higher level.

 Marketers often use advertising appeals or ad slogans that will activate (hopefully) these needs or motives. Try to find as many as three advertisements which are related to each of the levels of Maslow's hierarchy. Describe the ad and the specific need it appeals to.

Physiological needs

1 _____

2 _____

3 _____

Safety needs

1 _____

2 _____

3 _____

Belongingness needs

1 _____

2 _____

3 _____

Ego needs

1 _____

2 _____

3 _____

Self-actualization needs

1 _____

2 _____

3 _____

7

Why Organizations Buy: Business to Business Markets

*O*verview In this chapter the activities of business buyers and sellers is examined. How businesses and organizations are categorized, business buying behavior, and the business buying decision process are also discussed.

National Gypsum Company is the focus of the Real People, Real Choices segment. In this section student's will learn about the choices which National Gypsum had to make when their market share was declining and competition was increasing.

Objectives

1. Describe the general characteristics of business-to-business markets and business buying practices.

2. Tell how business and organizational markets are classified.

3. Explain the business buying situation and describe business buyers.

4. Understand the stages in the business buying decision process.

| Chapter Outline and Suggested Activities | **Introduction:** Begin by asking students how organizational markets differ from consumer markets. One way to approach this discussion would be to have students identify products which are purchased by both organizational and individuals. The Instructor's Manual mini-research project 7-B would be a good project to use for this discussion. |

1. **Business Markets: Buying And Selling When Stakes Are High.**
   ** Refer to Objective 1
   ** Use Video Mastercard Part II
   ** Use Marketing in Action: Real Choices at Pitney Bowes

   a. Like individual consumers, organizations make purchase decisions. The differences between the two and the risks involved in making a poor purchase decision however are different.

   b. ***Business-to-business marketing:*** *Marketing of those goods and services that business and organizational customers need to produce other goods and* services, for resale or to support their operations.

   c. Characteristics that make a difference in business markets.
   **Use Figure 7.1
       1).   Multiple buyers

➡ *Class Discussion*   Refer to Case I for Computer Friendly Stuff. Discuss with students the reasons why the firm wanted to win an account with a large retailer verses sales to individual consumers.

    2).   Number of customers
    3).   Size of purchase
    4).   Geographic concentration

   d. Business-to business demand
   ** Use Q#1 Marketing Practice: Applying What You've Learned
       1).   ***Derived demand:*** *Demand for business or organizational products derived from demand for consumer goods or services.*

➡ *Class Discussion*   Refer to Figure 7.2 and create a derived demand chart for Disney World or Honda cars.

    2).   ***Inelastic demand:*** *Demand for products that does not change because of increases or decreases in price.*

➡ *Class Discussion*   Refer to the Spotlight on Real People, Capitol Concierge. Is the demand for this service elastic, inelastic, or fluctuating? Explain.

    3).   Fluctuating demand: The ***acceleration principle*** *explains how a small percentage change in consumer demand can create a large percentage change in total industrial or business demand.*
    4).   ***Joint demand:*** *Demand for two or more goods that are used together to create a product.*

SPOTLIGHT ON REAL PEOPLE: Capitol Concierge

Summary: Mary Naylor's Washington, DC firm offers the same services executives expect in their home offices while they are on the road. Mary's business serves a variety of business customer's needs such as catering, gifts, tickets, valet services, and flowers. The company has a software tracking system which keeps client records and even can be used to remind customers of special occasions. The company's motto is, "Consider It Done".

Suggested Answers to Discussion Questions

1. **Why would Capitol Concierge be considered a business-to-business rather than a consumer company?**
   Capitol Concierge's clients, business executives, use her services as part of doing business. Although the firm does deal with individual clients who are purchasing services for individual use, the difference is that for these executives the services offered by Capitol Concierge help to make the executives job easier.

2. **Why is Capitol Concierge's business dependent upon derived demand?**
   If the executives in the firms which Capitol Concierge serves are doing well, then they will have a greater need for the services provided by Capitol Concierge. For example, when business is good, these executives may have less time to run routine errands.

3. **What unfilled need is Capitol Concierge addressing for its customers?**
   The services provided Capitol Concierge meet the need of time. Many people suffer from "time poverty" and the services provided by Capitol Concierge enable their clients to make better use of their time.

2. **Classifying Business-To-Business Markets**
   ** Refer to Objective 2
   ** Use Figure 7.3
   a. *North American Industry Classification System (NAICS): The numerical coding system that the U.S., Canada, and Mexico use to classify firms into detailed categories according to their business activities and shared characteristics.*
      ** Use Figure 7.4
      **Use Real People, Real Surfers: Exploring the Web
      ** Use Marketing Mini-Project: Learning by Doing
   b. *Producers: The individual or organizations that purchase products for use in the production of other goods and services.*
   c. *Resellers: The individuals or organizations that buy finished goods for the purpose of reselling, renting, or leasing to others at a profit and for maintaining their operations.*
   d. *Government Markets: The federal, state, county, and local governments that buy goods and services to carry out public objectives and to support their operations. Government buyers are usually required to obtain competitive bids.*
   e. *Competitive Bids: A business buying process in which two or more suppliers submit proposals (including price and associated data) for a proposed purchase and the firm providing the better gets the bid.*
   f. *Not-for-Profit Institutions: The organizations with charitable, educational, community, and other public-service goals that buy goods and services to support their functions and to attract and serve their members.*

3. **The Nature Of Business Buying**
   **Refer to Objective 3
   a.   The buying situation: Like individual consumers, business consumers spend more time and effort on certain purchases than on others.
          **Use Q#3 Marketing Practice: Applying What You've Learned
          1).   *Buy class: One of the three classifications of business buyers that characterize the degree of time and effort required to make a decision in a buying situation.*
                 a).   *Straight rebuy: A buying situation in which buyers make routine purchases that require minimal decision making.*
                 b).   *Modified rebuy: A buying situation classification used by business buyers to categorize a previously made purchase that involves some change and that requires limited decision making.*
                 c).   *New-task buying: A new business-to-business purchase that is complex or risky and that requires extensive decision making.*
   b.   The professional buyer
          **Use Instructor's Manual Marketing Mini-Project 7-A
          1).   A variety of titles are used to denote professional buyers
                 a)   Purchasing agent
                 b)   Procurement officers
                 c)   Directors of materials management
          2).   *Centralized purchasing: A business buying practice in which an organization's purchasing department does the buying for all the company's facilities.*
   c.   *The buying center: The group of people in an organization who influence and participate in purchasing decisions.*
          1).   The fluid nature of the buying center
          2).   Roles in the buying center
                 ** Use Figure 7.5
                 a)   Initiator
                 b)   User
                 c)   Gatekeeper
                 d)   Influencer
                 e)   Decider
                 f)   Buyer
   d.   Electronic Business-to-Business commerce
          1).   *Electronic commerce: The buying and selling of products electronically, usually via the Internet.*
          2).   *Electronic data interchange (EDI): EDI allows for limited communication through the exchange of computer data between two companies.*
          3).   *Intranet: Internal computer connections organizations use to distribute information among a company's different offices and locations.*
          4)   *Extranet: With extranets, marketers allow suppliers, distributors, and other authorized users to access data that the company makes available.*

4. **The Business Buying Decision Process**
   ** Refer to Objective 4
   ** Use Figure 7.6

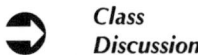

Class Discussion   Compare and contrast the business buying decision process (Figure 7.6) with the consumer buying decision process discussed in chapter 6 (Figure 6.1).

   a.   Problem recognition: As in the consumer process, the first step in the business buying decision process occurs when there is a purchase that can solve a problem.

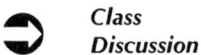 ***Class***
Discussion   How does problem recognition differ for each of the three buy classes?

   b.   Information search
        1).   Developing product specifications
        2).   Obtaining proposals
   c.   Evaluation of alternatives
        1).   Proposals are evaluated
        2).   Time is spend accessing which supplier best can satisfy the firms needs.
        3).   The more complex and costly the purchase, the more time spent searching for the best supplier.
   d.   Product and supplier selection: Consider these issues when selecting the supplier
        1).   Price is obviously an important consideration
        2).   Quality, reliability, and durability of materials must also be considered
        3).   ***Just in time (JIT):*** *Inventory management and purchasing processes that manufacturers and resellers use to reduce inventory to very low levels, but ensure that deliveries from suppliers arrive only when needed.*
        4).   ***Single sourcing:*** *The business practice of buying a particular product from only one supplier.*
        5).   ***Multiple sourcing:*** *The business practice of buying a particular product from many suppliers.*
        6).   ***Reciprocity:*** *A trading partnership in which two firms agree to buy from one another.*
        7).   ***Outsourcing:*** *The business buying process of obtaining outside vendors to provide goods or services that otherwise might be supplied "in house".*
        8).   ***Reverse marketing:*** *A business practice in which a buyer firm shapes a supplier's products and operations to satisfy its needs.*
   e.   Postpurchase evaluation: Organizations assess whether the performance of the product and the supplier meet expectations.

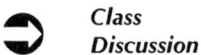 ***Class***
Discussion   The practice of outsourcing is increasing in firms. There have been incidents where a firm might downsize a department in the organization and then rehire some of those same individuals from the department on a contract basis. What are the advantages and disadvantages of outsourcing for the firm and the individual who is awarded the contract? When should the function of marketing be outsourced?

Real People, Bad Choices

Summary: The Hawaii State Public Library System contracted with Black & Taylor, a book wholesaler, to select and supply books to its branch libraries. The state was not pleased with Baker & Taylor's performance and terminated the contract.

Suggested Answer to Discussion Question

1.   **Do you think that there are certain kinds of firms for which outsourcing is a good idea? What firms?**
     It is difficult for some organizations to have the needed expertise in all of the areas required to do their business. It is also possible that some of the tasks required for the firm are small and are needed on a cyclical or fluctuating basis. Outsourcing is also a good option when the firm can afford to pay benefits to only a small number of employees.
          All firms at some time could use and benefit from the services provided through outsourcing.

Real People, Real Choices: How it Worked Out at National Gypsum

Summary: Craig Weishbruch is the Sr. V.P. of Sales and Marketing for National Gypsum, the world's second largest producer of gypsum wallboard. Gypsum wallboard is used to build walls and ceilings in residential, commercial, and manufactured housing construction. Problems with a new joint treatment product and increased competition from both the high end and the low end faced National Gypsum.

Option 1: Lower the price on high end products and try to cover costs by expanding marketshare.
Option 2: Abandon the idea of entering the low-end price market
Option 3: Market a new line of joint treatments designed for the needs of contractors and "DO-It-Yourselfers"

Mr. Weishbruch chose option 3.

Potential Discussion Questions

1. What was done to avoid confusion in the marketplace?

2. What are the needs of industrial (i.e., contractors) consumers and "Do-It-Yourselfers"?

Marketing Concepts: Testing Your Knowledge

1.   **What are some general characteristics of business-to-business markets? What is the primary difference between business customers and consumers?**
Business and organizational customers are usually few in number, may be geographically concentrated, and often purchase higher-priced products in larger quantities. Businesses purchase equipment, maintenance, repair, and operating products, as well as specialized services, and the materials and component parts needed to produce goods. Business demand is derived from the demand for another good or service, is generally not affected by price increases or decreases, is subject to great fluctuations, and may be tied to the demand and availability of some other good.
          Primary differences between business customers and consumers include:
a.   Purchase decisions made by organizations frequently involve many people.
b.   Organizational and industrial products often are bought according to precise, technical specifications, requiring rational criteria and knowledge about the product category.
c.   The decision process for some business products is lengthy and may involve price negotiations and complex financial arrangements.
d.   Impulse buying is rare. Business buyers are usually professionals.
e.   Many products are purchased directly from the producer.
f.   Organizational purchase decisions are frequently characterized by high risk.

2.   **How is business-to-business demand different from consumer demand? What are some of the factors that cause business demand to fluctuate?**
Derived demand is demand for business or organizational products derived from demand for consumer goods or services. Business demand is generally not affected by price increases or decreases (inelastic demand), is subject to great fluctuations, and may be tied to the demand and availability of some other good (joint demand).
          Some factors that may cause demand to fluctuate are the *acceleration principle* (or multiplier effect where a small percentage change in consumer demand may cause a larger change in business demand), business demand is linked to the changes in the overall economy and its up and down cycles, and shortages and prices create fluctuations in business demand.

3.   **How are business-to-business markets generally classified? What types of purchases do the three major types of firms make?**
Business-to-business markets can be broken into three general categories (See Figure 7.1 for more detail and explanation). The major categories are producers, resellers, and organizations.
          Producers purchase materials, parts, and various goods and services needed to produce other goods and services to be sold at a profit. Resellers purchase finished goods to resell at a profit. In addition, they also purchase other goods and services to maintain their operations. Governments and other nonprofit organizations purchase the goods and services necessary to fulfill their objectives.

4.   **What is the NAICS? What purpose does it serve? Of what use is it to business marketers?**
NAICS refers to the North American Industry Classification System. NAICS is the numerical coding system that the U.S., Canada, and Mexico use to classify firms into detailed categories according to their business activities and shared characteristics. This system replaced the U.S. Standard Industrial Classification (SIC) system in 1997 in order for NAFTA (North American Free Trade Agreement) countries to compare economic and financial statistics. These reports allow firms to determine how well (or how poorly) they are doing compared to their industry groups as a whole. NAICS can also be used to identify new customers.

5.   **Describe the three buy class situations.**
Straight rebuy is a buying situation classification used by business buyers to categorize routine purchases that require minimal decision making.

Modified rebuy is a buying situation classification used by business buyers to categorize a previously made purchase that involves some change and that requires limited decision making.

New-task buy is a buying situation classification used by business buyers to categorize a new purchase that is complex or risky and that requires extensive decision making.

6. **What is the role of electronic commerce in business-to-business marketing?**
Electronic commerce is the buying and selling of products electronically usually via the Internet. Using the Internet for e-commerce allows business marketers to link directly to suppliers, factories, distributors, and their customers. The result is a reduction in the time necessary for order and delivery of goods, tracking sales, and getting feedback from customers.

7. **What are the characteristics of business buyers?**
People who buy for organizations have a lot of responsibility. Even though they are generally considered to be professional buyers, some of their individual purchasing characteristics do creep into or affect their professional judgment. Therefore, business buying is often shaped by those that do the buying. How these buyers interpret and carry out the buy task is usually up to them. There tends to be more complexity and risk associated with the business buying situation. The situation will determine how much time and effort is put into the buying decision. The need to focus on economic considerations accounts for the primary differences between consumer buying and business buying.

Just like consumer buying, the buyer's age, income, education, personality, and attitudes can affect the purchase decision. In addition, communications and the buyer's role in the purchasing process are also to be considered. Lastly, expectations of the supplier, the organizational climate, and attitude toward risk are factors that are important considerations.

8 **What is a buying center? What are the roles of the various people in a buying center?**
A *buying center* is the group of people in an organization who influence and participate in particular purchasing decisions.

The various roles played by members of the buying center include:
a. *Initiator:* the member of a business buying center who first recognizes that a purchase needs to be made and notifies others in the organization.
b. *User:* a member of a business buying center who will actually use a business product after it is purchased.
c. *Gatekeeper:* the member of a business buying center who controls the flow of information to other members.
d. *Influencer:* a member of a business buying center who affects the buying decision by dispensing advice or sharing expertise.
e. *Decider:* the member of a business buying center who has the authority to make the final purchase decision.
f. *Buyer:* the member of a business buying center who has the formal authority and responsibility for executing the purchase.

9. **What are the stages in the business buyer decision process? What happens in each stage?**
The stages in the business buyer decision process (See Figure 7.3 for more detail and explanation) are:
a. Problem Recognition.
b. Information Search.
c. Evaluation of Alternatives.
d. Product and Supplier Selection.
e. Postpurchase Evaluation.
The business buying decision process involves a number of stages that are similar to but more complex that the steps followed by consumers when making a purchase decision. A single purchase may involve the recognition of a problem that can be resolved by making a purchase. The recognition stage is accompanied by the submission of a purchase requisition and initiates the subsequent steps of developing product specifications, identifying potential suppliers, requesting and obtaining proposals, evaluating the proposals, selecting a supplier, placing the order, and, finally, formally evaluating the performance of the product and the supplier.

10.   **What is single sourcing? Multiple sourcing? Outsourcing? Explain how reciprocity and reverse marketing operate in business-to-business markets.**

Single sourcing is the business practice of buying a particular product from only one suppler.

Multiple sourcing is the business practice of buying a particular product from many suppliers.

Outsourcing is the business buying process of obtaining outside vendors to produce goods or services that otherwise might be supplied "in house".

Reciprocity and reverse marketing are both types of buyer-seller relationships. In reciprocity an agreement is made where a buyer and seller agree to be each other's customers. In other words, I'll buy from you and you buy from me.

Reverse marketing is also a type of buyer-seller partnership. In reverse marketing a buyer firm shapes a supplier's products and operations to satisfy its needs.

Marketing Concepts: Discussing Choices and Issues

1.   **Do you agree with the idea that business-to-business marketing is more important to a country's economy than consumer marketing? Which one do you think provides better career opportunities for new college grads? Explain your answers.**

Business customers create vast opportunities for marketers and account for far more transactions in the marketplace than consumer purchasers. A single consumer purchase is the culmination of a series of buying and selling activities between many organizations. Therefore, most students should see that business-to-business marketing is very important to the economy.

Many students will not have had experience with business-to-business marketing and probably would not think of it as a first choice upon graduation. However, it worthy of their consideration, professional in its makeup, and has the potential for rapid advancement. If students like the thought of making important decisions that affect the viability of the firm, business-to-business marketing is a great field to explore.

2.   **A number of business buying practices may be criticized as being unfair to a one or more suppliers. What are the benefits of reciprocity to business firms? Is anyone hurt by reciprocity?**

Students may think that reciprocity is illegal, but it is not. Of course, the government does "frown" upon such agreements. Business firms benefit from reciprocity by having buyers for their products. The problem with reciprocity is that it can harm small manufacturers and buyers who cannot afford to form such agreements. Competition and the availability of a variety of goods to consumers may also be restricted as a result of reciprocity.

3.   **The practice of buying business products based on sealed competitive bids is popular among all types of business buyers. What are the advantages and disadvantages of this practice to buyers? What are the advantages and disadvantages for sellers? Should companies always give the business to the lowest bidder? Why or why not?**

Sealed competitive bids help to ensure fairness and a "level playing ground". The advantage for buyers is that this process eliminates bias from the decision process. The disadvantage is that typically only low price, and not often competitive factors are considered in the decision process.

The advantage for sellers is the ability to be considered unbiased. The disadvantage for sellers is that they have no knowledge of what their competition has included or excluded from their bid. This makes selling very difficult.

4.   **When firms engage in outsourcing, they relinquish control over how goods and services are produced. What are the advantages of outsourcing to a firm? What are some of the hazards of outsourcing? What can firms do to make sure that outsourcing benefits both them and the outsourcing firm?**

Note: You may want to refer to the "Real People, Bad Choice?" segment for an example of outsourcing.

The major advantage of outsourcing is that the firm does not have to pay a regular employee. This basically means no benefits! Another advantage is that the firm pays for services of an outside expert on an as needed or project basis.

The biggest hazard of outsourcing is that firms relinquish direct supervision and some control over the task being completed. To help ensure that problems do not occur and that outsourcing is a "win-win" situation, firms should:

- clearly state the responsibilities of the contractor and what is to be delivered
- Check references of all contractors
- Create a contract which is signed by both the firm and the contractor

Students may have other ideas. Ask students if they or someone they know performs some type of outsourcing task for an organization.

Real People, Real Surfers: Exploring the Web

All three Web sites, National Gypsum, Georgia Pacific and USG Corporation should be easy to access. Have students focus on answering questions two and three. One strategy would be to have half of the class answer questions two and the other half question three. Students could present their answers to these questions in class and discuss their findings.

Marketing in Action: Real Choices at Pitney Bowes

Summary: For over 75 years Pitney Bowes held a near monopoly in the postage meter business and was one of country's most profitable companies. Although there had been numerous attempts to undermine Pitney Bowe's position over the years, none had constituted a real threat, until now!

Suggested Answers to Case Questions:

1. **What is the problem facing Pitney Bowes?**
    Survival! The real issue is deciding what actions need to be taken in order to survive in a changing market. A second issue is selecting the best new direction for the firm to take.

2. **What factors are important in understanding this problem?**
    The following factors are important considerations.
    a.   The firm has an advantage with its established brand image.
    b.   Increased competition, especially from the U.S. Postal Service.
    c.   Technology changes: digital postmarks, E-stamp, E-mail, and mechanical meters.
    d.   Customers' increased demands for quick and efficient document communication.
    e.   New ventures into other markets are costly and the firm could lose money.
    f.   When should a firm deviate from its core product offering?

3. **What alternatives might Pitney Bowes consider?**
    The following list of alternatives might stimulate discussion.
    a.   Do nothing—Pitney Bowes has a strong core of loyal customers.
    b.   Expand internationally. Identify countries where there is little competition and where new technologies are not available.
    c.   Look for a joint venture or acquire a smaller firm which has more technology but little capital.
    d.   Pour resources into developing new services and technologically advanced products.
    e.   Build on the Pitney Bowes name and work on solving document communication needs rather than postage needs.
    f.   Focus on small businesses and home markets.

4. **What are your recommendations for solving the problem?**
    The recommendations cited by students will probably be varied. With the exception of "alternative a" all of the above alternatives have merit. Help students understand that Pitney Bowes needs to develop a long-term strategy, not a quick fix.

5. **What are some ways to implement your recommendations?**
    Pitney Bowes should build on its strong brand recognition. Establishing more relationships, similar to the one with NationsBank (now Bank of America), and working on solving document communication needs, rather than metering, would be a good solution. Pitney Bowes should also consider the needs of small businesses and home markets. Both of theses sectors of the business market are growing and represent a viable segment for the organization to pursue. Research needs to be conducted to determine how to best serve the business customer.
    Finally long term survival depends on the adoption of new technology. Pitney Bowes must either be the leader in developing new technologies or be the leader in delivering new technologies to the market.

Mini-Project 7-A
Buying Big Time

Purpose: to gain an understanding of business-to-business buying

When your bed linens begin to wear out, you will have to buy a couple of sheets and a couple of pillowcases. When Marriott's linens begin to wear out, (which they do on a regular basis) they have to buy thousands of sets of sheets and pillow cases. Understanding business-to-business marketing also means understanding organizational buying.

1. With several of your classmates, make arrangements to visit with a purchasing professional. In different organizations, these individuals may go by any number of different titles including

    ■   buyer
    ■   materials manager
    ■   purchasing agent

    You will probably want to tell the individual that you would like to learn more about their job and how they fit into the marketing of goods and services.

2. During your visit, you may want to ask some of the following questions:

    a.   What types of goods and services are they responsible for purchasing?
    b.   What type of training did they receive for their job?
    c.   What skills or abilities are most important for a buyer?
    d.   How is their job important to their organization?
    e.   What are the steps their organization goes through in buying goods and services? Do they request competitive bids, have specification buying, and do they have interdependent relationships with any of their suppliers?
    f.   What characteristics of products, of suppliers, and of sales people are most important in getting their business?
    g.   How important are green marketing activities to their organization?
    h.   Does their firm have a policy regarding gifts which the buyer may or may not accept?
    i.   Does their organization usually practice single or multiple sourcing? Why or why not?

3. Develop a report of your findings. Present your report to your class.

Mini-Project 7-B
Small Versus Large Customers

Purpose: to develop understanding of how marketing strategies for organizational customers differ from those used to attract individual consumers.

Some firms market both directly to consumers and to organizational buyers also. For example, Scott Paper company makes decorator paper products for home use and more heavy duty paper products for institutional use. IBM sells personal computers for home use and large main-frame computers and computer networks for business and industry. Coca Cola uses TV to advertise its product to individual consumers but also seeks to make themselves the supplier or choice for hotel and restaurant chains.

1.   Select a product (probably an individual brand) which you know is sold to both individual consumers and to large organizational customers.

2.   Using a variety of resources, find out how the firm markets its product to the two different customer types. You may want to seek out advertising on TV, in general audience magazines and in special business or professional periodicals (ask you librarian for suggestions). You may be able to talk directly with individuals in either the buying or the selling industry for help. In other cases, you may need to create your own ideas about how you think marketing strategies should be designed. Be sure to include the different strategies for each of the 4 Ps

Product/brand_____

Organizational Customers
Product Strategies _____

_____

_____

_____

_____

_____

Individual Customers
Product Strategies _____

_____

_____

_____

_____

_____

Organizational Customers

Pricing
Strategies _____

_____

_____

_____

_____

_____

Distribution
Strategies _____

_____

_____

_____

_____

_____

Promotion
Strategies _____

_____

_____

_____

_____

_____

8

Sharpening the Focus: Target Marketing Strategies

Overview   The focus of marketing efforts is sharpened by examining target marketing. In this chapter segmentation targeting, and positioning are discussed. An in-depth look at each of these principles is provided.

Burrell Communications is the focus of the Real People, Real Choices segment. One of Burrell's clients, McDonald's and the targeting decisions which had to be made in the development of an advertising campaign are discussed.

Objectives

1.   Understand the three steps involved in developing a target marketing strategy.

2.   Understand the need for market segmentation in today's business environment.

3.   Know the different dimensions used for segmenting consumer markets.

4.   Understand the bases for segmentation in industrial markets.

5.   Explain how potential market segments are evaluated and selected.

6.   Explain how a targeting strategy is developed.

7.   Understand how a firm develops and implements a positioning strategy.

Introduction: Ask students what type of bath soap or shampoos they most recently purchased and why they purchased this particular brand. As students begin to tell what brand they purchased and their reason(s) for purchasing the brand the instructor may want to point out the different reasons given for purchasing a brand. Discuss the concept of positioning and how consumers must perceive differences between brands for successful segmentation and positioning to occur.

1.   **Have It Your Way: Selecting And Entering A Market**
    **Refer to Objective 1
    ** Use video House of Blues
    **Use Figure 8.1
    a.   Consumers diverse interest and backgrounds have resulted in different groups who have distinct needs and wants.
        1).   *Market fragmentation: creation of many consumer groups due to a diversity of distinct needs and wants in a modern society.*
        2).   It is not realistic to provide a truly unique product to satisfy each individual consumers needs. Fortunately, some groups of consumers want the same thing.
        3).   *Target marketing strategy: Dividing the total market into different segments based on customer characteristics, selecting one or more segments, and developing products to meet the needs of those specific segments.*
    b.   *Segmentation: The process of dividing a longer market into smaller pieces based on one or more meaningful shared characteristics. There are many variables, segmentation variables, which can be used to divide the total market into fairly homogenous groups, each with different needs and preferences*
        Dimensions for segmenting consumer markets
        **Use Instructor's Manual Marketing Mini-research project 8-A
        **Use Q#2 Marketing Practice: Applying What You Learned
        ** Marketing Mini-Project: Learning by Doing
        1).   Demographics
            a).   *Age:*
                 Generation X: *The group of consumers between the ages of 18 and 29.*
                 Baby boomers: *Segment of people who are in their thirties and forties.*
            b).   *Gender*
            c).   *Family structure*
            d).   *Income and social class*
            e).   *Race and ethnicity*
            f).   *Geography:*
                 Geodemography: *Technique used by marketers to segment marketers the segment market that combines geography and demographics.*
        2).   Segmenting by Psychographics
            a).   Demographic information is useful, but more information is needed to divide consumers into meaningful segments. Psychographic profiles of consumers help to provide this additional information.
            b).   *VALS(Values and Lifestyles): Psychographic system that divides the entire U.S. population into eight segments*
                 **Use Real People, Real Surfers: Exploring the Web
                 **Refer to Figure 8.2

Real People, Bad Choices?

Summary: Should marketers be allowed to craft sexual appeals targeted to young people? Consider Calvin Klein (CK) and accusations that the firm used "Kiddie—porn" to sell apparel. Calvin Klein finally pulled the controversial advertising campaign, but not before CK received a lot of free publicity.

Potential Discussion Questions

1. Should CK have pulled the advertisements?

2. Consider the problems facing today's youth: do you think firms like CK are contributing to some of these problems by using sex appeals in their advertisements?

3).   Segmenting by behavior
  a).   *Behavior segmentation: Technique that divides consumers into segments on the basis of how they react toward, feel about, or use a product or service*
  b).   Segment the market based on characteristics such as users versus nonusers
  c).   *80/20 rule: A marketing rule of thumb that 20 percent of purchases account for 80 percent of product's sales*
  d).   *User occasions: Indictor used in one type of market segmentation based on when consumers use a product most.*

Spotlight on Real People: Orosi LLC

Summary: Orosi, the name of a river in Costa Rica, is not only a favorite Kayaking destination, but also the name of an innovative firm which designs Kayak helmets. Orosi's stylish products are popular with the twenty something Kayaking and white-water rafting group.

Suggested Answers to Discussion Questions

1.   **What dimensions could be used to segment the Kayaking market?**
  ■   *Demographics:* age, income
  ■   *Psychographics:* consider lifestyles
  ■   *Behavioral:* consider heavy users, those who Kayak regularly (80/20 rule)

2.   **What market segment is most likely to buy the product?**
     The twenty something group who enjoys Kayaking. This group is comprised of free spirited, rugged individualists who most probably go kayaking on regular basis.

3.   **How could Orosi expand their product line to appeal to other consumer segments?**
     The product line could be expanded to include not only Kayaking apparel but other non-kayaking apparel, such as shorts. Other brands such as Northface (skiing) and Bodyglove (surfing) both gained popularity in their respective sports before being accepted by other consumer segments.

3.   **Dimensions for Segmenting Industrial Markets**
      **Refer to Objective 4
  a.   The variables used to segment the industrial market are different than the variables used to segment the consumer market. However the underlying principle of why segmentation is necessary remains unchanged.

➜ **Class Discussion** Review with students the information about the Orosi Company found in the "Spotlight on Real People" (page 20). If Orosi wanted to sell the helmets to firms which lead kayaking expeditions (i.e., an industrial consumer), what dimensions should be used to segment the market?

    b.   Organizational demographics—used to help industrial marketers understand the needs and characteristics of potential customers. Some examples might include:
          1).   Number of firms in an industry
          2).   Size of each firm
          3).   Type of products needed
    c.   Company—specific characteristics
          1).   ***Operating Variables***—*the production technology used, the business customer's degree of technical, financial, or operations expertise, and whether or not the prospect is a current or non-user of the product.*
          2).   End-Use applications

4.   **Targeting**
       **Refer to Objective 1
       **Use Figure 8.1
    a.   Targeting is the second step in the target marketing process. In targeting marketers evaluate each potential segment and decide which of these groups they will try to turn into customers.
    b.   ***Target market:*** *Group or groups selected by a firm to be turned into customers as a result of segmentation and targeting*
    c.   Evaluate Market Segments
       **Refer to Objective #5
          1).   Identifying a segment does not mean that it's a useful one to target.
          2).   Requirements for a viable target segment.
              a).   Similarity of members in terms of needs and wants and different from consumers in other segments
              b).   Can the segment be measured?
              c).   Is the segment large enough to be profitable?
              d).   Can marketing communications reach the segment?
              e).   Can the needs of the segment be adequately served?
    d.   Develop segment profiles: A description of the "typical" customer in a segment
          1).   ***Market potential:*** *the maximum demand expected among consumers in a segment for a product or service.*
          2).   Firms need to forecast each segment's market potential

➜ **Class Discussion** Is it better to be a "small fish" in a big pond or a "big fish" in a small pond? Discuss the advantages and disadvantages of targeting segments where there is a lot of competition verses segments which may be smaller in number, but where there is less competition.

5.   **Choose A Targeting Strategy**
       **Refer to Objective 6
       **Use Q#3 Marketing Practice: Applying What You've Learned
       ** Use Computer Friendly Stuff Case II
       **Use Figure 8.3
    a.   ***Undifferentiated targeting strategy:*** *Technique of attempting to appeal to a broad spectrum of people.*

b.   ***Differentiated marketing:*** *Developing one or more products for each of several distinct customers groups and making sure these offerings are kept separate in the marketplace.*

c.   ***Concentrated targeting strategy:*** *Focusing a firm's efforts on offering one or more products to a single segment.*

d.   ***Custom marketing strategy:*** *Tailoring specific products and the messages about them to individual customers.*
   1).   An example of a firm which uses this strategy is Amazon.com
   2).   ***Mass customization:*** *Modifying a basic product or service to meet the needs of an individual*

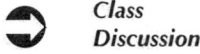

Class Discussion   Refer students back to the introduction exercise of this chapter. What type(s) of targeting strategies where used by the firm mentioned by students. For example, Proctor and Gamble, the manufacturer of Ivory soap, uses a differentiated strategy. Discuss with students the benefits and the risks of each type of targeting strategy.

6.   **Positioning**
   **Refer to Objective 7
   **Use Q#4 Marketing Practice: Applying What You've Learned
   **Use Instructor's Manual Marketing Mini-project 8-A
   a.   Positioning is the final step in the target marketing process (Refer back to Figure 8.1)
   b.   ***Positioning:*** *Developing a marketing strategy aimed at influencing how a particular market segment perceives a product or service in comparison to the competition.*
   c.   Developing a positioning strategy—four steps necessary to complete the positioning process
   1).   Analyze competitor's positions
   2).   Identify competitive advantage
   3).   Finalize the marketing mix
   4).   Evaluate the target market's responses and modify the strategy
      a).   Repositioning: Redoing a product's position to respond to marketplace changes

Class Discussion   What brands have been repositioned to respond to changes in the marketplace?

   d.   Positioning Dimensions:
   1).   Lifestyle image
   2).   Price leadership
   3).   Attributes
   4).   Product class
   5).   Competitors
   6).   Occasions
   7).   Users
   8).   Quality

Class Discussion   Refer to the CFS (Computer Friendly Stuff) case or the VW case at the end of Chapter 8. What dimensions were used to position each of these products?

e.   ***Brand personality:*** *A distinctive image that captures a product or service's character and benefits*

f.   ***Perceptual map:*** *A vivid way to construct a picture of where products or brands are "located" in consumers minds.*

**Refer to Figure 8.4 for an example of a perceptual map

Class
Discussion

Select a product or service category and construct a perceptual map for that category. You might want to refer to the introduction exercise for this chapter and use either soap or shampoo. Another option might be to use automobiles and discuss Marketing in Action: Real Choices at Volkswagen.

Real People Choices: How It Worked Out At Burrell Communications

Summary: Sarah Burroughs is the President and Chief Operating Officer of Burrell Communications Group, the country's largest minority-owned advertising agency. Burrell Communications was given the assignment of building awareness among African-American teens of the career opportunities available at McDonald's. Several creative alternatives were considered.

Option 1: Create a corporate "public service" campaign.
Option 2: Create a "real-life" profile featuring an African-American teen who worked his way up the McDonald's ranks.
Option 3: Build a campaign using a celebrity approach.

Option 2 was selected and a "typical" nice kid living in the inner city named Calvin was created.

Suggested Discussion Questions

1.   Why was the campaign successful?

2.   Why was Burrell Communications a good firm to use for this project?

Marketing Concepts: Testing Your Knowledge

1. **What is market segmentation and why is it an important strategy in today's marketplace?**

   Market segmentation is a process whereby marketers divide a large customer group into segments that share important characteristics.

   Market segmentation and target marketing are important strategies in today's marketplace because of market fragmentation—that is, the splintering of a mass society into diverse groups due to technological and cultural differences. Marketers must determine if they can better satisfy customers with a mass-marketing strategy or target marketing based on strategy efficiency and effectiveness.

2. **List and explain the major demographic characteristics frequently used in segmenting markets.**

   Age: consumers of different age groups have very different needs and wants.

   Gender: segmenting by sex starts at a very early age. Many marketers are looking to gender segmentation as means of expanding markets. For example, hair dryers sold to men dramatically expanded the industry's sales.

   Family structure: using the family life cycle, marketers can segment based on family status and position occupied. Newly marrieds will have different needs and desires than empty-nesters.

   Income and social class: the distribution on wealth has great interest to marketers because it determines what groups have the greatest buying power and market potential. Social class designations also affect purchasing patterns based on ones appreciation of status in their life.

   Race and ethnicity: membership in the various racial and ethnic groups within our country accounts for many changes in the way a consumer receives information, develops tastes, and makes purchases. Submarkets (such as the Hispanic market) are receiving increased attention from marketers because of their size and increased affluence.

   Geography: though not as dynamic as the other categories, geography does affect tastes and purchase behavior. Many marketers use geography to tailor their offerings to appeal to different regions of the country.

3. **Describe the three major ethnic groups in the United States (African Americans, Hispanic Americans, and Asian Americans) and tell how they provide unique market segments for many products.**

   African Americans are a significant racial segment. They account for 12 percent of the U.S. population. They have immense buying power. Many companies including McDonald's, Coca-Cola, and Carnation specifically target African Americans.

   The Hispanic Americans group described as a sleeping giant that is about to awaken. There are now over 19 million people in this category. The birthrate for this group is four times the national average, and its size is expected to continue to grow and become more of a market force. Pepsi and General Mills are at the forefront of marketing to this group.

   Asian Americans (surprisingly) are the fastest growing group in the U.S. They soon will be 6 percent of the United States population. Marketers are just beginning to recognize the value of appealing to this group. Many Asian Americans are prosperous and very status conscious, making them a prime target for luxury goods. They spend a significant percentage of their income on electronics. However, they are hard to reach because of subgroups within the larger category. Sears has been a leader in pursuing this market.

4. **Explain consumer psychographic segmentation.**

   Psychographics is useful to help understand differences among consumers who may be statistically similar to one another but whose needs vary. Psychographic segmentation examines shared attitudes, interests, and opinions. VALS (Values and lifestyles) is the most well-known system used to divide the American population into eight groups.

5. **How can consumer behavior be used for segmenting consumer markets?**
Behavioral segmentation divides consumers into segments on the basis of how they act toward, feel about, or use a product or service. By examining differences between users versus non-users, the amount of product used, and how the product is used information is gained which can be used to segment, target, and position the product.

6. **What are the major dimensions used for segmenting industrial markets?**
Categories similar to those in the consumer market are frequently used for segmenting industrial markets. Industrial demographics include industry and/or company size, Standard Industrial Classification (SIC) codes, or geographic location. Industrial markets may also be segmented based on operating variables, purchasing approaches, and end-use applications.

7. **List the criteria used for determining whether a segment may be a good candidate for targeting.**
There are several criteria for determining whether a segment may be a good candidate for targeting. To choose one or more segments to target, marketers examine each segment and evaluate its potential for success as a target market. Meaningful segments have wants that are different from those in other segments, can be identified, can be reached with a unique marketing mix, will respond to unique marketing communications, are large enough to be profitable, have future growth potential, and posses needs that the organization can satisfy better that its competition.

8. **Explain undifferentiated, differentiated, concentrated, custom, and mass customization marketing strategies.**
See Figure 8.3 for more information and explanation.
   Undifferentiated marketing strategy: a marketing strategy that (1) assumes the majority of customers have similar needs and (2) attempts to appeal to a broad spectrum of people.
   Differentiated marketing strategy: a market strategy in which a firm develops one or more products for each of several distinct customer groups.
   Concentrated marketing strategy: a marketing strategy in which a firm focuses its efforts on offering one or more products to a single segment.
   Custom marketing strategy: a marketing strategy in which a firm develops a separate marketing mix for each customer.
   Mass customization: a marketing strategy in which a firm modifies a basic good or service to meet an individual customer's needs.

9. **What is product positioning? Describe the three approaches marketers use to create product positions.**
Product positioning: the marketing practice of determining and influencing how a brand is perceived by consumers relative to the competition. The three approaches used to create product positions are to position the product like the competition, against the competition, or away from the competition.

10. **List the steps in developing and implementing a positioning strategy.**
The steps in developing and implementing a positioning strategy include:
   a.   Analyze the competitor's positions.
   b.   Identify competitive advantage (can include image, product, service, or people advantage).
   c.   Finalize the marketing mix.
   d.   Evaluate responses and monitor change (may include repositioning if necessary).

Marketing Concepts: Discussing Choices and Issues

1. **Some critics of marketing have suggested that market segmentation and target marketing lead to an unnecessary proliferation of product choices , which wastes valuable resources. These critics suggest that if we marketers didn't create so many different product choices there would be more resources to feed the hungry and house the homeless and provide for the needs of people around the globe. Are the results of segmentation and target marketing harmful or beneficial for society as a whole? Should these criticisms be of concern to firms? How should New Era firms respond to these criticisms?**

As far back as 1920 Al Sloan (a pioneering marketer at Ford's rival General Motors), realized that consumer's tastes and needs are different. There are many ways to deal with the need to improve to social environment but the dissolution of product choice for the American consumer is probably not one of the better alternatives. For many years the Soviet Union followed a policy of one product fits all needs. That solution did not satisfy consumers, nor did it fix their social system. In fact, one could argue that by striving to better match the needs and wants of the individual consumer, more social good will be the result because the consumer would be able to better direct her resources and use the remainder for social causes (if she so chooses).

New age firms should respond to this form of criticism by listening, evaluating, and taking action that will improve the overall good of the consumer. Some of this action will be in the form of new directed products and some will be in the improvement of action to social causes. The determination of the mix is up to the individual marketer.

2.   **One of the criteria for a usable market segment is its size. This chapter suggested that to be usable a segment must be large enough to be profitable now and in the future and some very small segments get ignored because they can never be profitable. So how large should a segment be? How do you think a firm should go about determining if a segment is profitable? Do firms ever have a moral or ethical obligation to develop products for small unprofitable segments?**
The students may produce a variety of answers to the questions cited above. Some of their answers will be the result of the role that they perceive that marketing plays in the firm and in society in general. With respect to size of market segments, demand must be measured and applied to short- and long-term goals and profit projections. There is no magic number. Profitability is a question of costs, resources, and competition. Most firms today are in business to make a profit and are responsible to their owners or shareholders for their performance record. Some unprofitable activities can be undertaken as long as they are subsidized by profitable activities (the unprofitable activities of today may become the profitable activities of tomorrow). The moral or ethical obligation is part of the corporate management and culture structure of the firm.

3.   **Some firms have been criticized for targeting unwholesome products to certain segments of the market—the aged, ethnic minorities, the disabled, et cetera. What other groups deserve special concern? Should a firm use different criteria in targeting such groups? Should the government oversee and control such marketing activities?**
The question of governmental control is dependent on one's viewpoint of government's role in business. Is government a rule maker and enforcer or a referee? Protection of such groups as children is accepted but a "hands-off policy" is used for most other groups. In addition to the groups mentioned above, children, AIDS victims, disaster victims, families of the recently deceased, and mental health situations are sometimes mentioned as groups that also need special attention and should probably be protected by different rules for targeting group members. What criteria can you name that would suggest caution in targeting a group?

4.   **Marketers are always looking for a better way to segment consumer markets. In the past they have used demographics, psychographics, lifestyles, and geodemographics. With a group of classmates, brainstorm to see if you can come up with other possible means for segmenting markets which might be useful to some firms.**
To aid students with their brainstorming attempt ask them to consider things that they all have in common or things they all do the same each day. Then ask for things that separate them as individuals and things that they do differently. Would an interesting way to segment be Internet usage, knowledge acquisition ability, technical knowledge amount, or ability to receive information (such as from television, radio, word of mouth, etc).

Real People, Real Surfers: Exploring the Web

Students will enjoy the exercise! Have students determine their own VALS type by taking the on-line survey. Have students bring to class the profile of their VALS type. See how many VALS types are represented in the class.

Marketing In Action: Real Choices at Volkswagen

Summary: Volkswagen needs to understand who is going to buy the new Volkswagen

Suggested Answers to Discussion Questions

1. **What are the problems facing Volkswagen?**
   The problem facing Volkswagen is understanding who is going to buy the new Volkswagen. Information from the case indicates that VW did not know who was going to buy the New Beetle and did not have a target marketing strategy.

2. **What factors are important in understanding these problems?**
   Not only did VW fail to identify a target market for the New Beetle, they were also pushing the new Passat; a luxury car to compete with BMW. Customers may be confused about the company VW. Is VW a luxury car provider or a provider of sub-compacts? The New Beetle also had a lot to "live up to". The classic Volkswagen Beetle was very successful and was a pop icon.

3. **What are the alternatives?**
   a). Wait and see who buys the car—do nothing.
   b). Clearly identify and define the target market for the New Beetle.
   c). Develop a new promotional campaign.
   d). Develop a unique position for the New Beetle

4. **What are your recommendations for solving the problem?**
   Options b, c, and d should all be considered.

5. **What are some ways to implement your recommendations?**
   Research needs to be conducted to determine who is the customer for the New Beetle and to determine what types of promotional messages should be used to reach these groups. Clearly the dimensions for segmenting the market need to be established. Rather than traditional survey research, VW might want to use a more creative approach for collecting consumer information. One suggestion would be to invite consumers to a focus group where they actually got to test drive the car.
   VW also needs to determine how to position the product. What should be promoted as the unique selling feature for the New Beetle?

Mini-Project 8-A
Designing Marketing for Different Segments

Purpose: to understand how marketers create strategies for different market segments.

1. With several of your classmates, select a product category which would typically be of interest to a number of different market segments. Some possible product categories might be

    ■ breakfast cereals
    ■ perfume or some other form of fragrance
    ■ bath soap
    ■ a restaurant

2. Next select 3 or more different market segments which might be targets for a new brand of the product category.

3. For each segment you have selected, create a new imaginary brand of the product category. Write out a description of the brand and design the product and/or its package. It may be a good idea for each member of your group to develop a brand for a different market segment.

4. Create a magazine advertisement for each new brand.

5. Make a presentation to your class in which you discuss each brand, how product characteristics are different for each market segment, and how you have designed your advertisements to appeal to each segment. Ask your class to add their suggestions for marketing strategies which might be used with this product category.

Mini-Project 8-B
Recognizing Target Markets

Purpose: to better recognize how marketers develop communications to attract different target markets.

While a few products (such as table salt and light bulbs) are generally marketed to a total market, most marketing strategies include the selection and targeting of specific market segments. As consumers, we can easily recognize whether the product is targeted toward us or someone else by the messages communicated in advertising and other promotional activities. For example, when you see a TV commercial for a nutritional supplement in which a child asks her grandfather if he will come to her wedding, you know that product is not aimed at college coeds.

1.   Select a highly advertised product category which you assume is marketed to different target markets. Some examples of product categories which would be good for this mini-project include

■   automobiles
■   beer or other alcoholic beverages
■   cigarettes

2.   Look for magazine advertisements and/or tv commercials for four different brands of the product which target different market segments.

3.   Use the spaces provided on the following pages to
      a.   Describe the ad
      b.   Identify the market segments which is being targeted
      c.   Identify specific elements of the ad which provide information about which segment is being targeted
      d.   Identify the appeal which is being used for this segment (more comfortable, tastes better, saves you money, etc.)
      e.   Give your evaluation of whether or not you think this is a good appeal for this target market and why you feel that way.

Product Category _____

Brand #1 _____

Describe the ad _____

_____

_____

_____

_____

What segment(s) is being targeted? _____

_____

_____

_____

Describe specific ad elements which identify the target for you _____

_____

_____

_____

_____

_____

What is the appeal used in the ad? _____

_____

_____

_____

Your evaluation of this appeal for this target market _____

_____

_____

_____

Brand #2 _____

Describe the ad _____

_____

_____

_____

_____

What segment(s) is being targeted? _____

_____

_____

_____

Describe specific ad elements which identify the target for you _____

_____

_____

_____

_____

_____

What is the appeal used in the ad? _____

_____

_____

_____

Your evaluation of this appeal for this target market _____

_____

_____

_____

Brand #3 _____

Describe the ad _____

_____

_____

_____

_____

What segment(s) is being targeted? _____

_____

_____

_____

Describe specific ad elements which identify the target for you _____

_____

_____

_____

_____

_____

What is the appeal used in the ad? _____

_____

_____

_____

Your evaluation of this appeal for this target market _____

_____

_____

_____

Brand #4 _____

Describe the ad _____

_____

_____

_____

_____

What segment(s) is being targeted? _____

_____

_____

_____

Describe specific ad elements which identify the target for you _____

_____

_____

_____

_____

_____

What is the appeal used in the ad? _____

_____

_____

_____

Your evaluation of this appeal for this target market _____

_____

_____

_____

9

Creating
the Product

*O*verview   Chapter 9 examines the process for creating new products and various degrees of product newness. Most students will be quick to realize that most new products are not truly new (i.e., discontinuous innovations) but rather represent continuous and dynamically continuous innovations.

The product layers and methods of classifying consumer and business-to-business products are discussed. Students will also learn that consumers do not accept or adopt products at the same rate. The stages in a customer's adoption of a new product and the diffusion of innovations help to explain how new products are adopted.

Eastman Kodak is the focus of the Real People, Real Choices segment, Kodak had to make decisions regarding the entry of a new photographic system called the Advantix Advanced Photo System (APS).

Objectives

1.   Explain the layers of a product.

2.   Describe the classifications of products.

3.   Explain the importance of new products.

4.   Describe how firms develop new products.

5.   Explain the process of product adoption and the diffusion of innovations.

Chapter Outline and Suggested Activities

Introduction: If possible, go to the store and purchase enough Oreo cookies for your class. While students are munching on the cookies discuss the variety of new Oreo products available. For example Oreo changes the traditional white cream filling to orange for Halloween, red for Christmas, and blue for Spring. Discuss the process of continuous innovations and explain the need for product innovations.

Other potential topics to discuss related to Oreos include:

- Layers of the product concept (Figure 9.1)
- Classification of consumer products (Figure 9.2)
- Adoption Process (Figure 9.4)

1. **Build A Better Mousetrap**
   **Refer to Objective 1
   ** Use Marketing Mini-Project: Learning by Doing
   a.   One of the goals of marketing is to create products that provide benefits sought by consumers. Many company's spend time developing features, but not focusing on the consumer benefit sought.
   1).   ***Good:*** *Tangible products we can see, touch, smell, hear or taste*
   2).   Products are viewed by marketers as a bundle of attributes that includes the packaging, brand name, benefits, and features of the physical good.
   b.   Layers of the Product
   **Use Instructor's Manual Mini-Project 9-B as a class discussion or break-out exercise
   **Use Q#3—Marketing Practice: Applying What You've Learned
   **Use Figure 9.1
   1).   ***Core Project:*** *All of the benefits the product will provide for customers.*
   2).   ***Actual Product:*** *A physical good or the delivered service that supplies customer benefit*
   3).   ***Augmented Product:*** *The actual product plus its supporting features*

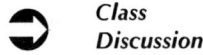 ***Class Discussion***   Refer students to the Real People, Real Choices segment on Eastman Kodak. Discuss the product layers for a basic 35mm automatic camera.

2. **Classifying Products**
   **Refer to Objective 2
   **Use Figure 9.2
   a.   Consumer product classes defined by how long a product lasts.
   1).   ***Durable goods:*** *Consumer products that provide benefits over a period of time such as cars, furniture or appliances*
   2).   ***Nondurable goods:*** *Consumer products that provide benefits for a short time because they are consumed (such as food) or no longer useful (such as newspapers)*
   b.   Consumer product classes defined by how consumers buy the product
   1).   ***Convenience product:*** *a consumer good or service that is usually low-priced, widely available, and purchased frequently, with a minimum of comparison and effort.*
   a).   Staples: Basic or necessary items that are available almost everywhere.
   b).   Impulse products: Products that people often buy on the spur of the moment.
   c).   Emergency products: products that people purchase when we're in dive need.
   2).   ***Shopping product:*** *A good or service for which consumers spend consider time and effort gathering information and comparing alternatives before making a purchase.*
   3).   ***Specialty product:*** *A good or service that has unique characteristics which are important to the buyer, and for which the buyer will devote significant effort to acquire.*

Class
Discussion
Create a list of products. Ask student to identify what type of consumer product class is represented by each product. Be prepared, student opinions may vary.

c. Business-to-Business products
   1). **Equipment:** *Expensive goods and organization uses in its daily operations and that lasts for a long time.*
   2). **Maintenance, repair, and operating (MRO) products:** *Goods that a business customer consumes in a relatively short time*
   3). **Raw materials:** *Products of the fishing, lumber, agricultural, and mining industries that organizational customers purchase to use in their finished products.*
   4). **Processed materials:** *Products created when firms transform raw materials from their original state.*
   5). **Specialized services:** *Services purchased from outside suppliers that are essential to the operation of an organization but are not part of the production of a product.*
   6). **Component parts:** *Manufactured goods or subassemblies of finished items that organizations need to complete their own products.*

3. **It's New And Improved! Understanding Innovations**
    *Refer to Objective 3

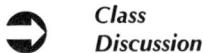

Class
Discussion
What does the term "new product" mean? Discuss the Federal Trade Commissions definition of the term "new product".

a. **Innovation:** *A product that consumers perceive to be new and different from existing products.*

Spotlight on Real People: Handcuff Sweatshirts

Summary: Chuck and Bob Mellon developed a new product called Handcuffs. The sweatshirt has cuffs that are fingertip length and feature a thumbhole.

Suggested Answers to Discussion Questions

1. **What is the core products the Mellon brothers developed?**
    A sweatshirt which protects your hands while allowing you freedom to use your hands.

2. **Are Handcuffs a continuous innovation, a dynamically continuous innovation, or a discontinuous innovation?**
    Students may very well debate about what type of innovation Handcuff represents. Focus the discussion on the amount of learning or change in behavior required to wear/use the sweatshirt. Very little learning or change in behavior is required. The sweatshirt is an example of a continuous innovation.

3. **What is the best way for the Mellons to demonstrate to consumers how Handcuffs are superior to ordinary sweatshirt?**
    An advertising campaign which shows people wearing the sweatshirt and the benefits received from wearing the sweatshirt should be developed. The focus should be on benefits and the novelty of the product.

---

b. **Types of Innovations**
   **Use Instructor's Manual Mini Project 9-A
   1). ***Continuous innovation:*** *A modification of an existing product that sets one brand apart from its competitors.*
      a). ***Knockoff:*** *A new product that copies with slight modification of the design of an original product.*
      b). Expensive clothing styles and brands are often knocked off by competitors.
   2). ***Dynamically continuous innovation:*** *A change in an existing product that requires a moderate amount of learning or behavior change.*
   3). ***Discontinuous innovations:*** *A totally new product that creates major changes in the way we live.*

Class Discussion   Most new products represent what type of innovation? - Answer: Continuous. Why are continuous innovations important to the organization? Why are there fewer discontinuous innovations?

4. **Developing New Products**
   **Refer to Objective 4
   **Use Figure 9.3
   **Use video New Product Showcase
   **Use Computer Friendly Stuff Case III
   **Use Real People, Real Choices at Eastman Kodak
   **Use Real People, Real Surfers: Exploring the Web
   a. The Visionary Phase
      1). Idea generation: Identifying ideas for new products that will provide customer benefits and that are compatible with the company mission
      2). Screening: Examining the chances that a product concept might achieve technical and commercial success.
      3). Business Analysis: The process of determining if a product can be a profitable contribution to the organization's product mix.
   b. Planning and development
      1). ***Commercial development:*** stage in new product development where marketers put together a marketing plan that builds upon the initial projections made during product screening and business analysis stages
      2). Technical development: *Stage in the new product development process where a firm's engineers work with marketers in refining the design and production process.*
   c. Testing and improving the product
      1). ***Test marketing:*** *Testing the complete marketing plan in a small geographics area that is similar to the larger market the firm hopes to enter.*

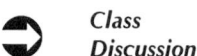

Class Discussion   Discuss the advantages and disadvantages of test marketing.

   d. ***Product launch:*** *The final stage of the new product development process that includes full-scale production, distribution, advertising, and sales promotion.*

5. **Adoption And Diffusion Processes**
   **Refer to Objective 5
   a. ***Product adoption:*** *The process by which a consumer of business customers begins to buy and use a good, service, or an idea.*

b.   ***Diffusion:*** *The process by which the use of a product spreads throughout a population.*

c.   Stages in a customer's adoption of a new product
       **Use Q#1, Marketing Practice: Applying What You've Learned
       **Use Figure 9.4
       1).   Awareness
       2).   Interest
       3).   Evaluation
       4).   Trial
       5).   Adoption
       6).   Confirmation

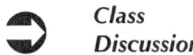 **Class Discussion**   What are some examples of marketing activities that could be used at each stage of the adoption process?

Real People, Bad Choices?

Summary: Students in Cincinnati who wanted to be the first to own and wear a new model of Nike's Michael Jordan sneaker skipped school in order to buy the $140.00 Air Jordan shoes.

Suggested Answer to Discussion Question

1.   Do you think marketers should feel good or bad about this Cincinnati incident?
    Marketers should feel bad for encouraging students to skip school to buy a pair of Air Jordans. Although marketing activities did not directly suggest or encourage students to skip school, students still somehow felt the need to own and wear the latest Air Jordan.
       Perhaps Nike could develop a program which would encourage and reward school attendance. Nike could also establish a policy where new products are made available for the first time on Saturday.

---

d.   The Diffusion of Innovations
       **Use Figure 9.5
       1).   Adoptor Categories
            a).   ***Innovators:*** *The first segment (roughly 2.5 percent) of a population.*
            b).   ***Early adopters:*** *Those who adopt an innovation early in the diffusion process but after the innovators.*
            c).   ***Early Majority:*** *Those whose adoption of a new product signals a general acceptance of the innovation.*
            d).   ***Late majority:*** *The adoptors who are willing to try new products where there is little or no risk associated with the purchase, when the purchase becomes an economic necessity or when there is social pressure to purchase*
            e).   ***Laggards:*** *The last consumers to adopt an innovation*

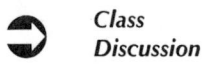 **Class Discussion**   Ask students about how quickly they adopt new products. Are they sometimes adopting in the early adoptor stage and other times adopting at the late majority or laggard stage? What factors influence how quickly they adopt a new product?

e.   Product factors affecting the rate of adoption
       **Use Figure 9.6

**Use Q#2, Marketing Practice: Applying What You've Learned

1).   Relative advantage: The degree to which a consumer perceives that a new product provides superior benefits.

2).   Compatibility: The extent to which a new product is consistent with existing cultural values, customs, and practices.

3).   *Complexity:* The degree to which consumers find a new product or its use difficult to understand

4).   Trialability: The case of sampling a new product and its benefits

5).   Observability: How visible a new product and its benefits are to others who might adopt the innovations.

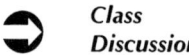 *Class Discussion*   What product factors affected the rate of adoption when Kodak invented an entirely new photographic system called the Advantix Advanced Photo System (APS)? (Refer to Decision Time At Kodak).

Real People, Real Choices: How It Worked Out at Eastman Kodak

**Use Kodak video

Summary: William Smith is the Category Manager and Director of worldwide marketing for the Advanced Photo system at Eastman Kodak. In the mid 1990s the industry as a whole was in a slump, and a lack of exciting new products was responsible for sluggish growth. What could break life into business?

Option 1: Maintain the current Kodak 35mm photo system and focus more attention on digital cameras.
Option 2: Form an industry consortium to introduce an entirely new photographic system.
Option 3: Forget the rest of the industry and launch a new Kodak film-based system.

     Mr. Smith choose Option 2 and in April 1996 the Advantix Advanced Photo System (APS) was on the market. The simultaneous introduction worldwide by 45 different companies made photo industry history.

Suggested Discussion Questions

1.   Why is the APS considered a discontinuous innovation?

2.   How did the consortium approach affect the rate of adoption of this new product?

Marketing Concepts: Testing Your Knowledge

1. **What is a product?**

A *product* is a tangible goods, a service, an idea, or some combination of these that through the exchange process, satisfies consumer or business customer needs; a bundle of attributes including features, functions, benefits, and uses.

2. **What is meant by the core product, the actual product, and the augmented product?**

See Figure 9.1 for more information and discussion.

The core product consists of the basic product category benefits and customized benefit(s) the product provides. The actual product is the physical good or delivered service including the packaging and brand name. The augmented product includes both the actual product and any supplementary services such as warranty, credit, delivery, installation, and so on.

3. **List and give examples of the different classifications of consumer products.**

Consumer products are classified according to how long they last and how they are purchased. *Durable goods* provide benefits for months or years (a washing machine). *Nondurable goods* are used up quickly or are useful for only a short time (chewing gum). *Convenience products* are purchased frequently with little effort (soda, cigarettes, gum, etc.). *Shopping products* are only after customers carefully gather information and compare different brands on their attributes and/or price (automobiles). *Specialty products* have unique characteristics and are important to the buyer (a wedding dress). *Unsought products* have little customer interest until a need arises (having a key made for your home or automobile).

4. **What types of products are bought and sold in business-to-business markets?**

Organizational customers purchase products to use in the production of other goods and services or to facilitate the organizations operation. Specific categories of products which are bought and sold in business-to-business markets include:

- Equipment
- Maintenance, repair, and operating (MRO) products
- Raw materials
- Processed materials
- Specialized materials
- Component parts

5. **What is a new product? Why is understanding new products so important to marketers?**

The FTC says that a company can call its products new if:
   a.   the product is entirely new or changed significantly from the past.
   b.   the product can only be called new for six months.
In reality, new products are anything that consumers perceive as being new and may also be classified as to their degree of newness.

Understanding new products is important to companies because of the fast pace of technological advancement, the high cost to companies for developing new products, and the contributions to society that new products can make.

6. **List and explain the steps in developing new products.**

New product development occurs in three phases (Figure 9.3). In the *visionary phase* a firm generates and screens ideas to identify those that will work best for the firm. The *planning and development phase* means turning those ideas into a product. The *test and improve phase* means trying out marketing strategies in test markets in order to improve the marketing plan and product, if needed, prior to full commercial launch

7.   **Explain the different types of innovations based on their degree of newness.**
A *continuous innovation* is a modification of an existing product. A *dynamically continuous innovation* provides greater change in a product. A *discontinuous innovation* is a totally new product that creates major changes in people's lives.

8.   **List and explain the stages in an individual's adoption of an innovation.**
Product adoption is the process by which an individual begins to use a new product, while the diffusion of innovations is how a new product spreads through a population. (Figure 9.4)

The stages in the adoption process are *awareness* that the innovation exits, *interest* in how a product may satisfy needs, *evaluation* of the costs and benefits of adoption, *trial* in which the potential adopter experiences the product, *adoption* in which an individual mentally and physically selects the product, and *confirmation*, which makes the adopter a loyal user of the innovation.

9.   **List and explain the categories of adopters.**
The categories of adopters are: (Figure 9.5)
a.   Innovator—the first consumer to know about and to try an innovation.
b.   Early adopters—the consumers that influence many other consumers' adoption.
c.   Early majority—a "follower" group that is neither first or last to adopt.
d.   Late majority—only adopt due to social or economic pressure.
e.   Laggards—may not adopt until all other customers have moved on to an even newer product.

10.   **Describe the product factors that affect the speed of adoption?**
Five product characteristics that have an important effect on how quickly (or if) a new product will be adopted by consumers are: (Figure 9.6).
a.   Relative advantage—a new product's ability to provide important benefits.
b.   Compatibility—compatibility with a consumer's normal way of doing things.
c.   Product complexity—how technical or complex is the product?
d.   Trailability—the ability to sample or try out a new product.
e.   Product observability—the likelihood that other people will be exposed to the new product.

Marketing Concepts: Discussing Choices and Issues

1.   **In this chapter we talked about the core product, the actual product, and the augmented product. Does this mean that marketers are simply trying to make products that are really the same seem different? When marketers understand these three layers of the product and develop products with this concept in mind, what are the benefits to consumers? What are the hazards of this type of thinking?**
Marketers have known for some time that consumers see products differently and purchase for different reasons and to fulfill different needs. When marketers look at the three different dimensions of the product as described above, they are attempting to find sets of needs that consumers will respond to. To some consumers the core product is a sufficient reason to purchase (fulfill the hunger drive by eating a steak). To others the actual product (a steak bought at their favorite steakhouse is what they really want). While still others want the "sizzle" or the augmented product (they not only want the steak but they want the entertainment and the atmosphere that might be present at their favorite steakhouse or the guarantee of satisfaction). The marketer is generally trying to find mechanisms to satisfy all of a customers needs when this approach is used. However, if the marketer does not concentrate on the proper need level, the consumer may not respond. For example (using the analogy above), if the marketer talks about the quality of the meat in a steak but the consumer is looking for a romantic setting, the consumer may make their purchase elsewhere.

2.   **The phrase "New and Improved" has been used so many times that, for many people, it is meaningless. Why has this occurred? What challenge does this present to marketers?**
New products and revisions of new products are introduced with ever increasing speed. In their attempt to feed the almost insatiable appetite of the stimulation oriented consumer, the marketers have dug themselves into a deep hole and consumers have begun to not believe claims of newness (especially for the revised

product). The challenge is to find significant ways to improve products that will solve consumers needs in different or unique ways. The consumers do not want new "bells and whistles" they want solutions to problems and quality and value for their dollar.

3. **Discontinuous innovations are totally new products—something seldom seen in the marketplace. What are some examples of discontinuous innovations introduced during the twentieth century? Why are there so few discontinuous innovations? What do you think the future holds for new products?**

    The answer to this question somewhat depends on the background and creativity of the student. Discontinuous innovations that might be cited to begin the discussion might include the computer, the television, the airplane, the rocket, the laser, nuclear power, and Velcro.

    The risk of failure is very high for discontinuous innovations. In addition, the venture capital necessary to get the invention and acceptability to the consuming public of the ground is very high. It is probably safer to produce products that are adaptations (less risky).

    As new technology and global marketing increases, the future for new products is bright. This is especially true in the fields of communication, electronics, aerospace, plastics, computers, and the use of the Internet. Business Week now devotes an issue once every two months to new products that are available for computers or the Internet.

4. **In this chapter we explained that knockoffs are slightly modified copies of original product designs. Should knockoffs be illegal? Who is hurt by knockoffs? Is the marketing of knockoffs good or bad for consumers in the short run?**

    Answer to the questions regarding knockoffs will probably vary. If you are a designer, whether it be apparel or trucks, you do not want your designs knockoff and would probably think that such an activity is illegal.

    Knockoffs not only hurt designers by taking away their sales, it may also hurt customers. In the short run it might seem like consumers and society benefit; however, if the product is inferior in quality consumers will ultimately pay more money for products.

5. **It is not necessary true that all new products benefit consumers or society. What are some new products that have made our lives better? What are some new products that have actually been harmful to consumers or to society? Should there be a way to monitor what new products are introduced to the marketplace?**

    Discuss with students new products that have been introduced during their lifetime and have made their lives better. Most of the discussion will probably center around technology equipment and entertainment (i.e., CD's and HD-tr). Another area of new products includes safety features on products.

    Some new products like car airbags and Redux a weight-loss medication, have actually been harmful to consumers the Food and Drug Administration (FDA) carefully monitors the introduction of new pharmaceuticals; however, there is a growing market of non-medicine treatments which do not require FDA approval. Products such as herbal teas and natural antidepressants like Saint Johns Wart, are available without a prescription and the products and the ingredients they contain are not monitored by the FDA. The result is that the consumer who purchases the products may be at risk.

    Firms which develop and introduce new products do have the responsibility of testing products to ensure that they are safe. These firms should also be quick to recall or remove from store shelves defective and/or dangerous products

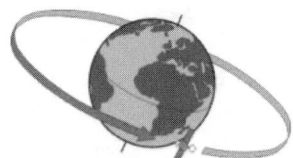

Real Real People, Real Surfers: Exploring the Web

This Web based exercise could be used with almost any topic in Chapter 9. You might wish to have students focus on questions one, two, and four and use responses to these questions for class discussion.

Marketing in Action: Real Choices at Idealab:

Summary: How can you tell which products and businesses will succeed and which ones will fail? Bill Gross, a 39-year-old entrepreneur, began starting businesses when he was in high school. He has continued to start successful businesses, which he then sells. In 1996, Mr. Gross founded Idealab, a company whose sole purpose is to turn creative ideas into successful products and businesses. Recently, he has been debating over whether or not to open the first Internet record label. Instead of buying CD's or tapes, consumers would download music from the company's Website.

Suggested Answers to Case Questions:

1. **What is the problem facing Bill Gross's Idealab?**
    Idealab needs to determine whether or not an Internet record label is a good investment for Idealab, or will it drain the firm's resources. Because of rapid innovation in technology and the infancy of Internet commerce, will Idealab have access to enough market information to make an informed decision and enough funds for R&D to support its development?

2. **What factors are important to understanding this problem?**
    The following factors are important considerations.
    a. Consumers, except for innovators, may be slow in their decision to try a new product, especially one that would replace other well established forms of media.
    b. Internet commerce remains limited to a small percentage of consumers.
    c. How easily can competitors copy the format of Idealab's record label?
    d. Will a new product be able to compete with established media forms such as CD's?
    e. How quickly will Idealab's format be obsolete?
    f. Does Idealab have the necessary funds to launch a successful promotion of the new company?
    g. How will Idealab find out what consumers want, how much they would pay for the product, etc.?

3. **What alternatives might Idealab consider?**
    The following are a series of alternatives that might stimulate discussion.
    a. Do nothing. Don't start the record label.
    b. Launch the product on a small scale in order to determine product demand.
    c. Design a web-based promotion which offers consumers music discounts for filling out surveys. Design the business based on consumer feedback.
    d. Develop the record label with another company, preferably an established record label, in order to benefit from brand recognition.
    e. Hire a consultant from the music industry to help with product development, testing, and promotions.

4. **What are your recommendations for solving the problem?**
    Given the solutions listed above, alternatives c and e would seem the most useful. Students should remember that not only is this a new product, but its distribution channel is new as well. The market may not be "ready" for the product yet. On the other hand, if they do not act now, they may lose the opportunity.

5. **What are some ways to implement your recommendations?**
    In order to prevent great losses if the label does not work, Idealab must utilize inexpensive and creative forms of advertising. The firm must collect consumer data to determine whether or not they are willing to buy such an innovative product and which markets to target. It would also benefit Idealab to find out if its products could benefit educational institutions. The firm needs to hire a knowledgeable consultant to assist in collecting market data and in designing the actual product.

Mini-Project 9-A
Is This Product Better?

** If you can solicit the assistance of a few students before class, this mini-project could be used an in-class experiment. You will probably want to ask for volunteers to participate in the actual experiment

Purpose: through simple experimental research, to understand the importance of every element of product design.

1.   With several members of your class, design one or both of the following two product tests. First, select a simple product category in which there is little difference among brands. Some possibilities are

- colas or non-cola soft drinks
- puddings
- liquid dish detergent

Different brands test
Ask research participants to sample (to taste for food product, to feel or smell for other products) different unmarked brands of the product category. Then ask the participants to identify

- which unmarked brand they like best
- which unmarked brand they like least
- which unmarked brand they think is normally their preferred brand (e.g., which brand is Pepsi)

After all participants are finished, report the results to the class. You will probably have several surprises.

Same product test
Alter samples of the same product so that they appear different. For example, you might use safe food colorings to color dish liquid or vanilla pudding yellow and green and pink.

Ask research participants to try each of the different samples of the product and to rate each one. You might want to ask them to describe the flavor or fragrance of the product and to evaluate how good they think the product is using a rating scale.

Present the results of your experiment to your class.

Important: Good research ethics say that when deception is used in research such as this, you must carefully tell all research participants the truth about the research. You should also make sure that they aren't upset that they were deceived and that they are ok—that almost everyone will identify products of different colors as tasting or smelling different.

Mini-Project 9-B
The Layers of a Product

Purpose: to identify the different layers of products and learn to recognize opportunities for product improvement

Most marketers know that all of the different layers of a product are important: the core product, the actual product, and the augmented product. For each of the product categories listed, specify one well-known brand if appropriate. Then, use that product/brand to do the following:

1.   Describe the core product benefits the consumer seeks in purchasing the product

2.   Describe the actual product

3.   Describe the augmented product

4.   Make one or more suggestions for how the product in any of its layers could be improved.

Fast food restaurant   Brand _____

Core Product _____

_____

Actual Product _____

_____

Augmented Product _____

_____

_____

Suggested Improvements _____

_____

_____

Athletic Shoes   Brand _____

Core Product _____

_____

Actual Product _____

_____

Augmented Product _____

_____

_____

Suggested Improvements _____

_____

_____

A Dental Check-Up

Core Product _____

_____

Actual Product _____

_____

Augmented Product _____

_____

_____

Suggested Improvements _____

_____

_____

Bank Credit Card   Brand _____

Core Product _____

_____

Actual Product _____

_____

Augmented Product _____

_____

_____

Suggested Improvements _____

_____

_____

10

Managing the Product

*O*verview In this chapter we will look at how companies manage products. The steps in product planning, how planners develop product objectives and factors influencing product strategies are all examined.

Emphasis is placed on branding and packaging, two of the more important tactical decisions made by product planners. The focus of the Real People, Real Choices is Intel. The problem of creating a brand identify for a computer processor is discussed. The Intel video could be used to introduce this chapter.

Objectives

1.   Explain the different product objectives and strategies a firm may choose.

2.   Explain how firms manage products throughout the product life cycle.

3.   Discuss how branding creates product identity and describe different types of branding strategies.

4.   Explain the roles of packaging and labeling play in developing effective product strategies.

5.   Describe how organizations are structured for new and existing products.

Chapter Outline and Suggested Activities

Introduction: The instructor's manual marketing mini-project 10-B provides an excellent exercise for beginning a discussion on products and product quality.

One way to use this exercise would be to divide the class into teams and assign each team a product category to examine.

·Potential Discussion Questions

1.   How does brand name impact perceptions of quality?

2.   How do distribution channels impact perceptions for quality? For example, some shampoos are only available in salons, does this mean that these brands are better than the brands sold at grocery stores?

3.   What other cues are used to symbolize quality? For example, the price of an apartment is based on location and the amenities provided by the apartment complex.

1.   **Chipping Away At The Competition: Creating And Nurturing Quality Products**
      **Use Marketing Plan for Computer Friendly Stuff
a.   Product planning is important to the development of tactical marketing plans
b.   The strategies in the product plan explain how the firm expects to develop a product that will meet marketing objectives.

2.   **Using Product Objectives To Decide On A Product Strategy**
      **Refer to Objective 1
      **Use Figure 10.1
a.   Product Objectives provide focus and direction
      1).   Support the marketing objectives of the business unit and the overall mission of the firm
      2).   Objectives need to specify how product decisions will support or contribute to reaching a desired market share or level of sales.
      3).   To be effective product-related objectives must be
             a).   Measurable
             b).   Clear and unambiguous
             c).   Feasible
             d).   Indicate a specific time frame

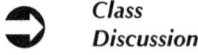
Class Discussion   Refer to the Introduction exercise and select one of the product categories examined. Have students explain how the manufacturer of the selected product might state its product objectives.

b.   Objectives and Strategies for Individual Products
      1).   Objectives and strategies for new products:
             For regional products, the strategy might be to introduce the product nationally.
      2).   Objectives and strategies for mature products
             These strategies might focus on breathing life into an existing product
c.   Objectives and strategies for multiple products
      **Use Figure 10.2
      Small firms might sell one product, but larger firms usually market a set of related products and must consider the portfolio of products offered to customers.

1. Product line strategies
   **Use Q#1 Marketing Practice: Applying What You've Learned
   a). ***Product line:** A firm's total product offering designed to satisfy a single need or desire of target customers*
   b). Product line strategies

   - full line
   - limited line
   - upward stretch
   - downward stretch
   - two-way stretch

   c). ***Cannibalization:** The loss of sales of an existing product when a new item in a product line or product family is introduced.*

2. **Product Mix Strategies**
   **Use Marketing in Action Real Choices at Polaroid
   a). ***Product mix:** The total set of all products a firm offers for sale*

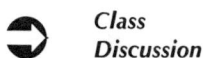 **Class Discussion**   Have students assist you in examining the product mix for a large consumer goods company. One good choice might be Campbells. You could have student go to the Campbell web site to identify all brands manufactured by the corporation.

Potential Discussion Questions

1. Discuss the width and depth of the product mix.

2. Which product categories appear to be strong and which categories appear to be weak? Explain.

   d. Quality as a Product Objective
   **Refer to the Introduction exercise
   1). Quality is tied to how customers think a product will perform.
   2). Quality is especially important in business-to-business products.
   3). The level of quality, in comparison with other brands, is important to consumers.
   4). Consumers are interested in consistency of quality
   5). The level of quality desired does change though and is dependent upon factors such as, the reason for buying the product, how long the customer expects to use and keep the product, and the environment where the product is purchased.

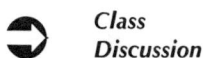 **Class Discussion**   Discuss why quality is an important product objective. Are there institutions and/or products for which quality is not an important objective?

3. **Marketing Throughout The Product Life Cycle**
   **Refer to Objective 2
   **Use Figure 10.3
   The ***product life cycle** is a concept that explains how products go through four distinct stages from birth to death: introduction, growth, maturity, and decline*
   a. ***The Introduction Stage:** The first stage of the product life cycle in which slow growth follows introduction of a new product in the marketplace.*

Refer to Figure 10.3. For each stage in the product life cycle discuss the following issues:

1. The relationship between sales and profits.
2. The amount and intensity of competition faced.
3. The introduction of new product variations.
4. The importance of brand name and branding strategies.

b. **Growth stage:** *The second stage in the product life cycle during which the product is accepted and sales rapidly increase.*

c. **Maturity stage:** *The third and longest stage in the product life cycle in which sales peak and profit margins narrow*

d. **Decline stage:** *The final stage in the product life cycle in which sales decrease as customers needs change.*

Spotlight on Real People: Music City Pasta

Summary: John and Carey Aron began their Nashville business by creating guitar-shaped pasta, hence the name Music City Pasta. The idea of shaped pasta has grown to include shaped pastas for 30 universities and shapes like dollar signs for thank you gifts.

Suggested Answers to Discussion Questions

1. **In what stage of the PLC (Product Life cycle) is the Aron's pasta?**
   The pasta should probably be considered in the growth stage. The instructor might want to discuss the factors which indicate that this product is in the growth stage. These factors include the rapid sales and consumer acceptance of the product as well as the continued introduction of new product variations.

2. **How is the couple creating a unique brand identity for their product?**
   First the name, Music City Pasta is unique. Second, the product variations which have been developed through licensing agreements provide a unique niche for the Aron's pasta.

3. **What are some potential avenues of expansion for these pasta shapes?**

   - Continue to add new colleges and universities
   - Create a line of Greek letter pasta for sororities and fraternities
   - Corporate pasta. Large firms might be interested in pasta shapes featuring their corporate logo. These packages of pasta could be given as gifts to clients.

---

4. **Creating Product Identify: Branding Decisions**
   **Refer to Objective 3
   a. Branding is an extremely important element of product strategies.
      1). What's In a Name (or a symbol)?
         Brand: *A name, a term, a symbol. or any other unique element of a product that identifies one firms product(s) and sets them apart from the competition.*

Class Discussion

How does a firm select a good brand name? Brand designers say there are four "easy" tests: easy to say, easy to spell, easy to read, and easy to remember.

Discuss with students brands which meet these four criteria. What brands do not meet these criteria? How important is a good brand name to the success of a product?

    2).   Trademarks

**Use Real People, Real Surfers: Exploring the Web

Trademark: The legal name for a brand name, brand mark, or trade character; trademarks may be legally registered by a government, thus, obtaining protection for exclusive use in that country.

Real People, Bad Choices

Summary: Because trademarks and copyrights are only protected in the U.S., brand piracy is a huge problem in international markets.

Suggested Discussion Question

1.   How can a company protect its precious brand identities from these brand pirates?
Students will hopefully have many suggestions for addressing this problem. The real issue is enforcement of laws protecting trademarks.

---

    b.   The Importance of Branding

        1).   *Brand equity: The value of a brand to an organization.*

        2).   *Brand extension: A new product sold with the same brand name as a strong existing brand*

Class Discussion

What are some examples of successful brand extensions? Why have these extensions been successful?

    c.   Branding Strategies

**Use Q#3, Marketing Practice: Applying What You've Learned

**Use Marketing Mini-Project: Learning by Doing

Class Discussion

At this point you might want to show the Intel video and discuss the branding decisions made by Dennis Carter at Intel. You could also discuss trademark protection.

        1).   Individual Brands Versus Family Brands

            Family brand: A brand that is shared by a group of individual products or individual brands.

        2).   National and Store Brands

            National Brand: Brands that are owned by the manufacturer of the product.

            Store or Private-Label Brand: Brands that are owned and sold by a certain retailer or distributor.

3). ***Licensing:*** *Agreement in which one firm sells another firm the right to use a brand name for a specific purpose and for a specific period of time. For example, Tommy Hilfiger allowing Springs Industries to use the Tommy name on a line of bed sheets.*

4). ***Co-Branding:*** *An agreement between two brands to work together in marketing a new product For example, Pillsbury slice and bake chocolate chip cookies with Nestle chocolate chips.*

Class Discussion   Why is a co-branding a "win-win" strategy for both partners? Consider the McDonald's "McFlurry". The McFlurry is basically a milkshake with candy of the buyers choice, added. The candy is actually chopped up and mixed into the milkshake. Customers can choose from toppings such as Oreo cookies, M&M candies, and Butterfinger candy bars. Why is the addition of these branded cookies and candies appealing? Would a milkshake with "candy coated chocolate pieces" be as appealing as a milkshake with M&M's?

5.   **Creating Product Identity: Packaging And Labeling Decisions**
**Refer to Objective #4
**Use Instructor's Manual Marketing Mini-Project 10-A
a.   Packaging Functions
**Use Figure 10.4
Package: *The covering or container for a product that provides product protection, facilitates product use and storage, and supplies important marketing communication.*

- Protects the product
- Easy storage and handling
- Communication

Class Discussion   Bring a package to class and discuss the function of a package.

Suggested Discussion Questions

1.   Does the package meet the basic functions of packing?

2.   How does the package communicate something about the product to the consumer?

Class Discussion   In the Computer Friendly Staff (CFS) Case #3, the packaging of the product was discussed. Discuss with students the issue of packaging for CFS. The concept of branding and brand extension could also be discussed.

b.   Designing Effective Packaging: Packages must also be useful. For example, resealable packages for cheese and meats.

Class Discussion   Many decisions must be made in designing the package. Refer to Exhibit 10.19 and discuss the reclosable cereal bag designed by Quaker Oats.

c.   Labeling Regulations

1). The Federal Fair Packaging and Labeling Act of 1996 controls package communications and labeling in the U.S.

2). Nutrition Labeling and Education Act of 1990

➡ *Class Discussion*   Examine the label on a product. Is the required information useful and easy to understand? Do you think consumers really want all of this information on their food packages?

Have international students discuss the labeling requirements in their country.

6. **Organizing For Effective Product Management**
**Refer to Objective 5
**Use Q#2 Marketing Practice: Applying What You've Learned

a.   Management of Existing Products

1). *Brand manager: An individual who is responsible for developing and implementing the marketing plan for a single brand.*

2). *Product category manager: An individual who is responsible for developing and implementing the marketing plan for all of the brands and products within a product category.*

3). *Market manager: An individual who is responsible for developing and implementing the market plan for products sold to a particular customer group.*

b.   Organizing For New Product Development

1). *Venture teams: A group of people within an organization who work together focusing exclusively on the development of a new product.*

Real People, Real Choices: How It Worked Out At Intel

**Use Intel video

Summary: Dennis Carter, Vice President and General Manager of Corporate Marketing at Intel Corporation, is responsible for making the "Intel Inside" logo a household name.

In the early 1990s, Intel was selling tens of thousands of its 386 microprocessors. Intel was not pleased however when other chip manufacturers began calling their microprocessors "386s" too. The courts ruled that "386" was a part number that Intel could not trademark. The company's solution was the "Intel Inside" logo, which created a branded product out of this bland computer part buried inside a faceless computer. Why did Dennis Carter chose the "Intel Inside" logo to create brand identify?

Reason 1: Microprocessor chips were in the introductory stage of the product lifecycle, and so Intel needed a strategy that provided detailed information about the product's properties.
Reason 2: Mr. Carter chose the logo because the Intel name was already well known among computer connoisseurs.
Reason 3: Mr. Carter choose "Intel Inside" because he wanted the company to develop a family branding strategy.

Dennis Carter chose option 2 because he wanted to encourage manufacturers to use the Intel brand name to add firepower to their own branding efforts.

Chapter Review

Marketing Concepts: Testing Your Knowledge

1. **List and explain some popular objectives and strategies used for individual and for multiple products.**

   Product objectives support a firm's broader marketing objectives and, ideally, focus on customer needs.

   Objectives for individual products may be related to introducing the product (Microsoft introducing Windows 95), introducing a brand that has been successful in a regional market to a nationwide market (Dr. Pepper was first marketed only in Texas and Mexico), rejuvenating an existing product (promoting orange juice for other uses besides breakfast), or harvesting a declining product.

2. **Explain what is meant by a full-line strategy and a limited-line strategy. How might a firm stretch or expand its product line?**

   When a firm has a large number of product variations in its product line, it is said to carry a *full line*. A company that adopts a *limited line strategy* markets a smaller number of product variations.

   In developing product strategies, organizations may decide to *extend* their product line—that is, add more items to an existing product line. Or if the company does decide to stretch its product line, it must decide on the best direction to extend itself. It can go upward to top of the line items, downward to items on the lower end, do both by implementing a two-way stretch, or follow a filling out strategy where only certain items are added to fill holes in the line.

3. **What is a product mix? What is meant by the width of a product mix.**

   A **product mix** is the total set of all products offered for sale by a firm, including all product lines sold to all customer groups.

   Width of the product mix means the number of different products produced by the firm.

   Consistency of the product mix refers to how closely related the items are in terms of technology, end use, channels of distribution, price range, or customer market.

   Length of product mix is the total number of different product items including all of the items in each product line.

4. **Why is quality such an important product strategy objective? What are the important dimensions of product quality?**

   Product objectives often address product quality or the product's ability to satisfy customers. Product quality is tied to customer expectations of product performance and can mean durability, reliability, degree of precision, case of use and repair, safety, or degree of aesthetic pleasure. Product quality objectives are likely to focus on the level and the consistency of product quality.

5. **How are products managed during the different phases of the Product Life Cycle (PLC)?**

   The product life cycle (PLC) explains how products go through four distinct stages from birth to death. In each stage product management decisions are crucial.

   **Refer to Figure 10.3
   a. Introduction: The goal in this stage is to get first-time buyers to try the product. Prices are often high in this stage and profits are basically nonexistent.
   b. Growth: In this stage marketing strategies may include the introduction of product variation to attract market segments and grow marketshare. Heavy advertising is also necessary as competition increases.
   c. Maturity: Sale peak, profit margins narrow, and competition is intense and shrinking. To remain competitive and maintain market share firms may tinker with the marketing mix, especially the product. Attracting new users is also crucial in this stage.
   d. Decline: The major decision is whether or not to keep the product. Decisions regarding how to phase out the product must be made.

6. **What is a brand? What are the characteristics of a good brand name? How do firms protect their brand?**

Brands are important because they help to develop and maintain customer loyalty and create value or brand equity.

A brand should be selected that has a positive connotation, is memorable, reproducible, and recognizable, and can be legally protected.

To protect a product legally, the brand name or symbol or other distinctive aspects can receive legal trademark protection.

7. **List and explain some of the different branding strategies.**

The types of brand strategies are:

a. Family brand—a brand used with a number of different product lines.
b. Individual brand—a brand used for one product only.
c. National or manufacturer brand—brand name owned by the manufacturer.
d. Private label or store brand—brand name use for products sold by a certain retailer.
e. Licensing—when a firm sells another firm the right to use a brand name for a specific purpose for a specific period of time. For example, Tommy Hilfiger name used on bed sheets.
f. Co-Branding—an agreement between two brands to work together in marketing a new product. For example, McDonald's McFlurry made with Butterfinger candy bars.

8. **What are the functions of packaging? What are some important elements of effective package design?**

A *package* is the covering or container for a product and serves to protect a product and allow for easy use and storage. In addition, the colors, words, shapes, designs, pictures, and materials used in the package design communicate a product's identity, benefits, and other important product information.

Package designers must consider cost, product protection, and communication in creating a package that is functional, aesthetically pleasing, and not harmful to the environment.

9. **What should marketers know about package labeling?**

Labels should:

a. Help consumers by providing useful information.
b. Be legally responsible in their description of their product.
c. Be accurate.

10. **Describe some of the different ways firms organize the marketing function to manage existing products. What are the ways firms organize for the development of new products?**

One way that firms manage existing products is with individual brand managers who supervise all the marketing activities for a single brand. Other firms may include product category managers to coordinate the activities of individual brands. Sometimes firms feel that it is best to focus on specific customer groups and structure product management with a number of market managers.

In large firms new product managers can develop marketing for the many different new products the firm develops, or new products can be managed by venture teams, groups of specialists from different areas who work together for a single new product.

Marketing Concepts: Discussing Choices and Issues

1. **Quality is an important product objective, but quality can mean different things for different products—durability, precision, aesthetic appeal, etc. What does quality mean for the following products?**

a. automobile
b. pizza
c. running shoes
d. hair dryer

e.   deodorant

f.   college education

Each student will have different impressions of what quality means for these products. So of what value are these impressions? They point out to the marketer a variety of issues that must be addressed in promotion and segmentation if the consumer is truly to be reached. If competitors reach the consumer better then they will probably get their business. Observe how many students put down more than one characteristic for each of the above items.

2.   **Many times firms take advantage of a popular well-known brand by developing brand extensions because they know that the brand equity of the original or parent brand will be transferred to the new product. But the transfer can go the other way. If a new product is of poor quality, it can damage the reputation of the parent brand while a new product that is of superior quality can enhance the parent brand reputation. What are some examples of brand extensions that have damaged and that have enhanced the parent brand equity?**

Some examples to get the discussion started are:

a.   Positive examples—Reese's, the maker of Reese's Peanut Butter Cups candy is now marketing a line of peanut butter; Grey Poupon, a product of the Nabisco Foods Group, has added salad dressings to its traditional mustard offerings; Bull's Eye Steak sauce is an extension of the Bull's Eye Bar-B-Que sauce.

b.   Negative examples—New Coke's addition to the established Coca-Cola line as a potential replacement for what is now called Coca-Cola Classic; in the 1980's Cadillac produced a "mini-Cadillac" to offset declining sales to imports and the Cadillac buyer saw it as an inferior and cheap version of the American classic luxury car.

3.   **Sometimes marketers seem to stick with the same old packaging ideas year after year, regardless of whether they are the best possible design. Below is a list of products. For each one, discuss what, if any, problems you have with the package. Then think of ways the package could be improved. Why do you think marketers don't change the old packaging? What would be the results if they adopted your package ideas?**

a.   dry cereal

b.   laundry detergent

c.   frozen orange juice

d.   a gallon of milk

e.   potato chips

f.   a loaf of bread

To do this project it would probably be better to get the students in small groups and let them exchange their ideas and present the results to the class. Common problems that they will have experienced with packages are that they are difficult to get into, they tear to easily, they won't reseal, the leak, they cause spilling or dripping, and they don't fit the place where they will be stored. Remind the students the function of packages and the costs associated with producing and then changing a package. Ask them if they can name some of the communication advantages and disadvantages to changing a package design. Can they remember a package change recently for one of their favorite products? What did they like or not like about it?

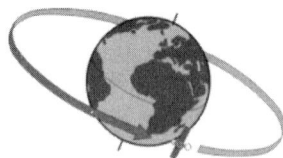

Real People, Real Surfers: Exploring the Web

In this exercise students are instructed to visit the U.S. Patent and Trademark Office Web site. This is a great exercise and one that provides useful information regarding the patent process and the benefits of federal trademark registration.

Marketing In Action: Real Choices At Polaroid

Summary: Polaroid needs to decide on the best strategy to address declining sales of the Spectra.

Suggested Answers to Case Questions:

1. **What is the problem facing Polaroid?**
   The main problem is how to improve the sales of Spectra, Polaroid' leading product.

2. **What factors are important in understanding the problem?**
   Sales for the Spectra had plateaued and the patents for the product would soon be expiring. Some of the important factors to consider include:
   a. Changes in consumer tastes for computer styles.
   b. Changes and new product introductions from competitors.
   c. The increase in the availability one-hour film developing.
   d. Cameras are in the maturity stage of the product life cycle.

3. **What are the alternatives?**
   a. Redesign the Spectra.
   b. Introduce a totally new camera.
   c. Increase the product mix by developing a line of camera accessories.
   d. Expand the product mix by offering a digital camera
   e. Focus on the immediate needs of Christmas sales by developing a promotion campaign aimed at increasing sales of the Spectra and other models on the market.

4. **What are your recommendations for solving the problem?**
   For the immediate need of Christmas sales, Polaroid should focus on developing a promotion campaign for Spectra and other models. Since the patent will soon expire for Polaroid, the firm needs to get the last sales burst from its products. Also, with Christmas only 9 months away there is probably not enough time to create and bring to market a new product.
   After Christmas Polaroid should consider increasing the product mix with a line of camera accessories and possibly with the addition of a digital camera.

5. **What are some ways to implement your recommendations?**
   Discussion should focus on the development of a promotional campaign. What should be the promotional message? How can Polaroid motivate consumers to buy the Spectra? The second part of the discussion should focus on product development for the digital camera and how to increase the product mix with camera accessories.

Mini-Project 10-A
Building a Better Package

Purpose: to develop an understanding of the various criteria for good package design.

1. Select a product category for which the package is important for using the product, that is consumers typically don't dispose of the package until they have used up the product. Some examples you might consider are

    ■   breakfast cereal
    ■   shampoo
    ■   orange juice
    ■   soft drinks
    ■   toothpaste

2. First, examine the traditional packaging yourself or with others in a student team. What is the shape of the package? Is there a reason why this shape is good? What material is used for the package? Does the package hold up under long-term use? Does the package make it easy to store and use the product? How do consumers dispose of the package when the product is gone?

3. Ask other consumers about the packaging. Do they find the existing packaging useful or do they encounter some problems is their use or storage of the product?

4. Based on your research, design and construct a mock-up of a totally new package for the product. Be sure to make the package attractive and as "real" as you can. Include important and useful package labeling information.

5. Show the package to other consumers and ask what they think of it.

6. Prepare a report for your class in which you discuss your research findings. Explain the reasons for your new design, and discuss how consumers feel about the new package. Finally, what would your recommendations about the old package and your new package be to firms which market the product?

Mini-Project 10-B
Enter Product Quality

Purpose: to learn more about how quality differs for different products.

More and more organizations are seeking product quality as a major objective of their firm. This is because they know that customers will only remain loyal to brands which provide the quality they want and expect to receive. But quality doesn't necessarily mean a pair of sneakers that never wear out or a refrigerator that runs forever. Rather, quality means that the product meets the expectations of the customer, that it provides the benefits customers seek. Sometimes this means high degree or precision. For other products it may be more related to ease of use, product safety, durability, or something quite different.

In the space below there are listed a number of products, both goods and services, which most college students purchase. Think about how you buy and use each product. Then describe how do you define quality in each product. Finally, list your current brand or supplier of the product and tell if you think the product quality deserves a grade of A, B, C, D, or F.

1.   Room or apartment

Quality for this product means _____

_____

_____

Current brand/supplier _____

Grade: A   B   C   D   F

2.   Concert

Quality for this product means _____

_____

_____

Current brand/supplier _____

Grade: A   B   C   D   F

3.   Stereo System

Quality for this product means _____

_____

_____

Current brand/supplier _____

Grade: A   B   C   D   F

4.   Shampoo

Quality for this product means _____

_____

_____

Current brand/supplier _____

Grade: A B C D F

5. Automobile

Quality for this product means _____

_____

_____

Current brand/supplier _____

Grade: A B C D F

6. Dry Cleaner

Quality for this product means _____

_____

_____

Current brand/supplier _____

Grade: A B C D F

7. College of University

Quality for this product means _____

_____

_____

Current brand/supplier _____

Grade: A B C D F

11

Broadening the Product Focus: Marketing Intangibles and Services

*O*verview This chapter examines the marketing of services, people, and ideas. The unique characteristics of services are explored as well as strategies for developing and managing services. Attention is given to the marketing of people and ideas as well. The Carolina Panthers are the focus of the Real People, Real Choices segment.

Objectives

1.   Explain the marketing of people, places, and ideas.

2.   Describe the four characteristics of services, and understand how services differ from goods.

3.   Explain how marketers measure service quality.

4.   Explain marketing strategies for services and nonprofit organizations.

Chapter Outline and Suggested Activities

Introduction: Begin by asking students to explain how services are different from products. Question one in Marketing Practice: Applying What You've Learned could be used to discuss the characteristics of services.

1. **Marketing What Isn't There**
    **Refer to Objective #1
    a. ***Intangibles:*** *Experience-based products that cannot be touched.*
    b. Does marketing work for intangibles?
        **Use Marketing in Action: Real Choices at Illinois Power Co.
        Although there are important differences in the types of marketing strategies which should be developed and implemented, nonetheless many of the same basic strategic steps can be taken to ensure that the organization does the best job of meeting consumer needs.

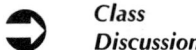 ***Class Discussion***   How would some basic marketing concepts apply to an art museum?

    c. Marketing People, Places, and Ideas
    1). Marketing People—categories of people marketing
        **Use Q#4, Marketing Practice: Applying What You've Learned
        a). Politicians
        b). Actors, musicians
        c). Athletes
    2). Marketing Places: For example, Vermont or Disney World

Suggested Speaker   If possible invite someone from local Chamber of Commerce to come and speak to your class about how the chamber markets your city. If this is not feasible, go to the website for a local chamber of commerce and examine how the Chamber helps to market the city.

    3). Marketing Ideas
    **Use Q#5 Marketing Practice: Applying What You've Learned
    a). ***Idea Marketing:*** *Marketing activities that seek to gain "market share" for a concept, philosophy, belief or issue by using elements of the marketing mix to create or change a target markets attitude or behavior. For example, "Don't drink and drive".*
    b). ***Cause Marketing:*** *Marketing activities in which firms seek to have their corporate identity linked to a good cause through advertising, public service and quality. For example, supporting the Susan Komer Research Center for Breast Cancer research.*

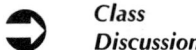 ***Class Discussion***   Today even churches are starting to market their churches. Ask students to discuss their feelings about churches which use marketing principles for the purpose of attracting new members.

2. **What Is A Service?**
    **Use Objective #2
    a. ***Services:*** *Intangible products that are exchanged directly from the producer to the customer.*
        1). Generate 74% of U.S. gross domestic product
        2). Account for 79% of all jobs.

b. Characteristics of Services
    1). Intangibility
    2). Perishability
    Capital management: The process by which the offering is adjusted in an attempt to match demand
    3). Variability
    4). Inseparability
        a). *Service Encounter: The actual interaction between the customer and the service provider*
        b). *Disintermediation: The process of eliminating interaction between customers and salespeople.*

Class Discussion

Ask students to comment on good and bad service encounters which they have experienced. What is the future of disintermediation? Are there businesses where disintermediation would be successful? In what businesses would disintermediation probably not be successful?

c. The Good/Services Continuum
    **Use Instructor's Manual Marketing Mini-Project 11-A
    **Use Real People, Real Choices: Exploring the Web
    **Use Figure 11.1
    1). Most products are a combination of goods and services
    The service continuum shows that some products are dominated by either tangible or intangible characteristics. As a product approaches the tangible pole of the continuum there is little emphasis on service. For products near the intangible pole, the service encounter is crucial in shaping the service experience.
    There are three positions on the continuum
    2). Good-Dominant Products—For example, a toll free 800 number.
        a). Including a service with purchase of a product
        b). *Embodying: The inclusion of a service with a purchase of a physical good.*

Class Discussion

What are some examples of embodying? Do you think that the practice of embodying could sway a consumer to purchase one brand over another?

    3). Equipment- or Facility-based services, facility driven services are concerned with three important factors. For example, car repair shop or hospital.
        a). Operational factors
        b). Locational factors
        c). Environmental factors

Class Discussion

Refer to the Real People, Real Choices segment on the Carolina Panthers. Discuss the importance of the three factors (i.e., operational, locational, and environmental) for the Panthers.

    4). People-Based Services—For example, a personal trainer.
        a). Tangible end of the continuum
        b). Growing availability of people-based services due to time-poverty and overall economic wealth.

d.   Core and Augmented Services
        **Use Q#2 Marketing Practice: Applying What You've Learned
       ** Use Video Yahoo-ing The World
           1).   *Core Service: The basic benefit that is obtained as a result of having a service performed.*
           2).   *Augmented Service: The core service plus additional services provided to enhance value.*

Class Discussion   Services often compete by offering superior augmented services that competitors lack. What are some examples of augmented services provided by:

    a.   Hairstylist
    b.   Department store
    c.   Restaurant

Does the augmented service enhance the core product? Explain.

3.   **Providing Quality Service**
    **Refer to Objective 3
    a.   Judging Service Quality
        1).   Quality is about exceeding expectations
        2).   Evaluative dimension of service quality
            a).   Search qualities
            b).   Experience qualities
            c).   Credence qualities

Real People, Bad Choices?

Summary: Sometimes a company lowers expectations of service quality so that it's sure to exceed them.

Suggested Discussion Questions

1.   Is this practice unethical?

2.   How do you think consumers would feel about firms which "bend" the truth?

3.   What are some practical solutions for increasing consumers expectations without bending the truth?

---

    b.   Measuring Service Quality
        1).   *Gap analysis: A marketing research methodology that measures the difference between a customer's expectation of a service quality and what actually occurred*
        2).   *The critical incident technique: A method for measuring service quality in which customer complaints are used to identify critical incidents, specific face-to-face contacts between consumers and service providers that cause problems and lead to dissatisfaction.*

Summary: Jonathan McNeill and William Haylon don't just fix cars, they provide a service. Their service facilities are clean and spacious. Sterling does not employ "damage estimators" but rather "service advisors" who manage the entire process.

Suggested Answers to Discussion Questions:

1. **What is the core service that customers who take their cars to Sterling receive?**
   The core service is feeling good about getting your car repaired.

2. **Unlike many auto repair businesses, why might this one fall toward the middle of the goods/services continuum in Figure 11.1?**
   The addition of augmented services places Sterling Collision Centers more in the middle of the goods/services continuum such as:
   a. Clean and spacious service facilities
   b. Use of "service advisors"
   c. Cooperative relationship with auto insurance carriers

4. **Strategies For Developing and Managing Services**
   **Use Table 11.1
   a. Service as Theater

Class Discussion   Use Figure 11.4 to explain how providing a service is similar to creating a theater performance. Be sure to include a discussion of the back stage and the front stage.

b. Targeting and Positioning Strategies for Service
   1). Targeting: Service marketers need to identify who is the target market.

Class Discussion   Refer to the Real People, Real Choices segment on the Carolina Panthers. What are some examples of targeting actions that might be taken by the Carolina Panthers? For each strategic goal below develop an example of a tactic which could be used.

- Audience Maintenance
- Audience Enrichment
- Audience Expansion
- Audience Development

   2). Positioning: There are five dimensions that successfully position a service.
   a). Tangibles:
      Physical evidence: A visible signal that communicates not only a product's quality, but also the product's desired market position to the consumer.
   b). Adopt a branding strategy
   c). Responsiveness
   d). Empathy
   e). Assurance

Class
Discussion

Refer to the Spotlight on Real People, at Sterling Collision Centers. Discuss how the positioning dimensions can be applied to Sterling Collision. What physical evidence is provided by Sterling Collision that communicates quality?

Real People, Real Choices:

How It Worked Out at the Carolina Panthers

Summary: Charles Waddell is director of marketing and sponsorships for the Carolina Panthers of the National Football League. He is responsible for the coordination of the Panthers sponsorship packages and team advertising. As a new NFL franchise, the Panthers had to develop a strategy that would feed the enthusiasm of its Charlotte fans and at the same time lure corporate sponsors. To maximize advertising revenues Waddell had to develop a television and radio advertising program that would ensure corporate backing of the Panthers. While at the same time bringing in needed funds for the team.

Option 1: Sell the advertising rights to a third party.
Option 2: Do all TV/radio advertising in house and have a production company produce the game.
Option 3: Do a mixture of both

Waddell chose option 3 because he was confident the Panthers would attract enough high-paying corporate sponsors to take a chance on the new team.

Marketing Concepts: Testing Your Knowledge

1. **What are intangibles? How do basic marketing concepts apply to the marketing of intangibles?**
    Intangibles are experienced based products that cannot be touched. The basic marketing concept applies to many types of product, including those we cannot touch. The concept of identifying needs and wants and developing goods/services which meet those needs and wants is just as crucial for intangibles as it is for tangible goods. Branding and brand important are also important when marketing intangibles.

2. **What do we mean by marketing people? Marketing places? Marketing ideas?**
    Like products, people, places, and ideas can all be marketed. Consider the following examples:
    a.   People: The marketing of a presidential candidate
    b.   Places: The marketing of the Orlando, Florida area and Disney World
    c.   Ideas: The marketing of ideas such as "Don't Drink and Drive" or "It pays to recycle".

3. **What is a service? What are the important characteristics of services that make them different from goods?**
    Services are products that are intangible and that are exchanged directly from producer to customer. Generally services are acts that accomplish some goal and may be directed either toward people or toward an object or possession. Important service characteristics include (1) intangibility (they cannot be seen, touched, or smelled); (2) perishability (they cannot be stored); (3) variability (they are never exactly the same); and (4) inseparability from the producer (most services are produced, sold, and consumed at the same time.

4. **What is the goods/services continuum? What are product-related services, equipment-or-facility-based services, and people-based services?**
    See Figure 11.1 for additional information and examples.
    It is sometimes difficult to separate products and services because of their interrelationship. However, the service continuum is a useful way of accomplishing this. Some products are dominated by either tangible or intangible characteristics (such as salt and teaching), while others tend to include a mixture of goods and services (such as flying on an airplane). Challenges come in formulating marketing strategy for product-related services, equipment- or facility-based services, and people-based services.

5. **How do marketers create augmented services to increase market share?**
    The augmented services are the core service plus additional services provided to enhance its value. See Figure 11.2 for more detail and description.
    Because in many cases the core service offered by the competitors is basically the same, a common strategic option is to provide competitive advantage by creating one or more augmented services unique to a company's service product. The augmented services are commonly cited as being innovative features, unique delivery systems, and the bundling of services together.

6. **How do consumers evaluate service quality? How do marketers work to create service quality?**
    Consumers evaluate product quality on tangible features such as appealing to the senses or styling, durability, dependability, et cetera. The satisfaction of service customers, on the other hand, is a perception and it is based on prior expectations.

7. **Describe some of the ways marketers measure service quality.**
    Both qualitative and quantitative research methods may be used to measure customer satisfaction. Gap analysis measures the difference between customer expectations of service quality and what actually occurred. Using a critical incident technique, service firms can identify the specific contacts between customers and service providers that create dissatisfaction.

8. **How may services marketing strategies be compared to directing a theater performance?**

A service is a show put on for an audience. Each service contact can be thought of as a dramatic performance, complete with actors, props, and costumes. The backstage, where the services is produced, and the front stage, where the service is delivered to the customer are the two areas where a service performance occurs.

Figure 11.4 illustrates how services marketing strategy can be compared to directing a theater performance.

9. **How does target marketing apply to the marketing of services?**

Not all people or organizations are interested in receiving a particular service. Most services can identify a target customer that they can serve well. Targeting actions taken by the firm might include:

    a.   audience maintenance

    b.   audience enrichment

    c.   audience expansion

    d.   audience development

10. **What are the five dimensions that successfully position a service?**

    a.   Tangibles: The physical evidence that communicates not only a product's quality but also the desired market position to the consumer.

    b.   Adopt a branding strategy: Develop a unique brand image for the product.

    c.   Responsiveness: An emphasis on speed and care with which the organization responds to customers' requests.

    d.   Empathy: An organization that understands its customer's needs and genuinely cares about their welfare

    e.   Assurance: AN organization an emphasize the knowledge or competence of its employees

Marketing Concepts: Discussing Choices and Issues

1. **Sometimes service quality may not meet customers' expectations because services are inseparable from the service provider and because of the variability in the performance of the service from one time to the next. What problems have you experienced with quality in the delivery of the following services? What do you think is the reason for the poor quality?**

    a.   hotel accommodations

    b.   dry cleaning

    c.   a haircut

    d.   your college education

The students should be encouraged to express their feelings and ideas about the above services. Point out how the characteristics of services (intangibility, perishability, inseparability, and variability) affect the perception of the service and its quality. What could they (as potential marketers) do to correct the wrongs that they have expressed? Did the wrongs cost the service provider any money? If not, why not?

2. **There have been a lot of criticisms of the way politicians have been marketed in recent years. What are some of the ways marketing has helped our political process? What are some ways the marketing of politicians might have an adverse effect on our government?**

Most students should have some sort of opinion about the role of marketing in politics and government. Critics point out that political marketing is deception at its finest. They claim that candidates tell voters what ever they want to hear just to get their vote. Though perhaps true in some sense, the voter still has the final vote on the credibility of the candidate. Hopefully bad candidates (like bad products) finish last.

With more communication and an attempt to understand the voting consumer, marketing may have brought the political process out of the smoke filled rooms and on to television. One of the benefits of the marketing application is the close inspection that the consumer is able to give the candidates. Strategies become clear and usually have to withstand the test of daylight if the candidate is to succeed.

3.   **Many non-for-profit and religious organizations have found that they can be more successful by marketing their ideas. What are some ways that these organizations market themselves that is like and different from the marketing by for-profit businesses? Should money that is donated to charitable organizations be used for marketing activities?**

Marketing is just as important for non-profit organizations as it is for profit organizations. There are basically no differences in marketing for-profit and non-profit organizations. However, non-profit organizations are held accountable by contributors for how they spend their money. Thus, it is important that they not spend too much money on "glitzy" marketing.

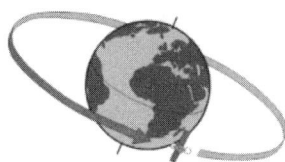

Real People, Real Surfers: Exploring the Web

In this exercise students are instructed to visit the web sites of McDonald's, Wendys, and Burger King, and to examine the target market, and positioning strategy of these fast food chains.

Additional Suggested Discussion Questions:

1.   Examine the product offerings of each restaurant. How are products offered used to position the restaurant?

2.   Have students visit each restaurant. (A team approach would be a good strategy.) Have each team report on the services provided and the level of service quality at each restaurant.

Marketing in Action: Real Choices at Illinois Power Co.

Summary: How do you apply marketing concepts to an intangible product like electricity? This is a question faced by Illinois Power Co. and will soon be faced by all utility companies. Deregulation of the utility industry means that consumers will be able to choose their utility supplier. This also means that utility firms must learn about marketing concepts such as brand loyalty and pricing strategies.

Suggested Answers to Case Questions:

1.   **What is the problem facing Illinois Power Co.?**
     Given the rapid changes brought about in the power industry by deregulation, how can Illinois Power Co. expand its base by adopting a branding strategy and secure its market position by employing marketing practices? This problem question is one of several issues facing the company.

2.   **What factors are important to understanding this problem?**
     Several important factors that should be considered by the company include:
     a.   The threat of wholesale power brokers.
     b.   The effect of deregulation.
     c.   Consumer knowledge and perception of the company.
     d.   Consumer brand loyalty.
     e.   The ability to establish loyalty.
     f.   The likelihood of new competition in the future.
     g.   Opportunities to enter new markets.
     h.   The development of a packaging strategy.
     i.   How to advertise in the future.
     j.   How to develop bundling strategies.
     k.   How to develop strategies where none have existed in the past.

3.   **What alternatives might Illinois Power consider?**
     The students have a wide open field with which to develop alternatives. Some areas that might generate discussion include the range of:
     a.   Do nothing—status quo.
     b.   Find ways better understand the consumers needs.
     c.   Study competitors strategies.
     d.   Adopt bundling strategies.
     e.   Create a new image and decide on a brand image.
     f.   Hire an outside marketing firm to assist in the transition.

4.   **What are your recommendations for solving the problem?**
     No matter which direction the students take they should address the issue of the need to meet competition and establish a new brand image with aggressive marketing and promotion. It might be easier for them to see these alternatives if the local power company is used as an example.

5.   **What are some ways to implement your recommendations?**
     The company has already implemented several steps that will move them in a direction of adding more marketing effort into their operations. The addition of Ralph Tschantz is a good first step. The escalation of the advertising budget indicates that there will be a serious attempt to either improve or establish a new image. Probably a good next step would be to do more aggressive research to find out what the current image is, what are perceived problems, and where is the company weak in the minds of the consumer. By attempting to move from a monopolist viewpoint and mentality to one of being one who is going to meet serious competition, the company can establish a relationship with their consumers that has not been there before. After this is done, new marketing strategies can be employed.

Mini-Project 11-A
Understanding the Service Industry

Purpose: to better understand how service organizations engage in marketing activities.

With other students in your class, arrange to visit a service organization in your area. You may consider some of the following

- a photography studio
- an advertising or public relations agency
- a hospital or other health care facility
- a television or radio station
- a restaurant
- a hair style salon

Plan ahead the questions which you will ask in order to learn as much as you can about the organization. You will probably want to develop questions which will allow you to learn about

- the mission and goals of the organization
- the market segments the organization targets
- how the organization has positioned itself
- the core and augmented product provided by the organization
- whether the service is customized or standardized
- specific strategies the organization uses to deal with the intangibility, the perishability, the variability, and the inseparability of the service encounter
- how the organization strives to create quality in its service
- how service quality is defined and measured
- the type of promotion the organization has used for its marketing
- how pricing strategies are developed

Based on the information you gain from the visit, write a report or present the information to your class.

Be sure in that report to include your evaluation of the strengths and weaknesses of the marketing practices of the organization and suggestions you would make for improvement.

Mini-Project 11-B
Marketing People

Purpose: to better understand how the marketing concept applies to the "selling" of people.

The marketing concept applies not just to goods and services but to other intangibles such as people and ideas. In fact, when you go to look for a job, you will be more successful at "selling" yourself if you do a good job of applying all you've learned about marketing to that process.

In order to better understand how the marketing concept applies to selling people including yourself, use the space below to prepare a profile of yourself.

1.   Describe yourself as the product you are trying to sell on the job market:
        a.   The core product

_____

_____

_____

_____

_____

_____

        b.   The actual product

_____

_____

_____

_____

_____

_____

        c.   The augmented product

_____

_____

_____

_____

_____

_____

2.   What is the cost of the product? (Note: be sure to include both salary and other monetary and non-monetary costs a company invests in a new hire.)

_____

_____

_____

_____

_____

_____

3.   Channel of distribution (where will the product be available?)

_____

_____

_____

_____

_____

_____

4.   Suggestions for promotion strategies

_____

_____

_____

_____

_____

_____

5.   What are some ideas for creating physical evidence of the product?

_____

_____

_____

_____

_____

_____

12

Pricing
the Product

*O*verview In this chapter we will first examine the question, what is price? Then we will see how price is related to product demand, to costs, and to other environmental influences. We will also discuss some of the psychological aspects of pricing. Finally some of the important legal and ethical considerations of pricing practices are presented.

Bojangles is the focus of the Real People, Real Choices segment. Randall Poindexter, the Vice President of marketing, had to decide the best pricing strategy to use in a competitive environment.

Objectives

1.   Explain the importance of pricing and how prices can take both monetary and nonmonetary forms.

2.   Understand the pricing objective that marketers typically have in planning pricing strategies.

3.   Describe how customer demand influences pricing decisions.

4.   Describe how marketers use costs, demands, and revenue to make pricing decisions.

5.   Understand some of the environmental factors that affect pricing strategies.

Chapter Outline and Suggested Activities

Introduction: Remember the television show "The Price Is Right"? Begin class by asking to give the price of a variety of products. You could either type a list of common consumer goods or just ask students the question "How much does an 8oz. can of Starkist tuna cost?" directly. If you are feeling creative and have time, you could bring in pictures of various products or actual products to use in the pricing exercise. You might even want to award prizes.

Suggested Discussion Questions

1.   What is price?

2.   Discuss non-monetary costs such as opportunity costs.

3.   How do consumers decide what is a "fair price" for a product or service?

1.   **"Yes, But What Does It Cost?"**
        **Refer to Objective #1
        **Use the video Watson Pharmaceuticals, Part 2
        a.   Monetary and Nonmonetary Prices
                **Use Instructor's Manual Marketing Mini-Project 12-B
                **Use Real People, Real Choices: Exploring the Web
                When you think of price, you probably also think about money. "How much will a new CD player cost?" is an example of a price related question. Most consumers think about price in terms of monetary value, in other words, cash! Not all exchanges involve cash; some exchanges involve the exchange of goods, services, or anything else of value in return for the desired product or service. This practice is called bartering.
                1).   *Price: The value that customers give up or exchange to obtain a desired product.*
                2).   *Bartering: The practice of exchanging a good or service for another good or service of lack value.*

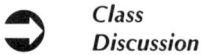
Class Discussion   What are some examples of non-monetary costs?

        b.   The importance of pricing decisions
                1).   Pricing is the least understood element in the marketing mix. Good pricing decisions are critical to a firm's success in the marketplace.
                2).   Even when the economy is good, most consumers rank "reasonable price" as the most important consideration in a purchase.
                3).   Price is also important to organizations and their purchasing agents.

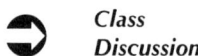
Class Discussion   What activities are used by consumers to help them obtain the "best price" for a product/service? What activities are used by purchasing agents to help them obtain the "best-price" for a product/service?

                4).   In general pricing decisions are important because:
                        a).   Price creates profits

            b).   Price influences customers
            c).   Price affects market share
    c.   Pricing and the Marketing Mix
            **Use Q#2, Marketing Practice: Applying What You've Learned
            **Use Marketing In Action: Real Choices at Hallmark
            Pricing decisions, like product decision, are interrelated with all other marketing mix decisions.
            1).   Price and Place:
                      Each member of the channel of distribution must be considered when developing the
                      pricing plan. The margins desired and needed by wholesalers and retailers must be
                      considered in pricing decision.
                      Selecting retail channels which match a product's price and image are also part of the
                      pricing plan.
            2).   Price and Product
                      Price sends a signal about product quality. For some products, like cosmetics, for
                      example, consumers are convinced that a higher price means a better product.
                      The stage of the product's life cycle also affects pricing. Early in the product life cycle
                      firms can charge a higher price because there is little or no competition. Later, as
                      competitors enter the marketplace, prices go down.

Class   What are some examples of products which consumers pay a high price for
Discussion   because they believe the quality is worth the price? Are products which are more
                   expensive actually better in quality? A discussion on apparel brands and retail
                   brands might prove to be interesting.

            3).   Price and Promotion
                      The costs of promotion activities need to be considered in pricing decisions. The firm
                      must generate enough revenue to pay for promotional expenses.
                      The promotions should also justify the cost of the product. Image building is very
                      important for premium priced products.

2.   **Developing Pricing Objectives**
        **Refer to Objective #2
        **Use Marketing Mini-Project: Learning by Doing
        **Use Table 12.1
        a.   Pricing objectives must support the broader objectives of the firm. Table 12.1 outlines five pricing
                objectives.

Class   Refer to the Real People, Real Choices segment on Bojangles or the Computer
Discussion   Friendly Stuff (CFS) marketing plan. For each of the five pricing objectives, provide
                   an example for either Bojangles or CFS.

        b.   Sales Objective
                Often the objective of pricing strategy is to maximize sales.

Class   Does setting a price intended to increase unit sales or market share mean that the
Discussion   price must be lower than the competition's price?

        c.   Profit Objectives
                Profit objectives focus on a target level of profit growth or a desired net profit margin.

➨ **Class**   Profits are critical for products which are fads and for seasonal products. Explain.
Discussion

d.   Competitive-Effect Objectives
Competitive-effect objective mean the pricing plan is intended to have a certain effect on the marketing efforts of the competition.

e.   Customer Satisfaction Objectives
Some firms prefer to focus on developing long-term relationships with customers. This philosophy embodies the belief that if we focus on customer satisfaction as the primary objective, sales and profits will follow.

f.   Image Enhancement Objectives
Price is used by consumers as a cheuristic, a mental shortcut, to denote product quality. Image enhancement is important for luxury and prestige products.
Low prices can also be used to communicate an image of good quality at a reasonable price.

➨ **Class**   Discuss with students the growth of private label brands in grocery stores. What
Discussion   type of image do store brands communicate to customers? Why are some store brands very successful?

g.   Flexibility of Price Objectives
Pricing objectives need to be flexible. Objectives may need to be tailored for different geographic regions and time periods.

➨ **Class**   1.   If you are teaching in a multimedia classroom with internet access, you
Discussion   may want to log onto the site of a hotel in a vacation resort area. Hotels in the Disney World area might be interesting. Select one or two hotels and examine the seasonal fluctuations in the price charged for rooms. You could also assign this activity to students. Discuss with students the market conditions which make these price adjustments necessary.

2.   Have students from different regions of the country and those from foreign countries discuss prices of commonly purchased products. Are prices for some products/services higher, lower, or about the same across geographic regions?

3.   **Estimating Demand: How Demand Influences Pricing**
**Refer to Objective 3
Demand is how much of a product consumers want and are willing to buy at different prices, all other things being equal. Thus, one of the steps in price planning is to estimate demand for a product.

a.   Demand Curves
**Use Figure 12.2
The typical or normal demand curve is downward sloping. As the prices increases, the number of units that consumers are willing to purchase decreases.
The demand for prestige products indicates that an increase in price may actually result in an increase in the quantity demanded because consumers see the product as more valuable.

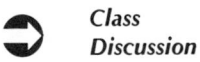

Class Discussion Toyota makes both the Toyota Camry and the Lexus. Both are nice cars, but the difference is price and prestige. Does the Lexus really drive and outperform the Camry? Students will differ on their views on this topic based on their knowledge of cars.

Some of the fresh fruits and vegetables available at specialty grocery stores are two to three times higher in price than those at a neighboring grocery store. Why would a consumer pay $1.00 a pound for bananas at a specialty grocer like Dean and Deluca when the same product is $0.59 a pound at a traditional grocery store less than a half mile away?

1). **Shifts in Demand**
**Use Figure 12.3
Products improvements and enticing advertising campaigns may cause an upward shift in demand. This upward shift in demand means that the company sells more of its product without lowering the price.

Class Discussion What factors, other than price and marketing activities, influence shifts in demand?

2). **Estimating Demand**
Understanding and estimating demand is important because
a). Production scheduling is based on anticipated demand. Ideally, the firm wants to produce only the amount demand.
b). All marketing planning and budgeting must be based on reasonably accurate estimates of potential sales.
To estimate demand the firm must first identify demand for an entire product category. Next, the firm predicts what the company's market share is likely to be.

Class Discussion Select a product category of your choice. Assume that you are developing a new brand for this category. What would be a good estimate of demand of the new entry?

You may want to do some preliminary research before class to identify the current demand for the selected product category. Another option would be to assign this task to students and ask them to estimate the demand.

b. The Elasticity of Demand
**Use Q#3, Marketing Practice: Applying What You've Learned
**Use Instructor's Manual Marketing Mini-Project 12-A
Price elasticity of demand: The percentage change in unit sales that result from a percentage change in price.

Class Discussion What factors might be influencing demand for Bojangles' biscuits and chicken? Under what types of buying situations are consumers willing to pay more? You may want to remind students of the various influences on consumer purchase decisions presented in Chapter 6.

1). Elastic and Inelastic Demand
**Use Figure 12.4
    a). When demand is inelastic changes in price and revenue are in the same direction. An increase in price causes total revenues to grow. A decrease shrinks total revenue .
    b). When a change in price results in a large change in quantity demanded demand is said to be elastic.

Class
Discussion
What are some examples of consumer goods for which demand is inelastic? What are some examples of organizational goods for which demand is inelastic?

Class
Discussion
The Instructor's Manual Mini-project 12-A could be used as an in class activity to help students understand the elasticity of demand.

Suggested Discussion Questions

1. For each product studied examine the differences and similarities between the demand curves. At what point does demand increase? Diminish? Ask students to explain factors which they think may be influencing demand for each product.

2. Under what types of buying situations are consumers willing to pay more?

2). Influences on Demand Elasticity
    a). Availability of substitute goods or service. If there is a close substitute, demand will be elastic.

Class
Discussion
Ask students what brand of toothpaste, laundry detergent and/or cereal they usually purchase. On a recent visit to the grocery store you find that the store is out of stock of your favorite brand. What do you do? Is there, in your opinion, a close substitute?

    b). The time period marketers are considering also effects demand. The longer the time period, the greater the likelihood that demand will be more elastic. The longer time periods allow time for substitutes to enter the market.
    c). Income effect on demand.
    d). Changes in prices of other products affects the demand for an item-cross-elasticity of demand.

4. **Determining Cost**
**Refer to Objective #4
a. Types of Costs
    1). *Variable costs: The costs of production (raw and processed materials, parts, and labor) that are tied to and vary depending on the number of units produced.*
    **Use Table 12.2
    2). *Fixed costs: Cost of production that do not change with the number of units produced.*

3). **Total costs:** *The total of the fixed costs and the variable cost for a set number of units produced.*

➡ **Class Discussion**   Ask students to provide examples of variable and fixed costs? You might also want to bring in an income statement and discuss the variable and fixed costs.

b.   Break-even Analysis
**Use Q#4, Marketing Practice: Applying What You've Learned
**Use Figure 12-5

1). **Break-even analysis:** *A method for determining the number of units that a firm must produce and sell at a given price to cover all its costs.*

➡ **Class Discussion**   Use questions 4 Marketing Practice: Applying What You've Learned as part of your lecture. One option would be to assign the problem and have students complete the problem before class and then to discuss the solution(s) during class. Another option would be for the professor to do the problems in class.

2).   At the break-even point, revenue or income from sales are equal to costs.
3).   Break-even can be calculated in units or dollars.
4).   After a firm's sales have met and passed the break-even point, the firm begins to make a profit. The break-even point can also be calculated with a dollar profit figure desired in mind.
5).   Break-even analysis does not provide all the answers for pricing decisions; the quantity demanded at a given price must also be considered.

c.   Marginal Analysis
**Use Figure 12.6
**Use Table 12.3

Marginal analysis: *a method that uses cost and demand to identify the price that will maximize profits.* Because most firms must lower their costs in order to sell additional units of their product, marginal revenue is also an indicator of demand. Profit is maximized at the point where marginal cost is exactly equal to marginal revenue.
1).   A method that uses cost and demand to identify the price that will maximize profits.
2).   The increase in total costs that results from providing one additional unit of a product.
3).   The increase in total revenue (income) that results from producing and selling one additional unit of a product.

5.   **Evaluating The Pricing Environment**
**Refer to Objective 5
The fourth step in developing pricing strategies (Figure 12.1) is to examine and evaluate the pricing environment. Presented below are some of the important external influences on pricing strategies.
a.   The Economy: Marketers need to understand how economic trends will affect their business.
**Use Q#1 Marketing Practice: Applying What You've Learned
1).   Trimming the Fat: Pricing in a recession
During a recession, consumers may switch to generics and shop discount or warehouse stores more frequently. Firms may cut their prices to levels where costs are covered, but no profit is earned.

Marginal analysis appears to be a straightforward procedure. However, nothing is ever as simple as it seems. Discuss with students how unexpected, unplanned, and uncontrollable events can skew a marginal analysis. For example, have students consider the pricing decisions which had to be made by Randall Poindexter at Bojangles.

Discuss how each of the following might impact costs and revenues. You and your student might even want to brainstorm and create your own "what if" scenarios.

1.   A shortage of biscuit flour.
2.   A severe storm such as a hurricane, tornado, or blizzard which slows the delivery of needed ingredients for food preparation and packaging
3.   Failure of the restaurant's oven.
4.   Economists predict that the economy is going to get worse, causing stock prices to fall drastically.
5.   The competition creates a new low fat biscuit which if eaten on a regular basis may help to lower cholesterol.

    2).   Increasing Prices: Responding to Inflation

In periods of inflation, marketers may also cut their prices and temporarily sacrifice profits.

b.   The Competition

**Use Bojangles video here

    1).   Consumers' expectations on what constitutes a fair price is highly dependent on what the competition is charging.

    2).   The type of competitive environment (i.e., oligopoly, etc.), also influences price decisions.

What are some examples of pricing objectives for each of the three types of competitive environments (oligopoly, monopolistic competition, and pure competition)?

You might want to select one industry, for example fast food, for this discussion.

c.   Consumer Trends

Culture and demographics determine how consumers think and behave and impact marketing decisions.

Consider the price of a cup of coffee at a specialty coffee store such as Starbucks. Now consider how much a cup of coffee made from a grocery store brand of specialty coffee made at home would cost. What factors are influencing the growth of the specialty coffee market and premium prices for coffee?

d.   International Environmental Influences

    1).   Currency exchange rates and national and/or local government policies may lead to differences in the prices competitors charge for products in global markets.

    2).   *Price subsidies: Government payments made to protect businesses or to reimburse them when they must price at or below cost to make a sale. The subsidy can be a cash payment or tax relief.*

Real People, Bad Choices

Summary: In 1993 Japanese and Canadian rod manufacturers were accused by Connecticut Steel and other U.S. companies of dumping. Dumping is selling excess inventory abroad cheaper than at home. The U.S. Department of Commerce investigated the claims of dumping and found Japanese and Canadian steel wire rod suppliers were guilty of price dumping; a duty (import tax) was levied against the offenders.

Suggested Answers to Discussion Questions

1. **Should companies be allowed to sell their excess inventory of products at any price they choose, or should they be penalized for dumping?**

   Some might believe that sellers should be able to sell goods at any price they choose. Other students might believe that price dumping is unfair to local firms; the U.S. government obviously takes a stand against dumping by penalizing firms which dump goods into the U.S. market.

2. **Does dumping really hurt anyone?**

   Again, responses to this question will vary, and will be dependent upon how the individual views dumping. Comments for class discussion might include:

   a. Competition is hurt when goods are dumped into the economy. It is often difficult for firms to compete against prices which are far below the standard level.

   b. Consumers in the home country of the offending dumpers may also suffer. Sometimes the price is raised higher in the home country to offset any losses which might occur in the foreign market.

 Class Discussion   Should the U.S. government offer subsidies to firms so that they can be competitive?

Real People, Real Choices: How It Worked Out At Bojangles

Summary: Randall Poindexter is Vice President of marketing for the Bojangles chain for fast-food restaurants. Bojangles specializes in Cajun-spiced chicken and homemade buttermilk biscuits. In 1995, Poindexter and his colleagues at Bojangles saw that the chain's lunch sales were down slightly due to the intensely competitive environment. Competitors had began to use combo menus and had also invested in substantial media support. Poindexter considered two options.

Option 1: Don't offer a combo option and do keep all sandwiches and individual dinners priced a la carte.

Option 2: Package all sandwiches and individual dinners as combos and price them at a 15 to 20 percent advantage to the customer versus the a la carte prices.

Randy Poindexter and his colleagues chose option 2.

Suggested Discussion Questions

1. Bojangles found that demand for their menu items was elastic. Explain what elasticity of demand means to Bojangles.

2. How did store managers and "front line crew members contribute to the success of the combo pricing strategy?

Marketing Concepts: Testing Your Knowledge

1. **What are some examples of monetary and nonmonetary prices?**
   Price, the amount of outlay of money, goods, services, or deeds given in exchange for a product, may be monetary (for example, dues, tuition, professional fee, rent, donations, and so on) or nonmonetary (for example, a vote for a candidate, or contribution of time and effort).

2. **Explain how pricing decisions are important to firms.**
   Pricing is important to firms because it creates profits, influences customers to purchase or not, and can be a competitive weapon useful in gaining market share.

3. **How are pricing decisions interrelated with other elements of the marketing mix?**
   Pricing relates with the other components of the marketing mix in the following ways:
   a.   Place—pricing decisions must be studied from the viewpoint of each channel partner's situation. Will your pricing plan allow them to be successful and will theirs allow you to be successful?
   b.   Product—a product's price must pay for the cost of production and other costs of doing business. Price is also an important communication tool that transmits information about the product's quality, status, and image. Price changes as the stage of the product life cycle changes.
   c.   Promotion—price is perhaps most strongly related to promotion activities. First, promotion costs must be covered. Second, the creative strategy and media strategy must justify the cost of the product. Promotion has to explain price to the consumer.

4. **How is demand influenced by price? What is elastic demand? What is inelastic demand?**
   Demand is the amount of a product customers are willing to buy at different prices. For most products lower prices increase demand, but with some prestige products demand increases as price goes up. Price elasticity of demand is the sensitivity of customers to changing prices. With elastic demand changes in price create large changes in demand, while when demand is inelastic price increases have little effect on demand and total revenue increases.

5. **What external influences affect demand elasticity?**
   See Figure 12.2 for additional material and explanation. In the real world, factors other than the price and other marketing activities influence demand. Such things as weather (demand for umbrellas), seasons (demand for garden tools), economic state (demand goes down in a recession for expensive items like furniture), new product development, and even consumer confidence can affect demand. In addition, substitute products, cross-elasticity of demand, the market time period, and product complements also affect the elasticity of demand.

6. **Explain variable costs, fixed costs, average variable costs, average fixed costs, and average total costs.**
   Variable costs are the costs of production that are tied to and vary depending on the number of units produced; variable costs typically include raw materials, processed materials, component parts, and labor.
   Fixed costs are the costs of production that do not change with the number of units produced.
   Average variable costs are the total spent on raw materials, labor, and so on divided by the number of items produced.
   Average fixed costs (fixed costs remain the same no matter the level of production) will decrease as the number of units produced increases. To calculate divide fixed costs by the number produced.
   Average total costs is the total cost (the total of the fixed costs and the variable costs for a set number of units produced) divided by the number of units produced.

7. **What is break-even analysis? How do marketers use break-even analysis?**
   Break-even analysis is a method for determining the number of units that will have to be produced and sold at a given price to break-even—that is, to neither make a profit nor suffer a loss.

Marketers use break-even analysis to help them in establishing and deciding on the price for a product. To make this calculation accurate the marketer must add in an estimation of demand. See Figure 12.5 for an example.

8. **What is marginal analysis? How do marketers use marginal analysis?**
Marginal analysis is a method of analysis that uses costs and demands to identify the price that will maximize profits. Marketers use marginal analysis in the same way as they use break-even analysis—to aid them in deciding and setting a price for the product. Changes in costs often cause this method to be in error. Therefore, all pricing must be flexible and responsive to changes in the environment and demand.

9. **What are some of the more frequently used pricing objectives?**
Refer to Table 12.1 for examples of each type of pricing objective

- Sales or market share
- Profit
- Competitive Effect
- Consumer Satisfaction
- Image enhancement

10. **What are some ways in which changes in the business cycle, the competitive environment, and consumer trends affect price planning?**
Business Cycle. During times of recession and inflation firms may need to cut their prices to a level where only production costs are covered. This type of price reduction not only helps the firm to remain in business but also demonstrates a "good will" effort by showing consumers in a tangible way (i.e., price reduction) that they are empathetic to their financial concerns.
    Competitive Environment. In an oligopoly, pricing objectives of firms are similar and this helps to avoid price competition. In a state of monopolistic competition firms differentiate their products and focus on non-price competition. Prices are directly influenced by supply and demand in a purely competitive market and firms have little opportunity to raise or lower prices.
    Consumer Trends. Marketers need to monitor the consumer environment for changes in attitudes and behaviors regarding price. For example, during cost-conscious periods marketers need to demonstrate to consumers the value and quality offered through their brand.

Marketing Concepts: Discussing Choices and Issues

1. **Governments sometimes provide price subsidies to specific industries; that is, they reduce a domestic firm's costs so that they can sell products on the international market at a lower price. What reasons do governments (and politicians) use for these government subsidies? What are the benefits and disadvantages to domestic industries in the long run? To international customers? Who would benefit and who would lose if all price subsidies were eliminated?**
Government (and politicians) say that subsidies are necessary in order to protect industries and the jobs they provide. The benefit to the domestic industry is that subsidies help them to be competitive in the international market. The disadvantage is that the industry may grow dependent on the subsidy and hence may not be as financial strong. International customers benefit by having more product choices at affordable prices available.
    If all price subsidies were eliminated, there would be both winners and losers. The winners would be the competitors in the foreign industry who would not have to worry about competition from U.S. firms. Customers in the international environment and the U.S. industry would both be losers.

2. **As the scope of marketing expands from producers of goods and services to marketing of such intangibles as ideas and people, the concept of pricing must also be expanded. What is the price and the benefit of marketing programs for a political candidate, keeping your cholesterol level down, donating blood to the Red Cross, or wearing a seat belt? Why do marketers sometimes find it more difficult to sell these "products" than to sell a pair of sneakers?**

If we consider price not only as a dollar amount but as a statement of value then the price of intangibles, such as those mentioned above, becomes a question of sacrifice (and the value of that sacrifice to the individual. The price of the political candidate becomes using your one-time vote, the issue of cholesterol becomes changing your life style, diet, eating habits, and health habits, donating blood involves fears, pain, and the use of time, and wearing a seat belt involves changing old habits and seeing the value of a safety device.

It is more difficult to sell intangibles than tangibles because and idea is always more difficult to perceive and experience than a physical good. Value to one may not be value to another—especially in terms of intangibles.

3. **Agricultural price supports are often hotly debated in Congress. Farmers say they can't get along without them. Opponents say that agricultural prices need to be left to the natural pressures of supply and demand. In what ways are price supports good for farmers? For consumers? For our country? What are some ways they hurt us? If you were in Congress, how do you think you would vote?**
Most students probably do not know much about the question of price supports unless they are from an agricultural area of the country. If the instructor would like more data on this question, most macro-economics texts have a section on price supports.

In general the pro arguments for support includes the ideas that price supports keep farmers in business during tough times and ease their debt burden. In addition, we in essence are subsidizing our own food and food for the poor by yielding to price supports. Price supports guarantees that all crops will be produced and supply will be balanced. Further we will not become dependent on foreign agricultural products.

In general, the con argument against supports includes ideas that price supports keep competition down and subsidize inefficiency. Farmers continue to grow or produce products that not really in demand or are high risk. There is no incentive to become more efficient. There is not incentive to compete in foreign markets. In the long-run, consumers pay more, and the poor do not really get the benefit.

4. **Critics of businesses often accuse marketers of taking advantage of consumers by setting prices that are far above the cost of producing the good or service—sometimes 10 or 20 more times the cost. How do you feel about this? What reasons might a manufacturer of luxury products have for setting very high prices? What might a pharmaceutical firm set the prices of its life-saving medications higher than the cost of production?**
Most students will probably think that this practice is wrong. Some may even agree that this is unethical. However, remind students of how a free market economy works and that buyers and sellers are free to set their prices as they see appropriate.

A manufacturer of luxury products might set the price very high based on demand. Consumers may want the product and may be willing to purchase the product at any price.

Pricing strategies used by pharmaceutical firms are the subject of much controversy and criticism. Production costs are not the only expenses which must be covered by the price. Research and development costs are enormous, and only a few products will actually make it to market. Finally, the bureaucracy of HMO's and managed health care has greatly impacted the pricing of pharmaceuticals.

Real People, Real Surfers: Exploring the Web

One way to use this exercise would be to have students complete the exercise prior to the class where you will be discussing NATE. Students answers to these questions could be used as part of your discussion of NATE.

Marketing In Action: Real Choices at Hallmark

Summary: Hallmark Cards, Inc. is the world's largest manufacturer of greeting cards. In 1998 Hallmark's future however, began to look less rosy.

Suggested Answers to Case Questions:

1. **What is the problem facing Hallmark?**
   How to revive sales in the stagnant greeting card industry?

2. **What factors are important in understanding this problem?**
   a. Consumers' perceptions that greeting cards prices were too high.
   b. Slotting fees and the increase of the amount required by retailers for placing cards in stores.
   c. Growing competition from discount retailers who sold Hallmark cards for 39 cents a piece.
   d. Growing popularity of electronic and e-mail greetings.

3. **What alternatives might Hallmark consider?**
   a. A change in the pricing strategy which is supported by a promotion campaign.
   b. Develop a product for electronic and e-mail greetings
   c. Work on developing stronger partnerships with retailers with the hope that slotting fees would be reduced.

4. **What are your recommendations for solving the problem?**
   A combination of both alternatives a and b should be used. A reduction of prices is obviously not enough to help revive stagnant sales. Consumers need to be convinced that Hallmark cards are worth the price and that cards are really a good value.
   The use of electronic and e-mail greeting by consumers ins growing. This form of sending greetings is in the growth stage of the product life cycle and there is still time for Hallmark to take advantage of this trend. Cannibalization of the traditional greeting card market might be a concern for Hallmark. However, the reality is that electronic greeting cards are already being used and appear to be growing in popularity.

5. **What are some ways to implement your recommendations? Hallmark needs to begin by developing a strong promotional campaign which supports their cards. This campaign should be used to persuade consumers that Hallmark cards are worth the price.**
   An Internet site which allows customers to create and send electronic greetings should be developed. Prices for the electronic greeting cards could vary from nothing to less than $1. This site could also be used to persuade consumers to go out and buy paper or traditional cards.

Mini-Project 12-A
Price Elasticity of Demand

Purpose: to better understand elasticity of demand

For this project you (and possibly several of your classmates) will be conducting a study on price elasticity of demand.

1. First, select 4 to 6 products which are frequently purchased by students like yourselves (such as soft drinks, gasoline, hamburgers, bottled water, pizza, etc.)

2. Next, develop a questionnaire which asks respondent how much of each product they typically purchase in a month or a week. (People may find it easier to think of buying a quantity of soft drinks per week but pizzas per month.) Also, ask them how much they usually spend on the items. Finally, you will want to set up a list of different prices from very high to very low and ask respondents to tell you how much they would purchase at each price. For example, a question about pizza might look like this.

How many times a month would you purchase a pizza for each of the prices listed below:

Price of a small pizza	Number of times per month I would purchase
$2.99	_____
$4.99	_____
$6.99	_____
$8.99	_____
$10.99	_____
$12.99	_____
$14.99	_____

3. After you have obtained responses to the questionnaire from a number of fellow students (you will probably want at least 25 students to participate in your study), calculate the demand for each of your products at each of the listed prices and plot the demand curves.

4. Prepare a report which explains your research and the results. Explain why some products have a demand which is more elastic while others show inelastic demand. Present your results to your class.

Mini-Project 12-B
Monetary and non-monetary prices

Purpose: to examine the monetary and nonmonetary costs of products.

To obtain most products, we consumers use dollars or the currency of the country where the product is being sold. When we are marketing people or ideas, the price may not be dollars and cents but still there are non-monetary costs involved. For instance, the politician is not seeking your money but does want your vote. For most products, there are both monetary and non-monetary costs. You can buy a gallon of milk for less money in a large super market than in the local convenience store but you have the added costs of time and effort to obtain the product. The decision to buy a product is made when consumers consider the cost-value relationship, that is, they consider if the value received is worth the cost.

For the products listed on the following page, estimate the monetary and nonmonetary costs that are normally exchanged for each. Then make suggestions for changes in the marketing mix that would allow consumers to perceive an improved cost-value relationship.

Product	Monetary Cost	Nonmonetary Cost	Recommendations
Your room or apartment	_____	_____	_____
	_____	_____	_____
A hair cut	_____	_____	_____
	_____	_____	_____
A hamburger and fries	_____	_____	_____
	_____	_____	_____
Rental of a movie	_____	_____	_____
	_____	_____	_____
Wearing your seat belt	_____	_____	_____
	_____	_____	_____
College education	_____	_____	_____
	_____	_____	_____
Your city's police protection	_____	_____	_____
	_____	_____	_____
A dental check-up	_____	_____	_____
	_____	_____	_____
Repairs on computer	_____	_____	_____
	_____	_____	_____
A pair of athletic shoes	_____	_____	_____
	_____	_____	_____

13

Pricing
Methods

*O*verview In this chapter methods use by companies to develop and manage pricing strategies will be examined. The psychological aspects of pricing will also be studied. Finally, some of the legal and ethical considerations in pricing will be presented.

Craig Lambert, Vice-president and Brand Manager of Courtyard by Marriott is the focus of the Real People, Real Choices segment. Lambert wondered if the traditional top-down pricing approach used in the hotel industry was the best pricing strategy for Courtyard to use.

Objectives

1.   Understand key pricing strategies.

2.   Explain pricing tactics for individual and multiple products.

3.   Describe the psychological aspects of pricing.

4.   Understand some of the legal and ethical considerations in pricing.

Chapter Outline and Suggested Activities

Introduction: Do customers actually like the no-haggle price policies used by some firms? Car companies, like Saturn for example, are promoting a no haggle price policy. What does a no-haggle policy really mean? For what other types of products could such a policy be used?

1. **Pricing Strategies**
   **Refer to Objective 1
   **Use Figure 13.2
   **Use the video Hain Food Group Part 2
   **Use Computer Friendly Stuff Part IV Case
   a. Pricing strategies based on cost
      These strategies are simple to calculate and relatively safe to use because they ensure that the price will cover the cost the company incurs in producing and marketing the product. There are two types of cost based strategies:
      1). *Cost-Plus Pricing: A method of setting prices in which the seller totals all the costs for the product and then adds the desired profit per unit.*
      2). *Price-Floor Pricing: A method for calculating price in which to maintain full plant operating capacity, a portion of a firm's only covers marginal costs of production.*

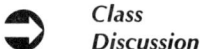 *Class Discussion*   What are some examples of products where pricing strategies bases on cost should be used?

   b. Pricing Strategies Based on Demand
      Demand-Based Pricing: A price-setting method based on estimates of demand at different prices. There are two types of demand based strategies:
      1). *Demand-Backward Pricing: Starts with a customer-pleasing price followed up with cost-management strategies to hold costs to a satisfactory level.*
      2). *Chain-Markup Pricing: A pricing strategy that extends demand-backward pricing from the ultimate consumer all the way back through channel of distribution to the manufacturer.*

   Class Discussion   Select any product or service and have students discuss the various costs which must be included when using either a demand-backward or chain-markup strategy. If you are using the Computer Friendly Stuff (CFS) case you could use CFS as the focus of your discussion.

   c. Pricing Strategies Based on the Competition
      1). Firms may choose to develop pricing strategies based on the competition. This makes sense in terms of costs and demands as it represents the sum of all industry wisdom and experience.
      2). There are basically three options:
         a). Price lower than the competition.
         b). Price higher than the competition.
         c). Price the same as the competition.
      3). In some industries there is a *price leader: the firm that sets price first in an industry; other major firms in the industry follow the leader by staying in line.*

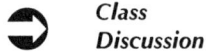 **Class**
Discussion
Usually firms which are in an industry with relatively few producers—an oligopoly, practice price leadership strategies. Consider an industry which might be best characterized as an oligopoly. Examine situations where firms in this industry should price their good lower, higher, or the same as the competition.

d.   Pricing Strategies Based on Customers' Needs
New Era firms look at the wants and needs of customers in developing pricing strategies.
The most common type of customer based strategy is value pricing.
**Use Case 13: Marketing in Action: Real Choices at Southwest Airlines
**Use Spotlight on Real People: Casket Royale
1).   ***Value pricing or every day low pricing (EDLP):** A pricing strategy in which a firm sets prices that provide ultimate value or price/benefit ratio to consumers*
2).   The BAR(Best Available Rate) system developed by Marriott Courtyard is an example of EDLP strategy.

 **Class**
Discussion
Many firms practice value pricing and have some type of EDLP policy or a "we will not be undersold" policy. Do you think EDLP policies are effective—even when the competition uses the same strategy? Ask students for examples of where they have seen pricing strategies based on customers' needs used. Are marketers *really* concerned with customer needs, or is this just a gimmick to increase sales?

Spotlight on Real People: Casket Royale

Summary: Casket Royale is one of the first discount coffin outlets in Canada. Owned by brothers Natale and Joe Roda, the company is taking advantage of laws that allow the deceased to "take his own casket" to a funeral parlor.

Suggested Answers to Discussion Questions:

1.   **What kind of pricing strategy does Casket Royale use?**
Students may differ on their responses to this questions. One answer would be that the firm is basing its price on the competition and is pricing its product lower than the competition; this is a very reasonable response.
        Value-based strategies is also a good response. Value-based strategies begin with considering the customer, then competition, and then the best pricing strategy.

2.   **What other pricing strategies might Casket Royale consider?**
Casket Royale might want to focus on expanding its customer need pricing strategy. Every-day low prices and/or a "we will not be undersold" strategies could be developed and promoted.

---

e.   New Product Pricing
**Use Q2 Marketing Practice: Applying What You've Learned
When a product is new to the market there are no established industry price norms. Below are the three commonly used pricing strategies for new products.
1).   ***Skimming Price:** A very high, premium price that a firm charges for its new, highly desirable, product.*
2).   ***Penetration Pricing:** A pricing strategy in which a new product is introduced at a very low price to encourage more customers to purchase it.*

3). **Trial Pricing:** *Pricing a new product low for a limited period of time in order to lower the risk for a customer.*

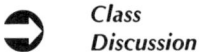

Class Discussion

Ask students to cite example of when each type of new product pricing strategy could best be used.

You might also want to look around your local grocery store or convenience store for examples of trial pricing. Penetration pricing is also often used in products sold at the grocery store. Both penetration and trial pricing encourage consumers to purchase a new product. What happens to sales when the price is raised? Will consumers continue to purchase the product?

2. **Developing Pricing Tactics**
**Refer to Objective 2
** Use video Watson Pharmaceuticals Part 2
**Use Figure 13.3
Pricing tactics are the methods used by companies to set their strategies in motion.

a. Pricing for Individual Products
Two tactics are commonly used
1). Two-part pricing: *For example, a fee to join the local YMCA plus a monthly fee.*
2). Payment pricing: *This strategy involves breaking the price into small payments. For example, "This CD player can be yours for 6 monthly payments of $15.99."*

b. Pricing for Multiple Products
These tactics are used for products which consumers typically buy together
1). **Price Bundling:** *selling two or more goods or services as a single package for one price.*
2). **Captive Pricing:** *A pricing tactic for two items that must be used together; one item is priced very low, and the firm makes its profit on another, high-margin item essential to the operation of the first item.*

c. Geographic Pricing
Geographic pricing is a tactic that establishes how firms handle the cost of shipping products.

Class Discussion

Question 3 in the Marketing Practice: Applying What You've Learned section could be used to discuss the advantages and disadvantages of geographic pricing.

1). **F.O.B. Pricing:** *F.O.B. stands for free on board which means the supplier will pay to have the product loaded onto a truck or some other carrier.* Title passes to the buyer at the F.O.B. location.
a). **F.O.B. origin pricing:** *A pricing tactic in which the cost of transporting the product from the factory to the customer's location is the responsibility of the customer.*
b). **F.O.B. delivered pricing:** *A pricing tactic in which the cost of loading and transporting to the customer is included in the selling price and is paid by the retailer.*
2). **Zone Pricing:** *A pricing tactic in which customers in different geographic zone pay different transportation rates*
3). **Uniform Delivered Pricing:** *A pricing tactic in which a standard shipping charge is added to the price for all customers regardless of the distance from the seller.*

> *Class Discussion*

Assume you are at a department store and are purchasing two identical wedding gifts for two friends who live in two different cities. One friend lives about 30 miles from you and the other lives 300 miles from you. You are having the store ship both presents because you will not be able to attend either wedding. When you see each of your register receipt you realize that the firm uses a uniform delivery pricing tactic and that you have been charged $5 to ship each present. What is your reaction? What do you think is the retailer's rationale for using the pricing tactic?

    d.   Discounting for Members of the Channel

           1).   Trade of Functional Discounts

                 Most price structures are built around a list price: the price the end-customer is expected to pay as determined by the manufacturer. When manufacturers develop pricing tactics for channel intermediaries, they may use a variety of discounting tactics.

                 Trade or Functional Discount: *Discounts off list price of products to members of the channel of distribution who perform various marketing functions.*

           2).   ***Quantity Discounts:*** *A pricing tactic of charging reduced prices for purchases of larger quantities of a product.*

                 a).   ***Cumulative Quantity Discount:*** *Discounts based on the total quantity bought within a specified time period.*

                 b).   ***Non-cumulative Quantity Discount:*** *Discounts based only on the quantity purchased with individual orders.*

           3).   Cash Discounts

> *Class Discussion*

What does 2/10 net 30 mean? What are the advantages of cash discounts for both the seller and the buyer?

           4).   ***Seasonal Discounts:*** *Price reductions offered only during certain times of the year.*

    d.   Pricing with Electronic Commerce

           The Internet has created a wired economy, enabling buyers to compare products and prices and enabling sellers to collect data about customer's buying habits.

> *Class Discussion*

Most consumers view airline reservations as a commodity. The airline industry views a seat on a flight as a perishable commodity. Using the Internet, have students identify the various airline fare alternatives available to a destination of their choice. Some airline carriers offer discounts only if a ticker is purchased over the Internet. Why would a carrier use this type of discounting tactic?

3.   **Psychological Issues In Pricing**
       **Refer to Objective 3
       **Use Marketing Mini-project: Learning by Doing

> *Class Discussion*

Question one in the Marketing Practice: Applying What You've Learned section could be used to discuss psychological issues in pricing.

a. Buyer's Pricing Expectations
Marketers need to understand the pricing expectations of their customers. Marketers should examine the factors which influence consumers' price expectations.

   1). ***Internal Reference Price:*** *A set price or price range in a consumer mind that she refers to in evaluating a product's price.*

➡️ ***Class Discussion***   What are some examples of tactics used by manufacturers to influence consumers perceptions of what a product should cost?

   2). Price-Quality Influences
   Often when consumers lack other product information they will use price as a cue or an indicator of quality.

➡️ ***Class Discussion***   Does it make sense to believe that a product is better quality just because it has a higher price tag? Ask students to comment on their experiences with higher priced and lowered priced versions of the same product. One product category you might want to discuss would be national brands and store brands of breakfast cereal.

b. Psychological Pricing Strategies
   1). Odd even pricing
   2). Price Lining: The practice of setting a limited number of different specific prices, called price points, for items in a product line

➡️ ***Class Discussion***   Why is price lining a good practice?

4. **Legal And Ethical Considerations In Pricing**
**Refer to Objective 4
There are a few manufacturers who are greedy and unscrupulous and thus engage in unfair pricing strategies.

a. Deceptive Pricing Strategies
   Unscrupulous businesses may advertise or promote prices in a deceptive way
   1). ***Bait-and-switch:*** *An illegal marketing practice in which an advertised price special is used as bait to get customers into the store with the intention of switching them to a higher-priced item.*
   2). The Federal Trade Commission (FTC), state lawmakers, and private bodies such as the Better Business Bureau (BBB) have developed pricing guidelines which are used to protect consumers and competitors from unfair pricing.
   **The instructor might want to refer students to the Real People, Real Surfers: Exploring the Web exercise from Chapter 2. This exercise examined the FTC and the BBB.

➡️ ***Class Discussion***   Sellers need to be aware that consumers are sometimes unethical. Instructor's Manual Mini-Project 13-A could be used to examine how unethical behaviors of customers impact pricing.

b. Unfair Sales Act
    1). ***Loss Leader Pricing:*** *The pricing policy of setting prices below cost in order to attract customers into a store.*
    2). Some states view loss leader pricing as wrong and have passed legislation called ***unfair sales act:*** *state laws that prohibit suppliers from selling products below cost and to protect small businesses from large competitors.*

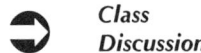

Class Discussion   Find out if loss leader pricing is legal or illegal in your state. Ask students for their views regarding the use of loss leader pricing.

Real People, Bad Choices?

Summary: The Sherman Act prohibits a company from predatory pricing. Three independent pharmacies successfully sued Wal-Mart Stores, Inc. for using predatory pricing tactics.

Suggested Answers to Discussion Questions?

1. **Should a company have a right to charge whatever it would like for its products?**
    Students responses to this question should generate a lot of discussion. Have students consider what would happen to competition and consumer choice if firms were allowed to charge whatever they pleased for products.

2. **Why is predatory pricing difficult to prove?**
    Predatory pricing is difficult to prove because reducing prices to stimulate business is the very essence of competition. Also, it usually involves larger firms with big wallets and good lawyers. Thus, the smaller competitors may be fearful, or financially unable to follow through with a formal law suit.

---

c. Price Discrimination
    **Use the Real People, Bad Choices? segment for discussion
    The Robinson-Patman Act includes regulations against price discrimination.
    1). ***Price Discrimination:*** *The illegal practice of offering the same product to different business customers at different prices and thus lessening competition.*
    2). There are exceptions to the Robinson-Patman Act
        a). The act does not apply to final customers only resellers
        b). Discounts to a large channel customer are legal if based on the large quantity ordered and if the discount is available to all customers who choose to buy that quantity.
d. ***Price Fixing:*** *The collaboration of two or more firms selling prices, usually to keep prices high.*
    There are two forms of price fixing:
    1). Horizontal price fixing
    2). Vertical price fixing

Real People, Real Choices: How It Worked Out at Courtyard by Marriott

Summary: Craig Lambert is Senior Vice President and Brand Manager of Courtyard by Marriott. Courtyard is a division targeted to individual corporate customers who travel during the week and to couples traveling on weekends. Courtyard is positioned to offer value to "road warriors" who want something nicer than an economy hotel but aren't willing to stay at an expensive facility.

In the early 1990's Courtyard was feeling some growing pains due to low occupancy rates caused by extensive over building in the hotel industry. Traditionally, hotels use a "top down" pricing strategy, quoting their highest price first and then reducing the rate if the guest-balks. Courtyard business travelers wanted a fair value for their travel dollar, and Mr. Lambert wondered if the top down approach was the best way to give it to them. He considered three options.

Option 1: Abandon "top down" pricing and instead adopt a "bottom up" strategy where the "best" price is quoted first.
Option 2: Keep the "top down" pricing strategy and wait out the storm.
Option 3: Keep the "top down" pricing strategy, but lower the "fall back" price quote even more to capture a greater share of guests who are price-sensitive.

Mr. Lambert chose option 1 and introduced a new strategy called Best Available Rate (BAR). Courtyard views its pricing policy as a way to let its regular guests know that they can always count on the chain for a good room at a fair price.

*** The Real People, Real Surfers: Exploring the Web could be used with a discussion of this segment.

Marketing Concepts: Testing Your Knowledge

1. **Explain cost-plus pricing and price-floor pricing.**
   Cost-plus pricing is a method of setting prices in which the seller totals all the costs for the product and then adds an amount for overhead and profit.

   Price-floor pricing is a method for calculating price in which, to maintain full plant operating capacity, a portion of a firm's output may be sold at a price that only covers marginal costs of production.

   Explain cost-plus and price-floor pricing.

2. **What are the advantages and disadvantages of pricing strategies based on demand? Explain demand-backward pricing and chain-markup pricing.**
   Demand based pricing is a method for setting price that is based on an estimate of demand at different prices. In order to use any of the pricing strategies based on demand, firms must conduct research to determine how much different target markets are willing to pay.

   One important strength of demand-based pricing strategies is that they generally ensure a firm that it will be able to sell what it produces—that there will be demand for the good or service at the determined price.

   A major disadvantage is the difficulty of accurately estimating demand.

   Demand-backward pricing starts with a customer-pleasing price and works backwards to costs. Firms first determine the price at which they need to sell the product and then work backwards, designing the product in such a way that they can produce it and make a profit at this price.

   Chain-markup pricing is a pricing strategy that extends demand-backward pricing from the ultimate consumer all the way back through channel of distribution to the manufacturer.

3. **Explain how a price leadership strategy works and how it helps all of the firms in an oligopolistic industry. Explain parity and limit pricing strategies.**
   Price leader strategy describes the firm that sets price first in an industry; other major firms in the industry follow the leader by setting similar prices.

   Price leadership is usually found in an oligopoly where it is in the best interests of all firms to avoid price competition. Price leadership strategies are popular because they provide an acceptable way for firms to agree on prices without ever talking with each other (thus avoiding the image of price fixing).

4. **What is every day low pricing?**
   Every day low pricing (*EDLP*) is also called value pricing characterizes a pricing strategy in which a firms sets prices that provide ultimate value or price/benefit ratio to customers.

   In practice, when EDLP strategies are used, products are perceived as offering strong benefits compared to similar products in their price range. Marketers hope that increasing what consumers get for their money will make them see the price as very reasonable and encourage them to remain loyal to that brand, rather than snapping up whatever happens to be on sale this week.

5. **For new products, when is skimming pricing more appropriate and when is penetration pricing the best strategy? When would trial pricing be an effective pricing strategy?**
   Rules for using a skimming price (high initial price) include:
   a. The product is highly desirable.
   b. It offers unique customer benefits.
   c. Demand in price-inelastic.
   d. Little chance that competitors will enter the market during the introductory stage of the product life cycle.
   e. Make sure that the market has several levels or customer segments that each have their own price sensitivity level.

Rules for using a penetration price (low initial price) include:
a.   Low prices encourage customers to try the product initially.
b.   Demand is increased in the introductory stages of the product life cycle.
c.   Low price tends to discourage competition and makes it difficult to be undercut in price.
d.   Demand should be elastic or price sensitive.

6.   **Explain how marketers may use two-part pricing, payment pricing, price bundling and captive pricing tactics.**
In *two-part pricing* two separate types of payments are required to purchase the product. An example is a golf club which charges yearly or monthly fees—plus fees for each round of golf.

    Payment pricing seeks to make the consumer think the price is "double" an example would by 3 payments of $39.99 each.

    Many firms sell several products together as a package. *Price bundling* is selling two or more goods or services as a single package for one price (a PC typically comes with a monitor, keyboard, and software). Price bundling usually involves a price savings for the consumer and reduces the number of buying decisions.

    Captive pricing is a pricing tactic for two items that must be used together; one item is priced very low, and the firm make its profit on another, high-margin item that is essential to the operation of the first item (an example would be popcorn in a movie theater).

7.   **What are the advantages and disadvantages of F.O.B. origin pricing, F.O.B delivered pricing, uniform delivered pricing, and freight-absorption pricing?**
F.O.B. origin pricing stands for *free on board*, which means the supplier will only have to pay to have the product loaded on board a carrier. Therefore the receiver will pay the majority of the freight cost. The method is simple and reduces the manufacturer's risk. The disadvantage is the higher cost and risk that has to be bore by the ultimate receiver of the goods.

    F.O.B. delivered pricing is a pricing tactic in which the cost of loading and transporting to the customer is included in the selling price and will be paid by the manufacturer. For example, a furniture company might say, "We offer 'free delivery' on all in stock purchases".

    Uniform delivered pricing averages shipping costs and spreads these costs among all receivers. This has all the advantages and disadvantages of averaging. This method is usually acceptable only when shipping costs are small.

    Freight-absorption pricing means that the seller absorbs all the total cost of transportation. Obviously, this is a benefit to the buyer. This method is usually used for high-ticket items. The method is also used to encourage business.

8.   **Why does it make sense for marketers to use trade or functional discounts, quantity discounts, cash discounts, and seasonal discounts in pricing to members of the channel?**
A list price is what is charged to the consumer. However, it is common practice to discount to members of the distribution channel on a temporary basis. Discounts should not be simply a means of price competition. Rather, most discounts to members of the channel are designed to meet a specific goal of the manufacturer. For example, with quantity discounts encourage larger purchases, cash discounts encourage prompt payments and speed cash flow, and seasonal discounts balance seasonal demand.

9.   **Explain these psychological aspects of pricing: price-quality inferences; odd-even pricing; internal reference pricing; the practice of price lining.**
A *price-quality inferences* means that consumers use price as a cue for quality.

    Odd-even pricing means that consumers respond to odd prices differently that to even prices. Odd pricing is now the usual practice and even pricing is looked as being usual by the consumer.

    Internal reference pricing means that one product might be displayed next to another (each has a different price) so that the consumer will assume that both have the same qualities and characteristics but just different prices (consumers assume the price differences, unless larger, are not significant).

    Price lining (see Figure 12.6 for additional information) is the practice of setting a limited number of different specific prices, called price points, for items in a product line.

10. **Explain these unethical or illegal pricing practices: bait and switch; loss leader pricing; predatory pricing; price discrimination; price fixing.**

   Bait-and-switch pricing is an illegal marketing practice in which an advertised price special is used as bait to get customers into the store with the intention of switching them to a higher-priced item.

   Loss leader pricing is when a firm sells a product at cost in order to attract customers.

   Predatory pricing is low pricing policies designed to drive competitors out of business.

   Price discrimination is the illegal practice of offering the same product to different business customers at different prices and thus lessening competition.

   Price fixing is the collaboration of two or more firms in setting prices, usually to keep prices high.

Marketing Concepts: Discussing Choices and Issues

1. **Many very successful retailers use a loss-leader pricing strategy, in which they advertise an item at a price below their cost and sell the item at the at price to get customers into their store. They feel that these customers will continue to shop with their company and that they will make a profit in the long run. Do you consider this an unethical practice? Who benefits and who is hurt by such practices? Do you think practice should be made illegal as some states have done?**

   Students will probably vary on their views regarding loss leader pricing. Some students may believe that the practice is illegal, while others may think that loss leader pricing is just part of the overall pricing strategy. The seller who is using loss leader strategy probably gains the most. However, small competitors who cannot afford to sell their products this low are probably the losers.

   Again students will vary on whether or not they think loss leader pricing should be made illegal. Ask students to explain why they think loss leader pricing should be made illegal.

2. **With a price leadership strategy, firms are able to avoid price competition and yet not be guilty of illegal collusion—getting together to set prices. Although it is legal, is a price leadership strategy ethical? How does price leadership strategy hurt, and how does it help, the industry? What benefits does it provide, and what problems does it pose, for customers?**

   Views on the legality of price leadership strategies probably depend upon who you ask. Firms who use price leadership probably view the strategy as part of their overall strategic plan. For these firms, it is ethical. Price leadership does hurt the industry by shutting out firms which cannot match the price. Price leadership does however help to stabilize prices in the industry.

   Customers can benefit from price leadership. When prices are the same between competitors firms are forced to differentiate their offerings on something other than price, like service. If the price set is high, customers will be the losers because there will be no lower price competitors from which to choose.

3. **Every day low pricing strategies have met with limited success. What do you think are the advantages and disadvantages of EDLP? Are some products more suited to EDLP than others? Why have customers not been more responsive to EDLP? What do you think will be the future of EDLP?**

   Value pricing is supposed to be based on what the consumer wants. However, the wants may be perceptual in nature. Marketers using this strategy have to "untrain" the consumer to always be looking for specials or ask distributors to reduce their reliance on using specials as a way to attract consumers.

   Obviously, something is good about the strategy because Proctor and Gamble have switched to it. Using this strategy, the company is stressing value instead of coupons. Consistency in pricing is the key according to those that use the strategy.

   Time has shown that not all product categories are as easy to modify as others. Laundry detergents have not done well with EDLP but liquid laundry detergents have. The disposable diaper market is still being researched. Most manufacturers would really like to get rid of costly coupons and "switcher" mentality.

4. **Two-part pricing, payment pricing, and pricing by priority are pricing tactics that are designed to make price more palatable to customers and to better meet their needs. But do these policies always benefit customers? What are the advantages and disadvantages of these pricing approaches for the average customer? For business customers?**

In two-part pricing, there are two separate parts to the price of the product (such as joining a health club and then having to pay for monthly dues). In payment pricing, the price of the product is spread over several less threatening payments (such as a camera that costs $200 being presented as a series of $25 payments). In pricing by priority, the seller sets prices for a first come first serve basis but may reduce prices later (such as with airline seating).

In many instances, consumers do not understand these pricing policies. However, in our use now and pay later society, deferment seems to be popular and prestigious. The disadvantages of the methods are that they obligate the customer to long-term payments and obligations that affect their monthly cash flow. The same could be said to be true for business customers. Most business customers do not prefer deferment because of the cash flow penalties that many times accompany the policies. Small companies that have difficulty getting credit sometimes use the above methods.

5. **Technology is said to be creating a pricing revolution. How is electronic commerce changing pricing strategies? In what ways are such changes good for consumers? In what ways are the changes good for sellers?**

Electronic commerce is making it possible for buyers and sellers to interact around the globe to connect. The Internet has created a wired economy, enabling buyers to compare products and prices and enabling sellers to collect data about customer's buying habits.

The good news for customers is increased access to a variety of sellers and a quick way to compare products and prices. Sellers also benefit by being able to quickly monitor competitors and make necessary changes in their pricing strategies. Another benefit to sellers is the ability to trace and record information about customers.

6. **Retailers sometimes display two products that are similar but that have different prices next to each other, hoping for an assimilation effect or for a contrast effect. Give some example of products that you have noticed displayed in this manner. What factors do think make it likely that one effect versus the other will occur? Do such practices help or hurt the consumer.**

Store brands are most often placed next to national brands hoping for an assimilation effect. Food products and health and beauty products, like shampoo and pain relievers, will probably be mentioned by students. Consumers are often swayed to purchase the lower priced product if the product package looks similar and if they can see no visible difference between the two products. When there is little difference between products consumers actually benefit from these products.

Real People, Real Surfers: Exploring the Web

This exercise provides students an insight into the overall marketing strategy of Marriott. Students will learn about the different hotels (brands) operated by Marriott, the market segments targeted for each brand, and the pricing strategies used by each brand.

Marketing In Action: Real Choices At Southwest Airlines

Summary: Southwest Airlines was the first airline to implement EDLP fares; and so far it has been the most successful. A number of airlines are becoming EDLP carriers, but Southwest was consistently profitable between 1990 and 1994. Southwest would like to increase its number of flights in the hope of becoming the first national low-fare carrier.

Suggested Answers to Case Questions:

1. **What is the problem facing Southwest Airlines?**
    Several problems may be cited. The most general and probably the most strategic in nature is how can Southwest airlines adapt its current strategies (EDLP and low costs) to their expansion objectives (become a true national carrier). A second problem that some may choose to address is that of what to do about increasing copycat competition. Either of the problems make for good discussion and somewhat address the same issues in the case.

2. **What factors are important in understanding this problem?**
    The following factors are important considerations:
    a.   Southwest's history in pricing, service, strategy, cost control, and expansion.
    b.   Southwest's reputation as a cost leader and the factors that contributed to cost reduction and control.
    c.   Old competitors that have begun to use EDLP.
    d.   New competitors that have begun to use EDLP.
    e.   Deregulation of the airline industry.
    f.   Southwest's future objectives.
    g.   The company's attitude change.
    h.   The effect of growth on the company and its management.

3. **What alternatives might Southwest consider?**
    The following are a series of alternatives that might stimulate discussion:
    a.   Do nothing—status quo—if it ain't broke, don't fix it.
    b.   Begin to seek other airlines to purchase.
    c.   Look for a joint venture partner.
    d.   Look for overseas routes.
    e.   Expand nationally.
    f.   Revise EDLP.
    g.   Reduce prices in targeted competitive areas.

4. **What are your recommendations for solving the problem?**
    The students should be creative with their recommendations dependent on which problem that they have stated. Expansion is definitely in the company's plans so the question becomes how to do that efficiently. Continuation of existing policy is advised. Cost containment is essential. A joint partner is an interesting idea that might allow for international expansion but would not do much domestically. EDLP seems to be a strategy that must be maintained by Southwest Airlines as they approach the 21st century.

5. **What are some ways to implement your recommendations?**
    In this case implementation becomes a question of how fast management wishes to move. Southwest has grown slowly but forcefully in the past and that seems to be the direction for the future. Some of their problems have been altered by changing current events (Valujet's removal from the market in 1996 because of air safety problems) and national competitors returning to discounting instead of maintaining EDLP. The company must carefully observe routes that are profitable and in high demand but are not being served well by existing competitors. The company must also secure a line of supply for its aging air fleet. Creative marketing will probably serve the company well (as it has in the past).

Mini-Project 13-A
Examining "Caveat Venditor"

Purpose: to aid in your understanding of the how retailers develop pricing strategies and how the problems faced by retailer due to unethical behavior of customers impact pricing.

The caveat venditor end of the Marketing Ethics Continuum shows that sellers must beware of unethical consumers. We all know that the cost of the products we buy in many stores is increased because of the losses the stores experience from shoplifting. But there are other types of unethical consumer behavior.

1. First, with a group of your classmates, visit a local retailer and discuss with them how the prices for products are established in their organization. Discuss the benefits to the store of this pricing strategy.

2. Also discuss with them the problems of unethical behavior—both shoplifting and other types of unethical consumer and employee behavior. Find out what the cost is to the store and how much that adds to the store's pricing of its products. Ask what, if anything, the store does to limit such losses.

3. Based on your research, develop a report which outlines
    a. The pricing strategies of the retailer
    b. The unethical behavior(s) you have learned about
    c. The perspective of the retailer
    d. Several original recommendations for improving the problem

4. Present your findings and your recommendations to your class.

Mini-Project 13-B
Market Basket Study

Purpose: to better understand different pricing strategies of food retailers.

In the space below, prepare a list of food items which a typical family might buy each week at the grocery store. Then visit three different grocery stores and record the price of each item at each of the stores. (Note: it might be a good idea to let the store manager know what you are doing and that it is for a class project. This might also be an opportunity to discuss how prices are established for that store.)

Also make note describing the atmosphere, design, customers, etc. in each store.

Finally compare the total prices of the market baskets for the three stores and the other information you have recorded about each store. Based on this information, what do you feel are the types of pricing objectives each store has. Does their primary objective appear to be total sales, customer satisfaction, or something else?

Item	Price Store #1	Price Store #2	Price Store #3

Instructor's Resource Manual with Video Guide t/a Marketing: Real People, Real Choices 2/e

Item	Price Store #1	Price Store #2	Price Store #3
Total			

Describe Store #1 _____

_____

_____

Describe Store #2 _____

_____

_____

Describe Store #3 _____

_____

_____

Summary and Conclusions _____

_____

_____

_____

14

Channel Management and Physical Distribution: Delivering the Product

*O*verview In this chapter students will learn about the science and art of distributing goods and services. Distribution channels and distribution strategies will be examined. The physical distribution process of moving finished goods from one point to another—and legal and ethical issues in distribution will also be explored.

The focus of the Real People, Real Choices segment is First Union National Bank. Banking today is not just about stuffy executives and elegantly decorated bank branches. Today the banking industry is quickly changing and the Internet is one of the distribution vehicles involved in the change of delivering goods and services to customers.

Objectives

1. Explain what a distribution channel is and what function distribution channels perform.

2. Describe some of the types of wholesaling intermediaries found in distribution channels.

3. Discuss the steps in planning distribution channels.

4. Describe the activities that are important in the physical distribution of goods.

Chapter Outline and Suggested Activities

Introduction: This opening activity is designed to be fun, but at the same time it can be used to demonstrate many of the aspects involved in distribution planning. Any set of objects you have handy will work for this activity. A can of tennis balls or a large bag of candy work well in this exercise.

Take your objects to class and hand them to student #1. Create your own scenario regarding the firm which is trying to distribute this product and this individual's role in the firm. Ask student #1 to use the most direct path possible for transporting the product to student #2. Tell the student that he cannot use any other student(s) to assist them. Ideally student #2 should be sitting two or three sets away. Watch out—students will often throw the object which they have, especially the tennis balls! If the student does not throw the object they will probably get up from their seat and actually hand the object to student #2.

Now that student #2 has the object, tell them that Joe (i.e., student #3) wants to purchase the object. Instruct student #2 to deliver the object to Joe. Instruct student #2 that they cannot get out of their seat to make this delivery. Ideally, Joe should be sitting three or four seats away. Hopefully, student #2 will somehow involve her classmates in delivering the product to Joe.

Now that Joe has the object, ask him to try and sell the object to a classmate. As part of the selling process, he learns that the buyer only wants to purchase a few of the items—not the whole bag of candy or a can of tennis balls. What should Joe do?

Discussion: Refer students to Figure 14.1 and Table 14.1. Discuss the definition of a channel of distribution. Explain what it means for a channel to be direct and indirect. Discuss some of the functions of channel members, for example, breaking bulk.

1. **The Importance of Distribution: You Can't Sell What Isn't There!**
    ** Refer to Objective 1
    ** Use Marketing Mini-Project: Learning By Doing
    ** Use Video DHL
    ** Use Figure 14.1
    a.   What is a Channel of Distribution?
        1).   A ***Channel of Distribution:*** *is the series of firms and individuals that facilitate the movement of a product from the producer to the final customer.*
        2).   Channels can either be direct or indirect. The purest form of a direct channel is when you buy produce from Farmer Joe at a roadside stand or at a farmers market. Indirect channels involve the use of one or more channel intermediaries.
        Channel Intermediaries: *are the firms or individuals such as wholesalers, agents, brokers, or retailers who help move a product from the producer to the consumer, or the business user.*
    b.   Functions of Distribution Channels
    Distribution channels perform many different functions. Some of the functions performed by channel members include:
        1).   Time, place and ownership utility for customers.
        2).   Increasing the efficiency of the flow of goods from producer to consumer.
        There are two ways which are used to create efficiencies by reducing the number of transactions necessary for goods to flow from many different manufacturers to a large number of customers.
            a).   ***Breaking Bulk:*** *Dividing larger quantities of goods into smaller lots in order to meet the needs of buyers.*
            b).   ***Creating Assortments:*** *Providing a variety of products in one location to meet the needs of buyers.*
        3).   Intermediaries also perform ***facilitating functions:*** *function of channel intermediaries that make the purchase process easier for customers and/or manufacturers. For example, credit to buyers.*

2.   **The Composition And Structure Of Channels**
         ** Refer to Objective 2
         ** Use Table 14.1
         a.   Types of Wholesaling Intermediaries
                  Wholesaling Intermediaries: *are firms that handle the flow of products from the manufacturer to the retailer or the business user.* Table 14.1 summarizes the important characteristics of each type.
         b.   Types of Distribution Channels
                  ** Use Figure 14.2
                  In developing place or distribution strategies marketers must first consider ***channel levels:*** *the number of distinct intermediaries that populate a channel of distribution.* Figure 14.2 summarizes the different structures a distribution channel can take. Different channels exist for both consumer and business-to-business markets.
                  1).   Consumer Channels. The simplest form of a consumer channel is a direct channel. Indirect channels are sometimes necessary in order to move the product from the manufacturer to the consumer.

➡ *Class*   What are the advantages to the consumer when a direct channel of distribution is
    Discussion   used? What are the advantages to the manufacturer when a direct channel of
                   distribution is used? What are the benefits to both the manufacturer and the
                   consumer when an indirect channel is used?

                  2).   Business-to Business Channels
                           ** Use Figure 14.2
                           These channels parallel consumer channels in that they may be direct or indirect. The simplest direct channel occurs when an industrial distributor buys products from a manufacturer and sells them to business customers.

➡ *Class*   Why are direct channels of distribution are more common to business-to business
    Discussion   markets than to consumer markets? You might also want to consider the various
                   channels of distribution which might be used by Peapod in the purchasing and
                   delivering of it's products to their customers. (Refer to Marketing in Action: Real
                   Choices at Peapod).

                  3).   Distribution Channels for Services. In most cases services travel directly from the producer to the consumer. Some services require an intermediary, called an agent. The agent is a facilitator and helps the parties to complete the transaction.

➡ *Class*   A travel agent is an example of an agent who serves as a facilitator and helps
    Discussion   parties to complete their transactions. What services are typically offered by travel
                   agents? What benefits do these services provide to buyers and sellers?

                  4).   Dual Distribution Systems
                           Manufacturers, dealers, wholesalers, retailers, and consumers may actually interact with more than one type of channel. This is referred to as a dual or multiple distribution system.

➡ *Class*   Explain how a manufacturer of packaged foods (like Kellogg, for example) might
    Discussion   use a dual distribution system.

c.   Environmental Influences on Distribution Planning

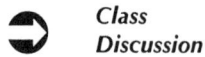

Class Discussion
Assume that you have just developed a new brand of premium ice cream. What are some examples of internal and external environmental factors that you should consider in planning the distribution of product?

3.   **Planning A Channel Strategy**
         ** Refer to Objective 3
         ** Use Figure 14.3
         a.   Channel Objectives
             Developing channel objectives is the first step in planning a channel strategy.

Class Discussion
The overall objective of any distribution planning is to make a firm's product available when, where, and in the quantities customers want and need at a minimum cost. How do channel objectives support the overall marketing goals of the firm?

         If you are using the Computer Friendly Stuff (CFS) case series you might want to refer to the Marketing Plan for CFS (Appendix A) and discuss the channels used by CFS and how these channels support the overall marketing goals of CFS.

         b.   Evaluating the Environment
             ** Use Q #3 Marketing Practice: Applying What You've Learned
             The internal and the external environment (see Chapter 3) must be considered when planning a distribution system. Some issues to consider include:
             1).   The ability of the manufacturer to influence channels members.
             2).   How the competition gets its product to market
             3).   The ability of the customer to access channels
             4).   The type of product
         c.   Choosing A Distribution System
             Planning distribution strategies means that at least three decisions must be made
             1).   Conventional, Vertical, and Horizontal Marketing Systems
                 a).   *Conventional Marketing System: A multiple-level distribution channel in which channel members work independently of one another.*
                 b).   *Vertical Marketing System (VMS): A channel of distribution in which there is cooperation among members at the manufacturing, wholesaling, and retailing levels. There are three types of vertical marketing systems: administered, corporate, and contractual.*
                 c).   *Horizontal Marketing System: An arrangement within a channel of distribution which two or more firms at the same channel level work together for a common purpose.*

Class Discussion
What are the advantages to manufacturers who use a vertical marketing system?

             2).   Intensive, Exclusive, and Selective Distribution
                 ** Use the Instructor's Manual Mini-Project 14-B
                 ** Use Q #1 Marketing Practice: Applying What You've Learned
                 ** Use Table 14.3

The level of market penetration sought is also an important part of distribution planning. There are three basic choices:

a).   *Intensive Distribution: Selling a product through all suitable wholesalers who are willing to stock and sell the product.*

b).   *Exclusive Distribution: Selling a product only through a single outlet in a particular region.*

c).   *Selective Distribution: Distribution using fewer outlets than in intensive distribution but more than in exclusive.*

 ***Class Discussion***   From the Marketing Plan for Computer Friendly Stuff (CFS) (Appendix A) we see that CFS chose to use a selective distribution strategy. Discuss the advantages of this strategy. In the future, should CFS consider an intensive or an exclusive strategy?

d.   Developing Distribution Tactics
      1).   Selecting Channel Partners

Class Discussion   If you are using the Computer Friendly Stuff (CFS) case series you might want to discuss this firm and the questions that they might ask in evaluating intermediaries. If you are not using the CFS series you might want to discuss the same topic but using any firm of your choice.

Real People, Bad Choices?

Summary: To avoid costly setback marketers must understand the basic legal constraints of channel arrangements. Some of the most common offenders are:

- Exclusive dealing contracts
- Exclusive territories
- Tying contracts

Suggested Answers to Discussion Questions:

1. **Why do you think these practices spell bad business and for whom?**
   All three of the situations restrict competition and can ultimately result in a loss of product availability to consumers.

2. **Do you think that these practices are wrong?**
   Students will probably differ in their opinions for this question. Try to help students realize that when a few firms begin to practice "bad business", others suffer.

---

      2).   Managing the Channel of Distribution
            All channels have a channel leader. The ***channel leader*** *is a firm at one level of distribution which takes a leadership role, establishing operating norms and processes that reduce channel conflicts, reduce costs, and enhance delivered customer value.* This power comes from different sources:
            a).   Economic power
            b).   Legitimate power
            c).   Reward or coercive power

e.　Distribution Channels and the Marketing Mix
** Use Real People, Real Surfers: Exploring the Web
Distribution decisions can sometimes give a product a distinct position in its market.

Class Discussion

Discuss with student's examples of products for which exclusive, intensive, and selective distribution channels are used. How does the selection and usage of these channels impact the position of the product in the marketplace. For example, would Godiva chocolates still perceived as a prestige product if it were available in the check-out lane at Wal-Mart?

4.　**Physical Distribution**
** Refer to Objective 4
a.　What is Physical Distribution?
Physical Distribution: The activities used to move finished goods from manufacturers to final consumers including order processing warehousing. Materials handling, transportation, and inventory control.
　1).　**Order Processing:** The activities that occur between the time an order comes into the organization and the time a product goes out the door.
　2).　**Warehousing:** *Storing goods in anticipation of sale or transfer to another member of the channel of distribution.*
　3).　**Materials Handling:** *The moving of products into, within, and out of warehouses.*
　4).　Transportation: Table 14.4 shows the various modes of transportation and summarizes the pros and cons of each mode.
　5).　**Inventory Control:** *Activities to insure that goods are always available to meet customers' demands—no more and no less.*

Class Discussion

Ask students to select the best mode of transportation for the following products:

- Ice Cream
- Lumber
- Apparel
- Fine china from England which is being sent to a US retail customer
- Buying tickets for a Broadway play

Spotlight on Real People: McAfee Associates

Summary: William Larson is the 40 year old CEO of McAfee Associates. McAfee licenses its network security and management software systems that detect viruses and facilitate backup storage for two-year periods. Unlike other companies that sell major upgrades every 18 months or so, McAfee send out mini-upgrades to licenses over the Internet—for free.

Suggested Answers to Discussion Questions

1. **What distribution channel does McAfee use?**
    McAfee uses a direct channel of distribution. The Internet provides the firm with direct access to their customers.

2. **What other channels are available to the firm?**
    Almost any of the other channel options are available to the firm. However, the firm's current strategy has been very successful and the firm has a strategic advantage in terms of price and delivery of products. The firm might consider some form of a dual distribution strategy where they maintain the Internet as their primary form of distribution and add either distributors or retailers in on to reach segments of the target market which they are not currently serving.

3. **How does McAfee's distribution strategy differ from other software manufacturers?**
    The competition does not use the Internet.

Real People, Real Choices: How It Worked Out At First Union

Summary: Cecelia Gardner is Senior Vice President and Project Manager for Consumer Re-engineering at First Union Corporation. First Union is the sixth largest bank in the U.S.A. Changes in consumers' lifestyles and technological advances are transforming the way banks deliver their services. In 1994 the bank hired Arthur Anderson Consultants to tell the bank how to re-engineer the retail bank so that customers could obtain fast, easy, error-free banking services where, when and how they want it. The team identified three segments. Ms. Gardner's team was challenged with creating the bank that would attract each of the three segments.

Option 1: Retail Center: A free-standing facility offering in-person sales and service.
Option 2: Telephone Bank: A center the offers full-service banking by phone.
Option 3: Mobile Sales Force: An external sales force catering to customers who want business conducted at the place of their choice.
Option 4: Home Banking: Rely to a great degree on multi-functional automatic teller machines and home PCs that let customers do their banking over the Internet.

In May 1997, First Union opened its first Future Bank in Atlanta to offer its customers better delivery choices, including the use of interactive video, mobile sales forces, remote/PC banking, and customer service centers as alternatives to visiting the branch. The bank also opened seven First Union Direct centers, where employees can access a profile of the customer in order to relate to his needs directly.

Marketing Concepts: Testing Your Knowledge

1. **What is a channel of distribution? What are channel intermediaries?**
    A channel of distribution is the series of firms or individuals that facilitate the movement of a product from the producer tot he final customer. Channel intermediaries are the firms or individuals such as wholesalers, agents, brokers, or retailers who help move a product from the producer to the consumer or business user.

2. **Explain the functions of a channel of distribution?**
    Certain functions help the consumer with their purchase decision. Channels provide time, place, and ownership utility for consumers.
    Channel members handle the physical distribution function for products, including the activities of breaking and accumulation of bulk, creating assortments, reducing the number of transactions necessary for the flow of goods, transportation, and storage. Intermediaries in channels of distribution also perform a variety of both communications and facilitating functions.

3. **List and explain the types of independent and manufacturer-owned intermediaries.**
    For more detailed information see Table 14.1 in the text.
    Independent intermediaries:
    Merchant wholesalers—buy goods (take title) from producers and sell to organizational customers. May be general or limited line wholesalers.
    Specific types of merchant wholesalers include:
    a. *Rack jobbers*—full function; limited line; and, call on retailers to provide display units and check on inventory levels.
    b. *Cash-and-carry wholesalers*—limited function; limited line; small retailers purchase at this wholesaler's location.
    c. *Drop shippers*—limited function; take orders from and bill retailers; products are drop-shipped from manufacturer; take title to product but do not have physical possession of it.
    d. *Mail-order wholesalers*—limited functions; sell through catalogs, telephone or mail order.
    e. *Truck jobbers*—limited function; sell perishable food and tobacco items.
    f. *Merchandise agents or brokers*—provide services in exchange for commissions but never take title of the product.
    Manufacturer-owned:
    Sales branches—wholesaler-type facilities owned and run by a manufacturer.
    Sales offices—like sales branches, are typically located in strategic geographic areas in order to be closer to customers.
    Manufacturers' showrooms—producer-owned facilities that customers visit to see the firm's products attractively displayed.

4. **What is a direct channel? An indirect channel?**
    A *direct channel* is a channel of distribution in which there are no intermediaries or middle levels. See Figure 14.2 for more information and detail.
    An *indirect channel* is the distribution of goods in which manufacturers reach end users through intermediaries—wholesalers, dealers, distributors, agents and/or retailers. See Figure 14.2 for more information and detail.

5. **Explain the steps in distribution planning?**
    Because of the intangibility of services, there is no need to be concerned and storage, transportation, and the other functions of physical distribution. Thus channels for the distribution of services tend to be relatively straightforward. In most cases, the flow of the service is directly from the producer to the consumer or to the business customer.

In some instances (like the travel business), an agent is involved. This agent helps to bring the producer and customer together and many times serves as a service entity (such as in insurance). This agent many times personalizes the service for the customer.

6. **What are conventional, vertical and horizontal marketing systems?**

A *conventional marketing system* is a multiple-level distribution channel in which members work and independently of one another.

Vertical marketing system (*VMS*)—is a channel of distribution in which there is cooperation among members at the manufacturing, wholesaling, and retailing levels.

Horizontal marketing system—an arrangement within a channel of distribution in which two or more firms at one channel level work together for a common purpose.

7. **Explain intensive, exclusive, and selective forms of distribution?**

Intensive Distribution: Selling a product through all suitable wholesalers who are willing to stock and sell the product. An example would be Coke. Coke is available in many locations from grocery stores to vending machines.

Exclusive Distribution: Selling a product only through a single outlet in a particular region. An example would be a specialty product/brand which is available at only one retailer in a particular region. For example, some brands of fine jewelry use exclusive distribution.

Selective Distribution: Distribution using fewer outlets than in intensive distribution but more than in exclusive. Many of the cosmetics available in department stores, for example Estee Lauder, use selective channels of distribution. Retailers which desire to stock Estee Lauder must meet specific requirements established by the manufacturer.

8. **What is a channel leader?**

A *channel leader* is a firm at one level of distribution which takes a leadership role, establishing operating norms and processes that reduce channel conflicts, reduce costs, and enhance delivered customer value. The power comes from different sources:

- Economic power
- Legitimate power
- Reward or coercive power

9. **What activities are involved in physical distribution?**

Physical distribution activities include:
a. Order processing—transferring title and handling paperwork related to distribution.
b. Warehousing—storing goods before they reach final customers.
c. Materials handling –moving products into, within, and out of warehouses.
d. Transportation—physically moving the goods from one location to another.
e. Inventory control—determining what amounts and types of goods should be kept on hand prior to sale.

10. **What are the advantages and disadvantages of shipping by rail? By air? By ship? By truck?**

See Table 14.4 for a detailed description of transportation alternatives.

	Advantages	Disadvantages
Rail	Accessibility, capability	Traceability
Air	Dependability, speed of delivery, traceability	Cost, accessibility
Ship	Cost	Dependability, speed of delivery, accessibility, traceability
Truck	Dependability, low cost for short hauls, speed of delivery, accessibility, capability, traceability	High cost for long hauls

Marketing Concepts: Discussing Choices and Issues

1. **You have probably heard someone say, "The reason products cost so much is because of all the intermediaries." Do intermediaries increase the cost of products? Would consumers be better off or worse without intermediaries?**

    An old saying is that "you can replace a middleman, but you can't replace their function." Consumer expectations (the desire for massive product choice, speed of delivery, and services that accompany the products) contribute to the number and (therefore) cost of middlemen. The consumer does have alternatives available. See the choices available on Figure 14.2. However, history has shown that the consumer is better off with middlemen. The reasoning is that each level of distribution (manufacturer, wholesaler, retailer, and customer) is better off specializing in what they can do best (their functions). The result or value of replacing a middleman must be weighted against the cost (both in time and money) of assuming that middleman's function in the distribution channel.

2. **Many entrepreneurs choose to start a franchise business rather than "go it alone." Do you think franchises offer the typical person good opportunities? What are some positive and negative aspects of purchasing a franchise?**

    The easy answer to the question is that franchising must be good because so many do it. The more sophisticated answer is that franchising is popular because the local owner can specialize in customer interaction and turn over other functional responsibilities to other members of the franchise network (i.e., product shipment and acquisition, promotion, national image, et cetera).

    Buying a franchise rather than starting from scratch often confers certain advantages:
    a. Using the franchise name give the merchant advertising clout, purchasing power, and name recognition.
    b. The franchise provides services for the operator such as employee training, giving access to lower prices for needed materials, and helping pick a location with visibility.

    There is a cost, however. Disadvantages include:
    a. The owner must pay a percentage of revenue for the right to be a franchise member.
    b. The business format of the franchise must be followed to the letter.
    c. If the franchise gets into difficulty, the individual operators are affected.

3. **As colleges and universities are looking for better ways to satisfy their customers, an area of increasing interest is the distribution of their product—education. Describe the characteristics of your school's channel(s) of distribution. What types of innovative distribution might make sense for your school to try?**

    To answer this question, students should be encouraged to think about how the educational product is delivered to themselves. They might remember that the educational product might come through classroom lecture, television, continuing education, extended or distance learning, video or audio tape, or foreign travel.

    New forms that might be explored are CD-ROM, surface transportation (such as on a train), the Internet, Web sites, teleconferencing, or other recorded means. The students should be encouraged to look at the factors (such as cost, competition, technology, mission identification, et cetera) that would impact the choice of these forms.

Real People, Real Surfers: Exploring the Web

Students who are familiar with the banking industry and/or those who desire to work in the banking industry should enjoy this exercise. On-line banking is predicted to represent the future of the banking students. Ask students who currently use on-line banking services to comment on their experiences with on-line banking.

Marketing in Action: Real Choices at Peapod

Summary: Peapod, founded by brothers Andrew and Thomas Parkinsar was the country's first on-line grocery business. Peapod provides a virtual supermarket by allowing shoppers to place their orders from home and have them conveniently delivered without ever leaving the house.

Peapod seemed like a great idea, but in January 1997, the jury was still out on whether the company would succeed. To become profitable, it seemed that Peapod would have to make changes in its marketing strategy—raise its prices even more, increase its volume to spread fixed costs over a larger number of customers, or perhaps cut the level of service it provided to customers.

Suggested Answers to Case Questions

1. **What is the problem faced by Peapod?**
   Peapod's primary problem seems to be how to achieve profitable long-term growth without losing current customers or market share.

   Students may also describe deeper problems of how to get the on-line service to a acceptable to the grocery shopper or they wish to discuss the future of on-line shopping in general.

2. **What factors are important in understanding this problem?**
   There are several environmental factors that might be considered. To list a few, consider:
   a. Characteristics of the virtual supermarket.
   b. Advantages of the system.
   c. Costs to the grocer and to the consumer.
   d. Changes in shopping style necessary to make the service a success.
   e. Loss of impulse sales for the grocer.
   f. Difficulties of overcoming the image of being a novelty and not being a serious service.
   g. Demographic characteristics of the target markets.
   h. Competitors.

3. **What alternatives might Peapod consider?**
   The following is a range of alternatives that might be discussed and adapted:
   a. Status Quo—do nothing and continue as is.
   b. Scrap the idea—it won't work.
   c. Look for a buyer and sell out.
   d. Look for a partner that could add needed capital (the partner could be from the food, grocery, or computer industry).
   e. Do research to discover how to make the service more acceptable.
   f. Add other services to the existing one so the consumer is buying a bundle of services.

4. **What are your recommendations for solving the problem?**
   The answer to this question is dependent on the alternative or series of alternatives that have been selected. The student should be challenged to make this service work, especially, in light of predictions that virtual shopping is a trend for the future. Alternatives d, e, or f seem to be the most likely if the company is to stay in business. What other sub-categories can the students think of that might be appropriate?

5. **What are some ways to implement your recommendations?**
   If the student has chosen any of the above three alternatives, they might be asked to supply a list of (a) potential partners, (b) forms of research that might be advised and a time line for accomplishing the research effort, and (c) a list of other services or other service businesses that might be considered or combined with Peapod. With respect to alternative f, the students might consider other products that are either found in or are natural match-ups with the grocery categories (consider fast food, video rental, small electric appliances, catalog clothing, et cetera).

Mini-Project 14-A
Channels are Not All Created Equal

Purpose: to better understand the structure and cooperative nature of channels of distribution.

With one or more members of your class schedule to visit an organization which is a member of a channel of distribution. This may be a retailer, a wholesaler or distribution, a manufacturer, or some other participant in a consumer or business-to-business channel. It would be a good idea if different members of your class planned to visit different types of channel members.

While visiting the organization you should plan to interview one or more people who are involved in some way in channel relationships. You will probably want to ask questions to get some of the following information:

- The type of channel system (conventional, VMS, etc.)
- The number of different levels and the number of different firms in the channel
- The types of intermediaries which participate in the channel
- The advantage of this type of channel for this industry
- The responsibilities of this channel member and of other members of the channel
- Which member is the channel leader? Why is this member the leader?
- How physical distribution is accomplished for the channel

Prepare a report of your findings and present them to your class. Be sure to include your evaluation of the effectiveness and efficiency of this channel structure and any recommendations you would make to improve the channel.

Mini-Project 14-B
How Many Channel Members

Purpose: to help in understanding how the number of channel members relates to marketing goals.

Distribution planning not only includes decisions about the number of channel levels but also the number of different channel members at each level, that is, how many wholesalers and retailers are needed to most effectively reach the marketing goals of the organization.

For some products *intensive distribution,* where the product is sold through every possible wholesalers or retailers is best. At the other end of the continuum is *exclusive distribution* in which only one wholesaler or retailer in a geographic market carries the product. Exclusive distribution may be selected for products with smaller markets or because of heavy service requirements or high price tags. *Selective distribution* may be best where demand is too great for exclusive distribution but other factors prevent intensive distribution from being a good option.

A number of product categories are listed on the following page. For each product, identify one or more brand which you think would best be suited to intensive, exclusive and selective distribution.

Hint: If your need help, call or visit a retailer who sells the product and ask them to tell you about different brands of the product and how they are typically distributed.

Product	Intensive Distribution	Selective Distribution	Exclusive Distribution
Women's makeup and beauty products			
Men's and Women's Wristwatches			
Men's shoes			
Writing Pens			
Automobiles			
Restaurant			
Candy			
Luggage			
Garden Tractors			
Women's clothing			

15

Retailing and Direct Marketing

*O*verview This chapter explores the many different types of retailers, comparing and contrasting them along some key dimensions. The strategic decisions retailers make as they position themselves in the minds of shoppers are also examined. How much and what type of merchandise to carry? At what prices? Where should the store be located? Alternatively, should merchandise be sold in a store at all—what about catalogs, television shopping, the World Wide Web? All of these issues are explored in this chapter.

IKEA, the world's largest-volume furniture chain, is the focus of the Real People, Real Choices segment. Göran Carstedt, the president of IKEA North American, was faced with identifying the best potential site for a store in Torrance, California.

Objectives

1.   Explain how retailing has evolved and how it continues to change.

2.   Describe how retailers may be classified by type or selection of merchandise.

3.   Understand the importance of store image to a retail positioning strategy, and explain some of the actions a retailer can take to create a desired image in the marketplace.

4.   Describe the major forms of nonstore retailing.

5.   Describe the opportunities and barriers to electronic commerce in retailing.

Chapter Outline and Suggested Activities

Introduction: One of the videos suggested for use in this chapter would be a good way to introduce the topic of retailing. The Forum or Starbucks video are both recommended.

1. **Retailing: Special Delivery**
   **Use Objective 1
   Retailing: *The final stop in the distribution channel by which goods and services are sold to consumers for their personal use.*

→ *Class Discussion*

What do retailers do? Discuss with students some of the following activities of retailers:

- Assemble and present products.
- Make products appealing and accessible.
- Develop unique and exciting store images.

   a.   Retailing: A Mixed (Shopping) Bag
       1).   Retailing provides many benefits to consumers.
             a).   Provide an assortment of merchandise under one roof.
             b).   Search the market, and sometimes the world, to find products.
             c).   Provide interesting environments in which to shop and spend leisure time.
   b.   The Evolution of Retailing
       1).   **The Wheel of Retailing Hypothesis:** *A theory that explains how retail firms change, becoming more "upscale" as they go through their life change.*
       2).   **The Retail life cycle:** *A process that focuses on the various retail life –cycle stages from introduction to decline.*
             a).   Introduction stage, after an aggressive entrepreneur who takes a unique approach to doing business
             b).   Growth stage, retailer catches on and sales and profits rise.
             c).   Maturity stage, intense competition and makes it difficult to maintain customer loyalty.
             d).   Decline stage, the retail format becomes obsolete as newer ways of doing business emerge.

→ *Class Discussion*

Discuss with students the wheel-of-retailing hypothesis. Is this hypothesis still applicable in today's retail environment? You might want to take a successful retailer, like Wal-Mart for example and discuss how the wheel-of-retailing hypothesis applies to Wal-Mart. At what stage in the retail life cycle is Wal-Mart?

   c.   The Evolution Continues: What's "In Store" For The Future?
       **Use Q#4 Marketing Practice: Applying What You've Learned
       Three important factors motivate innovative merchants to reinvent the way they do business:
       1).   Demographics—major factors to consider include
             a).   Convenience for working women
             b).   Catering to specific age segments
             c).   Recognizing ethnic diversity

➡ *Class*
Discussion

What changes have been made by retailers in your area in order to respond to changing demographics? Are there changes which need to be made?

2). Technology

    a). Technological innovations are changing the shopping experience, and the way information on customers is collected, stored, and used.

    b). ***Point of sale (POS) systems:*** *retail computer systems that collect sales data and are hooked directly into the store's inventory control system.*

➡ *Class*
Discussion

How do POS systems help to make stores more efficient? Should all retailers, even very small retailers have a POS system?

3). Globalization

➡ *Class*
Discussion

Discuss retailing concepts from other countries which have influenced American retailing? For example, Benetton and IKEA.

2. **Types of Retailers**
**Refer to Objective 2
**Use Instructor's Manual Mini-Project 15-B

  a. Classifying Retailers by What They Sell

    What a retailer sells is referred to as the ***merchandise mix:*** *the total set of all products offered for sale by a firm, including all product lines sold to all consumer groups.*

    1). Product Lines: What is Sold

        a). Product line: A set of related products offered by a retailer.

        b). ***Scrambled merchandising:*** *A merchandising strategy that offers consumers a mixture of merchandise that are not directly related to each other.*

    2). Product Type: Profit and Frequency

    Product differ in terms of the amount of profit each contributes to the business. The initial performance of a product is often examined by looking at the markup, gross margin, and inventory turnover. Successful retailers try to balance gross margin and inventory turnover.

        a). Markup: An increase in the selling price paid by consumers in order to make a profit.

        b). Gross margin: Revenue minus the cost of goods sold, calculated as a percentage of sales; the amount a retailer makes on an item

        c). ***Inventory turnover:*** *The average number of times a year a retailer expects to sell its inventory.*

  b. Classifying Retailers by Merchandise Selection
  **Use Figure 15.1

  Figure 15.1 illustrates the assortment differences for science fiction books. The merchandise assortment has two dimensions, merchandise breadth and depth.

    1). ***Merchandise assortment:*** *The range of products sold.*

    2). ***Merchandise breadth:*** *The number of different product lines available.*

    3). ***Merchandise depth:*** *The variety of choices available for each specific product.*

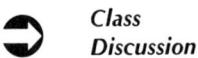
Class
Discussion

Have the class help you develop the merchandise assortment for a local retailer. Be sure to discuss the merchandise breadth and depth.

4). Some of the Major Forms Retailers Take Are:
a). *Convenience stores: Neighborhood retailers that carry a limited number of frequently purchased items, and cater to consumers willing to pay a premium for the ease of buying close to home.*
b). *Supermarkets: Foodstores that carry a wide selection of edibles and related products.*
c). *Specialty stores: Retailers who carry only a few product lines but offer good selection within the lines they sell.*
d). Discount stores may take several forms:
General Merchandise Discount Stores: retailers who offer a broad assortment of items at low prices with minimal service
Off-price Retailers: Retailers who buy excess merchandise from well-known manufacturers and pass the savings onto customers
Warehouse Clubs: Discount retailers who charge a modest membership fee to consumers that buy a broad assortment of food and nonfood items in bulk and in a warehouse environment.
Factory Outlet Stores: A discount retailer owned by a manufacturer, which sells off defective merchandise and/or excess inventory.
e). *Department Stores: Retailers who sell a broad range of items and a good selection within each product line.*
f). *Hypermarkets: Retailers with the characteristics of both warehouse stores and supermarkets; hypermarkets are several times larger than other stores and offer virtually everything from grocery items to electronics.*

Class
Discussion

Create a list of retailers which are found in your area. Have students identify the type of retailer for each firm on your list.

3. **Developing A Store Positioning Strategy: Retailing as Theater**
**Refer to Objective 3
** Use video Starbucks
**Use Figure 15.2
Today retailers have to do more than just sell products—they have to entertain too!
a. *Store Image: The way a retailer is perceived in the marketplace relative to the competition*
**Use Marketing Mini-Project: Learning by Doing
**Use Q#1 Marketing Practice: Applying What You've Learned
To create the desired image and shopping environment the atmospherics of the store are manipulated.
Atmospherics: The use of color, lighting, scents, furnishings, and other design elements to create a desired store image.

Class
Discussion

Discuss the atmospherics of Victoria's Secret. How do the retail environment entice customers to buy? (If you or students are not familiar with Victoria's Secret, you may want to choose another retailer for this discussion.

1). Store Design: Setting the Stage
Some specific decisions include
    a). Store layout (Use Figure 15.3)
        Traffic flow: The direction in which the shopper will move through the store and what areas they will pass or avoid.
    b). Fixture type and merchandise density
    c). Music—type of music and how loud should the music be played
    d). Color and lighting

Spotlight on Real People: MARS

Summary: Mark Begelman opened MARS (Music and Recording Superstore) in 1996. MARS is a retail concept that encourages customers to "jam their hearts out". Each store offers a performance stage for jamming, a fully functional recording studio, and numerous music clinics.

Suggested Answers to Discussion Questions.

1. **How would you classify MARS in terms of its merchandise assortment?**
MARS is a specialty retailer

2. **What elements of store design does MARS use to create an effect?**
MARS has created a unique store which offers a stage, recording studio, and music clinics. The atmosphere of the store encourages customers to touch and play the instruments.

3. **How is MARS positioned relative to other music stores?**
MARS is unique (See response to question 2) and offers customers a store where they can experiment with and try new products. Competitors do not offer this kind of environment.

---

2). The Actors: Store Personnel

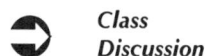
Class Discussion   How do store personnel impact the retail environment? Ask students to comment on their experiences with good and bad customer service in a retail store.

3). Pricing Policy: How Much for a Show Ticket?
Price points play an important role in the image consumers form of a retailer. Strategies such as EDLP create an image of a store which is concerned with offering consumers the price.
Stockouts occur when inventory is poorly managed.
- ***Everyday low pricing (EDLP) strategy:*** *A strategy which involves setting prices that are between the regular price and the deeply discounted price offered by stores that compete on price only.*
- ***Stockouts:*** *An inventory problem that results when desired items are no longer available*

b. Building the Theater: Store Location
**Use Q#2: Marketing Practice: Applying What You've Learned
1). Types of Store Locations
**Use Figure 15.4
    a). Business districts
    b). Shopping centers

     c). Freestanding retailers

     d). Nontraditional store locations

   2). Site Selection: Choosing where to build

     Location planners look at many factors when selecting a site. They want to find a place convenient to customers in the store's trade area, a geographic zone that accounts for the majority of a store's sales and customers.

4. Nonstore Retailing

**Refer to Objective 4

**Use Instructor's Manual Marketing Mini-Project 15-A

**Use Real People, Real Surfers: Exploring the Web

**Use the Computer Friendly Stuff Part V Case

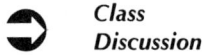

Class Discussion Use Q#3 Marketing Practice: Applying What You've Learned
Divide the class into teams and have each team consider opportunities for the marketing of Elegant Evenings in the various types of non-store retailing formats.

Nonstore retailing: Any method used to complete an exchange with a product end user that does not require a customer to visit a store.

There are several forms of nonstore retailing

Direct Marketing: Exposing a consumer to information about a good or service through a nonpersonal medium and convincing the customer to respond with an order.

a. Mail order

   1). *Catalog: A collection of products offered for sale in book form, usually consisting of product descriptions accompanied by photos of the item.*

   2). *Direct Mail: A brochure or pamphlet offering a specific product or service at one point in time.*

b. *Direct Selling: An interactive sales process that involves a salesperson presenting a product to one individual or a small group, taking orders, and delivering the merchandise.*

   1). Door-to-Door Sales

   2). Parties and Networks

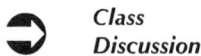

Class Discussion People who attend parties often buy things they would not normally buy if alone. Why?
     Discuss the party plan system:
A sales technique that relies heavily upon people getting caught up in the "group spirit" buying things they would not normally buy if alone.
     Ask students who have attended a home shopping party to comment on the experience.

a. Part of the popularity of in home parties is attributed to stay at home moms. Many of these women were in the workforce before they decided to stay home with children and now use their business skills to operate successful businesses. Some examples of popular companies which use in home parties to sell products include Kelly's Kids (children's apparel). Creative Memories (Scrapbooks and Photo journalizing), and the Pampered Chef (cooking utensils).

b. Multilevel networks is another form of nonstore retailing.

   Multilevel network: A system in which a master distributor recruits other people to become distributors, sells the company's product to the recruits, and receives a commission on all the merchandise sold by the people recruited. Some examples of networks include Amway and Mary Kay Cosmetics

Some network systems are illegal and are usually ***pyramid schemes***. *An illegal sales technique where the initial distributors profit by selling merchandise to other distributors, with the end result being very little product ever gets bought by consumers.*

1).   ***Telemarketing:*** A sales technique where direct selling is conducted over the telephone.
        **Use Real People, Bad Choices?

Real People, Bad Choices?

Summary: Telemarketing does provide direct access to prospective customers, but sometimes it's hard to tell the difference between a legitimate sales call and a scam. Congress is now considering tougher regulations on the telemarketing industry.

Suggested Answers to Discussion Questions

1.   Should marketers be allowed to use the telephone to push their products, even if what they are selling is legitimate?
        If the sales call is legitimate, there is usually no problem. However, it is very difficult for consumers to determine which calls are legitimate and which are scams. Most households today receive these phone calls frequently, and many consumers are annoyed by the frequency of these calls.

2.   What rules would you impose on telemarketing?
        Some students may feel that no rules need to be established. For those students who believe rules should be imposed, a variety of responses might be given. These might include time of day restrictions for making calls, types of products which can be sold, and the use of credit card information.

---

c.   Automatic Vending
        1).   Coin-operated vending machines are not new. These machines require minimal space and personnel to maintain and operate.
        2).   In the US we typically think of convenience goods as being sold through vending machines.

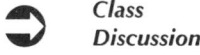

Class Discussion   The text discusses how vending machines are used to sell Levi jeans in France and fresh flowers in Japan. What product(s) do you think should be included in the vending machines at your college and/or place of business?

d.   Direct Response Television
        1).   Infomercials are ***direct response tv:*** a half-hour or hour commercials that resemble a talk show but in actuality are intended to sell something.
        2).   Home Shopping Networks
e.   Electronic Commerce: Back to the Future
        **Refer to Objective 5
        1).   Electronic retailing allows buyers to have access to millions of stores without leaving their desk or home.
        2).   The Allure of Electronic Commerce Benefits to Customers include:
                a).   Browse stores quickly and easily
                b).   Increased ability to search for product information
                c).   Retailers can update price and product information continuously

| Class Activity | Send students on a virtual shopping trip. Assign individual or teams of students to find and "almost" purchase a product using the Internet. You might wish to assign a variety of products to be purchased. (** You could also Real People, Real Surfers: Exploring the Web here) |

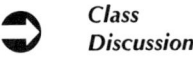

Suggested Discussion Questions

1. How easy was it to find the item which you sought? How many sites offered your product?

2. Would you actually consider buying the product via the Internet? Why? or Why not?

3). Barriers to Success
   a). Customers must wait a few days to receive the product.
   b). Some products require more "touch-and-feel" information before a purchase decision can be made.
   c). Security concerns.
   d). Inventory sold on-line may cannibalize store sales
4). On-line Shopping: Surfer's Paradise or a Drop in the Bucket?
   **Use the video Land's End: The Internet
   **Use Marketing in Action: Real Choices at the Gap
   The success of on-line shopping will depend upon the ability of retailers to offer sites that are entertaining and informative

| Class Discussion | If you are using the Computer Friendly Stuff (CFS) case series, refer to Case V and the Marketing Plan for CFS (Appendix A). Evaluate the usage of on-line retailing by CFS. Why is on-line retailing a secondary strategy for CFS? |

Real People, Real Choices: How It Worked Out At IKEA

Summary: Göran Carstedt is the president of IKEA North America. IKEA is the world's largest-volume furniture chain with outlets in countries all over the world. The company sells about $700 million worth of products per year in North America. Stores are usually located outside city limits but close to main roads.

In January 1992 IKEA acquired one of its competitors, STØR. STØR was an American-owned clone of IKEA which operated stores on the West Coast. With the acquisition, Carstedt now had four stores operating in the L.A. area and there was not one close enough to attract the customers who had shopped at a recently closed STØR in Torrance, California. IKEA began to shop for sites near Torrance.

Option 1: Choose the STØR site in Torrance
Option 2: Three possible properties in the same area as the STØR site but all three sites have problems.
Option 3: A site at Carson Mall, a strip mall with three department stores.

Göran Carstedt and his colleagues choose option 3. They decided to enter the Carson Mall site, but only on the condition that the mall owner do a major renovation.

Potential Discussion Questions

1. Why was option 3 the best choice for IKEA?

2. Why would the owners of Carson Mall agree to spend $12 to $17 million to do a complete renovation of the center?

Marketing Concepts: Testing Your Knowledge

1. **How does the Wheel of Retailing explain changes in retail outlets? How does the Retail Life Cycle Concept explain these changes?**

   The *wheel-of-retailing hypothesis* is a theory that explains how retail firms change, becoming more "upscale" as they go through their life cycle. The suggestion is that retailers compete on price and then move "upscale", leaving room for other new low-price entrants.

   The *retail life-cycle concept theory* is a theory of retailing that focuses on the various life-cycle stages from introduction to decline. The suggestion is that retail institutions are introduced, grow, reach maturity, and then decline. Their degree of aggressiveness and innovation rise and then decline with the stages of the cycle.

2. **What are some of the environmental trends that will have a major impact on the future of retailing?**

   A number of environmental trends will continue to drive the evolution of retailing. These include demographic changes such as an aging population, increasing affluence among ethnic groups, time poverty resulting from increased numbers of working women, and technological developments such as advanced POS systems that enable retailers to provide more personal service. Environmentally conscious consumers look for retailers who are environmentally sensitive. Market globalization will continue to offer new opportunities for retailing innovation.

3. **How are gross margins and turnover rates used to classify retailers? Describe the differences in merchandise assortments for convenience stores, supermarkets, specialty stores, discount stores, department stores, and hypermarkets?**

   For additional information see Figure 15.1.

   Gross margin is revenue minus the cost of goods sold, calculated as a percentage of sales; the amount a retailer makes on an item.

   Inventory turnover is the average number of times a year a retailer expects to sell its inventory.

   Retailers often confront a basic trade-off between margin and volume, and they sometimes must adjust their merchandise mix as their strategy evolves. In some cases retailers try to develop a "portfolio" of products with low and high margins. They reason that by making a relatively large profit on some items, they can use these revenues as a buffer against price wars in other areas that may erode profitability.

   Differences in merchandise assortments for the following types of retailers include:

   a. *Convenience stores*—neighborhood retailers that carry a limited number of frequently purchased items, including basic food products, newspapers, and sundries, and cater to customers who are willing to pay a premium for the ease of buying close to home.

   b. *Supermarkets*—food stores that carry a wide selection of edibles and related products.

   c. *Specialty stores*—retailers who carry only a few product lines but offer good selection within the lines they sell.

   d. *Discount stores*—retailers who offer a wide variety of inexpensive brand-name items in a self-service, "no-frills" setting.

   e. *Department stores*—retailers who sell a broad range of items and a good selection within each product line.

   f. *Hypermarkets*—retailers with the characteristics of both warehouse stores and supermarkets; hypermarkets are several times larger than other stores and offer virtually everything from grocery items to electronics.

4. **What is meant by store "atmospherics"? How can the elements of atmospherics be used to increase the store's success? How are store personnel a part of the store image?**

   For additional information see Figure 15.2 in the text.

   Atmospherics use color, lighting, scents, furnishings, and other design elements to create a desired store image.

The primary use of atmospherics is in store design. Good store design has a lot to do with the success of the individual retailer. Store design decisions include those on store layout, the use of store fixtures and open space, the use of sound to attract (or to repel) certain types of customers, and the use of lighting and color to influence customer mood.

Store personnel contribute to a customer's perception of the image of the store. Factors that are influenced by the store personnel include each employee's role in the operation of the store (complete with props and costumes), serviced to customers begins with the personnel, competency of personnel, personnel are a major factor in holding down costs, and personnel are many times what the customer remembers the most about the retail store and the shopping experience.

5.   **What are some of the different types of store locations? What are the advantages and disadvantages of each?**
The major types of locations include:

Business districts such as the central business district (CBD), the secondary business district, and the neighborhood business district. The advantages of business districts is that they tend to be places where traffic and consumers converge. However, the very congestion that includes many customers also includes traffic and human congestion problems.

Shopping centers such as the neighborhood shopping center, the community shopping center (or strip mall), the regional center, and the super-regional center are common locational forms for suburban areas. Shopping centers attract many consumers to their different retail outlets and offer the advantages of heavy traffic, sharing the costs of promotion among retailers, and a clean and safe environment in which to shop. However, not all locations in the centers are equally attractive, many competitors are attracted, there is competition among centers, and traffic can be overwhelming at times.

Freestanding retailers are those located by themselves in a separate building. The advantage is that they distance themselves from competition, usually have lower rents, they have adaptability, and the retailer is free to alter its selling space to meet its own needs. On the other hand, the store had better be popular because it cannot rely on the drawing power of neighbor stores to provide it with customer traffic.

Nontraditional store locations house innovative retailers who experiment with designs to reach consumers who are unwilling or able to reach the retailer in the traditional way. Putting small stores aboard Navy ships, kiosks in high traffic areas, and automation of some form are a few examples. The advantage is the uniqueness and the disadvantage is the inability to be able to grow with competition copying the concept or the limitations of space.

6.   **How do retail store location planners evaluate potential store sites?**
Evaluation may be done is several ways. One method is *Reilly's law of retail gravitation* (a theory to explain how a store's trading area is affected by its proximity to a population center). This method does not seem to work for urban environments.

A second method or consideration is to determine whether an area needs another new store or not by evaluating whether the market (in terms of locations) is saturated, understored, or overstored.

Third, the consumer segment itself may dictate whether a location is favorable or not. Consider whether the market is growing, size of existing stores, traffic flow, parking spaces available, visibility from the street, et cetera.

Lastly, the retailer can consider the buying power index (BPI) to examine an area's buying income, retail sales, and population relationships. Such things as new families entering the market, a community life cycle, and mobility are often considered.

7.   **Describe the major types of non-store retailing.**
Non-store retailing includes mail-order shopping, direct-selling operations, and vending machines as well as the newer forms of direct marketing such as television shopping and electronic retailing.

Mail-order houses are catalog retailers (almost 15 billion catalogs were mailed in 1990). Direct-selling establishments are where retail sales occur either on an in-person basis or by telephone. Automatic merchandising machine operators are fancy descriptions for vending machine companies.

8.   **Explain the different types of direct selling.**
Home shopping parties, door-to-door selling, and telemarketing are popular direct selling techniques.

Home shopping parties are popular in neighborhoods and useful if the product needs intimacy and demonstration to execute a sale. Many times, party participants buy out of obligation to the host and purchase items that they normally would not purchase. Tupperware is famous for the method.

Door-to-door selling is one of the oldest forms of retailing. However, the method is declining in the United States because of the high labor costs, large number of homes that are empty during the day, and an increasing reluctance of those who are at home to admit strangers. Today, consumers tend to buy more in the office than in the homes. Therefore, door-to-door selling is having to make modifications.

Telemarketing (wherein customers are contacted by phone) is on the rise. It is cheaper than door to door but has a bad reputation (one of three shoppers said that they had been cheated). Many consumers hate being disturbed at home and the method is limited to those that have phones. Again, many customers are not home during the day (and therefore not available for contact).

9. **Describe some of the changes that are expected in the growing electronic marketplace.**
The growing electronic marketplace utilizes the power of more traditional television infomercials, home shopping networks and the growing popularity of computer on-line services, the World Wide Web, and CD-ROM sales presentations to reach prospective customers. The electronic marketplace is here to stay and currently is very popular with young computer literate consumers.

Many believe that home shopping channels are tacky imitations of retail establishments but the fact remains that $2 billion in sales were recorded in 1992 on these channels and more are being added all the time. The future for computer on-line assisted retailing is bright and is high in growth potential.

Marketing Concepts: Discussing Choices and Issues

1. **Some people nostalgically believe retailing was better in the "good old days." What are some of the ways in which modern retailing makes your life better? What are some negative aspects of modern retailing?**
For students to answer this question, it may be easier to have them focus on a specific shopping trip (such as a trip to the mall or to purchase clothes). Once that they begin to brainstorm, more ideas will occur to them.

Some positive aspects of retailing that might be used to begin a discussion include expanded merchandise selection, scrambled merchandising, one-stop shopping, expanded buyer services, higher quality merchandise, store warranties, expanded store hours, highly specialized (trained) service personnel, store credit, catalog shopping, speed of purchase processing, et cetera.

Some negative aspects of retailing that might be used to begin a discussion include tight store security, congested store environments, lack of personalization by sales people due to their stocking responsibilities, encouragement to "max out" credit, high pressure selling, difficulty in seeing all of the merchandise, too many impulse items (especially at checkout for children) at checkout stands, et cetera.

2. **Retailers use store atmospherics to create a certain image. Describe some ways in which creative marketers might use atmospherics to create an image for (a) an antique store, (b) a vintage-clothing store, (c) a bank in a Hispanic neighborhood, and (d) a bookstore.**
To best answer this question, students might be asked to recall creative atmospherics that they have seen and then determine if those unique atmospherics could be applied to the situations described in Question #2.

Some examples that might be used to begin discussions about the variety of retail forms might include:
a. An antique store—dress personnel in period costumes, have lectures about the period pieces, play music from the period, use special lighting to highlight featured items, et cetera.
b. A vintage-clothing store—dress personnel in the clothing, have periodic in store fashion shows, use television monitors to show clothing or to illustrate occasions for usage, use theme mannequins to display clothing, et cetera.
c. A bank in a Hispanic neighborhood—decorate the interior in Spanish art, build the building in adobe, require that all personnel be bi-lingual, specialize in minority loans, have children's programs (such as art exhibits from area schools), feature Hispanic artists (painting, books, poetry, music), et cetera.

d.	A bookstore—design so there are reading areas, feature artist signing parties, have poetry readings, design a special children's corner, have theme sales days (such as Dickens, Poe, Stephen King, as so on), have training sessions for consumers on how to use on-line reading and ordering services, et cetera.

3.	**Some people have suggested that retailers have gone too far in using lighting, color, and even smells to entice shoppers to buy. What do you think? Can the use of atmospherics be unethical?**
Since most students are from a younger generation (younger consumers tend to enjoy sensory stimulation while shopping), they will probably not be negative toward the use of atmospherics. If they are negative, determine if the negativism is toward retailers with which they regularly shop or ones that they avoid. For example, a student might not like the smells that emit from a gourmet coffee shop or a tobacco shop, but she doesn't drink coffee or smoke tobacco.
Some students might have objections toward certain lighting or music. Determine what these objections might be. Some retailers' approaches to special occasions might be objectionable, such as the overplay on Halloween, Valentine's Day, or the 4th of July. Do they have pet peeves about Christmas?

4.	**As the twenty-first century dawns, the potential of electronic media is in its infancy. How do you think electronic media will change retailing in your lifetime?**
To begin this discussion, the instructor might ask students how electronic media has already changed retailing. Examples might be store security, bar codes, electronic cash registers, television monitors in the store environment, telemarketing, catalog shopping, on-line shopping, Web sites, computer search capabilities, et cetera.
Some ideas to stimulate applications for the future might be processing an entire basket of goods (such as in a grocery store) at one time (already being experimented with), virtual shopping including virtual clothing fitting and design, expanded computer ordering, expanded on-line services including Web cash, and expanded Web capabilities.

Real People, Real Surfers: Exploring the Web

Many students have probably used the web to search the products offered by some of their favorite retailers. Although the exercise suggests using the Internet sites for Proffitts, Sears, Macy's and the Gap, any retailer could be used for this exercise. One option would be to have students visit the sites from different types of retailers. For class discussion you might want to focus on students' responses to questions two and three.

Marketing in Action: Real Choices at Gap

Summary: Under the leadership of Chief Executive Mickey Drexler, Gap has grown to become one of the most recognized American and global brands. Gap's success is not just about clothing. Gap does a better job of marketing itself than the competition.

Gap Kids, Old Navy, and Banana Republic are all successful retail chains which are owned by the Gap. Each chain serves the needs of a specific customer group. Despite this success, Drexler wants to continue to see Gap's market share grow.

Suggested Answers to Case Questions

1. **What are the problems facing Mickey Drexler?**
   The key issue centers around how to continue to grow an already successful retail business. Gap's 4 percent market share is good, but Drexler wants 8,10,12 percent.

2. **What factors are causing the problems?**
   The following factors are important considerations.
   a.   Increased competition from other retailers
   b.   Increased competition from Electronic Retailing
   c.   Perhaps boredom with the "The Gap" store and the need for an exciting new shopping venue.
   d.   The continued growth of discount and off-price stores

3. **What are the alternatives?**
   The following are a series of alternatives that might stimulate discussion.
   a.   Open more Gap stores
   b.   Develop new retailing approaches
   c.   Electronic Retailing
   d.   Focus on global expansion
   e.   Improve existing outlets

4. **What are your recommendations for solving the problems?**
   Although all of the alternatives have merit, Gap would be wise to focus on alternatives b, c, and e. Consumers are easily bored with existing retailing environments; thus, new shopping venues must be created in order to keep existing customers. Electronic retailing is here! There are still many issues and concerns associated with retailing on the Web, but retailers must consider how they are going to use the Web for conducting business. Improvements in existing outlets should be made. Stores that become "dull" unexciting do nothing to help attract customers and sell merchandise.

5. **What are some ways to implement your recommendations?**
   Those involved in store planning for the Gap should continually be scanning the environment looking for new trends in store design and types of stores desired by consumers. A brainstorming or visioning session which includes store planners, retail developers, and consumers might help the Gap to develop the next generation of Gap stores.

   The Gap needs to be aware of how other retailers are using the web and how the Gap can do business better than their competitors on the Web.

Mini-Project 15-A
Non-Store Retailing in the Future

Purpose: to focus your attention on how retailing may evolve in the future to meet the needs of customers.

During the past couple of decades, non-store retailing has grown dramatically as consumers are increasingly relying on catalog merchandisers and home shopping networks. Since the mid 1990s, the electronic marketplace has offered consumers the opportunity to learn about and purchase goods and services with their home computer. Many of the college students of today will probably be employed in marketing through the Internet and/or CD-ROMs. The most important question about the electronic marketplace is no longer whether or not it will succeed but rather what path will that success follow. Who will use the Internet for shopping? For what products? What will be the important advantages to customers? And will in-store retailing as we know it disappear?

1. With one or more of your classmates, develop a study of consumers attitudes toward shopping on the Internet. For this study, you should plan to conduct personal interviews with a number of consumers. Depending on how many of your classmates are working with you on this project, you may interview as few as 10 consumers or as many as 50. Ideally, you will be able to interview consumers from a variety of different demographic groups.

2. First develop a brief questionnaire. For this kind of study, it is good to include a lot of open-ended questions—the type of question you can use to probe for the specifics of why an individual feels of thinks the way they do.
    For example, you might ask

    "What do you see as the advantages of Internet shopping?"

    If the respondent says,

    "I think it's fun."

    You might probe

    "In what ways is it fun?"
    Or
    "Are there any other advantages for you?"

    You will probably want to include 10 to 15 questions for your study.

3. Prepare a report of your findings. Include in the report

    - a summary of your findings
    - a discussion of any differences you observed in the attitudes or feelings of different demographic groups
    - conclusions that you have drawn from your study about the future of the electronic marketplace
    - recommendations for marketers considering entering this marketplace

Mini-Project 15-B
Differences in Retail Prices

Purpose: to better understand how the characteristics of the retailer relate to prices.

One of the more important ways in which retailers differ is in price. Prices tend to be higher at specialty stores which offer good selection and the latest in fashion and at convenience stores which, as their name states, offer convenience to the shopper. On the other end of the spectrum, discount stores offer lower prices on a limited variety of items in a no-frills atmosphere. Similarly, non-store retailing—whether vending machines, telemarketing, door-to-door sales or catalog shopping—may offer consumers products at the same, lower, or higher prices than can be found at local retail stores.

In the space below, a number of products are listed along with some of types of retailers which typically carry the product. Find the price of the product at each of the locations. Be sure to identify and price equivalent items

Product	Location	Price
Chewing gum		
	Vending machine	
	Convenience store	
	Supermarket	
	Mass merchandiser	

A 21" piece of soft-sided luggage		
	Mass Merchandiser	
	Specialty store	
	Discount store	

Product	Location	Price
A board game (such as Monopoly)		
	Department store	
	Mass merchandiser	
	Specialty store	
	Catalog	

Product	Location	Price
Hand lotion		
	In-home shopping	
	Specialty store	
	Convenience store	
	Supermarket	

Product	Location	Price
Men's jeans		
	Specialty store	
	Department store	
	Mass merchandiser	
	Catalog	

Instructor's Resource Manual with Video Guide t/a Marketing: Real People, Real Choices 2/e

16

The Promotion Superhighway

*O*verview This chapter provides an overview of the communication tools that marketers use to connect with consumers. The chapter begins by reviewing some of the basic elements of promotion strategy, including the many diverse communication methods that people use to learn about products, to form impressions of companies and to choose some alternatives over others. Promotion is a vital part of the marketing mix and how promotion plans are developed and implemented is explored.

Tom Eppes, the President of Price/McNabb, is the focus of the Real People, Real Choices segment. Price/McNabb develops communication programs for clients that combine the promotional elements of advertising, public relations, database marketing and sales promotion.

Objectives

1.   Explain the goals of marketing communications.

2.   List and describe the elements of the promotion mix.

3.   Explain the steps in developing a promotion mix.

4.   Compare the traditional model of communications with the current trend toward interactive promotion strategies.

5.   Explain why database marketing is increasingly popular and how databases are developed and managed.

6.   Explain integrated marketing communications and its implementation, and why some marketers resist it.

Chapter Outline and Suggested Activities

Introduction: Begin by asking students, "What is promotions?" Many students will answer advertising or some form of mass media, such as television. Assemble examples of various types of promotions that a firm might use and discuss the concept of the promotion mix.

    ** The video "Lands' End: Teaching Consumers About Lands' End" could also be used to introduce this chapter.

1. **Tailoring Marketing Communications to Customers**
   a.   To reach consumers, it is essential to know them and to talk their language.

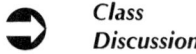 ***Class Discussion***   Have students identify television commercials and/or print advertisements which are targeted to different age groups. How is "the talk" used to reach each group different? How are the images and people included in the advertisements different? Discuss with students the concept of communicating with customers.

    b.   ***Promotion:*** *The coordination of a marketer's marketing communication efforts to influence attitudes or behaviors.*

    c.   In the past promotion was a one-way conversation from marketer to consumer. Innovations in technology has allowed marketers to become interactive and talk with the customer.

    d.   Promotion is intended to accomplish four goals:
    **Refer to Objective 1
    1).   Inform
    2).   Remind
    3).   Persuade
    4).   Build relationships with customers

2. **Promotional Strategy**
   **Use Marketing in Action: Real Choices at Virgin Cola
   a.   The Promotion Mix
       **Refer to Objective 2
       **Use Q#1 Marketing Practice: Applying What You've Learned
       The ***promotion mix:*** *the major elements of marketers—controlled communications including advertising, sales promotions, publicity, and public relations, and personal selling.*
       Each of the different elements of the promotion mix has both pros and cons.
       ** Use Table 16.2

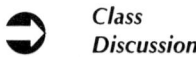 ***Class Discussion***   Assume that you are responsible for deciding on which promotion mix elements to use in each of the following situations. Justify your decision. (Refer students to Table 16.2 which compares the elements of the promotion mix.)

    ■   A new brand of cereal targeted to senior adults
    ■   A new medication for treating arthritis
    ■   A new style of jeans targeted to young teens who are between the ages of 11 and 13
    ■   A new variety of fresh fruit

    b.   Categories of Communication
    **Use Table 16.1 and Table 16.2
    1).   Personal appeals—an example would be personal selling
    2).   Mass appeals—examples include

a). *Advertising:* nonpersonal communication from an identified sponsor using the mass media.

b). Sales promotion, programs such as contests or store demonstrations.

c). Publicity and public relations

c. Managing the Promotion Mix

**Refer to Objective 3

The *promotion plan* is a framework that outlines the strategies for developing, implements, and controlling the firm's promotional activities.

**Use Figure 16.1

Spotlight on Real People: Beach'n Billboard

Summary: Patrick Dori is founder of Beach'n Billboard, a startup company that makes impressions in the sand that form an ad or product logo. Dori calls the results "the world's largest and first environmentally safe billboard."

Suggested Answers to Discussion Questions

1. **What type of promotion does Beach'n Billboard use?**
The firm uses a mass appeal, specifically advertising.

2. **Who is the target market for this promotion?**
Obviously the target is beach goers. However, firms should consider the demographic composition of different beaches and the different times of year some groups are most likely to visit the beach. For example, Florida, Spring Break and college students is a known promotional mecca for many firms desiring to reach the college market. During the Winter the West Coast of Florida is a haven for wealthy senior adults. Finally, the beaches surrounding Orlando are often filled with families who are visiting DisneyWorld.

3. **What are the drawbacks to this kind of promotion, and how might they be overcome?**
The biggest drawback is rain. The firm currently offers "rainchecks" and gives credit for rainy days. Other drawbacks include unpredicted ocean waves and people stumbling over the sand sculpture.

---

1). Establish Promotion Objectives

**Use Q#2 Marketing Practice: Applying What You've Learned

**Use Figure 16.2

Establishing the promotion objective is the first step in the promotion planning process. There are five types of promotion objectives which a firm may choose from. These objectives represent an uphill climb.

a). Create awareness

b). Inform the market

c). Create desire

d). Encourage trial

e). Build loyalty

2). Identify Influences on the Promotion Mix

One element is determine whether to use a push or pull strategy.

a). *Push strategy: The company tries to move its product through the channel by convincing channel members to offer them.*

b). *Pull strategy: The company tries to move its products through the channel by building desire for the among consumers, thus convincing retailers to respond to this demand by stocking these items.*

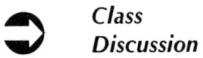

Class Discussion

Consider the promotion plan developed for Computer Friendly Stuff (CFS) (Appendix A). Did CFS use a push or a pull strategy?

    If you are not using the CFS series you could discuss with students other examples of push and pull strategies. For example, large manufacturers of cereal other packaged consumer goods most often use a push strategy. Today many pharmaceutical firms are using a pull strategy and are targeting the actual user of the prescription drug. These messages often end with the phrase, "go ask your doctor or pharmacist."

c). The stage of a product in the product life cycle influences promotion mix decisions.

Class Discussion

Assume that you have just created a new brand of cologne targeted to college aged females. Discuss how the promotion mix for this product would change as it moves through the product life cycle.

    If you are using the Computer Friendly Stuff (CFS) series you could use the above mentioned discussion using CFS as your focus.

3). Determine and Allocate the Promotion Budget

Is communication viewed as an expense or an investment? How a firm answers this question influences the approach it chooses for determining and allocating their promotion budget.

There are two budgeting techniques:

a). ***Top-down budgeting techniques:*** *require top management to establish the overall amount that the organization wishes to devote to promotion activities, and this amount is then divided up among advertising, public relations, and other promotional departments.*

- ***Percentage-of-sales:*** *A method for promotion budgeting in which the promotion budget is based on a certain percentage of either last year's sales or on estimates for the present year's sales.*
- ***Competitive-parity method:*** *Matching whatever the competition is spending.*

b). ***Bottom-up budgeting techniques:*** *Allocation of the promotional budget based on identifying promotion goals and allocating enough money to accomplish them.*

- ***Objective-task method:*** *A promotion budgeting method in which an organization first defines the specific communications goals it hopes to achieve and ten tries to calculate what kind of promotional efforts it will take to meet the goal.*

4). Allocate the budget to a specific promotion mix—Factors to consider

a). Organizational factors

b). Market potential

c). Market size

5). Evaluate the effectiveness of the Promotion Mix

The final stage in managing the promotion mix is to decide whether the plan is working.

Class Discussion

What are some ways to monitor and evaluate the company's promotion efforts? For example, some firms might ask new customers "how did you hear about us?" Responses to this question help the organization to evaluate its promotion efforts.

3.   The Promotion Superhighway: Interactive Marketing
   a.   The Traditional Communications Model
            **Refer to Objective 4
            ** Use Instructor's Manual Mini-Project 16-B
            ** Use Figure 16.3
            Communications model: The elements necessary for meaning to be transferred from a sender to a receiver.
            1).   Encoding by the marketer
                      Encoding: The process of translating an idea into a form of communication that will convey meaning.
            2).   The Source*: An organization or individual that sends a message.*

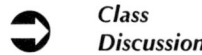

Class   Are celebrity endorsers effective?
Discussion   Discuss with students the use of celebrities in communication efforts.
                 How is a celebrity selected? Does a celebrity have to actually use the product in
                 order to endorse the product?

            3).   *The Message:* The communication in physical form which is sent from a sender to a receiver.
                      a).   The message should communicate four objectives
                      b).   *AIDA model: The communication goals of Attention, Interest, Desire, and Attention.*
                      c).   There are two types of message appeals
                                ■   Rational appeal
                                ■   Emotional appeal
                      d).   The structure of the appeal
                                ■   Supportive argument or one-sided argument
                                ■   Two-sided argument

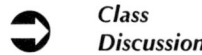

Class   Have students bring to class examples of promotion messages. The easiest to bring
Discussion   would be a newspaper or magazine advertisement. In class, have students use the
                 advertisement to discuss the communication model.

                                   Suggested Discussion Questions

            ■   Who is the source?
            ■   What type of message appeal is used?
            ■   What is the structure of the appeal?
            ■   What is the meaning of the message?

            4).   *The medium: A communications vehicle through which a message is transmitted to target audience.*
            5).   Decoding by the receiver
                      a).   *Decoding: The process of assigning meaning to the message by a receiver.*
                      b).   *Receiver: The organization or individual that intercepts the message.*
            6).   *Noise: Anything that interferes with effective communication.*
            7).   *Feedback: The reactions of the receiver to the message that are communicated back to the source.*

b.   Redrawing the Traditional Communications Road Map: Interactive Marketing
1).   ***Interactive Marketing:*** *A promotional practice in which customized marketing communications elicit a measurable response from individual receivers.*
2).   Customizing the Message: De-Mass Marketing.
Companies are slicing the mass market into smaller, more manageable pieces. For example, the Coca-Cola Company is creating alternatives to big budget commercials. They range from a "quick-cut" style for MTV to a *Star Trek*-style spot to appeal to teenagers.
3).   Levels of Interactive Response:
a).   ***Transactional Data:*** *An ongoing record of individual or organizations that buy a product.*
b).   First-order response. A product offer that directly yields a transaction.
c).   Second-order response. Customer feedback to a promotional message that is not in the form of a transaction.

c.   The Bedrock of the Promotion Superhighway: Database Marketing
** Refer to Objective 5
** Use Instructor's Manual Mini-Project 16-A
1).   The goal of interactive marketing is to track consumer responses to its messages and to create a dialogue with the customer. The secret to effective interactive marketing is the development of a customer database.
2).   ***Database marketing:*** *The creation of an ongoing relationship with a set of customers who have an identifiable interest in a product or service and whose responses to promotional efforts become part of future communications attempts.*
3).   The following list explains what database marketing can do
a).   Database marketing is interactive.
b).   Database marketing builds relationships.
c).   Database marketing locates new customers.
d).   Database marketing stimulates cross-selling.
e).   Database marketing is measurable.

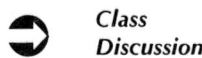

Class Discussion   If you are using the Computer Friendly Stuff (CFS) case series, discuss the benefits of database marketing for CFS.
Another option would be to discuss the ethical issues of database marketing as presented in the "Real People, Bad Choices?" segment.

Real People, Bad Choices?

Summary: Many companies buy response lists from professional called list managers. These contain addresses of people who have an interest in the product or who have bought a related item in the past. The growing use of sophisticated databases worries some consumer groups, who are concerned about invasion of privacy.

Suggested Answer to the Discussion Question

1.   **Should marketers have the right to buy private information about the purchasing habits of consumers in order to sell other products and services to them?**
Responses to this question will no doubt be varied. Some may say yes, that databases and using the information they contain to solicit customers is just a tactic for conducting business. Others might believe that consumers' privacy is being invaded.
Discuss with students whether or not laws, like the one passed in Europe in 1998, should be passed which limit the ability of companies to sell consumer data.

---

4. **Putting It All Together And Hitting The Open Road: Integrated Marketing Communications**
**Refer to Objective 6
When a traditional promotion campaign is used, there is little effort to coordinate the messages consumers receive.
   a.   Driving in Multiple Lanes: Coordinating Promotion Messages
        **Use Figure 16.4
        Integrated Marketing Communication (IMC): *A strategic business process used to plan, develop, execute, and evaluate coordinated, measurable, persuasive brand communication programs over time with targeted audiences*
        1).   The basic idea is to anticipate every opportunity in which a customer will see information about a good, service, or organization. Then to make sure each of these different exposures communicates the desired message and elicits the intended response.
        2).   IMC is still an emerging perspective.
   b.   The IMC Planning Model: Begin With the Driver Not the Engine
        **Use Marketing Mini-Project: Learning By Doing
        **Use Figure 16.5
        Steps in developing an IMC promotion strategy
        1).   Start with a Customer Database—this means that the customer, not profit or sales goals, is the focus of the communication strategy
        2).   Develop Promotional Strategies—insights from the database are used to devise strategies that reach targeted customers.
              Contact Management: *A communication strategy that provides communications exposures where and when the targeted customer is most likely to receive them.*
        3).   Implementing Specific Promotional Tactics
        4).   Evaluating IMC Communications: The following dimensions matter when evaluating an IMC promotion strategy.
              a).   First-order responses: The firm can track transaction to determine the campaign's effectiveness.
              b).   Second-order responses: Customers' request for more information can be used to determine if the campaign stimulated interest.
              c).   Attitudes toward the brand and/or the organization: When attitudes are tracked over time, they can be used to help predict purchases.
                    **Use Real People, Real Surfers: Exploring the Web
   c.   Roadblocks on the IMC Superhighway
        Some barriers to acceptance include:
        1).   Changes in the way marketers plan and implement promotion
        strategies
        2).   The IMC approach assigns relatively more importance to aspects of promotion other than advertising.
        3).   The IMC approach requires upper-level management to view other aspects of marketing mix (such as packaging and pricing decisions) as part of the communications strategy.

Real People, Real Choices: How It Worked Out At Price/McNabbs

Summary: Tom Eppes is the President of Price/McNabb, a fully integrated marketing communications company. One of Price/McNabb's clients is Browning-Ferris Industries (BFI). Head quartered in Houston, BFI sees to the removal of solid waste, medical waste, and recycling for clients ranging from department stores and office complexes to hospitals and school systems.

In 1996, BFI restructured its organization around its customers businesses and created six division—healthcare, office/commercial, publication, manufacturing, small businesses and general business services markets. Price/McNabb was hired to help implement BFI's new aggressive customer-driven business strategy. An integrated promotional strategy was needed to make the new strategy work. Mr. Eppes and his colleagues considered three options:

Option 1: Continue to compete on a price basis just like the competition.
Option 2: Customize the tactical plan for each customer group.
Option 3: As in option #2, begin with the development of a positioning recommendation for each subject.

Tom Eppes selected option #2.

Potential Discussion Questions

1. Consider option 2, what are the advantages to BFI and its customer groups?

2. Why is option 1 not the best solution for BFI?

Marketing Concepts: Testing Your Knowledge

1. **What is promotion? What are the goals of promotion?**
   Promotion is the coordination of a marketer's marketing communications efforts to influence attitudes or behavior. The goals of promotion are to:

   - Inform
   - Remind
   - Persuade
   - Build relationships

2. **List and describe the elements of the promotion mix?**
   For additional information refer to Table 16.2.

   Advertising is nonpersonal communication that is paid for by an identified sponsor using mass media to inform or persuade an audience.

   Sales promotions are marketing activities used to stimulate immediate sales by providing extra value or generating interest in a product.

   Publicity and public relations consists of marketing efforts or activities to portray an organization and its products positively by influencing the perceptions of various publics, including customers, government officials, and shareholders.

   Marketers also communicate with customers through product and package design. Word-of-mouth communication from one consumer to another is often the most influential factor in consumer decisions.

3. **List and explain the steps in the development of a promotion plan.**
   The promotion plan is a framework that outlines the strategies for developing, implementing, and controlling the firm's promotional activities. Figure 16.1 outlines the stages in the development of the promotion plan.
   a. Step 1: Establish promotion objectives. Figure 16.2 depicts the different types of communication objectives a firm might have.
   b. Step 2: Identify influences on the promotion mix. Should a push or a pull strategy be used? At what stage is the product in the product life cycle? How a firm responds to these questions influences the promotion mix
   c. Step 3: Determine and allocate the total promotion method. The firm must decide what type of technique, top-down or bottom-up will be used for determining and allocating the promotion budget.
   d. Step 4: Allocate the budget to a specific promotion mix. Organizations need to consider:

      - Organizational factors
      - Market potential
      - Market size

   e. Step 5: Evaluate the effectiveness of the promotion mix. In this final stage the organize attempts to determine whether the promotion objectives are adequately translated into marketing communications that reached the right target market.

4. **Why should promotion objectives be phrased in terms of communications tasks? What are some examples of communications task objectives?**
   For additional information see Figure 16.2 in the text.

   The whole point of developing a promotion strategy is to connect the marketing plan to consumers—to let them know that the organization has a product that has been developed to meet their needs in a timely and affordable way. In many instances promotional objectives do not equal marketing objectives. Marketing objectives are stated in terms of measurable tasks to be performed with respect to sales or consumer response. Promotion objectives need to be defined in terms of the specific communications tasks that will deliver the desired message to the target audience.

Some examples of communications task objectives are:

a. Create awareness.
b. Inform the market.
c. Create desire.
d. Encourage trial.
e. Build loyalty.

5. **How does the promotion mix vary with push versus pull strategies? How does it vary in different stages of the product life cycle (PLC)?**

In a push strategy, the company tries to move its products through the channel by convincing channel members to offer them. Promotion efforts focus on personal selling and sales promotions such as exhibits at tradeshows. In a pull strategy the company tries to move its products through the channel by building desire for the among consumers, thus convincing retailers to respond to this demand by stocking these items. Promotion efforts focus on media advertising to stimulate interest among end consumers.

The stage of the product life cycle also influences the promotion mix.

a. Introduction stage: Advertising primary promotional tool for creating awareness. Publicity is also used.
b. Growth phase: Specific product benefits are communicated through advertising and trial is encourage.
c. Maturity stage: The goal is to entice people to switch from a competitors product. Sales promotions, especially coupons, are used in this stage.
d. Decline phase: As sales decline, so does spending on all elements of the promotion mix.

6. **Explain each of the following budgeting methods:**

a. percentage-of-sales
b. competitive-parity
c. objective-task.

Percentage-of-sales—the promotion budget is based either on last year's sales or on estimates for this year's sales. The percentage is often based on an industry average.

Competitive-parity method—match whatever competitors are spending.

Objective-task—the firm first defines the specific communications goals it hopes to achieve and then figures out how much and what kinds of promotion efforts it will take to meet the goal.

7. **Describe the traditional communications model.**

The traditional communications model identifies the elements necessary for meaning to be transferred from a sender to a receiver. Figure 16.3 depicts this model. The elements in the model include:

- Encoding
- Source
- Message
- Medium
- Decoding by the receiver
- Noise
- Feedback

8. **What is interactive marketing?**

Interactive marketing is a promotion practice in which customized marketing communications elicit a measurable response from individual receivers. An example might be an ad that is inserted into an automatic teller machine at a bank that asks the consumer questions and gets specific interactive responses.

9. **What is database marketing? What are some reasons that database marketing growing in popularity?**

Database marketing is interactive marketing activities that utilize a customized database of customers who have an identifiable interest in the product . The database has become a major component in marketing plans and is no longer just a place to get or store information. The database is important because it allows the marketer to learn about the preferences of its customers, to fine-tune its offerings to their needs, and slowly but surely to build an ongoing relationship with them.

A marketer can obtain lists of names from many sources, but the quality of a list is usually the single most important determinant of success. In this context, quality refers to the proportion of prospects contacted who will eventually be converted into customers. In general, "quality" prospects are people who are likely to be interested in the product and who are willing to make such a purchase by mail or phone. The single best predictor or purchase is whether the person has bought a similar product recently.

Marketers can buy or rent lists, can hire specialists who will compile lists (usually broken into a complied list and a response list), or they can create in-house lists. The company should probably consider integrating transactional data with other information eventually.

10. **What is integrated marketing communications (IMC)? What is contact management and how is it part of IMC?**
See Figure 16.4 and Figure 16.5 for additional information and detail.

Integrated marketing communications (*IMC*) is the coordination of messages and media to maximize the effectiveness of a promotion strategy in reaching targeted consumers on a continuous basis.

Contact management is a communications strategy that seeks to provide communications exposures where and when the targeted customer is most likely to receive them. Contact management is the second step in an IMC planning model (See Figure 16.5 for more detail). Whereas the primary goal of those devising promotion strategy used to be creating a persuasive message, a bigger concern of IMC planners (and addressed in contact management) now is identifying the times, places, or situations where marketing communications are most likely to reach each of the customer types.

Marketing Concepts: Discussing Choices and Issues

1. **Increasingly, marketers are seeking new ways to communicate with consumers. Advertising is being placed on bathroom walls, in high school cafeterias, and even in the halls of university classroom buildings. Develop debate arguments for and against this proliferation of commercial messages.**
Students should be encouraged to express their true feelings about message proliferation. Some points that begin the debate are listed below.

    For arguments:
a. It is good for the economy.
b. Any mechanism that presents more information is good.
c. Is the argument about the quantity or the quality of the messages.
d. It is a price to pay with a freedom of speech society.
e. Advertisers are provided rental revenues for entities that only received government support in the past. Now they are less of a burden on government and therefore taxpayers.
f. If people reacted badly toward the ads and the sponsoring companies, they wouldn't be there.
g. It is a natural extension of relationship marketing.

    Against arguments:
a. It is visual pollution at its finest.
b. We know that people don't like it because of the increasing legislation that is designed to prevent it.
c. There are no controls on what is advertised (such as tobacco and alcohol).
d. School administrators are selling out to big advertisers and big money.
e. There is no room for positive messages (such as those regarding behavior or habits).
f. Where do you draw the line between free speech and privacy?
g. Most of these new ads are designed to reach the young.
h. It makes us an even more consuming nation' instead of one concerned with solving world and environmental problems.

2. **Still another reason to build a database is to advance a political or social agenda by identifying and mobilizing a core of supporters. For example, Philip Morris has built a database with 26-million-names that the tobacco company uses to rally customers to the cause of smokers rights. What are the ethical issues related to this usage of databases?**

Perhaps the best way to approach this question is by asking for pro and con arguments from the students. Be careful to not just center the discussion on controversial issues, such as that of tobacco. Mention what many would deem to be positive issues, such as the environment, drug abatement, animal rights, or minority rights.

For (pro) arguments:
a. Its their money and they can do with it as they wish.
b. The database can be used for many positive issues as well.
c. The database can be used to present information (even if it is biased) but it cannot make people do something that do not want to do.
d. How is this different from what politicians do?
e. It brings the company closer to the customers lifestyle.

Against (con) arguments:
a. It distorts the truth.
b. It invades privacy very subtlety.
c. It doesn't present all the issues or both sides.
d. It mixes advertising and political issues and sometimes confuses the consumer.
e. It is wrong to get people's names under one pretense and then try to influence them in other ways.

3.   **Consumers are becoming concerned that the proliferation of databases is an invasion of the individual's privacy. Do you feel this is a valid concern? How can marketers use databases effectively and at the same time, protect the rights of individuals?**

This question might be harder for the students to answer if they are not on many databases. An interesting way to begin the discussion (and to make it different from the ones in Question #1 and #2 above) is to ask students what they would think about the University selling their database data to private companies. When would this be OK? When would it be bad?

Most would agree that there is more information floating around about us than ever before. There are really no rules that govern this. What type of rules would the students like to see?

The answer might be for companies to guard information that they have on you in the same way that the registrar guards your private records. No one gets it without your permission, or no one gets it, period, or you are notified if someone does get it.

4.   **There are some who argue that IMC is just a passing fad in marketing communications. What do you think?**

Literature and practical business experience has shown that there is an increasing trend to coordination of communication efforts. This coordination has led to IMC. The difficulty seems to be in the precise model that might best. As firms experiment and customize more form will most certainly emerge.

One major barrier will be that of tradition. However, notice how tradition has given way in broadcasting (through the use of cable TV), office procedures (using computers), interactive advertising, and the Internet. Obviously, new methods are emerging. Firms can resist, or they can take a lead role and gain advantage.

If the students choose the membership approaches they might want to review the changes that have been made at Sam's Wholesale Club as a basis for their recommendations.

The problem of customers who no longer purchase should probably be explored with a primary research effort. Continual customer satisfaction data should be obtained.

 **Real People, Real Surfers: Exploring the Web**

This exercise can be used to explore how the Internet is used to both build a database and to communicate one-on-one with customers. Instructors might want to focus on responses to questions 2, 3, and 4 for class discussion.

Marketing in Action: Real Choices At Virgin Cola

Summary: Which elements of the promotion mix would be most beneficial to Virgin Cola? Richard Branson, the creator of the Virgin label, faces the problem of challenging Coca Cola and Pepsi. The company has been successfully launched in the U.K. and now Mr. Branson wants to introduce the product line in America. He faces the issue of entering a mature market. On his side however, are American consumers, who are usually willing to give new products a chance.

Suggested Answers to Case Questions:

1. **What is the problem facing Virgin Cola?**
    Advertising is a major form of promotion used in the cola market. In 1997, Coke spent $113 million on advertising Coke Classic alone. Based on the facts that Virgin Cola does not have the advertising budget that Coca Cola and Pepsi have and that the U.S. cola market is a mature one, how will Richard Branson best promote Virgin Cola to capture the largest market share?

2. **What factors are important to understand this problem?**
    The following factors are important considerations.
    a.   Virgin lacks the level of brand recognition enjoyed by industry giants.
    b.   Very small budget compared to industry giants.
    c.   Introduction of Virgin Cola is likely to start price wars.
    d.   Can a firm as small as Virgin Cola compete on price with industry leaders regardless of price wars?
    e.   The chance that channel wars will prevent Virgin from finding distribution channels.
    f.   How will Virgin budget its money to most effectively compete with the larger firms?

3. **What alternatives might Virgin Cola consider?**
    The following are a series of alternatives that might stimulate discussion.
    a.   Do nothing.
    b.   Concentrate on advertising as the major form of promotion.
    c.   Plan an extraordinary media event to accompany product introduction.
    d.   Development of an interactive communications program utilizing the development of a database through direct mail or the Internet.

4. **What are your recommendations for solving the problem?**
    Students must keep in mind that Virgin Cola is a much smaller company than the soft drink giants, Coke and Pepsi. Also, they need to recognize that the firm is competing against other small firms as well. One possible solution would be for Virgin Cola to develop an integrated communication strategy (option d). Virgin Cola may get promotion ideas from studying smaller firms to reveal their strategies for competing on a small budget. Virgin Cola also needs to develop a media event for the introduction of the product to the U.S. market (option c).

5. **What are some ways to implement your recommendations?**
    Virgin Cola has already tested its product in a market much smaller than the U.S. and experienced success. Some of these earlier strategies should be tested in American markets. Mr. Branson should market in a variety of test areas throughout the United States. The firm should also conduct taste tests in the U.S. to establish if Americans favor the products as the British do. Virgin Cola can develop more effective integrated communication strategies by utilizing these various test results.
    The firm should also begin developing a database of customers. One strategy would be to include a request for personal information such as name, address, etc., on all coupons. If consumers provide the requested information, they could be entered into the database and sent a follow-up coupon for a free cola.
    The firm must also consider how they are going to build a relationship with distributors. The success of this relationship will be crucial to the success of the brand. Some distributors might be willing to assist in the introduction of the product to the U.S. market.

Mini-Project 16-A
Database Marketing for a Small Business

Purpose: to give you experience at developing a database marketing strategy.

It seems that every day we see new examples of how large businesses are using database techniques to improve their marketing strategies. From grocery stores to movie rentals to office supply stores, businesses are enticing customers to allow them to monitor their purchases with money-saving offers. But what about the small private business. Most entrepreneurs have yet to discover the benefits of database marketing. This mini-project allows you to be of assistance to such a business.

1.   First, with several of your classmates, identify and obtain cooperation of a small business "client" in your community. You will probably need to spend a fairly large amount of time visiting the business and talking with the owner and/or employees. Find out what the business currently does to build relationships with customers and what problems it currently faces.

2.   Based on what you have learned, develop some recommendations for database marketing for the client. Your recommendations may include some of the following:

   - how to create a database with existing customers
   - how to obtain data on potential new customers
   - a plan for adding demographic or other useful information to the database
   - strategies to attract new customers
   - strategies to reactivate one-time buyers and other lapsed customers
   - techniques for building bonds with customers

   You may also wish to develop examples of direct mail communications or other types of materials which might be used to implement your recommendations

3.   Present your findings and your recommendations to your client and to your class.

Mini-Project 16-B
Product and Package Design

Purpose: to increase your understanding of how product and package design provide an important source of communications about a product.

The design of a product and its package don't happen accidentally. A lot of effort goes into deciding on the best color, shape, size, use of lines, type styles, pictures, information, etc. Consumers, however, seldom think about these things.

Below are listed a number of product categories. Visit a retail store that sells each of these and make notes on the product and package design. You will probably want to think about some of the following questions:

- Do all the brands look alike?
- Does one or a couple of brands stand out from the rest?
- Why do you think the colors used were selected?
- What do the colors say to you?
- What does the material and the shape of the package communicate?
- What information is on the package?
- How is this information useful or not useful for consumers?
- What message does the overall package design give to the customer?
- Which package do you feel is best and why?
- Which do you think does the poorest job of communications?

Canned pasta sauce

_____

_____

_____

_____

Computer software

_____

_____

_____

_____

Women's or men's cologne or perfume

_____

_____

_____

_____

Laundry detergent

_____

_____

_____

_____

Power hand tools (drills, saws, sanders, etc.)

_____

_____

_____

_____

Vitamins

_____

_____

_____

_____

Breakfast cereals

_____

_____

_____

_____

Cough syrups

_____

_____

_____

_____

Snack crackers

_____

_____

_____

_____

17

Advertising

*O*verview Most students have heard of advertising, but few will understand what advertising is and its role in marketing. This chapter begins by exploring advertising's role in the marketing mix. Next how advertising objectives, creative strategy, and media strategy affect advertising campaigns is discussed. Finally, students will learn how marketers evaluate the effectiveness of campaigns. Ann Olofsson, account manager at A&O Analys is the focus of the Real People, Real Choices segment.

Objectives

1.   Tell what advertising is and describe the major types of advertising.

2.   Describe the major players in the advertising process.

3.   Tell how advertisers develop an advertising campaign.

4.   Describe the major advertising media and the important considerations in media planning.

5.   Explain how advertisers evaluate the effectiveness of the campaign.

6.   Discuss the challenges facing advertising.

Chapter Outline and Suggested Activities

Introduction: Use the "Got Milk" Part 1 video to introduce the topic of advertising . Discuss how the message "Got Milk" evolved. Was the "Got Milk" campaign a success? Does the campaign represent product or institutional advertising?

1. **Promotional Messages: And Now a Word From Our Sponsor**
    **Refer to Objective 1
    a.   Types of Advertising
            Advertising: Nonpersonal communication paid for by an identified sponsor using mass media to persuade or inform.
            Common types of advertising
            1).   ***Product advertising:*** *an advertising message that focuses on a specific good or service*
            2).   ***Institutional advertising:*** *an advertising message that promotes the activities, personality, or point of view of an organization or company.*
                    a).   ***Advocacy advertising:*** *a type of public service advertising provided by an organization that is seeking to influence public opinion on an issue because it has some stake in the outcome.*
                    b).   ***Public service announcements:*** *advertising run by the media without charge for not-for-profit organizations or to champion a particular cause.*
    b.   Who Does Advertising?
            **Refer to Objective 2
            **Use Real People, Real Surfers: Exploring the Web
            Advertising Campaign: a coordinated, comprehensive plan that carries out promotion objectives and results in a series of advertisements placed in media over a period of time.
            1).   In-house agency— firms do their own advertising.
            2).   Limited-service agency provides one or more specialized services such as media buying or creative development
            3).   Major players in the development of an advertising campaign
                    a).   Account Management: Supervises the day-to-day activities on the account, and is the primary liaison between the agency and the client.
                    b).   Creative Services: These are the people who actually dream up and produce the ads.
                    c).   Research and Marketing Services: They collect and analyze information that will help account executives to develop a sensible strategy.
                    d).   Media planning: The media planner helps to determine which communications vehicles are the most effective and recommends the most efficient means for delivering the ad by deciding where, when, and how often it will appear.

2. **Developing the Advertising Campaign**
    **Refer to Objective 3
    **Use Marketing In Action: Real Choices at Postum
    a.   Identify the target market

Class Discussion   Refer to the Introduction and the video "Got Milk" who is the target market for the "Got Milk" campaign?

    b.   Establish Message and Budget Objectives
            1).   Setting message goals—some examples
                    a).   To increase brand awareness
                    b).   To boost sales by 2%
                    c).   To improve brand image
            2).   Setting the Budget

c. Design the Ad
    **Use Q#1 and/or Q#2 Marketing Practice: Applying What You've Learned
    **Use Instructor's Manual Marketing Mini-project 17-B
    1). *Creative strategy: the process that turns a concept into an advertisement*
    2). *Advertising appeal: the central idea or theme of an advertising message.*
    3). *Common advertising appeals*
        a). *Unique selling proposition (USP): An advertising appeal that focuses on one clear reason why a particular product is superior.*
        b). Comparative advertising
        c). Demonstration
        d). Testimonial
        e). Slice-of-life
        f), Lifestyle
        g). Feel-good
        h). Fear appeals
        i). Sex appeals
        j). Humorous appeal

Class Discussion   Bring to class or have students bring to class examples of these common advertising appeals. For each advertisement discuss who is the target market and whether or not the advertisement is effective.

Real People, Bad Choices?

Summary: Smith & Wesson introduced the Lady-Smith, a revolver with a slimmed-down grip. The company's ads have been criticized for preying on the fear of women.

Suggested Answer to the Discussion Question

1. Should advertisers be allowed to use fear as a reason to buy their client's products?
    As you begin a discussion of the use of fear appeals, focus on other products for which fear appeals are used. For example, car companies often use fear appeals to persuade consumers that their family will be safe on rainy days while riding in their car. Should car companies be allowed to use fear appeals?
        We may not always agree with the tactics some advertisers use, but their right to do so is protected by law, unless the results of their advertisements might result in harm to consumers.

---

d. Pretest What Will Be Said
    1). *Pretesting: a research method that seeks to minimize mistakes by getting consumer reactions to ad messages before they are placed in the media.*
    2). *Copy testing: marketing research method that seeks to measure the effectiveness of ads by determining whether consumers are receiving, comprehending, and responding to the ad according to plan.*
    3). Copy testing techniques
        a). Concept testing
        b). Test commercials
        c). Finished testing
e. Choose the Media
    **Refer to Objective 4
    Media planning: the process of developing media objectives, strategies, and tactics for use in an advertising campaign.

Aperture: the best place and time to reach a person in the target market group.

1). Types of Media: Where to Say It
**Use Table 17.2

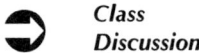

Class Discussion

Use Q#2 Marketing Practice: Applying What You've Learned for class discussion. Divide the class into teams and have each team discuss the pros and cons for one type of media vehicle.

a). Television
b). Radio
c). Newspapers
d). Magazines
e). Directories
f). *Out-of-home media: a communication medium that reaches people in public places.*
g). *Computer media: a communication medium that transmits information through the World Wide Web (WWW) or via e-mail messages.*

Spotlight on Real People: Lava Mind

Summary: Lava Mind makes weird CD-ROM business simulation games such as Gazillionaire and Zapitalism. Competing against big publishers with massive advertising budgets was tough, so Steven and Naomi (the owners) created the Virtual Pet Cemetery to attract visitors to their Web site. The strategy worked.

Suggested Answers to Discussion Questions:

1. **Who is the target market for the Virtual Pet Cemetery?**
   Web surfers

2. **What are Lava Mind's message goals?**
   The primary message goal is to create awareness of Lava Mind and to expose potential buyers to the products offered by the firm.

3. **What other advertising media might Lave Mind use?**
   TV, newspapers, and magazines are all very expensive, probably too expensive for Lava Mind to consider at this point. Lava Mind may want to consider radio. In a radio ad spot sound effects that allow listeners to imagine that they are playing the video game could be used.

---

2). Media Scheduling: When to Say it
**Use Figure 17.1

a). *Media schedule: The plan that specifies the exact media to use and when.*
b). When analyzing the media the planner is interested in assessing

Advertising exposure: The degree to which the target market will see an advertising message placed in a specific vehicle.

Impressions: The number of people who will be exposed to a message placed in one or more media vehicles.

Reach: The percentage of the target market that will be exposed to the media vehicle.

Frequency: The number of times a person in the target group will be exposed to the message.

Gross rating point (GRPs): A measure used for comparing the effectiveness of different media vehicles: average reach times frequency.

> ***Cost per thousand* (CPM):** *A measure used to compare the relative cost-effectiveness of different media vehicles that have different exposure rates; the cost to deliver a message to 1,000 people or homes.*

       3).   Media Scheduling: How Often to Say It
           a).   Continuous schedule
           b).   Pulsing schedule
           c).   Flighting schedule

3. Evaluating Advertising
**Refer to Objective 5
**Use Instructor's Manual Marketing Mini-project 17-A
a.   Posttesting
       Three ways to measure the impact of an advertisement:

       1).   ***Unaided recall:*** *a research technique conducted by telephone survey or personal interview that asks how much of an ad a person remembers during a specified period of time.*

       2).   ***Aided recall:*** *a research technique that uses clues to prompt answers from people about advertisements they might have seen.*

       3).   ***Attitudinal measures:*** *a research technique that probes a consumer's belief or feelings about a product before and after being exposed to messages about it.*

b.   Challenges Facing the Advertising Industry
       **Refer to Objective 6
       Threats facing the industry
       1).   Erosion of brand loyalty
       2).   Technology gives power back to people
       3).   Greater emphasis on point-of-purchase factors
       4).   The rules are changing
       5).   The advertising environment is cluttered
       6).   Some consumers are turned off by advertising

c.   How the Advertising Industry is Meeting the Challenges
       1).   Global research
       2).   Diversity
       3).   Technology
           **Use Marketing Mini-project: Learning by Doing as a summary activity

---

Real People, Real Choices: How it Worked Out at A & O Analys

Summary: Anna Olofsson is account manager at A&O Analys, a Swedish advertising agency focusing on strategic marketing consultation. The Swedish Brewers Association ask Anna Olofsson to create a public service message that would discourage young people from drinking.
    Olofsson considered three options.

Option 1: Focus on the risk of looking stupid in front of your friends while drunk.
Option 2: Focus on the fear of violence.
Option 3: Ask the kids themselves to help find a solution.

Olofsson used a combination of options 2 and 3.

Potential Discussion Questions

1.   Why was a fear appeal used?

2.   Why were rising young actors and actresses, rather than famous teenagers or young adults chosen as spokespersons?

Marketing Concepts: Testing Your Knowledge

1. **What is advertising and what is its role in marketing?**

   Advertising is a nonpersonal communication paid for by an identified sponsor who is using mass media to persuade or inform.

   Advertising informs, reminds, and creates (persuades) consumer desire. In other words, advertising is intended to bring about some change in its audience, whether to create awareness of a product, to change the way we think about it, or to get us to run out and buy it immediately.

2. **What are the types of advertising that are most often used?**

   Consumer product advertising is used to persuade consumers to choose a specific product or brand. Trade advertising promotes products to people and businesses in a specific industry. Institutional advertising is used to promote an entire organization (corporate image advertising), to promote a local store (retail advertising), to express the opinions of an organization (advocacy advertising), or to support a cause (public service advertising).

3. **List and describe the various departments in an advertising agency.**

   Advertising begins with the client or advertiser, who may be a manufacturer, a distributor, a retailer, or an institution. Some companies have an in-house advertising department, but most rely on the services of advertising agencies to create ads (or other promotions) and arrange for their delivery to the target market.

   Typical agency personnel and departments include:

   a. Account management—described as the "soul" of the agency. The account executive is in charge of developing the overall strategy for the client and making sure that the advertising that is created will meet the client's needs. The account executive supervises the day-to-day activities on the account and is the primary liaison between the agency and the client.

   b. Creative services—the "heart" of the communications effort. These are the people who actually dream up the ads. Different job tasks and roles include the creative director, copywriter, art director, and producer.

   c. Research and marketing services—the "brains" of the operation. They collect and analyze information that will help account executives develop a sensible strategy. They assist creatives in designing and evaluating ad executions by doing copy testing to gauge consumer reactions to different versions of ads and by providing copywriters with information about the target group.

   d. The account planner—is not attached to a department. The account planner works with researchers and creatives to be sure that ads will appeal to the target market. This person talks to consumers in the field about a product and then shares their opinions with the client and creatives.

   e. Media planning—the media planner helps to determine which communications vehicles will be the most effective at accomplishing the campaign's advertising objectives.

4. **What is an advertising campaign?**

   An advertising campaign is a coordinated, comprehensive plan that carries out promotion objectives and results in a series of advertisements placed in media over a period of time.

5. **What is a creative strategy? Describe some of the different advertising appeals.**

   Creative strategy is the process that turns a concept into an advertisement. Some of the different advertising appeals used in advertising include:

   a. Unique Selling Position: An appeal that focuses on one clear reason why a particular product is superior.

   b. Comparative Advertising: An appeal that explicitly names two or more competitors.

   c. Demonstration: The ad shows the product "in action" to prove that it performs as claimed.

   d. Testimonial: A celebrity, an expert, or a "typical person" states the product's effectiveness.

   e. Slice-of-Life: This format presents a dramatized scene from everyday life.

f.   Lifestyle: Shows person(s) attractive to the target market in an appealing lifestyle.

g.   Feel-good: Messages that are warm and friendly.

h.   Fear Appeals: The negative consequences of using or not using a product.

i.   Humorous Appeals: Humorous ads can be an effective way to break through advertising clutter.

j.   Sex Appeals: An appeal that relies on sexuality to get consumers' attention.

6.   **What are the strengths and weaknesses of television, radio, newspapers, magazines, directories, out-of-home media, and computer media for advertising?**
See Table 17.2 for additional information and description.

	Strengths	Weaknesses
Newspapers	Wide exposure Flexible format	Short time reading Low readership
Magazines	Targeted audiences Long life and repeat reading	Expensive Long deadline dates
Television	Extremely creative High impact message	Message impression is fleeting Fragmented audience
Radio	Targeted audiences Low cost	Lack of attention Not appropriate for some products
Outdoor	Low cost Good supplemental medium	Hard to communicate complex messages Visual pollution image
Place-based	Can break through clutter	Relative high cost in popular areas

7.   **What information does a media planner use in developing an effective media schedule?**
Media schedule is the plan that specifies what media will be used and when the messages will be sent.
Considerations include:

a.   The match between demographic and psychographic profiles for the audience and media vehicles.

b.   Sales patterns of the media and their associated markets.

c.   The advertising patterns of competitors.

d.   The amount of attention that viewers or readers profess for each media form.

e.   The capability of each medium to convey the desired messages and information.

f.   The quality of the media environment.

8.   **What are continuous, pulsing, and flighting media schedules?**
A *continuous schedule* maintains a steady stream of advertising throughout the year. This is appropriate for products that sell on a regular basis.

A *pulsing schedule* varies the amount of advertising throughout the year based on when the product is likely to be in demand. Advertisements for suntan lotion and Christmas ornaments would use a pulsing schedule.

A *flighting schedule* is an extreme form of pulsing in which advertising appears in short, intense bursts alternating with periods of little to no activity.

9.   **What are the challenges facing advertising today? How have advertisers responded to these challenges?**

a.   Erosion of brand loyalty—image oriented advertising that stresses intangible qualities of the brand

b.   Technology gives power back to the people—to face the challenges caused from channel surfing, advertisers must make ads more exciting and find new ways to reach consumers, such as the Internet.

c. Greater emphasis on point-of-purchase factors—focus on store sales promotions and publicity events

d. The rules are changing—advertising agencies are now competing with other industries for business. Advertisers are moving toward an integrated marketing communication approach in order to face this challenge.

e. The advertising environment is cluttered—Messages are often simpler and the media schedule is more varied.

f. Some consumers are turned off by advertisements—Finding new ways to lend credibility to advertisements

10. How can advertisers make sure their advertising is effective before it is placed in the media and after the audience has been exposed to the advertising in the media?

Although it is clear that advertising does increase sales, advertisers need to conduct research to determine whether specific advertisements are effective. One method of doing this is to conduct pre-testing or *copy testing* (a procedure that measures whether an ad is received, comprehended, and responded to in the desired manner). Versions of this form of testing include concept testing, testing of TV advertising animatics or storyboards, and finished ad testing.

Advertisers often need more solid evidence that a campaign is doing what it set out to do. In order to do this advertisers can conduct post-testing research to make sure that ads are doing well. Several methods make sure that ads are remembered, liked, and understood. Common methods are the *Starch Report* for magazines and *Burke Day-After Recall* for television. Both of these services interview consumers to determine who read or saw the ads and what they came away with afterward.

Three ways to measure the impact of an advertisement are unaided-recall (can consumers remember ads—no prompting is allowed), aided-recall (prompting is allowed to aid consumers in remembering ads), and attitudinal measures (probes deeper by examining consumer's beliefs or feelings about the product before and after being exposed to messages about it).

Marketing Concepts: Discussing Choices and Issues

1. Some people are turned off by advertising because they say it is obnoxious, that it insults their intelligence, and that advertising claims are untrue. Others argue that advertising is beneficial and actually provides value for consumers. What are some arguments on each side? Hoe do you feel?

Most students will probably not have an opinion on this issue because they will have experienced advertising rather than thought about advertising in a strict consumer sense or strict business sense. To begin a discussion in this area consider the for and against arguments listed below. Students should be able to add to the list. Ask them whether they would be better off with or without advertising?

Arguments for advertising:
a. Provides needed information about the product or service.
b. Increases demand (which affects more areas than one might imagine).
c. Encourages the production of more goods and services (which is good for the economy and jobs).
d. Makes economies of scale possible.
e. Gives a signal about product quality.
f. Helps consumers know about goods that they normally would not have information about.
g. Promotes efficiency at the local retail level because of heightened sense of competition.
h. Helps to create desire for products and services.

Arguments against advertising:
a. Effectiveness can't really be measured.
b. Increases costs.
c. Makes us want things that we can't have.
d. Discriminates between rich and poor.
e. Tries to sell us products that have no socially redeeming value.
f. Distorts the truth.
g. Makes children want things that they shouldn't have.
h. Makes us want to throw away things before their useful value is over.

2.	**In recent years, for various reasons, many advertisers have been decreasing the amount spent on advertising. What are the reasons for this change? What do you think will happen to advertising spending during the next five to ten years?**

Among commonly cited reasons for a reduction in ad spending in recent years are the following:

a.	Erosion of brand loyalty.
b.	Technology gives power back to the people.
c.	Greater emphasis on point-of-purchase factors.
d.	The rules are changing in the industry.
e.	Advertising is expensive.
f.	The advertising environment is changing.
g.	Some consumers are turned off to advertising.
h.	Leveraged buyouts and uncertainty have caused a reduction in spending.
i.	Relationship marketing has encouraged a different form of customer communication.

3.	**Advertisers who spend millions of dollars for Super Bowl ad spots may be more interested in achieving esthetic goals—that is, having the most highly rated ad—than in selling products. Does it make sense for advertisers to focus on esthetic goals rather than marketing goals? Explain.**

As noted in the previous chapter, promotion goals and objectives (and therefore advertising goals and objectives) are not necessarily consistent with marketing goals and objectives. One of the functions of integrated communications strategies is to bring these two more in line with one another. When marketers have esthetic goals such as the one mentioned above, their rationale might be more deep than meets the eye. This does not mean that the expenditure is justified. It means that the critic must carefully examine the reasons for the esthetic reason. The student in formulating their answer should also be reminded of the several goals of promotion (and therefore advertising) mentioned in the previous chapter. The goal might not always be to stimulate immediate sales. What might some of the other goals and objectives be?

4.	**Technology through television remotes, VCRs, computers, and cable television is giving today's consumers more and more control over the advertising images they see. How has this affected the advertising industry so far, and do you think this will affect it in the future? What are some ways that advertising can respond to this?**

These technologies have given "power back to the people" by making it easy for them to turn-off and/or tune-out advertisements. For example, a favorite television show is tapped, and when the show is watched at a later time, the viewer fast forwards over the advertisements. This means that advertisements have to more exciting and creative in order to get the customers attention. Advertisers must also find new methods for communicating with consumers, for example, interactive Web sites.

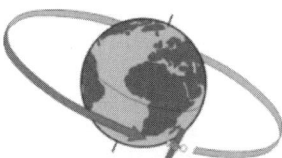

Real People, Real Surfers: Exploring the Web

In this exercise students are instructed to visit the Web sites of several advertising agencies. Students will learn about the mission of each agency investigated and the major clients of each agency. (If you have students who are interested in advertising as a career, this is a great exercise for them to complete.)

Marketing in Action: Real Choices at Postum

Summary: Postum is a 100 year old coffee substitute of which many of today's consumers have never heard. Postum is made from roasted wheat, bran, and molasses, the powder is added to hot water to make a tasty morning beverage.

Suggest Answers to Case Questions

1. **What is the problem facing Postum?**
   Though the basic question facing Postum can be stated in a variety of ways (from very general objectives to specific media initiatives) the simple answer to this question is how can Postum expand its market.

2. **What factors are important in understanding this problem?**
   Important factors that should be considered when addressing this problem are:
   a.   The history of the brand.
   b.   The previous advertising strategy of the brand.
   c.   The sales goals for the brand.
   d.   The budget.
   e.   The current users, their needs, and problem solutions fulfilled by the brand.
   f.   New market desires.
   g.   Position of the brand.
   h.   The new proposed message of the brand.

3. **What alternatives might Postum marketers consider?**
   The following are a series of alternative choices that are designed to stimulate discussion in this area:
   a.   Status quo—do nothing—the brand is still doing OK.
   b.   Abandon the brand.
   c.   Sell the brand.
   d.   Private label the brand and quit supporting the brand as a national product.
   e.   Do research to examine how to attract new users and determine who the new users might be.
   f.   Develop a positioning strategy to re-vamp the brand and its image.
   g.   Develop an advertising strategy to re-vamp the brand.

4. **What are your recommendations for solving the problem?**
   The students should see (even though they will probably have no interest in this product) that a product can be successful with no advertising. They should also ask the question about the viability of this product for a younger generation. Why has it been so successful for an older generation? How have those consumers found out about this product?

   Because of the questions mentioned above, the first step to solving the brand's problem is probably to adopt alternative "e" and do research. It would probably be premature to devise an advertising campaign given the limited data provided in the case. If the students choose this alternative, they should be asked about the type of data that would be necessary for the planners to develop a new and expanded image approach for the brand.

5. **What are some ways to implement your recommendations?**
   Similar to the material presented in the previous question, students should outline a process whereby they would gather information to make the advertising decisions necessary to construct a new and dynamic campaign for the brand. One further consideration is the rather limited budget that has been proposed. How far will a $1 million dollar budget get you? Not very far if new (and as yet undetermined) markets are to be pursued. Can the students outline a series of one year events that might be undertaken? How much would this cost? What could be the potential benefits? When is it time to call it quits on an old brand?

Mini-Project 17-A
Copy Testing Ad Ideas

Purpose: to better understand the importance of copy testing in creating effective advertising

Advertising costs firms millions or even hundreds of millions of dollars every year. Quite obviously, marketers want every assurance they can get that their money is being spent wisely. For this reason advertising agencies frequently test advertising at several different stages in the creative process—from the basic concept to the finished ad.

1.   With several of your classmates, create a new imaginary brand of a product that students like yourselves typically buy and use.

2.   Next, each of the members or your group should develop a story board of a television commercial. (It will probably be more fun if you do this without discussing your ideas with each other.)
        A story board is a series of drawings that show what will happen in a finished commercial along with the dialogue and information about any music, sound, special effects, etc.

3.   Present the story boards to your class. Show them the drawings and explain the dialogue, music, effects, etc.

4.   Ask the students to rate each commercial. You will probably want them to rate the ads on such factors as whether

    ■   they like the ad
    ■   the ad provides them with the information they want and need about the product
    ■   they would be likely to buy the product based on the ad
    ■   they feel they would remember the ad including the brand name and the message

(You may want to develop a short questionnaire for these ratings.)

5.   After the ratings are completed, the results tallied, and the preferred ad announced, ask your class to discuss exactly what they feel is good about the ads and what recommendations they would make for improving any of the ads.

Mini-Project 17-B
Examining Advertising Messages

Purpose: to recognize different types of advertising appeals.

Whether in television commercials, magazine advertisements or infomercials, the guts of an advertising is the message. Advertising messages are generally categorized based of

- the appeal and
- the format

Some types of communications appeals are

Rational Appeals
- *a Unique Selling Proposition (USP)* that gives consumers one clear reason for buying the product
- *comparative advertising* which compares the advertised product with a competing identified brand

Emotional Appeals
- *fear appeals* which highlight the negative physical or social consequences of not using the advertised product
- *sex appeals*
- *humorous appeals*

Ad formats include

Lecture format in which the source of the message speaks directly to the audience
    Lecture formats include
- *demonstration* in which the product is shown in action
- *problem solution*
- *testimonial*

Drama format which means that the ad is similar to a play or a movie
    Drama formats include
- *metaphor* involving the use of comparison
- *allegory* in which an abstract trait or concept is personified as a person, animal, vegetable of mythical figure
- *story line* where the ad tells a story about the product itself
- *slice-of-life* presents a dramatized scene from real life
- *lifestyle* in which a person or persons calculated to be attractive to the target market are shown in an appealing setting with the product

Search through magazines your read regularly for examples of each of the following types of advertisements. Describe the elements in each ad that categorize it.

Unique Selling Proposition (USP)

_____

_____

_____

_____

comparative advertising

_____

_____

_____

_____

fear appeals

_____

_____

_____

_____

sex appeals

_____

_____

_____

_____

humorous appeals

_____

_____

_____

_____

demonstration

_____

_____

_____

_____

problem solution testimonial

_____

_____

_____

_____

metaphor

_____

_____

_____

_____

allegory

_____

_____

_____

_____

storyline

_____

_____

_____

_____

slice-of-life

_____

_____

_____

_____

lifestyle

_____

_____

_____

_____

18

Sales Promotion, Public Relations, and Personal Selling

Overview This chapter focuses on three important elements in the promotion mix. Sales promotion, public relations, and personal selling. These communications are crucial to many marketing strategies, and each can be implemented separately or ideally—coordinated with a firm's advertising activities. Bunny Richardson, coordinator for media relations at BMW Manufacturing Corp, is the focus of the Real People, Real Choices segment.

Objectives

1. Explain the role of public relations and its function.

2. Describe the steps in developing a public relations campaign.

3. Explain what sales promotion is and describe some of the different types of trade and consumer sales promotion activities.

4. Explain the important role of personal selling in the marketing effort.

5. List the steps in the personal, selling process.

6. Explain the job of the sales manager.

Chapter Outline and Suggested Activities	**Introduction:** Discuss with students the difference between sales promotion, public relations and personal selling.

The video NASCAR: Racing for Sponsorships could also be used to introduce this chapter.

1.   Public Relations
**Refer to Objective 1
**Use Table 18.1
a.   ***Public Relations: Communications strategies to build good relationships with an organization's publics, including consumers, stockholders, and legislators.***
  1).   ***Publicity:*** unpaid communication about an organization appearing in the mass media.
  2).   Public relations is important in shaping and communicating the company's image.

➡ *Class Discussion*   You have just received word that two children have been slightly injured while playing with your company's new water gun toy. What should you do?

b.   Objectives of Public Relations
  1).   Introducing new products to manufacturers
  2).   Introducing new products to consumers
  3).   Influencing government legislation
  4).   Enhancing the image of a city, region, or country.
  5).   Calling attention to a firm's involvement with the community.

➡ *Class Discussion*   Have students provide an example for each of the public relations objectives listed above.

c.   Planning a Public Relations Campaign
**Refer to Objective 2
**Use Marketing in Action: Real People at Hawkeye Bank
There is a three-step process of developing objectives, executing, and evaluating.
  1).   Develop clear objectives—define the message you want people to hear.
  2).   Creating and executing a campaign strategy.
    a).   The most common way for public relations specialists to communicate is a press release
    b).   ***Press release:*** *information distributed to the media by an organization about its activities, intended to appear as publicity.*
    c).   Common types of press releases
      ■   Timely topics
      ■   Research stories
      ■   Consumer information
  3).   Evaluate the effectiveness of the campaign
    **Use Table 18.2

2.   Sales Promotions
**Refer to Objective 3
**Use Real People, Real Surfers: Exploring the Web
**Use Table 18.3

Sales Promotion: A program designed to build interest in or encourage purchase of a product during a specified time period.

   a.   Trade Promotions

        1).   Discounts and deals

             a).   ***Merchandise allowance:*** *reimburses the retailer for in-store support of the product.*

             b).   ***Case allowance:*** *A discount to the retailer or wholesaler based on the volume of product ordered.*

        2).   Industry Boosting and Boasting

             a).   ***Trade shows:*** *Events at which many companies set up elaborate exhibits to show their products, give away samples, distribute product literature, and troll for new business contacts.*

             b).   Promotional products

             c).   Incentive programs

                 ■   ***Push money:*** *a bonus paid by a manufacturer to a sales-person for selling its products*

   b.   Consumer Promotions

        **Use Instructor's Manual Marketing Mini-project 18-A

        **Use Q#3 and/or Q#4 Marketing Practice: Applying What You've Learn

        1).   Price-Based Promotions

             a).   Coupons

             b).   Price deals, refunds, and rebates

                 ■   ***Rebate:*** *sales promotions that allow the customer to recover part of the product's cost from the manufacturer.*

             c).   Special packs

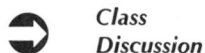 ***Class Discussion***   Evaluate the effectiveness of each of the price-based consumer promotions.

        2).   Attention—Getting Promotions

             a).   ***Premiums:*** *an item included without charge when a customer buys a product.*

             b).   ***Sampling:*** *distributing trial-size versions of a product for free to encourage people to try it.*

             c).   ***Point-of-purchase (POP) promotion:*** *the use of signs or displays to influence purchases at the store level*

             d).   ***Cross-promotion:*** *two or more products or services combine forces to create interest using a single promotional tool.*

3.   Personal Selling

        **Refer to Objectives 4 and 5

        **Use Computer Friendly Stuff (CFS) Case VI

   a.   The role of personal selling

        **Refer to Objective 4

        1).   **Telemarketing:** *the use of the telephone to sell directly to consumers and business customers*

        2).   **Order taker:** *a salesperson whose primary function is to facilitate transactions that are initiated by the customer.*

Real People, Bad Choices?

Summary: A Pepsi promotion in the Philippines offered to pay out $37,000 to holders of specially marked bottle caps. A computer glitch put out the wrong winning number and half a million people claimed the prize! Riots erupted when Pepsi refused to pay. As a gesture of goodwill, Pepsi offered to pay each cap holder 500 pesos (about $18.50).

Suggested Answer to the Discussion Question

1.   **Should a company be obligated to pay up even when an honest mistake is made?**
     The error which occurred was clearly a mistake and was probably caused by human error. Since no one was physically harmed by the mishap, Pepsi should not be held accountable and be required to pay. Pepsi did do the right thing by offering the disappointed cap holders a mall sum of money.

          3).   ***Technical specialist:*** *sales support personnel with a high level of technical expertise who assists in product demonstrations.*

          4).   ***Missionary salesperson:*** *a salesperson who promotes the firm and tries to stimulate demand for a product but does not actually complete a sale.*

          5).   ***Order getter:*** *a salesperson who works creatively to develop relationships with customers or to generate new sales.*

    b.   Approaches to Personal selling

          1).   Transactional Marketing: Putting on the Hard Sell

          Transactional selling: *a form of personal selling that focuses on making an immediate sale with little or no attempt to develop a relationship with the customer.*

          2).   Relationship selling: Countering the Tarnished Image

          Relationship selling: *a form of personal selling in which the salesperson seeks to develop a mutually satisfying relationship with the consumer so as to work together to satisfy each other's needs.*

Class Discussion   You have just accepted a position as a pharmaceutical sales representative. Your company is number two in the market and many of the products they sell are generic brands. The person who previously held your position left many of the company's clients dissatisfied. What can you do to help restore your firm's tarnished image and rebuild a relationship with these dissatisfied customers?

    c.   The Role of Personal Selling in the Promotion Mix

Class Discussion   Discuss the role of personal selling in the promotion mix of Computer Friendly Stuff.

    d.   The Selling Process
        **Refer to Objective 5
        **Use Instructor's Manual Marketing Mini-project 18-B
        **Use Figure 18.1
        1).   Prospect Customers

Use Marketing Mini-project: Learning by Doing

Prospecting: a part of the selling process that includes identifying and developing a list of potential or prospective customers.

2).   *Qualifying prospects: a part of the selling process that determines how likely prospects are to become customers.*

3).   Do a Preapproach

Preapproach: part of the selling process that includes developing information about prospective customers and planning the sales interview.

Spotlight on Real People: Danny Hahn, the Beer Man

Summary: Danny Hahn is a 34-year-old who sells beer at Baltimore's Camden Yards Stadium. Hahn does not just sell beer, he entertains his customers.

Suggested Answers to Discussion Questions

1.   **What kind of salesperson is the beer man?**
Danny Hahn is an order getter because he works creatively to develop relationships with customers.

2.   **What kind of sales presentation does Danny use?**
His approach uses entertainment and is tailored to meet the needs of each individual customers.

3.   **How does Danny Hahn sell relationships in addition to beer?**
Danny knows his customers by name. When other vendors leave during the eighth inning, Hahn returns to the stands to shake hands with his customers and thank them for coming.

---

4).   Make the approach

Approach: the first step of the actual sales presentation in which the salesperson tries to learn more about the customer's needs, create a good impression, and build rapport.

5).   Make the Sales Presentation

Sales Presentation: the part of the selling process in which the salesperson seeks to persuasively communicate the product's features and the benefits it will provide after the sale.

6).   Overcome Customer Objectives

7).   Close the Sale

Sale Closing: the stage of the selling process in which the salesperson actually asks the customer to buy the product.

8).   Follow up after the sales

Sales follow up: Sales activities that provide important services to customers.

e.   Sales Management

**Refer to Objective 6

Sales Management: the process of planning, implementing, and controlling the personal selling function of an organization

1).   Setting Sales Force Objectives

    a).   Performance goals

    b).   Behavioral goals

2).   Creating a Sales Force Strategy

Sales territory: a set of customers often defined by geographic boundaries, for whom a particular salesperson is responsible

3).   Recruiting, Training, and Rewarding Salespeople

Real People, Real Choices: How it Worked Out at BMW

Summary: Bunny S. Richardson is coordinator of media relations at BMW's first full manufacturing facility in the United States. In 1992, BMW selected Spartanburg County, South Carolina as the site for its first full manufacturing facility outside of Germany. After the first year of operation BMW decided to expand the South Carolina factory. Richardson and her colleagues needed to find a way to get favorable publicity for BMW.

Option 1: Schedule a press conference at the existing South Carolina factory.
Option 2: Visit the reporters and editors on their home turf to talk about the expansion and to use the opportunity to educate people about the factory.
Option 3: Make the event a more broad-based South Carolina story about an international company investing for a second time in a state where the automobile industry is relatively new.

The BMW team chose combination of options 2 and 3.

Potential Discussion Questions

1.   What are the advantages to options 2 and 3?

2.   When BMW announced that it was expanding it's facility, who were the winners?

Marketing Concepts: Testing Your Knowledge

1. **What is public relations? What is publicity?**

   Public relations—activities of organizations aimed at influencing the way consumers, stockholders, and other feel about brands, companies, politicians, celebrities, not-for-profits organizations, and even governments.

   Public relations is crucial to an organization's ability to create and manage a favorable long-term image. It is especially valued by marketers who understand the importance of also satisfying non-customer groups (those who can affect the fortunes of an organization apart from individual purchase decisions, such as government regulators and the investment community).

   One way that public relations specialists do their job is by creating publicity for the organization. *Publicity* is any unpaid communication about an organization appearing in mass media.

2. **What are the objectives of public relations?**

   The following are objectives of public relations:
   a. Introduce new products to manufacturers.
   b. Introduce new products to consumers.
   c. Influence government legislation.
   d. Ease public acceptance of corporate changes.
   e. Enhance the image of a city, region, or country.
   f. Encourage recruitment and patronage at not-for-profit institutions.
   g. Enhance the image of a company by linking it to activities that benefit society.

3. **What are the steps in planning a public relations campaign?**

   The following are suggested steps in planning a public relations campaign:
   a. A statement of the problem.
   b. A situation analysis.
   c. The development of program goals and objectives.
   d. Specifications of target audiences (publics), messages to be communicated, and specific program elements.
   e. A timetable and budget.
   f. Discussion of how the program will be evaluated.

4. **What is sales promotion? When is sales promotion more likely to be an important part of the promotion mix?**

   Sales promotion—short-term programs to build interest in, or encourage purchase of, a good or service during a specified time period.

   Sales promotion has become more important in recent years because advertising has become very expensive and less effective, brand loyalty has deteriorated, sales promotion activities are effective for smaller markets, and marketers can measure the results of sales promotions. Sales promotions are a very useful component of the promotion mix when the firm has an immediate objective, such as increasing sales for a brand quickly or encouraging consumers to try a new product.

5. **Explain some of the different types of trade promotions frequently used by marketers.**

   See Table 18.3 for additional information and explanation of trade promotions.

   Trade promotions can roughly be divided into two types: First, there are efforts to make retailers' lives easier by giving them a break on what they pay for a product or on advertising. Second, there are efforts to generate product awareness and orders by creating opportunities for the retailer and other members of the distribution channel to be exposed to one's products.

   With respect to the first form, manufacturers provide local advertisers support (cooperative advertising allowances) or sales training. Next, they may give a may give a break on prices (*price allowance*—a type of trade sales promotion in which a manufacturer reduces prices to retailers).

   Lastly, trade shows, specialty advertising, and incentive programs can aid sales force effectiveness and industry promotions.

6. **Explain some of the different types of consumer sales promotions frequently used by marketers.**
Consumer sales promotions may be classified as attention-getting activities, point-of-purchase (POP) activities, or price-based promotions.

Attention-getting promotions involve the consumer in the company's marketing efforts and include giveaways, contests, and sweepstakes, and premiums delivered to the consumer in, on, or near the package or through the mail.

POP activities include in-store sampling, product displays, and signs, and in-store media.

Price-based consumer promotions include coupons, which are most often delivered via newspaper free-standing inserts (FSIs), price-offs, rebates, and special packs such as bonus packs.

7. **What is the role played by personal selling within the total marketing function?**
For most firms, some form of personal selling is essential for a transaction (the sale) to occur, so this type of promotion is an important part of an organization's overall marketing plan. Through one-on-one selling, the salesperson can directly address customer objections, can furnish other customer services (such as installations, setup, and instruction), can provide the company with feedback on the marketing effort, and is a source of competitive intelligence.

8. **What is the difference between transactional selling and relationship selling?**
Transactional selling—a form of personal selling that focuses on making an immediate sale with little or no attempt to develop a relationship with the customer.

Relationship selling—a form of personal selling in which the salesperson seeks to develop a mutually satisfying relationship with the customer so they can work together to satisfy each others' needs.

9. **What are order getters, order takers, missionary salespeople, and technical specialist?**
Order getter—a salesperson who works creatively to develop relationships with customers or to generate new sales.

Order taker—a salesperson whose primary function is to facilitate transactions that are initiated by the customer.

Missionary salespeople—salespeople who promote the firm and try to stimulate demand for a product but do not actually complete a sale.

Technical specialist—are sales support personnel who have a high level of expertise and who assists in product demonstrations.

10. **List the steps in the creative selling process.**
See Figure 18.1 for additional material and discussion.

The steps in the creative selling process are listed as:
a. Prospecting and qualifying.
b. Preapproach.
c. Approach.
d. Sales presentation.
e. Handling objections.
f. Close.
g. Follow-up.

11. **Describe the major decisions made by sales managers.**
a. Setting sales force objectives.
b. Creating a sales force strategy.
c. Recruiting, training, and rewarding salespeople.

Marketing Concepts: Discussing Choices and Issues

1. **Some critics denounce public relations specialists, calling them "flacks" or "spin doctors: whose job is to cover up the truth about company's problems. What is the proper role of public relations within an organization? Should PR specialists try to put a good face on bad news?**
In order for students to answer this question, please refer to "Marketing Concepts: Testing Your Knowledge" Questions 1 and 2.

It is the job of PR specialists to try to make the company look good, even when the news is bleak. For example, after an airline crash, the airline carrier involved in the crash and the airline industry promptly issue PR messages to reassure customers that it is ok to fly. The objective is not to cover up the fact that a crash occurred, but rather to respond to consumer's fears and to reassure them that it is safe to fly. If prompt PR measures were not taken, the entire airline industry and affiliated industries (such as travel agencies and tourism) would suffer.

2. **Companies sometimes teach consumers a "bad lesson" with the overuse of sales promotion. As a result, consumers expect the product always to be "on deal." What are some examples of products where this has occurred? How do you think companies can prevent this?**

    Most products that students will be able to name come from the grocery area. Some examples might include cereals, milk, beer, soda, candy, many canned goods, and bread. Others that they might recall are the "value meals" at fast food restaurants and quantity discounts in certain clothing stores.

    One method for preventing the phenomenon is to avoid constant sales promotion campaigns. Or the marketer can have clear sales promotional goals, vary the campaigns, and make clear to the consumer what the "real" retail price is an stick to it.

3. **In general, professional selling has evolved from "hard sell" to transactional selling. But does the hard sell still exist? If so, in what types of organizations? What do you think the future holds for these organizations? Will the hard sell continue to succeed?**

    To some extent hard sell organizations still exist. The text uses the examples of encyclopedias, refrigerators, and televisions. In general, organizations whose purpose is to sell to the consumer only once or a few times use the hard sell technique. But as consumers, the hard sell technique makes us feel manipulated and resentful. The truly professional salesperson, on the other hand, plans for the long term and works hard to build a relationship with customers.

    The future is not bright for the hard sell organization (even though the form will probably continue for some time). Relationship selling is rapidly replacing the hard sell. As more success comes to those that use relationship selling and as consumers grow to appreciate and expect its benefits, the hard sell will end up being no sell at all.

4. **One reason cited by experts for the increase in consumer catalog shopping is the poor quality of service available at retail stores. What do you think about the quality of most retail salespeople you come in contact with? What are some ways in which retailers can improve the quality of their sales associates?**

    To be fair this discussion should probably be begun by asking what students like and dislike about retail sales experiences and retail salespeople. Can these statements be categorized into several common areas? If so, then those negative areas are a place to begin to remedy the problem of the retail sales environment.

    Common complaints are that the retail salespeople are rude, inexperienced, do not know about the products or services offered, are only trying to make a sale rather than satisfy the customer, don't really want to wait on the customer, don't pay any attention to the customer, and (even though they are underpaid—sometimes only receiving minimum wage—or over worked) they aren't worth their salary. This list should generate discussion on how to fix the situation at the retail sales level.

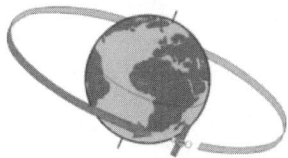

Real People, Real Surfers: Exploring the Web

In this exercise students are instructed to visit several Wed sites which have been developed for the sole purpose of distributing coupons. You may want to focus class discussion on responses to questions 1 and 3.

Marketing in Action: Real Choices at Hawkeye Bank

Summary: United States Bank (USB) a $50 million financial institution had been in business in Cedar Rapids, Iowa for over 70 years. The company was purchased in 1982 by Hawkeye Bank Corporation. Originally USB retained its name, but recently all 22 banks owned by Hawkeye voted to adopt a common name: Hawkeye Bank.

Suggested Answers to Case Questions

1. **What is the problem facing USB?**
   The problem might be simply stated as how can USB adopt a name change without alienating their traditional customer base.

2. **What factors are important in understanding this problem?**
   Several factors must be considered by USB. They are:
   a.   Understand the insecurity that might occur from a name change.
   b.   Understand how the existing markets currently view the bank.
   c.   Understand how the existing markets might react to a name change.
   d.   Review the relationship with the new banking partners.
   e.   Review competition plans for proposed name changes.
   f.   Review any name change (actual names) options.

3. **What alternatives might USB consider?**
   Alternatives must be put into perspective to the actual actions that the bank is probably forced to take. Some alternatives that might generate discussion among the students are:
   a.   Research the attitudes in the market before a name change is adopted.
   b.   Make the name change right away and let the customers adjust.
   c.   Determine what forms of promotion or publicity might make the name change transition more smooth.
   d.   Determine if there is any way to avoid the name change.

4. **What are your recommendations for solving the problem?**
   The problems facing USB are rather straight forward. Recommendations should probably be considered more as planning devices. Alternatives "a" and "c" seem to be the best of the ones offered above. The bank must research attitudes and then prescribe promotional alternatives to aid in solving any negative aspects.

5. **What are some ways to implement your recommendations?**
   The only group that the bank thinks will be resistant to any name change is their older traditional market. Therefore, research on this market is probably a good first step. The research could be a survey or a focus group. The focus group would probably provide quicker answers as to how to best approach the change.
   Once the results of the focus group are in, the bank should develop a roll-out promotional program to implement the proposed change. The bank must also remember that the success of the effort will depend heavily on the existing bank employees and the confidence that show to the customer about the impending change. Some portion of the promotion effort might be directed toward these employees (such as incentive rewards).

Mini-Project 18-A
Consumer Sales Promotion

Purpose: to learn about the different types of consumer sales promotions.

Companies spend billions of dollars every year on consumer sales promotions—from coupons to rebates to the prize in the bottom of the box of cereal. But sales promotions are used for several different purposes. Some of the objectives of sales promotions are to motivate

- consumers to try a product or
- non-users to try an existing product
- users of competing brands to buy the promoted brand
- users of the product and/or brand to use more of the product
- users of the brand to buy more of the brand and stock pile
- image enhancement

Below are listed some of the different types of consumer sales promotions. For each one, find one or more examples. Describe the example and then tell what you think the objective of the sales promotion is. Finally, evaluate how effective you feel the promotion will be in meeting its objective and, if possible, make recommendations for changes in the sales promotion program.

Describe the Sales Promotion Example	What is the Objective of the Sales Promotion	What is Your Evaluation of the Sales Promotion
Coupons		
Rebates		
Sweepstakes		

Describe the Sales Promotion Example	What is the Objective of the Sales Promotion	What is Your Evaluation of the Sales Promotion
In-pack Premium		
Bonus Pack		
Continuity Plan		
Sampling		
Self-liquidating Premium		
Store Displays		

Describe the Sales Promotion Example	What is the Objective of the Sales Promotion	What is Your Evaluation of the Sales Promotion
In-Store Video		
Reusable Container		

Mini-Project 18-B
Making a Sales Presentation

Purpose: to experience planning and delivering a sales presentation

Many young people begin their careers in marketing as a professional salesperson. Some continue in professional selling because they find it an enjoyable and rewarding career while others use selling as a foundation for other jobs in marketing. In any case, the skills of the good salesperson are of value. In this mini-project you will have the opportunity to begin developing your skills in making winning sales presentations.

1.   First, you should decide on a product that you feel you could enjoy selling. This is important since very few of us will ever be successful selling a product we dislike or don't believe in. You will probably find that developing your sales presentation will be easier if you select a product which is typically sold though personal sales, that is, it is easier to develop a sales presentation for a new improved personal computer than for a bottle of shampoo.

2.   Develop an outline of your sales presentation. You may want to include some or all of the following:

   - an approach which initiates the contact with the prospective customer
   - questions about the customer's product needs, the benefits wanted, etc.
   - information about the benefits the product will provide for the customer
   - details about such aspects of the augmented product as warranties, service, etc.
   - facts, data, or other proof statements to support the statements made about the   product
   - good visuals
   - an opportunity for the customer to ask questions and raise objections
   - a closing which asks for the sale
   - after the sale is agreed upon, a summary of what all parties involved are expected to do and when

3.   VERY IMPORTANT: Practice your sales presentation. Then practice again. Finally practice some more. In rehearsing your presentation you will want to be sure that you are

   - enthusiastic
   - well mannered
   - friendly
   - energetic
   - animated

4.   Ask a member of your class to serve as your "customer" and with him/her present your sales presentation for your class.

5.   Ask for feedback and a critique from your classmates and/or your Instructor.

Computer Friendly Stuff (CFS)

Case Notes

Prepared by:

Chris Cole, President
Computer Friendly Stuff

End of Case Answers to Questions

1. **Q:** *What concepts from Chapters 1–4 apply to this case?*

    A: Computers are plain looking. No one can really argue that point. Depending on what's in the computer and what's on the computer, they can be boring too. There are all kinds of innovative and entertaining software programs (screen savers, wallpapers, etc.) that bring life to a computer and give it texture in the stale environment that is sometimes the office cubicle, reception desk or home office. There are also colorful screen frames that are designed for computers, and there are always little toy figurines (trolls, action figures and such) that consumers can purchase to set on top of their computers. However, until the Computer Bug, there were no toy figurines that were designed not only to be integrated into the exterior of the computer but that also existed inside the computer. Create an entertaining character that exists inside and outside of the computer and that also makes sense in this artificial environment, create additional characters that can be added to the line in the future, do it at a price that allows a high margin of profit, and what have you done? You have fulfilled the **basic marketing concept**. You have focused on identifying and satisfying consumer needs to ensure the organization's long term profitability objectives. The consumer's actual state of wanting products to decorate the outside of his computer and to beautify the computer screen as well belied the actual need—to have a product that conceptually becomes part of the computer and satisfies both desires, "the desired state." Being that entertainment could be considered a need of any larger society, the **social marketing concept** applies in this case too. Fortunately for Computer Friendly Stuff, the humor and entertainment value of their products seems to be multicultural with initial sales on three different continents. While the concept of **relationship marketing** was not directly addressed, some elements do apply to the content of this case. Computer Friendly Stuff was seeking to set a price that both allowed for a good margin of profit while also preserving the image of their product. The "image" would only be important if Computer Friendly Stuff were looking for ongoing business with their customers.

2. **Q:** *What is meant by "good marketing makes good luck?" Do you think Computer Friendly Stuff made its own luck at the New York Toy Fair?*

    A: While it could be argued that Computer Friendly Stuff was a bit naïve in planning for the Toy Fair, it did some fairly good fly-by-the-seat-of-your-pants marketing. The company was stuck in an old, decrepit, model train section of the Toy Building and they were restricted on where they could go with the Computer Bug costume. Had they simply stayed within the confines of their booth space and braved the harsh weather conditions outside of the Toy Building with the Computer Bug costume as the show rules allowed, it's highly likely their original plan would have resulted in abject failure. They weren't reaching potential customers inside of the building, and the only action outside of the building was the rush to reach the warmth within. Better research and better planning would have resulted in more favorable conditions for Computer Friendly Stuff at its first Toy Fair, but that knowledge would only prove helpful for future Toy Fairs. Their situation was their situation. They had to bend the rules a little. The idea of handing out chocolates was great because it greatly decreased the likelihood that other exhibitors would complain about Computer Friendly Stuff wandering the building. After all, who wants to remove their supply of chocolate? Also, when you're handing out something for free, it is a rare individual who doesn't feel some responsibility to allow at least a little lip service from the gift giver. Staying one step ahead of security and probably risking expulsion from the show, Computer Friendly Stuff did finally do what it had to do, and managed to pull an order out of a situation where none were likely to come had they played by the rules. Was the order from New Zealand good luck? What is the old saying? "The harder you work, the luckier you get." Computer Friendly Stuff's guerrilla marketing strategy, developed on the fly, did result in an early, important piece of business, so, yes, Computer Friendly Stuff did make its own luck at the show.

3. **Q: *How would Computer Friendly Stuff's strategy change if the international sales had not occurred? What makes their product desirable to an international market?***
   A: Chances are that Computer Friendly Stuff would not have elected to pursue more flea markets and consumer direct sales as it was "backbreaking" work. One option would have been to look at how to better attack the domestic market. As was stated in the case, Computer Friendly Stuff learned that, "when we marketed directly to our customer, the product sold off of the shelf." Since selling direct to consumers is not an option, Computer Friendly Stuff could have helped develop their existing domestic business by doing sales meetings and in-store detailing with the sales people. To develop new accounts, and since they had inventory, they could offer to place merchandise for free in the stores and also provide sales education or even sales training by spending a day with the sales force in each new store. These are things that can be accomplished with personnel resources and very little expense. Since Computer Friendly Stuff had "no money," it would have to have used its personnel as efficiently as possible to better service existing customers and to attract the attention of potential customers. Small store chains would probably welcome the personal attention. The partners in Computer Friendly Stuff could have also decided to dilute their stock ownership to make available enough shares to attract investment capital for marketing expenditures. Of course the biggest problem in bringing in investment capital is that you also likely bring in another person, and there's no guarantee that this new person will work synergistically with the existing personnel. Because computer users worldwide cannot take full advantage of the internet without having a working knowledge of the English language, Computer Friendly Stuff has an edge with its product. While it is an English-only product, this product has English speaking customers all over the world. Therefore, if the product is satisfying a desire within its domestic English speaking market, why couldn't that same desire exist in other English speaking markets? Judging from the order from the New Zealanders and other orders received from Asia and the Middle East, the humor does at least translate to those cultures. So, what makes Computer Friendly Stuff's product desirable to an international market?: the satisfaction of a recognized desire of English speaking computer users wherever they may be.

4. **Q: *English, in many ways, is the language of the Internet. What makes the Original Computer Bug a good product to sell on-line, especially in a global market? What are the pros and cons of selling this type of product over the Internet?***
   A: Because the Original Computer Bug is a product that exists both inside and outside of the computer, on-line viewing of the product can provide the viewer an instant sensation of what it would be like to own it. Also, goofiness is a universal concept, and the figurine is certainly goofy enough to (at least on a surface level) convey the overall concept of the character's humor. Also, computer users worldwide all deal with the same computer problems. Some people may choose to cry over their problems, but some people may choose to make fun of them. Since English is basically the language of the Internet, the terms associated with computers and especially computer problems are the same worldwide. A bug is a bug is a bug. A crash is a crash is a crash, etc. Those consumers who don't take their computer problems too seriously are those who are more likely to purchase a Computer Bug. Additionally, the ease and security with which consumers can now purchase over the Internet makes the impulse buy that much more likely to take place. The con selling the Computer Bug over the internet is that there is a lot of artwork that can be copied off of the web sites and then used to counterfeit or infringe on Computer Friendly Stuff's trademarks. Also, if Computer Friendly Stuff is offering the product to individual consumers, the same old problem exists of selling one Computer Bug at a time. Each Bug has to be individually shipped which means higher costs in materials, shipping and personnel time. If the product doesn't weigh very much, it's highly likely that shipping six Computer Bugs in one box might cost the same to ship as one Computer Bug and probably takes the same

or less time to package. Selling distributors or store chains would seem like the ideal way to go, but selling one at a time over the Internet might also build awareness of the product and possibly interest from store chains and distributors.

MARKETING PLAN QUESTIONS AND ANSWERS

Refer to the Sample Marketing Plan in Appendix A as you answer the following questions about developing and modifying a marketing plan for CFS.

1.   For this year's marketing plan, how would you define CFS's distinctive competency, which is one of its key strengths and a critical component of its competitive strategy?

Answer: A distinctive competency is defined as a superior capability of a firm in comparison to its direct competitors. The distinctive competency of CFS is its ability to develop unique and creative integrated toy/software products to make using computers more fun. No competitors are offering screen savers that are fully integrated with adhesive toy attachments for computers.

2.   Looking ahead to next year's marketing plan, what additional information about global markets should CFS be gathering as it gets ready to expand distribution to more countries?

Answer: Students will offer a variety of answers, depending on the direction they believe CFS should take in its future global expansion. For example, students may suggest some of the following:

- CFS should research computer ownership trends and demographics of targeted market segments in selected countries or regions to identify promising new global markets.
- CFS should examine the competitive environment in other countries, looking at competing screen savers, computer toys, and similar accessories.
- CFS should look into the latest import/export rules governing software, especially any changes in the rules for exporting from the United States and the regulations for bringing software into other countries.

CASE #2

End of Case Answers to Questions

1. **Q:** *At the consumer level, CFS makes products that appeal to a wide demographic (computer users). Within that demographic, CFS thought their products appealed most to professional women aged 20–50 and boys/girls ages 7–14. Do you think the "professional women" category can be refined even more into distinct subgroups? Do you think there are other primary segments of consumers that CFS may have overlooked? Why?*

   A: One thing that has to be constantly kept in mind when discussing the "professional women" category is the fact that computers have slipped under the $1,000 mark. This means that a lot of people, especially home-based women, are surely contemplating something they hadn't previously considered; a computer purchase. On-line shopping for clothes and groceries can save hours and hours of time, and managing the checkbook, recipes and the children's schedules is a walk in the park for any mother who knows how to utilize a computer. Plus, computers are much more user friendly than they used to be and don't require a steep learning curve. In other words, a lot of people, including mothers, who may have been intimidated by technology are becoming less and less so as time and marketing by computer manufacturers continues. CFS may be overlooking the home-based woman. They shouldn't. Everyone wants to have fun, and everyone wants to be entertained. The CFS line is "G" rated, so mothers can be entertained by the Computer Bug without fear of some of the entertainment being inappropriate for their children. Other subgroups can include less affluent professional women who either work part time or who work in jobs that normally wouldn't supply the disposable income for a computer purchase. Almost anyone can now afford a computer, and all human beings are the same where entertainment and laughter are concerned. We all want it. Hopefully CFS is continuing to pay attention to the availability of computers because less affluent men are also likely to want to buy gadgets for their computers soon after their purchase.

2. **Q:** *CFS decided to use an undifferentiated target marketing strategy when launching their first product. Was this a good decision? Describe a scenario where they would want to move to a differentiated approach. A custom approach.*

   A: In CFS's case, it probably was a good idea to use an undifferentiated strategy. Firstly, they had no money to spend on market research, and secondly they got the opportunity to make mistakes on a small scale without doing damage to themselves on a large scale. They got to test the waters on a lot of different levels by doing the hard work themselves. They exhibited at various trade shows, got to meet directly with consumers and store owners and didn't have to filter information received from a market research firm that may have had ulterior motives (like keeping CFS coming back for more answers and spending more money with them). Of course CFS didn't have the money to pay a market research firm, but CFS could have been less patient and could have jumped the gun on crucial packaging and marketing decisions. By doing things the hard way, they allowed themselves the flexibility to make changes in the middle of the game. At a time when CFS has more money and has managed to get their products into large retailers, they will of course have to change their strategy. They won't have the luxury of making mistakes without taking a real hit on how their customers perceive them. Making a mistake with Toys 'R Us could have much graver consequences to CFS's long term picture than making a mistake with Tony's Toys just around the corner. A custom approach would likely come much later in the game, assuming that CFS has been successful on a large scale and has arrived on the national stage. When the CFS line has expanded, and there are many Computer Bug characters with their own CD ROMs, CFS could go the direction of making their Computer Bugs collectible in a similar fashion to Beanie Babies or Star Wars toy figurines.

3.   **Q: *What are some of the difficulties encountered from a target marketing perspective when you develop a product that must appeal to all age groups?***
     A: In CFS's case with the Computer Bug, which is a product of a humorous nature, CFS has the problem of marketing the Computer Bug's humor across the spectrum of children, adults, males and females. Fortunately for CFS, people of all ages use computers, and everyone who uses a computer has dealt with "bugs" in their systems. One of the problems CFS could have encountered that other companies surely have is the problem of communicating the concept of their product in a way that consumers of all ages can understand and want to hear at the same time. All generations communicate in different fashions. They all have their own slang and their own sensibilities. Because computers on the consumer level have not been around for more than a generation, virtually everyone who uses a computer is familiar with the same computer lingo and joking about computer malfunctions. The Internet aids in this common familiarity because people are constantly passing emailed jokes and animation files around and also spend a lot of time in chat rooms. So, the problems that CFS doesn't have in the translation of its product's humor are the problems that many other non-technical products have that are aimed at the populace as a whole. For instance, you can't market something with a rap music theme and hope to communicate a message that everyone over the age of 35 wants to hear. Additionally, if humor is going to be used to communicate a product's value and identity, the humor can't be too specific or sophisticated, or too many people won't get the message.

4.   **Q: *A company always does market research when it observes and talks to its customers as CFS did at trade shows. Can you think of inexpensive yet effective ways that start-up companies can use to obtain market research?***
     A: Apart from trade shows and depending on how company personnel perceive the value of their time, a company could choose to offer a deal to different small store chains or mom and pop stores that have a customer base that fits within the target consumer group. The company could offer their products free of charge to these stores providing the store owner agrees to fill out a questionnaire designed to give answers as to why the product sold or why they couldn't give it away. The company could work out a deal on a half dozen items at no charge and then accept reorders at the regular rate. After all, if something is selling, the store owner is going to want to continue carrying it. If the product doesn't sell in the particular store or store chain, then at least via the questionnaire the company will have answers as to why the product didn't move in that retail environment. Additionally, if a company has the financial and personnel resources to construct and put up a web site, a great deal of market research can be achieved simply by offering something for free to anyone visiting the web site who is willing to fill out a consumer questionnaire. The "free" item could be a letter opener, key chain or some other inexpensive item that is also inexpensive to mail.

MARKETING PLAN QUESTIONS AND ANSWERS

Refer to the Sample Marketing Plan in Appendix A as you answer the following questions about developing and modifying a marketing plan for CFS.

1.   For this year's marketing plan, what brand personality should CFS develop for each of its products? Is there a positioning strategy that runs through all of its products?

     Answer: Brand personality is defined as a distinctive image created for a brand that captures its character and the benefits it delivers. Students will use their imaginations when answering this question. One example:

- Brand personality for the Computer Bug: "A funny, irreverent, friendly creature that keeps you smiling throughout the day with its unexpected antics." (Note that the phrase "smiling through the day" reflects the product's benefits.)

2. Looking ahead to next year's marketing plan, how can CFS use behavioral segmentation to identify additional subgroups within the overall market for its products?

    Answer: Behavioral segmentation is defined as a way to segment consumer markets based on how they act toward, feel about, or use a good or service. This is another question likely to provoke diverse and creative responses from students. Two sample answers:

    - CFS can further segment consumer markets by identifying users versus nonusers of computer toy/accessory products. Consumers who are already using one CFS product (or a competing product) may well be excellent prospects for another CFS product.
    - CFS can further segment consumer markets by use at home versus use at work. A segment of consumers may want to use a computer toy/accessory at home but not at work, for example, a distinction that suggests a different marketing mix approach than for a segment that wants to use the product at work.

End of Case Answers to Questions

1. **Q:** *CFS chose to develop a new product before building on the Computer Bug line. Do you think this was a good decision? The obvious way to develop this product is to develop additional Computer Bug characters. Can you think of other ways to develop this product? Describe other possible characters. What do they build on and how do they extend the line?*

   A: If it's true that the large retailers don't take a new company seriously until it shows its ability to produce additionally interesting or creative products, then it was a very good idea for CFS to develop a different product that still adheres to the company's aim: to make products that make computers more fun to use. If they had simply added a Computer Bug character to the line-up, it's possible that the company could still be perceived as a one-product company that's just expanding on their one good idea. Two good ideas that have "franchise" or "license" written all over them would be enticing to any buyer that appreciates where Computer Friendly Stuff is coming from in general. The obvious items that can be added to the Computer Bug line-up would include a mouse pad and maybe interactive software that uses the Computer Bug as the main interface. CFS could also develop educational software using the Computer Bug as the main interactive feature for kids in the same way that Elmo is used in "Elmo's Reading Basics." There are already characters on the CD ROM that have not been developed into products, but new characters could include an evil Computer Bug that is goofy like the Dr. Evil character in Austin Powers or a female character which seems to be lacking on the CD ROM as it is now. Doesn't CB need a female counterpart?

2. **Q:** *CFS developed Monitor Morphs after developing the Original Computer Bug. Do other new products come to mind? Describe a new product?*

   A: (When students describe new products, ask them to include products that can adapt to laptops and Personal Digital Assistants, and flatscreen monitors as well.)

3. **Q:** *Can CFS set up a regular process to ensure that it develops new products on a regular basis?*

   A: The more financially successful CFS becomes, the more its creative team will have time to spend on product development and the more it will become possible to set up a product development process. Right now CFS seems to have very limited personnel resources. Everyone wears several hats and probably many of the duties that the CFS personnel perform do not come naturally to them. How many actor/accountants have you known? Still, while the unorthodox process CFS utilizes for its product development has produced results, it goes to follow that a more structured development process would probably produce better results. As busy and fragmented as the CFS staff probably is, they can surely find a way to create a product development regimen.

4. **Q:** *Are Monitor Morphs a fad, as CFS claims, or a potential franchise? If Warner Bros. is interested, who else might be interested? What would you like to see as a Monitor Morph product?*

A: The term "fad" is usually applied to a product that has no utility. Take the pet rock for instance. Where's the utility? The Morphs have utility. As they are right now, they couldn't be more generic, so, by way of the Morph concept, there is a way to put more characters into the computer monitor without them being computer bugs. It makes sense that computer bugs live inside a computer, but other companies that have tried to put characters into the computer have failed, probably because the characters didn't belong there in the first place. With arms or something that exists outside of the computer, then it makes some sense to put whatever you want inside the computer monitor. You're bringing together the outside world with something that exists inside the computer. The Morph arms, as mentioned, are generic. They can be changed by adding sleeves, costuming, tattoos, and other things to clearly identify them as belonging to a specific character. It seems like anyone could be interested in doing a Monitor Morph product. There's supposedly another Terminator movie going into production. How about Terminator Morph Arms and a Terminator screen saver? What about other cartoon characters? Bugs Bunny with attachable ears too? Mickey Mouse? Computers aren't going away, but more and more kids are spending time in front of their computer screens rather than the television screen. Why wouldn't other studios want to do a licensing deal?

5.   **Q:** *How does one establish a brand with a toy that is easy to copy? What does branding mean here?*
A: In this case, branding means establishing a unique image for a product which may otherwise be fairly easy to copy or imitate. CFS often faces the problem of creating products which can be imitated. They deal with this in several ways. First they use unique product names such as "Monitor Morphs" and "The Original Computer Bug" and "Chubby Stubby Stuffed Animals." Unique names are used in the hopes that the consumer will want the original as opposed to an imitation. "Beanie Babies" serve as a good example of this strategy. Even so, some companies have tried to mimic the unique "Beanie Babies" name with names such as "Beanie Buddies," etc. Another way to establish a brand is to throw a lot of money into advertising. This isn't an option for a lot of smaller companies, but it drives home the point that companies have to focus on promotion (even if by only using guerrilla tactics). They have to get that unique product name out to the consumer before the competition does. A good example of this is Monster.com. They spent over one million dollars to advertise during the 1999 Super Bowl even though that was a major part of their annual income for that year. Their reasoning? They wanted to be the first job search internet site to establish a brand with consumers. Did it work? They don't know yet.

6.   **Q:** *Develop your own package for Monitor Morphs. Draw a prototype. What is most important in this package?*
A: (The Student designs own packaging. Look for size, color, etc. Is it appealing? Does it convey the product concept? Does it stack or stand by itself? Can it hang from a peg? All of these are important considerations.)

MARKETING PLAN QUESTIONS AND ANSWERS

Refer to the Sample Marketing Plan in Appendix A as you answer the following questions about developing and modifying a marketing plan for CFS.

1.   For this year's marketing plan, identify the current location of The Computer Bug, Monitor Morphs, and Chubby Stubby stuffed animals within the product life cycle.

   Answer: The Computer Bug, introduced in 1997, appears to be entering the maturity stage of the product life cycle, with the most rapid sales growth starting to peak. Monitor Morphs, introduced in 1998, are still in the growth stage, with rapid growth in sales still projected for the coming year. Chubby Stubby stuffed animals are a new product in the introduction stage of the product life cycle.

2.   Looking ahead to next year's marketing plan, describe the screening methods and business analysis CFS should use as part of its new product development process.

Answer: Students are likely to suggest various ideas for screening and business analysis during the new product development process. Two sample questions that CFS can ask to screen potential product concepts are:

- What benefits will this product deliver to satisfy the needs and wants of the targeted segment?
- Can CFS make this product significantly different (and better) than competing products to gain a competitive edge?

For the business analysis step in the new product development process, two sample questions would be:

- Can CFS profitably develop, produce, and distribute this product, given its somewhat limited financial resources?
- What is the projected demand for this new product, and how many units can CFS reasonably expect to sell in the first year, in the second year, and in subsequent years?

CASE #4

End of Case Answers to Questions

1. **Q:** *In grid format, list the advantages and disadvantages of all three pricing strategies: tight profit margins, reasonable profit margins, and very good profit margins. Which pricing strategy do you think is the best?*

    A:

	Advantage:	**Disadvantage:**
TIGHT PROFITS:	+Low price is appealing to consumers +Can undercut competition on price	–Consumers may think low price means low quality –May not make enough profit to sustain business
REASONABLE PROFITS:*	+Customers get a fair price +Company makes enough profit to grow, advertise, etc.	–Cannot compete with low priced competition –Profits exist, but are somewhat limited
VERY GOOD PROFITS	+Very high profit margin +Can make money on new products before competition hits market	–Customers pay very high price –Not a good long term strategy

    *Reasonable profits are probably the best long-term pricing strategy. It allows room for growth, and delivers a good product at a fair price to customers.

2. **Q:** *For the most part, CFS looked at a static pricing strategy. How easy will it be to change prices? Does CFS have to change its objective to change prices? What future events could cause CFS to change its pricing strategy?*

    A: Changing prices is a fairly complicated procedure because CFS deals with so many different types of customers. If they were to change prices, they would have to sure that everyone was treated equally. With some clients, the hassle associated with changing prices might not be worth the trouble and the product line might be dropped. That is why it is important to give careful thought to pricing strategy from the beginning.

    CFS does not have to change its objective to change prices. For example, the product could become an instant success tomorrow, causing orders to skyrocket. Facing this type of demand, CFS could ask for a higher price. That does not mean that CFS would be changing its long-term strategy. On the other hand, changing a firm's objectives may very well result in a price change. Other future events that could cause CFS to change its pricing strategy include increased production costs, increased advertising plans, more product competition, or a company merger with a large distributor.

3.   **Q:** *Compare CFS with other consumer products such as Starbucks Coffee and Coca-Cola. How important is promotion to Starbucks and Coca-Cola? How important is advertising? How important is a sales staff? Make a grid with your answers.*

	CFS:	**Starbucks/Coca-Cola**
Promotion:	As the product has a low level of brand awareness, promotion is key. If CFS fails to get the product out in front of people, it has no chance of selling.	These companies have a high level of awareness due to ongoing promotion. However, there are many competitors waiting in the wings for them to stumble. Thus, they must continue to expand and promote the products.
Advertising:	As CFS does not have a budget for advertising, there is very little activity in this area currently. As it the company grows and increases distribution, it will be forced to develop advertising strategies if they want to experience significant sales increases.	Advertising is key to the marketing strategy of Coca-Cola. It has created some of the most well known campaigns in the USA. Of course, the main reason for this is Coca-Cola's ongoing competition with Pepsi. Starbucks, on the other hand, does not advertise nearly as much as Coca-Cola, yet the brand is a household name. This is a fairly unique situation, due in part to their rapid growth and, perhaps, well executed PR strategy.
Sales Force:	Very important to the future growth of the company.	Not as important. Sales force takes on more of a fulfillment role. Marketing takes precedence.

4.   **Q:** *A South American distributor contacted CFS and wanted to buy Computer Bugs that were converted into Portuguese (CD-ROM, packaging, pamphlet). Given that they will have to spend time and money creating this version, how should CFS settle on a price for 5000 units?*
      A: This can be done several different ways. If the distributor is trustworthy, they can localize the package themselves, which is much easier for CFS. They can pay royalties for the right to do this. However, this is a risky strategy and leaves CFS open to being exploited. It is not realistic for CFS to be able to monitor the activities of an overseas distributor, so they must proceed with caution. If CFS decides to do the localization, they must take into account the cost for translating and printing new packaging. They must also account for the cost of converting the contents of the CD-ROM. In general, 5000 units is probably not enough to warrant CFS doing the work unless the distributor is willing to pay for their time. They could also try to get the distributor to settle for a pamphlet which translates the CD contents and not actually reprogram the CD itself.

MARKETING PLAN QUESTIONS AND ANSWERS

Refer to the Sample Marketing Plan in Appendix A as you answer the following questions about developing and modifying a marketing plan for CFS.

1.   For this year's marketing plan, explain how CFS is using price lining to develop a specific price point for each of the items in its product line.

      Answer: Price lining is the practice of setting a limited number of different specific prices, called price points, for items in a product line. CFS is using price lining by setting different retail price points for each item in its product line. For example, the Computer Bug has a retail price of $17.99, while Monitor Morphs have a retail price of $19.99. This pricing allows CFS to capture sales for each product within the range of prices that consumers consider acceptable for that product. Consumers will not buy products with prices outside the acceptable range. So if consumers are unwilling to pay more than $20 for a computer toy/screen saver combination, the Monitor Morphs price of $19.99 keeps this product within the consumer's price range—which means CFS will have a better chance of selling to those consumers.

2.   Looking ahead to next year's marketing plan, what type of new-product pricing is appropriate for CFS's forthcoming Chubby Stubby products? Why?

Answer: Students may offer different answers for this question. Some students may argue for a skimming price (to skim the "richest" product sales off the top by charging a premium price). This is most successful when customer segments have different levels of price sensitivity. Ask students whether they think that customers who buy stuffed toys are likely to be price sensitive.

Some students may argue for penetration pricing (using a low price to quickly capture sales and market share). However, the viability of this option depends on CFS's financial condition. If it needs to cover its development and production costs by generating solid profits immediately, penetration pricing may be unacceptable.

Some students may argue for trial pricing, offering a low introductory price for a short time to induce trial purchasing and reduce perceived risk. (Ask students what risks consumers might perceive in buying Chubby Stubby products.) If CFS anticipates that Chubby Stubby products will become a fad like Beanie Babies, the company may want to use trial pricing to get customers to buy once, then return to buy at full price as they collect more of these products.

End of Case Answers to Questions

1. **Q:** *The Internet can be an advertising medium as well as (or rather than) a sales medium. Why does a company such as Coca-Cola see it this way? (you want to sell a can of pop over the Internet?)*
    A: There are several reasons for this. First, the Internet provides a cheaper alternative to traditional advertising through the strategic use of banner ads and other promotions. In fact, this is changing the way that many advertising agencies do business. Because there are so many advertising options available to companies today, ad agencies are finding that they cannot command the high commission rates that they have in the past. Second, as the Internet is a new and hip medium, companies such as Coca-Cola are careful to be sure that they are not left behind. A good example of this is MTV. MTV recently announced new plans for its web site. The strategy is very ambitious in that MTV wants to be both the Amazon.com and Yahoo.com of music on the web. What is interesting is that MTV took so long to begin establishing this type of presence on the web. Analysts wonder why they didn't begin two years ago and some wonder if it is too late for them to try and catch up with more established portholes and selling sites. Finally, at this early stage it is impossible to determine how large a presence the Internet will eventually play in our lives. For example, ordering groceries on-line may become much more common than it currently is. It may become the rule rather than the exception. If this happens, a company such as Coca-Cola will certainly want to have a significant advertising presence on the Internet.

2. **Q:** *Go to CFS's web site. Has CFS done a good job advertising their product? Why or why not? What would you suggest they do?*
    A: CFS does a fairly good job of advertising their product on their web site. They present the information in a fun manner and they provide free downloads. However, they could do more to bring customers to the site, via banners, advertising on other sites, etc. This is not a direction that they have chosen to go, but it may be a strategy for the future. A particularly good form of guerrilla advertising that is suited to CFS is the use of free email animations. These are short funny animations that are sent as attachments from office worker to office worker for amusement. "The Dancing Baby" started this way, for example. Such animations often catch on and reach hundreds of thousands, even millions of computer users. At the end of the animation, CFS can have a hot link to their site. CFS has chosen to wait until after the Y2K issue is over to pursue this tactic, so the issue is not confused. However, it will most likely be an advertising strategy during the year 2000.

3. **Q:** *The Internet can be seen as a product information medium. Go to CFS's web site and comment on its effectiveness in conveying product information. What are some of the benefits of Computer Bugs and Monitor Morphs, as described in the Web site?*
    A: As you know from the case, CFS uses its web site primarily as an on-line catalogue. The do a fairly good job of presenting their product in a fun and detailed manner. As these are unusual products and fairly hard to describe, CFS also includes free downloads so that visitors can better understand the products.

The benefits of both products center on making your computer more fun to use. They also promise to keep you company as you work and amuse your friends. They are also careful to point out that the special adhesives used on each product won't leave a mark on your computer.

4.   **Q: *Comment on the usefulness of the product name "computer bug" considering the problems that came up with Internet search engines. What product names does the Internet force one to avoid? What are the characteristics of a good product name for the Internet?***
       A: Computer Bug is both a good and a bad product name. It is good because everyone understands what a computer bug is, and because computer bug as a term is understood in most languages. The global possibilities for this character are limitless. It is a bad name because it is very generic. There are many people who use the term in its original context (to describe glitches, viruses, etc). If CFS is successful in developing their character as the bug "that you want to have in your computer," it will be a great name that could become synonymous with computer/internet use.

       The Internet forces one to avoid generic product names. Sites such as Yahoo.com, Amazon.com, and Ebay.com are well suited to the web because the names are unique and new. For this reason, Computerbug.com is not a very good web site name, as discussed previously in this case. At some point, CFS will probably change the name. However the decision for a new site is a tough one. ComputerFriendlyStuff.com is too long, CFS.com is too generic. Also, CFS first has to grapple with the issue of what direction the company will take. Will it become a toy company or a computer toy company? If it moves in the direction of toys, perhaps it should consider changing the name to Fun Stuff, inc. or something similar.

5.   **Q: *Should CFS consider advertising for its products on other company Web sites? If so, what sites?***
       A: Although this is not a direction that CFS wants to pursue currently, it is an issue that will come up as they continue to grow. One of the advantages that the Web offers is the ability to target customers very accurately. For that reason, advertising on web sites is a very attractive option. It is also a very cost effective way to reach customers. Sites that would be appealing to CFS would be Nickelodeon, Disney, Computer User Groups, and Gift sites.

MARKETING PLAN QUESTIONS AND ANSWERS

Refer to the Sample Marketing Plan in Appendix A as you answer the following questions about developing and modifying a marketing plan for CFS.

1.   For this year's marketing plan, indicate whether CFS's Internet strategy should emphasize the direct channel or indirect distribution to take advantage of the explosive growth of electronic commerce. Explain how this emphasis affects the company's plans for physical distribution.

       Answer: Based on CFS's previous experience with selling its products directly from its own Web site—and the company's limited resources—this year's marketing plan should emphasize indirect distribution via on-line retailers, particularly those that sell gifts, toys, and computer accessories. This emphasis means that CFS must implement an efficient process for processing retailers' orders, storing products before they are sent to retailers, shipping products to retailers, and controlling inventory to be sure sufficient quantities are available to fill retailers' orders.

2.   Looking ahead to next year's marketing plan, what kind of channel conflict could CFS encounter if signs up a much larger number of Internet retailers to sell its products? Does CFS have sufficient power to become a channel leader on the Internet? Explain your answer.

       Answer: If CFS signs up many more Internet retailers to sell its products, it may encounter horizontal conflict, which can occur between two firms at the same level of a distribution channel. For example, a large on-line computer retailer (such as CompUSA) may have some reason to object to CFS selling its products through smaller on-line computer retailers. At this point, CFS lacks sufficient power to become a channel leader on the Internet. However, if its products become wildly popular, it will gain considerable channel power and have much more control over its product distribution.

End of Case Answers to Questions

1. **Q:** *At what point do you think it is reasonable for CFS to take on a salaried sales force? Is it a question of company size or the characteristics of a particular industry?*

    A: The most obvious answer to this question is "not until they can afford to pay for one!" While the characteristics of a particular industry will play into this decision, the size of a company is really the main factor.

    CFS will certainly have to grow in size and revenue before considering such a move. Joel Wildman estimates that he would want to see a product line reach $25 million in annual sales before making the move to a 100% salaried sales force. Of course, there are many options for CFS prior to reaching that point. For example, CFS can slowly decrease the number of freelance reps as their revenue grows (large established accounts can be handed off to Joel to manage directly). CFS can also decrease the commissions that reps receive as income grows (as Mark Grill described in the video). In a way, this is similar to the law of diminishing returns. As the income grows, CFS will have to decrease the rate that reps are rewarded so that they are not overcompensated. The money saved should be applied towards marketing the product. As discussed in the case, the reps will then take on more of an order-taking role and the marketing managers will become responsible for the marketing/selling of the product. For example, CFS recently attended a large computer trade show. Sony had a huge booth that cost over 5 million dollars to build! Yet, you couldn't find a single sales rep at the show. Why? The marketing managers were there instead. They were dealing with the buyers, building relationships, schmoozing, etc. All orders were placed after the show (with the sales reps doing the facilitating).

    Let's look at another example. Let's say that in a given year, CFS sells 1 million dollars worth of Computer Bugs. Assume they used 20–30 freelance reps who each work on a 10% commission. Obviously, ten percent of revenue, or $100,000, is enough to pay commissions, but not enough to pay fixed salaries for all of those reps. Hence, the use of freelance reps. Next, let's say that CFS sells 25 million dollars of Computer Bugs in a given year. Ten percent of that is 2.5 million dollars. Why pay out 2.5 million dollars in rep commissions when you can hire 5 or 6 great reps for $100,000+? The 2 million that is saved can go toward marketing or advertising the product.

    Internationally, CFS will probably not change its organization, as it does not work with rep groups overseas. Currently, Bill Martens, in consultation with Joel Wildman, negotiates all deals with overseas distributors and the distributors buy from CFS in bulk. Since this horizontal structure has worked very effectively, CFS does not see a need to incorporate additional middlemen.

2. **Q: What are the similarities and differences between commissioned multi-line reps and a salaried sales force? Make a grid.**

	Freelance Reps	Salaried Reps
Work on Salary	No	Yes
High Commissions	Yes	No
Low Commissions	No	Yes
Carry other company's products?	Yes	No
Require strong selling skills	Yes	Yes
Require strong buyer relationships	Yes	Yes
Heavy travel requirements	Yes	Yes
Self-motivated personality	Yes	Yes
Strong Knowledge of markets	Yes	Yes
Can negotiate complex deals specific to individual retail mkts	Yes	Yes
Constantly out selling line	Maybe	Yes
Works in more than one mkt	Not usually	Yes
May take on an order-taking role as company grows	N/A	Yes

3. **Q: Does it matter that Joel Wildman does not work at the CFS home office? What are the advantages and disadvantages of this type of arrangement?**
A: As you know, CFS is based in Chicago. Joel Wildman, their National Sales Manager, is based in Florida. This situation works fine for both parties. However, several factors make this possible. First, Joel is an extremely honest, hard-working, reliable sales manager who does not require day to day supervision. He speaks with the CFS team at least three times a day. If he were not doing his job, it would be obvious to Chris and Bill. Second, since both CFS and Joel are located near major airport hubs (Orlando and Chicago), travel is very convenient. Third, both Joel and CFS are proficient with technology (email, fax, cell phones) and use these methods to communicate on a daily basis. Finally, neither location provides a geographic advantage in the toy or computer industry (most large retail clients are based in NY, NJ, or TX), so moving Joel to Chicago wouldn't make a significant difference from a strategic standpoint.

4. **Q: What type of special promotions would you offer the CFS Sales Force? Draw up a flyer announcing a special promotion.**
A: When a company is starting out, finances dictate that promotions be somewhat limited. Start with a newsletter that recognizes superior performance. Next, move up to awards, such as plaques, boxes of steaks, and gift certificates. All of these can serve as excellent prizes for sales performance. The next step in promotions might be to offer a vacation. However, when it comes to trips, it is best to combine them with sales meetings. This way, the company gets the most "bang for its buck." For example, CFS can offer to hold a sales meeting in a warm location at a very nice hotel and allow reps to bring their spouses. They can reward top selling reps by providing them with deluxe suites. The important thing is that CFS must set reasonable goals for the reps and then they must track the sales carefully. CFS can aim to either increase sales or to get orders in by a certain date. Most significantly, the promotions must keep pace with the growth of the company in order to ensure a sense of fairness and motivation with the sales force.

MARKETING PLAN QUESTIONS AND ANSWERS

Refer to the Sample Marketing Plan in Appendix A as you answer the following questions about developing and modifying a marketing plan for CFS.

1.   For this year's marketing plan, design a trade promotion to attract potential buyers to CFS's exhibit at the upcoming Toy Fair. Indicate how the sales reps, the buyers, and CFS will benefit from this promotion.

       Answer: Students should be able to come up with some imaginative trade promotions to attract potential buyers to CFS's Toy Fair exhibit. One sample: create a "Match the Computer Bug" contest in which potential buyers receive a colorful, numbered Computer Bug trading card (like a baseball or other sports trading card) inside their convention registration packets. Buyers bring the trading card to the CFS exhibit and find out whether they win a valuable prize. The trading card would list funny "player stats" for the Computer Bug and include useful information such as product features and wholesale and retail pricing. The sales reps would benefit from this promotion because it would bring buyers into the exhibit, where they would interact with the sales reps and possibly place orders for CFS products. The buyers would benefit because they would have the opportunity to win a prize while learning about CFS products that would be attractive to their retail customers. CFS would benefit because its exhibit would have more buyer visitors and the company would therefore have more opportunities to sell its products in the retail channel.

2.   Looking ahead to next year's marketing plan, what sales force objectives should CFS set for its sales reps? How will these objectives help CFS reach its overall goals?

Answer: The details of students' answers will vary. CFS should define specific sales performance objectives that support the company's overall marketing and sales objectives, as stated in the marketing plan. Because the marketing plan calls for increasing gross sales by 300 percent within one year, CFS should set corresponding sales performance objectives to reach that goal. CFS would also want to set customer development goals for sales reps, aiming to increase the number of orders and the value of each order placed by retailers. In addition, CFS might want to set profitability goals as well as behavioral goals, such as specifying the number of new prospects each rep must identify.

$\mathcal{V}$ideo Guide

Table 1: Guide to Video Cases for Solomon/Stuart 2nd. Edition

Name of Video \ Chapter Number	1	2	3	4	5	6	7	8	9	10	11	12	13	14	15	16	17	18
Terra Chips	1																	
WNBA: We Do More!	2																	
CFS 1	1																	
Nike: Playing to Win		1																
FD & B Part 1		2																
Patagonia			1															
Ritz Carlton			1															
Lands' End: Hello Japan!				1														
MTV				2														
Sputnik					1													
M/A/R/C Group					2													
Mercedes Benz					3													
Sebago						1												
MasterCard Part II							1											
House of Blues								1										
MasterCard I								1										
CFS2								1										
New Product Showcase									1									
Kodak									1									
Intel: The Power Behind the PC Part 1										1								
Yahoo-ing the World										1								
DuPont: The Right Ingredients for Success										2								
Hain Food Group Part 1										1								
Nivea: Managing an Umbrella Brand (Parts 1 and 2)										2								
CFS3										1								
Yahoo-ing the World											1							
Lands' End: Perceptual Recipe for Success											2							
Bojangles												2						
CFS4													1					
DHL														1				
Hain Food Group Part 2														2				
Forum															1			
Starbucks															2			
Yahoo: Yahoo-ing the World!															1			
Mountain Travel Sobek															1			
Lands' End: The Internet															2			
CFS5															1			
Lands' End: Teaching Consumers about Lands' End																1		
FD & B Part 2																2		
Got Milk Part 1																	1	
Intel: The Power Behind the PC Part 2																	1	
Mad Dogs and Englishmen Part IV: Creating Advertising																	2	
NASCAR: Racing for Sponsorships																		1
CFS6																		1
Personal Selling with Kathleen Carroll Mullen of GE																		1

Legend: 1 = Best Video(s) for Chapter 2 = Second Best Video(s) for Chapter
Note: Yahoo is associated with three chapters. It could be used with any one of these, but is best used with Chapter 11.

Terra Chips

Should Accompany Chapter 1 of Solomon/Stuart

Summary:

Content of Video: Terra Chips is a nice case to introduce students to the elements of the marketing mix and a close up look at two entrepreneurs. This case illustrates the development of a niche marketing strategy using a product with a competitive advantage and higher pricing (psychological pricing) and innovative distribution channels to enhance the perceived value of the product.

The Product: The company was started by two chefs from New York who had begun making chips from exotic vegetables such as sweet potato, batata, yucca, taro and parsnip. When they served these at catered events, the chips were quickly gone and customers wanted more. So the two chefs went into business.

The Company: They began making chips in an apartment working 14 hours a day to produce 5 cases of chips. Their big break came when Saks placed an order for 50 cases. Saks sold out in two weeks and ordered more. So, Alex and Dana took a deep breath and went into mass production.

Price and Packaging: Because the ingredients for the product cost more, the price for the chips had to be higher. To support the higher price, Dana and Alex turned to Keith Black of California to create a silver and black sophisticated package that would lend style to the product.

Distribution and Promotion: Given the high price, these chips could not compete in the typical grocery store. So, they are distributed through upscale outlets such as Saks and Neiman Marcus; through delis, health food stores and a few select grocery chains. Promotion occurs through the distributive outlets and packaging rather than through extensive advertising.

The Future: Alex and Dana are considering new products, expanded distribution and going global. The problem with the latter is that the ingredients that seem exotic in the U.S. will not be exotic abroad and the allure of the chips will decrease. The video asks students what recommendation they would make with regard to going global.

Description of Video: There are many shots of the production of Terra Chips, still pictures of the founders and an interview with Dana Sinkler.

Teaching Tips: Before showing this video, instructors should cover the basics of the marketing mix. Explain what targeted marketing is (Finding and reaching a target market) and review briefly the elements of Product, Place, Price and Promotion (Marketing's Tools).

It is helpful to give students a handout that lists the terms target market, product, place, price and promotion. Ask them to make notes about each of these as they watch the video. After showing the video, discuss why the marketing strategy for Terra Chips has worked. Go over each element and define the target market. Stress that it is the consistency that makes the market mix appropriate: a high price demands an unusual product with higher value and that needs slicker packaging and higher priced outlets. You cannot sell Terra Chips at the local low-priced supermarket. They don't fit there.

Ask students to write a positioning statement that describes Terra Chips. This will force them to consider the entire marketing mix and market and how they relate to each other.

Last, discuss how the company should grow: new products, expanded distribution or selling abroad. Try to list the advantages and disadvantages of each. The importance of this discussion is to bring out the factors that affect expansion decisions, not to actually answer the question. There really isn't enough information given to reach a definitive answer. If you want to avoid this discussion, you can turn the video off after Dana says "This is music to our ears." The screen goes blank after that before the issue of international is mentioned in the voice-over and shown on the screen.

WNBA: We Do More!

Should Accompany Chapter 1 of Solomon/Stuart

Summary:

Content of Video: This video focuses on three aspects of the WNBA. The first is the excitement and feelings of fun that are generated at WNBA games. This is reinforced by comments from Welts and Miller.

The second is the demographic that the WNBA appeals to which is women and family. When the league was founded, most of those involved really expected more men in the audience. Today, 70% of the attendance at games is women and 50% of the television audience is women. And when women come, they bring their families. So, the WNBA is much more of a family event than is the NBA. There are several reasons for this. One is pricing. WNBA game tickets average $13 a piece which makes them an affordable evening out for a family; whereas NBA games cost much more. Another reason involves the players. The women players are much better at being role models. They are better behaved and more responsive to fans. One might hypothesize that it took so long for them to get their own basketball league that they are just thankful for the opportunity and don't want to blow it. Because of the positive environment and role models, one sees many little girls at the game sometimes with their brothers—both of whom are WNBA fans. The younger generation sees little unusual about women as sports role models.

The third foci of the video concerns the community involvement of teams in the WNBA. The league has adopted two national causes which receive support from them. These are breast cancer and physical fitness. Breast cancer is an obvious cause because it afflicts women regardless of age, income, social class, etc. Physical fitness also ties in with idea of athletes who would be physically fit. Some teams have also associated themselves with programs to eliminate violence against women.

Along with these major elements, the video briefly describes the founding of the WNBA, its association with the NBA and the fact that the WNBA plays in the summer.

Description of the Video: This video contains scenes from WNBA and basketball games along with interviews with Cheryl Miller (Head Coach Phoenix Mercury), Val Ackerman (President WNBA), Rick Welts (Executive Vice President and Chief Marketing Officer) a college player, Katie Carpenter and several WNBA ads featuring WNBA players.

Teaching Tips: This video can be used with several sections in Chapter 1: Anything can be marketed, People marketing and Social issues in marketing. The WNBA is a grand example of sports marketing and the video tries to communicate the enthusiasm and fun involved in a WNBA game. Given the level of support and positive associations with the WNBA, one wonders why it took so long!

Show the video and then ask students the following questions: What makes the WNBA successful? Is it the experience? Is it the audience?

Has the WNBA really targeted women/children/families? Would it make a difference if most of the audience were male?

What is the effect of having good sports role models in Cheryl Miller and Rebecca Lobo? How can the WNBA change the perception of women? How does this affect little girls? Little boys?

Does it make sense for an organization to support social causes such as breast cancer, physical fitness and eliminating violence against women? Do the causes they've chosen make sense? Are there other causes that the WNBA should support?

How can supporting social and charitable causes help the image of the WNBA? How does this demonstrate the positive side of marketing? How can this help to eliminate criticisms of marketing?

Computer Friendly Stuff:
It's a Small World Market After All

Should Accompany Chapter 1 of Solomon/Stuart

Summary:

Content of Video: This is the first of six new videos in this series to accompany Solomon and Stuart, 2nd. Edition. The first video describes the founding of Computer Friendly Stuff—a firm that makes a computer "bug" that you would want in your computer. The bug "lives" in your computer, popping up now and then as a screen saver, cleaning the glass on the monitor and telling jokes. The idea behind the computer bug is to make computers less—to make them fun.

In starting this firm, Chris Cole, founder, began with an idea and little else. He describes his original marketing plan as "starting at the top." He mailed 18 sample packages to the 18 largest retailers in the U.S. and got no response. Thus, he and his team were forced to sell the computer bug at Christmas fairs and flea markets throughout Illinois, Michigan and Wisconsin.

Their next step was to sublet a space at the International Toy Fair in New York, but they were in a booth of a train company and customers entering the booth weren't interested in computers. They made a 7 foot Computer Bug costume, but the bug was just one of 25 mascots standing outside the fair. This segment illustrates the importance of being in the right location and be agile in devising ways to attract attention. For Valentine's Day, the bug mascot gave buyers catalog sheets, chocolates and wished them a Happy Valentine's Day. A couple from New Zealand who ran a distributorship selling to 150 computer and toy stores responded with a $15,000.

The order from New Zealand catapulted this firm into the international business arena. The computer bug was a hit in New Zealand with children and the company received letters from kids attesting to its success. Chris comments that international sales are a nice, clean, simple way of doing business because the buyer has to pay for the goods before they are shipped. By the next Christmas, the couple in New Zealand ordered $20,000 of computer bugs. By then, the company, CFS was selling in England, the Middle East and Asia, but not the U.S. (Unfortunately, how they got these sales is not explained.)

Because they did not want to sell in flea markets in the U.S. again, they decided they needed a better marketing plan. Before deciding on a marketing plane, Chris takes stock of what they have learned:

- Find a need and fill it.
- You have to market
- International sales are significant (even for small companies)
- Good marketing creates it's own luck.

At this point, the video ends.

Description of the Video: This video is mostly an interview with Chris Cole, founder of CFS. There is some footage of their efforts to sell at the International Toy Fair, but most of the video is Chris talking supplemented with footage of him or some associate acting out he is describing. The accompanying music is 1940s band-style music and the major points of the presentation/video are reinforced with still screens containing the important information.

Teaching Tips: Because the computer bug is not explained very well in this video, you might ask students to visit the computer bug web site (www.computerbug.com) before you show the video in class. That way, they will understand the product. Visiting the web site is not redundant with what they will see in the video.

Show the video and write the points from the last screen in the video on the blackboard. These are the bullet points provided in the content of the video section. Ask students how the video/the example of CFS illustrates each of these points. This will reinforce the textbook sections on: Marketing satisfied Needs and (Almost) Anything can be marketed. Ask the class to describe the marketing plan of CFS after their first Christmas.

At that time, the plan was to go to the International Toy Fair. Although this led to some success, the company still needs to create a better marketing plan.

Ask the students how the company could market the computer bug in the future. This should force a discussion of who would buy the bug? (Target market section of text). The product is defined and it would be difficult to establish price, but the promotion and distribution tools can be discussed. Where should they advertise/promote the computer bug, assuming that they have any money to do so? Where should it be sold?

Draw up a simple plan in class and make a paper version of it that can be distributed to the class. In later class sessions when you use other videos about CFS, you and the students can compare the original plan that the class developed with the changes described by CFS personnel in the later videos.

Video Case 4

Nike Playing to Win

Should Accompany Chapter 2 of Solomon/Stuart

Summary:

Content of Video: The Nike video focuses on four aspects of the company's success: (a) its founding and growth, (b) mission, (c) communication and (d) extension of the mission to their international strategy.

Founding: Nike was founded in the early seventies by Phil Knight because he wanted to design and sell a better shoe for runners. His goal was to enhance the performance of runners. By following this simple goal, Nike has grown into a more than $6.5 billion company.

Mission: Knight's original goal is now Nike's mission: to serve the athlete. Marketing personnel at Nike explain in the video that the mission means being inside the sport, understanding it from the participant's perspective and creating a great product that enhance the athlete's performance. The key to their success, they believe, is a great product.

Communication: To communicate their message, they chose athletes to endorse products because they understand how the product works to enhance performance. To be chosen as an endorser, an athlete must excel at his/her sport and be motivating. The communication goal is touch people, to move them, to create an emotional bond with them through fresh, unexpected communications. Bill Zeitz, Global Director of Advertising Development, comments that Michael Jordan was involved in the design of the products he endorsed; that he was not just a spokesperson. This reinforces the centrality of the product in Nike's strategy.

International: Nike's initial attempts to enter international markets were not successful because they did not pay enough attention to the sports played in those markets. Although Nike is a great basketball shoe, basketball is not that popular outside the U.S.. So, Nike had to re-learn its own creative process by getting close to the athletes in the popular sports whether it's rugby in Australia or soccer in Europe. They had to learn the sport from the inside; they had to know what it takes to excel at the sport and they had to create good products for the sport. Liz Dolan, Marketing Director, admits on the tape that they made mistakes; that the Nike soccer shoe was not that good. But today, Nike has worked on improving its products and signing celebrity athletes to endorse the product. Nike is obviously using the same strategy as in the U.S. Improve your product, i.e. a better soccer shoe and sign the major stars to endorse the product.

What has Nike learned from this experience? One thing is that the company should never be afraid to make mistakes. Liz Dolan comments that Nike has the same values as a big company that it had as a small company and that it is highly entrepreneurial. Tolerating mistakes is important in stimulating the entrepreneurial spirit.

Description of Video: This tape consists of comments by Liz and Bill interspersed with many action shots of athletes in action and advertising clips. It is relatively fast paced and likely to keep student's attention. The video shows clips from a controversial ad Nike used in Europe in which Nike endorsers play against the devil and his team and win. Eric Cantona (of the Manchester United team) takes on devil to score the winning goal. It would be interesting to see student reaction to the ad. They may fail to understand why it would offend Europeans.

Advice to Marketing Students: Near the end of the video Liz Dolan and Bill Zeitz advise students that they should train their powers of creativity and observation. They should ; take on all jobs that are offered and learn to have fun doing them. Finally, they should not settle for anything less than what they are passionate about—what they truly enjoy doing.

Teaching Tips: Before showing the video ask students to think about the following questions:

1.   What is Nike's mission statement?
2.   What is Nike's growth strategy?
3.   What is the key to their success?
4.   Describe their internal environment and explain how that facilitates success.
5.   What is their distinctive competence?
6.   What is their objective in each of their markets?
7.   How do they communicate with the market?

You might give the students these questions on a handout with room for them to jot notes during the video.

The short answer to each question is:

1.   The mission is to serve the athlete that translates into viewing the sport as s/he does.
2.   Their growth strategy is to constantly seek out new markets, determine what sport is important to the populace and develop a great product for that market.
3.   The key to their success is their focus on sports and creating a strong bond of communication and understanding between athletes and Nike for each sport.
4.   Their internal environment is highly supportive. People are encouraged to be entrepreneurial even if it means making mistakes. As Liz Dolan says, she has learned that nothing is too outlandish—even a soccer game against the devil.
5.   Their competence is their willingness and ability to develop a great shoe for each sport.
6.   Their goal is to be number one in each of their markets.
7.   They communicate through creative and daring ads using well-known athletes. The message in the ad is always enhanced performance. When discussing communication, ask students how they felt about the ad using the devil. This caused quite a stir in Europe although it might not do so in the U.S.

Discussing these questions will cover many of the topics covered in Chapter two of the text.

The Nike video demonstrates how to take a simple mission, adhere to it and use it to create success in markets all around the globe. Emphasize that what does not change in Nike's strategy is the mission. The sports may change, the products may change and the celebrity endorsers may change, but the basic mission remains the same.

Student Project: At the end of the video, Bill Zeitz indicates new markets for Nike could be Eastern Europe, China and India. Students could be divided into teams and asked to determine what the main sports in these areas are, and to develop a strategy for Nike's success in each country. Students would need to identify not only the popular sports, but also athletes in developing a strategy. This would require some library research, but would give them an opportunity to engage in the same strategy development process that Nike does.

FD&B Part I

Should Accompany Chapter 2 of Solomon/Stuart

Summary:

Content of Video: This video primarily describes FD&B—a full-service marketing firm located on Long Island that handles the accounts of such clients as MasterCard, Watson and Hain Foods. Although they do deliver advertising, FD&B sees itself as a marketing firm, not an ad agency. They claim that the ad agency concept is outdated. The video focuses on the way that FD&B markets itself. This illustrates attention to the fundamentals of good marketing planning.

FD&B knows that a full service firm must be able to control communications and provide all the necessary resources needed for strategic planning and thinking. They believe that even though they are a small firm, they can provide the same services as a larger firm thanks to improvements in technology. In addition, they can turn things around faster and offer personalized service. They believe that clients expect more commitment from a smaller agency.

Throughout the video, the partners discuss the need for a marketing firm to be service oriented and to establish partnerships with their clients. To do this a firm must be consumer oriented, market driven, value-based, integrated and goal oriented. To do this, a marketing service firm must understand the clients' business and their needs. FD &B personnel often work for a new client for several weeks in order to understand their business.

To make sure that they understand the situation fully, FD & B uses lots of research—both secondary and primary; quantitative and qualitative. They try to understand the product category, who the competition is, the dynamics of the product that they're doing communication for, who is the target consumer, what are they looking for and how can the product be positioned to provide a unique need.

FD&B seeks clients that are dedicated to their mission, looking for growth, want strategic planning, direct follow through, and executions carried out with the highest quality. That would create a match between the client and FD &B.

Description of Video: There are interviews with three partners at FD&B: Philip Franznick (President), Kevin P. Franznick (Executive VP) and Todd Bernard (Senior VP). There are scenes of people working at the agency, meetings with clients, planning sessions and excerpts from 8 o'clock coffee ads done by FD&B.

Teaching Tips: The main value of this video is in demonstrating how a firm markets itself. Therefore, before showing the video, talk about the importance of planning and strategy. Ask the students to think of themselves as potential clients who are considering hiring a marketing/advertising agency. What would they look for in an agency? What evidence would they want to know that this is the agency for them? What services would they expect? Would they want a small or large agency? Why or why not?

After looking at the video, ask them what FD & B's mission is? What are their objectives? What is their competitive advantage? (These are all discussed in the first few sections of Chapter 2.) How would they feel about hiring FD & B. Did what they saw and heard make them feel good about FD & B? What evidence was most important? Was it what people said? The services discussed? The list of clients? Why would they want to pick FD &B? If they do, then FD & B did a good job of marketing themselves. If they didn't, it's important to discuss why. What was missing? What should FD & B have said?

Patagonia

Should Accompany Chapter 3 of Solomon/Stuart

Summary:

Content of Video: This video focuses on three subjects: (a) Patagonia's relentless pursuit of quality; (b) the company's decision to limit growth and (c) to be as environmentally conscious as possible.

The pursuit of quality is driven by the founder's goals and the company's target market. Yvon Chouinard founded the company for the express purpose of providing rock climbers with better equipment. The target market consists of serious users who use Patagonia's products under extreme conditions where product failure could be fatal.

The decision to limit growth comes from the recession in the 1980s when Patagonia found its warehouses full of unsold goods. Company management contemplated various means of selling off these goods, but concluded that maintaining growth was a drain on the environment. The company made a conscious effort to limit growth by restricting distribution of the catalog, making multi-use garments and accentuating product quality so that goods would last longer and consumers would buy less frequently. Through high quality, the company is trying to reduce the increasing role of consumption.

The environmental stance relates to the quality and growth issues. The founder, Chouinard, developed chocks for climbers that would not damage rock faces, so in a way, Patagonia has always had an element of environmentalism. The recession of the 1980s strengthened this element and led the company to begin an environmental grants program. Believing that national efforts already had plenty of backing, Patagonia supports smaller, grassroots efforts that frequently have a harder time finding funds. The company also conducted an extensive environmental assessment of itself and its suppliers in order to determine how to reduce the impact that it has on the environment. This has resulted in hefty recycling efforts and the use of more natural materials in the production of their products.

Description of Video: Company personnel interviewed in the video are: Ian Yolles, Marketing Director; Jil Zilligen, Environmental Grants Program; Mike Brown, Environmental Assessment Director and Lu Setnicka, Public Affairs.

The video makes use of zip ins to prepare students to learn about the following subjects which are listed on the screen: the Marketing Environment, Actors and Forces in Target Markets, Macroenvironment Influences, Understanding of the Natural Environment, Shortages, Regulation and Consumer Awareness have affected the company's marketing plan. In response, the company has used a societal marketing approach to respond to outside marketing forces.

There are plenty of shots of company personnel going about their jobs from which students can learn that this company has a relaxed dress code. The environment of the firm is highly informal.

Teaching Tips: This video case relates very well to the following sections of Chapter 3: creating quality, people centered corporate cultures, relationships with the public, and responses to the competitive and sociocultural environments. Actually all of these subjects are interrelated. Before showing the video, tell students to pay close attention to how quality has affected the operations of Patagonia. After showing the video, ask what quality means to Patagonia and how it permeates their operations. Because price and quality are usually directly related to one another, bring up the issue of higher prices for Patagonia products and discuss how this affects their operations and reinforces the goals of the company (higher prices "force" consumers to use goods longer and buy fewer).

At the end of the video, students are asked to explain how Patagonia has chosen to respond to the macroenvironment. Instructors might stop the video before this comes on and discuss the effect of quality first. When that discussion is finished, then move on to discuss the effect of macroenvironmental forces. Patagonia's main response to macroenvironmental forces has been to show regard for the physical environment through its grants, recycling and assessment efforts. Through its environmental programs, it avoids the effect of much regulation while at the same time responding favorably to consumer issues and changes in the sociocultural environment. It has shown almost total disregard for the competitive environment and uses technology to reduce its impact on the environment.

Students are usually very positive about the Patagonia case. One of the major learnings to take away from this case is that being a good guy—treating employees and the environment right and focusing on quality—leads to higher prices. Everyone whether corporations or individuals have to make expensive decisions where the environment and doing the right thing is concerned.

Ritz Carlton
Should Accompany Chapter 3 of Solomon/Stuart

Summary:

Content of Video: This video focuses on Ritz Carlton's use of Total Quality Management to increase customer retention and improve profitability. It believes that by relentless dedication to high levels of customer service, it can build strong, lasting customer relationships that increase customer satisfaction and enhance the value and quality of its services. Their approach is characterized by detailing planning, quality teams, defining objectives, developing action plans and rigorous monitoring of the environment.

The key to their successful 97% customer satisfaction rating is employee empowerment. Employees are selected (1 out of 100 applicants is hired), well trained, empowered to resolve bills, and are asked to tell management what they need to provide quality service. Special emphasis is given to greeting customers and anticipating problems before they arise by both management and employees. Currently, Ritz Carlton is moving toward self-directed work teams which turns daily decision making over to employees.

Total Quality at Ritz Carlton involves everyone. Quality teams set objectives, develop detailed plans and teams meet weekly to review key statistics defining success. Each hotel has a quality leader responsible for problem solving, strategic planning and quality certification standards.

This attention to guest recognition, retention and preference is stimulated by the knowledge that it costs five times as much to attract a new guest as to keep an old one. Thus, adherence to TQM not only improves service, it also reduces costs and helps to build long term relationships with customers.

At the end of the case, the president, Horst Schultze, is described as setting a new goal for Ritz Carlton: meeting the 6 sigma standard which is 3.4 defects per million or 100% customer satisfaction. Arguments for and against this goal are presented. Because this new goal can be used as the focus for using this video in class, the arguments are presented in the teaching tips section.

Description of Video: This video revolves around interviews with Ralph Vick, General Manager Phoenix, and Sharon Alexander, Sales and Marketing Division Phoenix. These interviews are mixed in with mostly still shots of hotel operation, quality team meetings, employee training and a shot of the president, Horst Schultze.

Teaching Tips: This video goes well with the Total Quality Management and Relationships with Publics sections of Chapter 3. Discuss these concepts in class before showing the video. Use the issue raised at the end of the video for a basis of class discussion after the video.

The issue raised is whether or not Ritz Carlton <u>should</u> attempt to meet the 6 sigma standard. Arguments in favor of doing so revolve around a study that shows a 5% reduction in customer defection can lead to as much as an 85% increase in the bottom line, and that all of their efforts to date are based on building long-term relationships with customers. They also point out that it costs five times as much to attract a new customer as to keep an old one. Arguments against are that the cost of satisfying all customer complaints can spiral out of hand and that it's impossible to anticipate, let alone, solve customer problems beforehand.

Warn students before showing the video that the discussion will be based on this issue. You might even divide the class in half. One half will focus on gleaning information from the video that supports the 6 sigma goal and the other half focuses on the argument against. After the video discuss this issue and bring in the importance of employee empowerment, the gold standards and the use of quality teams into the discussion. Make sure that students understand how these affect Ritz Carlton's ability to reach the 6 sigma standard.

Lands' End: Hello Japan!

Should Accompany Chapter 4 of Solomon/Stuart

Summary:

Content of Video: In this video, Lands' End expansion abroad is described. In 1987, Lands' End first tested the international waters by sending their catalogs to Canada. Based on success there, they began in 1991 to send catalogs to the U.K. where they ran into some problems.

The main difficulty was the difference between the Queen's English and U.S. English. The two are not the same. In the U.S. the term pants refers to trousers, but in the U.K., pants are underwear; in the U.S. thongs are a type of shoe, but in the U.K., they're a skimpy bathing suit and in the U.S., we have diaper bags, but in the U.K., they're called nappy bags. But Lands' End persevered and put together their own creative team and artists and by 1993, they were able to open facilities in England and be a success.

Their next stop was Japan. There advertising for products was primarily done through full color newspaper inserts crammed with products. Lands' End resisted this trend and advertised as they do at home with few products on the page, but they did accede to the Japanese habit of using newspaper inserts. Their next problem involved payment. In Japan, the merchandise is delivered and then people pay. Again Lands' End had to go with the cultural flow of billing after delivery. Another issue was the guarantee. Land's End wanted to use their guarantee, but such a practice was unknown to the Japanese, so Lands' End had to explain their guarantee in the media and practice what they preached for a while until the Japanese believed. Finally, Lands' End found the letters and stories it prints in its catalogs to be very powerful as consumer testimonials in Japan. With the Japanese, Lands' End found that it could build trust by sending the merchandise first, supporting their guarantee and using customer testimonials.

In entering any market, Lands' End looks for three ingredients:

1.   Stable infrastructure—populace must be able to buy the goods
2.   A good distribution system—mail service
3.   A good telephone system

Near the end of the case, students are asked where should Lands' End go next? It is considering Germany, the Netherlands or France.

Description of Video: The video consists of many shots of English operations, the British catalog, shots of Japan and Japanese advertising and catalog. There are also interviews with Andrew Gallant, U.K. Copywriter and Frank Buettner, VP International.

Teaching Tips: In international markets, there is always an issue of standardization vs. customization. Both of these are highlighted in the Lands' End case. Lands' End would like to standardize its international operations as much as possible which is why it wants catalogs, advertising and operations to be alike in all countries. But it had to adapt to a small extent in the U.K. in terms of language. How did it have to adapt in Japan? Why? Were these cultural values, norms, customs? (The Cultural Environment) Which of elements of its marketing mix did Lands' End have to adapt? Products? Promotion? Price or Distribution? (Choosing a marketing mix)

Student Assignment: You might assign students to explore the catalog markets in Germany, the Netherlands and France and write a paper explaining which country they think Lands' End should enter and why. All three meet the criteria outlined in the case. Students may be shocked to know that Germany has the largest catalogers in the world. Ottohandelsgruppen which owns Eddie Bauer and Spiegel is the largest catalog company in the world. This means that German consumers are very accustomed to shopping by catalog, but think of the competition. Which country would fit with the Lands' End understated non-trendy look? Which country is the largest in market size? (Don't forget that they speak German in Switzerland and Austria.)

Lands' End chose to enter Germany in spite of the fact that their guaranteed violates German law that goods must be returned within 15 days. So far, they have been successful. Their guarantee is still tied up in the courts.

MTV

Should Accompany Chapter 4 of Solomon/Stuart

Summary:

Content of Video: In this video, we are introduced to the global marketing of MTV which has a single brand that is customized locally in many places, but also has a very standardized look and feel around the globe. In many countries it broadcasts in English.

MTV was born on August 1, 1981 and was immediately known as unpredictable and irreverent. It imitated the cutting edge of rock and roll with its graphic look, video jockeys or vjs, music news, rockumentaries, original programming and seemingly endless music videos.

Its programming consists of what young people are interested in—whether its sports, movies, music news, news from a different perspective or specials. It has become an American Institution—a cultural monolith.

When cable growth began to slow in the U.S., MTV took its show on the road with such success that it has more viewers in Europe than in the U.S. It has been hailed as the ultimate new-age multinational and is seen in more than 256 million homes in 64 countries.

Producing a single global brand with customized local programming costs more, takes longer and is harder, but it must be localized to bond with viewers.

MTV has six affiliates: MTV Europe (Pan-european and in English with 40% of videos not in English); MTV Latino (from Miami and aimed at the U.S. hispanic population, Latin and South America); MTV Brazil (in Portuguese); and MTV Asia (which reaches 30 countries in English and Mandarin) and MTV Japan (which is customized for Japanese youth).

While there are standardized shows, they are frequently dubbed with the local language and presented from the local point of view although the footage may have been sent from the U.S.. To localize, stations use local artists and videos. But the mix and the programming is constantly changing.

At the end, the video asks if this is the homogenization of youth internationally—whether they are losing their cultural identity? Comments from the VP of International Operations indicate that each MTV affiliate has its own style. MTV Brazil is very rock-oriented; whereas MTV Europe is more pop and MTV Asia is very glossy and stylish. So, maybe the youth are not being exposed to such a standardized product, after all. But what will it be like in ten years?

Description of Video: This video is full of footage from MTV which is counterbalanced with interviews with Tom Hunter, Sr. VP of International Operations.

Teaching Tips: This video zeros in on the cultural issue. Does MTV lead to homogenization of youth? Surely MTV does not do this alone. It has plenty of American movies and consumer products on display and for sale around the globe to help it out. MTV is only one element of this homogenization issue.

The localization issue responds to political environmental issues as politics may be the basis of some programming. Good issues to discuss are the commonality of values espoused through MTV as well as symbols and language. It would appear that MTV is active in promoting the common use of the English language and common symbols to youth. All of these are issues that can be discussed around the MTV video.

Sputnik: Insights from the Streets

Should Accompany Chapter 5 of Solomon/Stuart

Summary:

Content of Video: This video describes the operations of a New York firm that conducts interview research among progressive youths to look for trends that will cross over into the mainstream. Janine Lopiano-Misdom and Joanne De Luca founded Sputnik to overcome deficiencies they perceived in current research. They thought it was important to get into contact with the leaders and movers of the youth culture and that quantitative research and focus groups didn't get at the motivations of people and failed to capture the individual's personality.

Sputnik research is conducted by correspondents, young artists who videotape interviews with trendsetters wherever they find them—whether it's nightclubs, in stores, cafes or poetry readings. Joanne and Janine call the interviewees visionaries because these are people who can create, explore and experiment.

Once the interviewing is done, the tapes are reviewed by staff and common themes are filtered from the content. The final report to the client is a video and thick book that details the common mind trends uncovered in the research. From this, Sputnik finds new product ideas, positionings and promotions.

Sputnik's client list is most impressive and includes firms like Coca-Cola and Pepsi-Cola—both firms with a heavily youth-driven market.

The video opens with scenes from previous interviews and the end of the video follows a typical correspondent as she interviews people about jeans. A common theme emerging from these interviews is the idea of many pockets on jeans to carry such items as a Nokia phone and the other clutter that consumers carry around with them. At the end, the founders hypothesize that we will see many new products and messages that have real depth.

Description of the Video: There are many shots of interviews taking place, interviewees and scenes in Sputnik facilities along with interviews with Janine Lopiano-Misdom and Joanne De Luca, founders of Sputnik and Rachel, the correspondent.

Teaching Tips: This video can be used with the section on determining the research technique, gathering data, validity, reliability, representativeness and predicting the future.

After showing the video, ask students what kind of research Sputnik does? (Exploratory) Then discuss the pros and cons of their data gathering technique. (It provides more in-depth research and is not a summary of respondent comments. By seeing the videos, one knows that the interviews were done, what was asked and what the response was. Actually this is a clever way of 'supervising' interviewers.)

Some of the cons of this research are questions about validity, reliability and representativeness. Reliability would require that respondents say much the same thing; validity would require that the research be investigating the right subjects and would be difficult to judge in Sputnik research; and representativeness would require that they interview a sample of the 'right' respondents. Given the nature of the interviewing process, one can assume that interviews are likely to be long, but relatively limited in number. This is definitely small sample, exploratory research.

Does it accurately identify trends among this group? We have no direct way of answering this question, but the firm is selling to many big name clients and hopefully, they have been satisfied with past research. How does Sputnik's means of predicting future trends compare with the futurists described in the text?

The M/A/R/C Group

Should Accompany Chapter 5 of Solomon/Stuart

Summary:

Content of Video: This video describes the activities of the M/A/R/C Group—one of the ten largest marketing research firms in the U.S. The M/A/R/C group uses effective information systems to assess information needs and develop an information plan for collecting data and distributing information and interpreting the results. The focus is on information, not data. As Scott Bailey of M/A/R/C says, marketing research doesn't provide answers to problems, it provides intelligence that helps to solve problems. Data needs to be interpreted and analyzed to become information and intelligence.

M/A/R/C works with clients through a team approach in which teams consist of a senior partner, an account executive, an analyst, a project manager and staff experts. The team approach is used to provide clients with the range of M/A/R/C expertise and to build a long run relationship.

M/A/R/C has two core businesses. The first is its custom research division which does market segmentation, forecasting and simulation and tracking studies. It also conducts customer satisfaction research, quality programs and brand equity consulting. It's strongest attribute is its emphasis on simulation and sophisticated analytical systems.

It can collect data through telephone, in-person or one-on-one interviews and mail surveys. Of these, telephone is the fastest and most representative; one-on-one is used when the respondent has to see a stimulus such as a new product or an ad; and mail is the least expensive, but most time consuming. Because quality and speed of information collection makes the difference, M/A/R/C is constantly improving its computer and analytical resources.

The second M/A/R/C business is TargetBase—a full service database agency. It engages in targeted, direct marketing. An example is helping a pet food company find households with pets, developing a direct mail promotional piece for them and then evaluating the results.

What sets M/A/R/C apart is its tight connection to the customer.

At the end of the video, students are asked which data collection technique they would use to test a new, nonfat chocolate dessert product—either a mall intercept or a central facility testing site? Why?

Description of Video: This video has many shots of the M/A/R/C facility of clients and teams, computers, analysts at work and interviews with Scott Bailey, Sr. VP of MARC Research and Michelle Stephens, Director TargetBase Marketing.

Teaching Tips: Pick up with the project given at the end of the video tape? Ask students what type of research is being done with the nonfat, chocolate dessert? Exploratory, Descriptive or Causal? How should they gather the data? This is the mall intercept or central facility testing question. Either is a possible data collection situation, but central facility would be more expensive. Because special equipment such as projectors or viewers are not needed, the mall intercept might be best. Students should asked how one could ensure reliability, validity and representativeness. Then ask which division of M/A/R/C would conduct this research. (Custom Research)

Now, supposed the manufacturer is Jello and they want to run a promotion for the product, which M/A/R/C division would do this? TargetBase is the answer. How could TargetBase help the manufacturer? Find the right households, send them a promotion such as a coupon and measure the results.

Mercedes Benz

Should Accompany Chapter 5 of Solomon/Stuart

Summary:

Content of Video: This video describes research at Mercedes Benz an example of recent Mercedes research. Throughout the video, the following marketing research terms are highlighted on the screen and defined: Marketing Information System, Marketing Decision Support System, Ongoing Information, Monitored Information, Requested Information, Exploratory Research, Problem Solving Research, Reliability, Validity, and Representativeness.

The marketing research example used in the case involves image research conducted for Mercedes. From dealer reports and focus groups, Mercedes found that consumers were not comfortable with the car—they even questioned whether they could sit in a car in the showroom. An additional report from a company specializing in product personalities revealed that although consumers realized that Mercedes was glamorous and had a lot of integrity (superior engineering and high product quality), they also thought Mercedes was aloof, non-caring, not youthful and definitely not fun.

In the video three options that Mercedes could take are outlined on the screen. They could (a) ignore the studies, (b) change the car's market position by downscaling it for younger consumers or (c) change the communications strategy. Bob comments that Mercedes thinks of itself as a serious company, but also recognizes that times change and that the psychological fit between the consumer and the car is important. Therefore, Mercedes chose to change its communication strategy—to make its ads more light hearted and humorous while retaining the core values of engineering and product quality. Several ads are shown in this part of the video to demonstrate the new communication strategy.

Bob ends by commenting that communication must take lifestyles into account and create the perception of a friendlier car. Doing so may makes consumers less afraid of sitting in the car in the showroom!

One of the positive features of the video is that emphasizes the need for information rather than focusing on data collection. Bob even points out that information is for people in the firm to use. This is the major function of marketing research: to collect information for decision-making purposes.

Description of Video: The only person interviewed in this video is Bob Baxter, Manager of Marketing Research for Mercedes Benz, North America. There are several shots of people conducting telephone research and in-dealer showroom research. Ads depicting the new Mercedes communication strategy are shown near the end of the video.

Teaching Tips: Before showing the video talk about the importance of information as opposed to data. A set of numbers and research findings may or may not contain information. The value of information is its usefulness. In collecting it, it is important to use the right techniques and make sure that the information is of high quality (reliable, valid and representative). Use only a short lecture on marketing research to precede the video.

When you reach the part of the video where the question "If you were Bob Baxter, what would you do?" is posed on the screen, stop the video. Bob's three options have already been given. Briefly discuss the options to make sure that everyone understands what they are. Then let the class discuss what they would do in small groups. Give them 5–10 minutes for this. Hold a class discussion about what the various groups would do. Then show the rest of the video so students can compare their responses to what the company actually did.

It is important to note that this video illustrates the use of marketing research information rather than how to do marketing research.

Sebago

Should Accompany Chapter 6 of Solomon/Stuart

Summary:

Content of Video: This video is designed to go with the chapter on consumer behavior. While it centers on Sebago shoes, it has many screens that list the factors that affect consumer behavior and a model of internal and external influences that affect consumer decision-making.

Sebago Shoes have a reputation for quality. They are American made from all high quality materials and this results in a higher price. This price, however, should be viewed as an indicator of the value of the product and is reasonable given the workmanship and quality of materials in the shoe.

Sebago's traditional product was the penny loafer, popularized by James Dean who is an example of an influential or social influence on consumers. In the 1970s, another social influence, the mini-skirt damaged sales of the product.

Sebago's response was to team with another firm to make boating shoes in response to the increased popularity of sailing. After 22 years, the other firm moved off-shore. This left Sebago with a decision. They could either accept the lower price, create a new brand name or stop production of boating shoes.

Sebago chose to create a new brand, but then encountered resistance from consumers and retailers who insisted that Sebago was a loafer, not a boating shoe. The name was changed to Dockside with Sebago in small letters and sales skyrocketed. Dan Wellehan of Sebago comments that within a few months one summer, the Kings of Norway and Sweden and Spain were all pictured on magazine covers wearing Docksides. A company could never afford to buy such promotion. This is another example of influentials. Most of the purchasers of Docksides have never been near a boating shoe.

Dan describes the typical Sebago consumer as traditional, not at the cutting edge of fashion, a bit conservative, likely to all natural fiber clothing and to be interested in buying quality products.

The factors identified in the video as influencing consumer decisions are perception, learning, influentials, reference groups and social influences. One screen shows a model of consumer decision making as being affected by individual influences (perception, motivation, learning, attitude and personality), personal influences (age, gender, income, family life cycle, and lifestyle), situational influences (time, mood and shopping environment) and social influences (cultural, sex-role identities, subculture, social class, reference groups and influentials).

Description of Video: The video shows scenes of sailing, scenes in a shoe store and of production in the Sebago factory along with the interview with Dan Wellehan, son of the founder of Sebago shoes.

Teaching Tips: The value in showing this video is to provide a concrete example of a purchase decision to which students can relate the factors that influence purchase. In class, you might walk through the purchase decision process (problem recognition to postpurchase evaluation) and ask students to identify the actions that Sebago might take to influence the decision process. (Example: Problem recognition can be stimulated through advertising and in-store signs and displays and through influentials seen to be wearing the shoes; information search through advertising and promotion; evaluation through comments of sales clerks, etc.)

Then widen the scope by looking at internal, personal, social and situational influences affect purchase and how Sebago could affect those. (Example: Sebago could increase learning through advertising and through selling materials given to sales clerks to learn about the company; celebrity endorsements are examples of social influence; situational influences could include in-store promotions and displays). The goal is to tie corporate action directly to factors that affect consumers and make students aware that firms can and do influence consumer learning, attitude, perception, etc.

MasterCard Part II

Should Accompany Chapter 7 of Solomon/Stuart

Summary:

Content of Video: This video discusses the importance of MasterCard's Health Care Division responding to changes in the consumer environment to help member banks and health care providers improve their profitability.

This division of MC helps members through ongoing support, identification of new markets to penetrate and new pilot of testing of services, promotions, or strategies. Competition forces focusing of activities and MC uses its partnerships with members and providers to develop the level of innovation need to provide increasing levels of value.

The marketing planning process MC uses begins with constant feedback from its members. Several times yearly it holds meetings with key banks to determine what problems they face in using specific promotions and programs. This reinforces the importance of marketing research in understanding member's needs and environments.

The growth of Health Care Maintenance Organization, HMOs, is a major change in the consumer environment affecting the use of credit cards in the health care industry. Growth of HMOs has led providers to pay more attention to their bottom line and to increased use of credit cards to pay for health care. Those not enrolled in an HMO find their deductibles and copay are increasing so that use of the credit card becomes more viable in paying these bills. Those in HMOs find that some procedures and doctors outside their area are not covered so that they too have higher bills to pay.

A major challenge for MC's health care division is increasing awareness among consumers that credit cards are a preferred means of payment. Awareness is created through signs at checkout desks and materials provided by MC. **Although not in this video, MC knows that customers are more likely to buy and pay quickly for health care when they use a credit care. This explains why credit cards are preferred.**

At the end of the video, on screen statements inform students that when marketing plans are properly integrated, they are unified, consistent, coordinated and use a total quality approach for members' long run, moderate length and short run plans. They are also informed that different strategic business units require separate marketing plans. It concludes with a statement by MC's director of health care marketing that satisfying ultimate consumers need to obtain health care when they need it is the best means of meeting the needs of member banks and businesses.

Description of Video: This video is an interview with Melanie Breen Moelis, Director of Health Care Marketing for MC. The interview is interspersed with shots in a dentist office, ads for MC in health care settings, examples of MC health care promotions and on-screen statements stressing the goals of MC's health care division and the characteristics of properly developed marketing plans.

Teaching Tips: This video is especially useful for discussing the characteristics of business markets, derived demand, the classification of member banks and health care providers and the buying situation in adopting the use of MC.

Discuss all of these concepts in class and list them on the blackboard. Show the video and afterwards, ask:

1.   How it illustrated the concept of derived demand? MC must pay attention to the consumer market because demand is generated there for the services of healthcare providers and member banks.

2. What are the characteristics of MC's business members/partners? Banks are normally very profit oriented, there are fewer of these than health care providers and each represents a large account for MasterCard. There are more health care providers who are more geographically dispersed and whose individual transactions are much smaller.

3. How to classify member banks and providers? Banks may be perceived to produce the MC service and providers as resellers.

4. What is the buying situation and how is it affected by the use of MC? Banks are trying to find means of increasing their bottom line and to provide more valuable services to their customer accounts. MC is one means of meeting both of these goals. This is a New Task buying when the bank partners with MC. Providers on the other hand are trying to encourage purchase of their services and quick payment. By adopting the use of MC, they are removing an obstacle or barrier that prevents the consumer from buying. Both are trying to increase their bottom line.

Student Assignment: Once students understand this business-to-business situation, they could be given an out of class assignment to devise promotions that banks could use to sell MC to health care providers and promotions that health care providers could use to generate more payment by credit card. Give them specific objectives such as increasing the number of health care providers of a certain type that sign up for MC or how providers could increase consumer awareness or usage of MC to pay for services. In the next class, students could report on their efforts in class.

This assignment should only be used if you have not shown the MasterCard Part I video. That video describes such promotions by MasterCard. If you do use this assignment, you might show the MC Part I video after the students have made their presentations to compare their ideas with what MC has actually done.

House of Blues:
Singing the Blues?

Should Accompany Chapter 8 of Solomon/Stuart

Summary:

Content of Video: This video relates the House of Blues to the concept of Segmentation. First of all, the blues are one form of music that appeals to specific fans. Selling the blues is a matter of culture. According to founder Tigrett, most music originates from the blues and the Southern Culture.

Second, the HOB segments the market geographically. There are seven Houses of the Blues and each has its own decoration and theme. Some are large (Chicago and Los Angeles) while others are small (Cambridge, Massachusetts). Some are domestic and some are international such as Tokyo, London and Paris.

Third, each House of Blues segments it market according to local musical types. There are evenings when the music may be spanish, hip-hop or white boy—it depends on local tastes and local bands which get a chance to perform to attract the local crowd. And it finds target groups to attract to the HOB. Stephensen talks about have S.I.N. night which is Service Industry Night to attract people employed in service businesses.

Fourth, the House of Blues actually has three target markets—consumers (discussed above), employees and performers. Most employees find that they are treated well and really like working at the HOB. The idea is to treat everyone with respect. HOB also targets musicians by providing the best of equipment and stages for them to work with. They also manage concerts, so they provide musicians with a place to play (the HOB facilities) and they will manage their tours.

Fifth, the HOB is able to micro-segment the consumer market through narrowcasting. They are the largest promoter of live concerts. You can buy concerts from their web site, but when technology catches up with them and you can watch the concerts on your web-enabled TV, you will be able to select just the concerts that you want to watch. This means that 5,000,000 viewers could watch 5,000,000 different programs—each specially designed for the individual viewer. That's as finely segmented as you can get.

The HOB is more than just a for-profit business. It has established a foundation that targets school children (among others) in educational programs of all sorts. And it is committed to demonstrating that a business can be principled. The HOB tries to be principled through the Foundation, and by demonstrating the five Vedic values of love, truth, peace, righteousness and non-violence.

And the HOB is entering other ventures—internet auctions and digital radio.

Description of Video: The video contains shots from the L. A. House of Blues and interviews with Charlie Musselwhite (musician), Isaac Tigrett (founder), Kris Stephenson (   ), Arick Berghammer (Manager, L.A. House of Blues).

Teaching Tips: This video was designed to illustrate various ways to segment the market. After showing the video, ask students the HOB adapts itself to its consumer market? This will bring out the various bases for segmentation mentioned above.

Then, ask it has other targeted markets? This should elicit responses about the employees and musicians. Some may argue that the Foundation is targeted toward various groups (children through education, blacks through Martin Luther King celebrations, etc.).

Ask students if the HOB engages in differentiated marketing or concentrated marketing.
The answer would seem to be concentrated if it only focused on the blues, but given its inclusiveness (Espanol rock), it appears to be more differentiated.

You might ask students to write a positioning statement for the HOB—one that captures its cultural interests as well as its for-profit endeavors and principled "nature."

Before showing this case, go to the House of Blues web site (www.hob.com). You will find a world of information about the House of Blues there—about their philosophy, their venues, their concerts, the activities of the Foundation, etc.

Student Assignment: Because the HOB has a wonderful web site, you might ask students to visit the web site and write a short report on the extent of HOB's segmentation activities that they find there. They should think very carefully about who the target audience is for each program. You might check the web site before class and give them a list of activities and programs that they are to check on. (This list can't be provided in advance because the web site changes daily.)

MasterCard Part I

Should Accompany Chapter 8 of Solomon/Stuart

Summary:

Content of Video: This video illustrates how MasterCard segments its markets, selects target market segments and how it designs unique offers for each segment.

Segmentation: MC's market is segmented into three groups: member banks, businesses that accept MasterCard and customers who use the cards. MasterCard itself is organized into three divisions: health care, government and travel. This video illustrates MC's marketing strategies for the health care division.

Example of Promotional Strategy: Each division develops marketing materials, strategies and promotions for member providers' use in selling to the health care market. A specific example is the For a Clean Bill of Health promotion. Based on the marketing research finding that most customers who postponed health care did so for financial reasons, MC's health care division developed the Clean Bill of Health promotion to encourage health care providers to accept MasterCard. It had three components: a brochure emphasizing the ease of accepting MC, preauthorization forms health care providers could use for customers to authorize payment of their bills with MC and invoice stickers providers could attach to invoices stating that they accept MC. If MC holders used their card to pay health care bills, they were given the For a Clean Bill of Health Kit. It contained a guide filled with information about health care (Ex. questions to ask when selecting a doctor), coupons for discounts on partners' goods and services (Ex. NordicTrack), and a collection of preprinted materials from health care associations (brochures on cancer and osteoporosis). Eight million of these were mailed out by member banks and the campaign was backed by public relations efforts, free standing inserts in newspapers and marketing on the internet. It was extremely successful in increasing the use of MC for health care payments.

Near the end, the video indicates that MC segments the provider market into existing penetrated markets (physicians, dentists and hospitals) and new, emerging markets (nursing homes, home health care agencies, hearing aids and laboratories). The new market presents opportunities for MC to understand the market, identify their needs and develop sales materials for their members to use in penetrating these markets.

MC's strategy is summarized in a series of on-screen statements about its ability to study target markets' needs, develop well conceived strategies and unique benefits that members can use to attract new businesses and credit card users.

Description of video: The video is an interview with Melanie Breen Moelis, Director of Health Care Marketing for MasterCard, interspersed with shots in a dentist office, a payment transaction and on-screen lists of target markets, description of differentiated marketing and summaries of MC's segmentation and targeting strategy.

Teaching Tips: Use this video to illustrate the segmentation and targeting of a service industry. Before showing the video, discuss the concepts of segmentation, targeting and positioning. Then show the video. It is a relatively straightforward description of MC's segmenting and targeting efforts.

Afterwards, ask students to describe MC's market segments and talk about the different goals of each. Ask them to identify how the Clean Bill of Health promotion targeted all three segments and explain why it was successful.

Discuss the differences in the existing and new market segments. Ask and discuss how promotions such as the Clean Bill of Health would be useful in selling into these segments.

Because positioning is not really discussed in the video, a good way to bring closure to the discussion and get active student participation is to ask students to develop a positioning statement for the MasterCard health care division's strategy. This statement should be broad enough to apply to both market segments, but specific enough to capture the benefits that MC provides for each segment.

Computer Friendly Stuff, Case 2:
Different Keystrokes for Different Folks

Should Accompany Chapter 8 of Solomon/Stuart

Summary:

Content of Video: This video focuses on knowing the customer(s) and how to reach/target them. It begins with the folks at CFS going to a department store in Michigan and standing between ladies lingerie and infants' wear with no one coming to see them. The lesson they learned was that this was a mismatch between them and the customer.

Fortunately, they had learned that their market consisted of two segments: (1) professional women between the ages of 20 and 50 and (2) children between the ages of 7 and 14. They had made the product fun to appeal to children with humor sophisticated enough to appeal to adults.

Once they had the product and target market right, they needed to figure out how to reach their market segments. This led them to think in terms of business to business markets. They realized that they could sell to: computer stores (primary market), gift stores (women) and toy stores (children). When dealing with retailers, they focused on brand awareness. Because their product could be easily copied, they needed to get to market first (beat the competition) so that retailers would recognize it.

They developed three strategies for selling at the three types of trade shows to reach the three types of retailers. (1) *Computer shows*—they built a giant monitor out of a big screen TV, with an oversized keyboard with a styrofoam bug stuck to the side. Even so, they found it difficult to compete with giants like Sega, Nintendo and Microsoft. Their solution to creating awareness came from working with a consulting firm, Creative Solutions. They created a card with a picture of the computer bug on it that could be stuck on the buyer's name badge. The bug was depicted looking at the buyer and saying things like "This person stole towels from the hotel room." This worked because it was cheap, took advantage of vacant real estate and was noticed by everyone.

(2) At *toy shows*, the card strategy wouldn't work because toy buyers are conservative and don't like the idea of something stuck to them. Hence, CFS used the computer bug mascot to attract attention.
(3) At *gift shows*, buyers would be intimidated by the big monitor, so CFS ditched the big monitor, used the computer bug costume, plush versions of the bug and small regular-size computer screens.

This strategy worked because they targeted their efforts at the three different types of buyers.

The video ends with Chris saying that they needed to move on to another problem—that they needed a new product. Customers in New Zealand were asking for new products. In addition, a one product company cannot survive because the margins are too small.

Description of Video: Again, this video is mostly an interview with Chris interspersed with footage from their trade show and department store experiences.

Teaching Tips: You might begin discussion of this video by contrasting the approach to the market developed here with that described in the first video. Begin by going over the current strategy of three different types of retailers to reach the two types of consumers. Ask students to explain why this system works to reach the final consumer. Be sure to include some discussion of the buyer's mind set for each type of distribution channel—this harks back to chapter 7 on organizational buying. By elaborating the three markets (computer, gift and toy) which can be reached at the appropriate trade shows, the current strategy is set in everyone's mind.

Next, to relate the discussion to the segmentation section of chapter 8, ask students what are the different characteristics of each segment (note: this may already have occurred in the discussion of buyers). How does Chris segment these buyers? Is it psychographics or behavior or some of both? (Certainly, it's partly psychographics—remember the differences in appearance and willingness to have something stuck on them of the computer and toy buyers.)

Now, backtrack to the first video in which Chris' initial strategy was to mail samples of the product to the 18 largest retailers in the U.S. Conduct a discussion of why the first strategy worked and the new one (from this video) did. This should illustrate the differences in undifferentiated marketing (the first strategy) and differentiated marketing (the second strategy). By aiming at the largest retailers and the mass market, Chris and company were ignoring whether these were the right outlets to reach computer users.

Ask students to explicitly delineate the advantages of differentiated marketing for CFS. (This is mainly avoiding the expense and effort of winding up at the wrong trade shows . By focusing, all their energy and talent can go into tailoring their approach which makes them more successful at the trade show.) The discussion should bring out why differentiated marketing involves less effort and possibly less cost than mass marketing and can be more effective. This discussion relates to the targeting section in chapter 8.

As a last activity, ask the students to write a positioning statement for CFS. This statement should be strongly related to the brand personality as described by Chris in the video.

The New Product Showcase:
A Museum of Losers

Should Accompany Chapter 9 of Solomon/Stuart

Summary:

Content of Video: This video is a visit to the New Product Showcase in Ithaca, New York. Bob McMath, owner of the Showcase, has spent decades collecting new products in the health and beauty and grocery categories. All of these over 60,000 products are now cataloged and/or displayed at the Showcase.

Corporations are Bob's main clients. As groups of executives or new product teams, they come to the Showcase to look for new product ideas, to find out if an idea has been used by others and to study why new products fail. Lawyers also use the Showcase to check for trademark infringement

To be successful, new products have to meet a need, be timed right, have a good name, be packaged well and be backed by adequate marketing, advertising and market entry support. They also need to avoid being me-too products.

Bob gives several examples of losers. One is a new hand sanitizer he has received. He asked why do we need another hand sanitizer—this is a me-too product with no unique selling proposition. He also mentions Teddy Graham cereal which was rushed to market without adequate testing. RJR Nabisco found out too late that their cereal formed a glop in the cereal bowl when mixed with milk. Then, there's the Maxwell house refrigerated coffee product packaged in a carton like milk. The idea was that consumers would pour out a cupful and heat it in their microwave. Some decided to heat the whole carton in order to have a pot of coffee. When the carton collapsed, they had a mess instead.

There is a new product that Bob does like. It's Water Joe which is caffeinated water for use in a place such as the Chicago exchange where the only beverage allowed is water. But because traders need to stay on their toes, the caffeinated water satisfies a real need for them. Marilyn Raymond of his staff also thinks that single servings of cottage cheese and Campbell's soup in resealable mugs are good new product ideas.

Marilyn has also identified several promising trends. Cool fusion which is a mix of contradictory elements used in one product such as chocolate on a healthy product. Functional foods such as nutriceuticals (St. John's Wort) on chips is another trend. Then, there's comfort foods like Mother used to make such as mashed potatoes. Only you don't have to do the peeling, cooking and mashing and make the mess that Mother did. You use refrigerated mashed potatoes so you can have the comfort foods and clean cuisine which is no mess.

Description of Video: This video consists of shots of new products at the New Product Showcase along with interviews with Bob McMath, Owner of the Showcase, Marilyn Raymond, Home Economist at the Showcase and Jean McMath, wife of the owner.

Teaching Tips: After showing the video in class, ask students what are the characteristics of successful and unsuccessful new products mentioned in the video. It's important to get a fix on these before proceeding to discuss specific products.

Then, ask the class whether or not they think that the single portion of cottage cheese or the soup in the resealable mug will be successful. Evaluate each of these using the criteria that students listed for success of new products.

Next introduce the concept of innovations. Discuss how they differ from new products. Ask if the cottage cheese or resealable soup is an innovation, and if so, what type. Use the Water Joe product to discuss innovations. Is it an innovation and what type? Why would it be successful? (Use the criteria of relative advantage, compatibility, etc. to evaluate it).

What about the comfort foods, the nutriceuticals and cool fusion products? Are these innovations? Ask if the students found any examples of these when they visited stores (see assignment below). Ask if those are innovations and evaluate the likelihood of success of these.

Student Assignment: Before the class on new products, you might assign students to visit drug, convenience, discount and grocery stores to find new product ideas. They should jot those down to use in the class discussion.

Kodak: Taking Pictures Further

Should Accompany Chapter 9 of Solomon/Stuart

Summary:

Content of Video: This video describes the introduction of the Picture CD—a new product from Kodak that enables any consumer with any kind of camera to have the advantages of digital pictures.

Running through the video is the theme that Kodak began as a company that made it easy for everyone to take pictures. One of their original slogans was "You push the button, we do the rest." When they introduce digital imaging to the mass market, that slogan might change to "You click on the icon and we do the rest."

Kodak is committed to the digital imaging business as they think it is the next growth spurt of photography (the previous ones being black and white home photography and then color photography). Initially, Kodak tried to sell consumers on digital imaging from the ground up—meaning that consumers had to buy a digital camera and learn to use it and to work with their pictures on a computer. That's too much behavioral change for consumers, not to mention the expense.

So, the Picture CD is a vastly pared down means of getting consumers into digital imaging. The only change that a consumer has to make in picture taking is to ask for the CD when they get their pictures developed. However, that CD enables them to store their pictures on disk or on-line, rotate the pictures, remove red eye, crop pictures, e-mail pictures, etc. The goal is get people to using their pictures rather than just taking them home and sticking them into an album.

Putting pictures on CD or disk enables consumers to better organize and more efficiently store their pictures. This advantage is one of the key benefits stressed in advertising for the CD.

But Kodak is not a technology company. To make the CD and all of the digital imaging and support that is needed for this new way of taking pictures, Kodak had to partner with Intel, Microsoft, Adobe and Hewlett Packard to have the software, processing and printing capability needed to bring consumers fully into the digital picture age.

Their hope, of course, is that the Picture CD will turn people on to digital photography so that you and I will eventually buy digital cameras. One element missing in the video is that Kodak has a service called PhotoNet On-line. What Kodak ultimately hopes, is that we will all use that service to store pictures, to rotate, crop them, etc., to email them and to have them printed on baseball caps, t-shirts, etc. The Online service brings Kodak closer to consumers and enlarges the ways in which Kodak can profit from extending the use of pictures.

The video also briefly describes the test marketing for the Picture CD. This was done in Salt Lake City and Indianapolis, IN. These two cities were picked because they are very self-contained. Promotions in one market do not spill over into others. Each city also has a different level of PC penetration, so that Kodak can test how that will affect demand for the Picture CD. In each test site, they ran different advertising and promotions to see which worked best.

Description of Video: This video contains shots of the Kodak facility in Rochester, shots of old Kodak cameras and still shots taken from Kodak files along with interviews with William Gray (Manager, Corporate Branding and VP, Corporate Marketing) and Carl E. Gustin Jr. (Chief Marketing Officer and Sr. VP).

Teaching Tips: This video fits very well with Chapter 9. After showing the video, you can ask students to explain what the core, actual and augmented product aspects of the Picture CD are.

Then use the Picture CD to talk about innovations. What kind of innovation is the digital camera? (Dynamically Continuous) What kind of innovation is the Picture CD? (Continuous Innovation) Discuss why.

Evaluate the both the digital camera and Picture CD as an innovation on the bases of relative advantage, compatibility, complexity, visibility, and trialability.

Finally, discuss Kodak's attempts to target the Picture CD to consumers. Are they stressing the right benefits in advertising? Will consumers understand the partnership of Kodak (pictures) with Intel, Adobe, Hewlett Packard and Microsoft (technology)? Is that combination of pictures + technology important to consumers? Does it matter whether or not they understand it.

How can Kodak stimulate awareness? Interest? Trial?

Intel: The Power Behind the PC Part I

Should Accompany Chapter 10 of Solomon/Stuart

Summary:

Content of Video: This video focuses on the branding strategy used by Intel—especially on the question of why Intel engages in heavy branding efforts. Prior to 1990, Intel like other chip manufacturers targeted its marketing efforts at buyers of computers for businesses and parts buyers for manufacturers because these were the people who know about and understood the importance of the microprocessor. As sales of PCs began to take off in the early 1990s, consumer ignorance about how computers work and the importance of a microprocessor posed a big challenge to Intel. The company thought that consumers could make better choices if they knew more about the microprocessor. Thus, Intel started a campaign designed to convince consumers that the microprocessor should be a key element in their computer purchase decision and to build preference for Intel's products.

The first campaign focused on advertising for the 486SX chip and was quite successful, but two things happened to dampen Intel's success. First, the market moved on to the 486 and second, a court ruling defined 386 and 486 as parts numbers, not trademarks or brands. As parts numbers, anyone could use them. Intel responded quickly.

Literally over a weekend, the Intel Inside campaign was born. Its goals were to establish Intel as an umbrella brand that could be used to communicate the specific benefits of other and future products without the Intel Inside element changing; to lead the consumer to ask "what's inside?" so that they would seek more knowledge about the microprocessor; and to enhance the computer manufacturer's brand image.

Intel chose to use a coop advertising campaign because that would encourage more advertising and work synergistically in enhancing the manufacturer's brand as well as Intel's. Intel's brand would then benefit from being coupled with other well known, quality brands. While some manufacturers balked at this, others climbed on board so that the campaign was a success.

Dennis Carter of Intel defines the essence of a brand as defining it, establishing a link with the consumers in order to provide them with predictability and reliability in products. The result is better choices made by consumers. Incorporating the company name in their brand, Intel identifies the source of the brand and serves to reassure the customer.

Description of Video: This video consists of an interview with Dennis Carter, VP and Director of Sales and Marketing for Intel. It is interspersed with scenes of chip manufacturing, ads for Intel and shots of workers using computers.

Teaching Tips: This video can be used to discuss the Product Life Cycle and Branding sections of the chapter. A key comment in the case occurs when Dennis Carter refers to the increasing sales of PCs in the early 1990s. At this point, the marketing strategy of Intel changed dramatically. PCs were moving out of the office and into the home. Because this enlarges the market for PCs, they entered the growth stage of the product life cycle. As Dennis Carter comments, the PC was becoming a consumer product and was being purchased by final consumers rather than knowledgeable professional buyers. This changes the dynamics of the marketplace.

As products enter the growth stage, competition enters the market, distribution expands, promotion is intensified and branding becomes more important in an attempt to establish consumer preference and hopefully, loyalty—all of which describes the actions taken by Intel in building their brand.

Of course, there are some specific branding issues for Intel—the use of umbrella branding and the need to make an invisible ingredient brand visible.

Discuss the PLC and branding before showing the video. Afterwards ask students to explain the positive benefits of the Intel Inside campaign to consumers and computer manufacturers. Then, ask them about the relationship between this branding strategy and the PLC. This is a good opportunity to get them to relate what they have just seen to a concept that was not mentioned in the video.

You can extend and update this case by pointing out that the market has moved toward purchase of less expensive computers (under $1,000). What does this imply about the life cycle of PCs? What stage are they in? What does this mean for companies such as Intel? Should it put the Intel Inside logo on these cheaper computers? Does that damage their image? What should Intel do as their traditional market (the over $1,500 computer) stagnates?

Yahoo-ing the World!

Can be Used with Chapters 11, 10 or 15 of Solomon/Stuart

Summary:

Content of Video: This video briefly describes the founding of Yahoo by Jerry Yang and David Filo—two PhD students at Stanford who explored the web to relieve the boredom of their graduate studies. When they published their favorite sites on the web, Yahoo was born. Although originally the name of rude, insensitive people in Gulliver's Travels, they adopted the name for their internet service and adapted it to mean Yet Another Hierarchical Officious Oracle. Since those early days, Yahoo has grown to over 165,000,000 viewings per month. But the company cannot rest on its laurels.

Yahoo's goals are to attract new users and keep current users at their site longer. They attempt to do this through products: providing a multitude of services that target a large number of segments in the market. They want to be the one place that anyone needs to go to find anything, buy anything and connect with anyone. By collecting information about users through My Yahoo, they can tailor offerings to individuals. So, they have chat rooms and clubs for teens, Yahooligans for children and lots of finance for business types and they can send the right information to shoppers about products that they want to buy. Because Yahoo is a service, it has to have a broad range of services to constantly build loyalty and attract new users.

To expand markets, Yahoo has gone global. It is now available in fifteen countries. Obviously, the idea of the world wide web ought to be global. While many of the services and features of Yahoo are the same around the globe, it also adapts its offerings to the local market. For example, there would be local news and local people and events might be featured.

They also engage in brand building through a funky campaign that aims to persuade potential users that Yahoo is easy, fun, convenient and human rather than a serious techy sort of brand. Management's thinking is that if consumers perceive Yahoo to be fun, that will translate into easy which translates into convenient. From their perspective, Yahoo is a consumer brand, an enabling brand that helps people do what they want to do. Management wants to give it a sense of personality by creating an image and personality that's irreverent and a little off beat through their advertising. This ad campaign is supported through kazoos, yoyos, tee-shirts and surfer shirts and the Yahoo colors of yellow and purple.

Yahoo also seeks to expand its brand through co-branding. It has three different branding partnerships. The first is brand partners. These are groups that work with Yahoo on events, teams or other sponsorships so that both get credit. The second is distribution partnerships in which the co-branding firm enables Yahoo to expand its distribution. An example of this is distribution through AT & T. The third is content partnership in which Yahoo gets information from organizations such as CNN and CBS MarketWatch and puts that information in the appropriate Yahoo category, but also labels it from CNN and CBS.

In building this brand image, Yahoo not only makes themselves consumer-friendly, they also set themselves apart from the competition. While Yahoo is zany and creative, the competition tries to come across as highly respectable and serious. But new firms are entering the arena. Among them is Disney which unlike the previous competition, really understands the consumer market and is highly creative. What does Yahoo have to compete with them? Well, it's more creative than most and smaller than many so that it can be more nimble—get there more quickly with the new, right products. As Karen Edwards (head of branding says), the future will be tough and before long some firms are going to be gone. Yahoo doesn't intend to be one of them.

Description of Video: This video is quite lively. It features interviews with Karen Edwards, Director of Brand Management, Jasmine Kem, International Marketing Manager and Ken Greff, Brand Manager Yahooligans as well as excerpts from interviews with the founders and Chief Yahoos, Jerry Yang and David Filo. Several Yahoo ads are shown during the video which help to give the flavor of that funky Yahoo personality. Also included are shots of Yahoo offices, people at work and play and multiple shots of Yahoo.com online.

Teaching Tips: There are three major topics to discuss about Yahoo. These are branding (Chapter 10), services (Chapter 11) and retailing Chapter 15.

If you use the video with Chapter 15, the discussion might focus on the advantages and disadvantages of electronic retailing as opposed to catalogs and store. Be sure to point out that Yahoo can target offerings to consumers (which catalogs and stores find more difficult to do). Also, it is easier for consumers to browse and find merchandise than in stores where moving around may be difficult physically, things are easily overlooked and frequently sales people are not available or knowledgeable. Online retailers are less likely to be out of stock. The major disadvantage is that consumers must have a computer or have access to one and to the internet. But as PCs penetrate more homes and technology changes such as web-enabled TVs hit the market, more and more people will be logging onto the net. When they do, they have a choice of Yahoo, AOL, Disney. Which they choose may be influenced by branding considerations.

Branding—Chapter 10: It is important to discuss first of all what Yahoo's brand image consists of. The elements are fun, easy, convenient, human and irreverent. Students will pick up on those easily, but follow that discussion with why those elements would entice consumers to Yahoo and why that brand image will be more attractive than say the image of Infoseek? Could these two firms attract different types of users? Maybe Yahoo attracts an audience that is younger and less information oriented. Infoseek may attract more serious people who are more interested in the internet for information than for connection with others. Discuss how the variety of products and services help to build the Yahoo brand. What is the value of Yahooligans? If you have a good site for children, will that carryover to brand preference among parents? What is the value of their co-branding partners? Does being associated with AT & T, Compaq, CBS, etc. enhance the Yahoo brand? If so, how? Why?

The last thing to emphasize is the service aspect of Yahoo. What are the characteristics of Yahoo as a service? Karen Edwards mentions "making it tangible". What does that mean? Is it perishable? Is it variable? Inseparable? How would you judge the quality of the service? How is Yahoo like a theater? What are the front and back stage aspects of Yahoo? How does Yahoo identify/target its services? What is its positioning statement? Ask the class to write a positioning statement for Yahoo. If you used the student assignment with the class, now is the time to discuss the comparisons that students made between Yahoo and other portals. The results will be useful for discussing the future of Yahoo vis-à-vis the competition.

Student Assignment: Before showing the video in class, tell students to visit the Yahoo site and one other portal (AOL, Infoseek, etc.) Ask them to count the number of subject areas on the screen and services available to user. Tell them to pick one area (automobiles or health) and investigate each on Yahoo and the other service that they pick. The goal is to have comparisons of Yahoo and other providers across a range of services to attempt in class to decide which provides a better service. Is Yahoo hype or does it deliver? If it doesn't, all the clever brand building probably won't save it.

DuPont: The Right Ingredients for Success

Should Accompany Chapter 10 of Solomon/Stuart

Summary:

Content of Video: This video focuses on the branding strategy employed by DuPont. Because DuPont makes ingredient products used in the production of other products, branding is a major challenge for this company—especially when one considers that the company has two markets. First, it sells directly to other manufacturers, but to be successful, it must understand and respond to the needs of final consumers and communicate to them. DuPont picks its direct customers carefully because the company wants not only to sell to them, but to partner with them. The customer should become a partner in designing the final products to be made from the DuPont ingredient brands. For final consumers, DuPont engages in marketing research in order to understand the needs of consumers, how they are living and what they are thinking in order to turn that knowledge into products meeting needs that consumers sometimes didn't even know they had.

To accomplish its goals, DuPont uses an umbrella strategy when the DuPont name is the umbrella under which the ingredient brands such as Corian, Kevlar, Nomex, Teflon and Stainmaster are sheltered and marketed in a proactive manner. Thus, advertising and communication for the individual brands is also associated with the DuPont logo and slogan "Better things for better living." As the umbrella or parent brand, DuPont is presented as standing for respect for the individual, safety, health and the environment, honesty and ethics. The ingredient brands are then promoted on the basis of the benefits that each provides.

DuPont adheres to five principles of Brand Management that are illustrated with comments by individual brand managers and DuPont personnel. The five principles are:
(A) Personality—the company's culture, its goal of bringing solutions to consumer needs
(B) Visibility—projecting the company to its markets through a variety of advertising and promotional means that create awareness of the company's brands and make them visible in the marketplace as well as connecting with consumers.
(C) Target Management—selecting partners and customers: Whom do we connect with?
(D) Marketing management—managing the brand by understanding the dynamics of the marketplace: by seeing, feeling and touching them.
(E) Reputation Management—present DuPont globally in a way that builds on the core values of respect, health, environment, honesty and ethics.

Description of Video: This video contains interviews with the following DuPont personnel: Kathy Forte, DuPont Public Affairs; Jamie Murray, DuPont Brand Director; Barbara Pandos, U.S. Programs Manager; Steve McCracken, VP, General Manager, Corian; Mary Kopf, Brand Manager—Kevlar and Nomex; David McAndrews, VP, General Manager DuPont-Flouroproducts; Roszann Graham, Global District Director—Automobile Finishes; and Gary Johnston, National Marketing Communications Manager, Nylon Furnishings. The interviews are interspersed with pictures of the founder, shots of the logo and slogan and ads for the various ingredient brands.

Advice to Marketing Students: To be good marketers, they should be totally tuned into the needs of customers so that they can translate those needs into an offering that meets the need in a timely fashion and quality way at a price that the customer is willing and can afford to pay.

Teaching Tips: Before showing the video, ask students what type of brand is DuPont? While it is a national brand, it does not fit neatly into any of the other branding types discussed in the textbook. Ask what DuPont means to them? What does it stand for? What kind of personality does it have?

Then shift to a discussion of the ingredient brands. Ask what products does DuPont make? Students should be able to provide a list of some of the products discussed in the video and other products such as Lycra. Point out that these products' names are also brands just as the name DuPont is a brand. Ask students what is the relationship between the two types of brands.

Conclude this part of the discussion by asking why DuPont engages in heavy brand management. This sets the stage for showing the video. The main issues of types of brands, relationships between brands and the personality and reputation of the brands as well as why DuPont advertises its brands to final consumers have been raised.

Now show the video. Point out that students should take note of the five principles of brand management. After showing the video, compare the students' answers with the information in the video. They were probably pretty close. If they are, this indicates that DuPont has done a good job of communicating about their corporate and product brands.

Discuss how the approach used by DuPont differs from/is similar to that used by Intel or another ingredient branding firm (Intel sells to computer manufacturers, but does not partner with them) and General Motors or another umbrella branding firm (sells directly to the final consumer). Conclude with a discussion of whether this approach is worth the cost and extensive marketing and financial resources it requires. What are the benefits? Good corporate reputation, builds demand with final consumers, attracts topnotch partners who want to be affiliated with DuPont, enables the company to charge higher prices and build brand loyalty/repeat purchase and build esprit de corp among employees who are proud to work for a firm with the core values that DuPont has. Balance this against cost and drain on resources. The result should be greater benefit than cost, but only if the corporate claims are believable. Underlying all the advertising and reputation building is a focus on quality products that deliver the promised benefits. In the end, it comes down to the product—a point made early on in the video.

Hain Food Group Part 1

Should Accompany Chapter 10 of Solomon/Stuart

Summary:

Content of Video: Hain sells natural, diabetic and kosher products. It engages in systematic product planning which means it questions every product in its mix to be sure that the product belongs. It asks questions such as why does it exist? Is there a demand for it? Is there a niche for it? Does it taste good? If the answer is negative, the product would be gone. Their positioning emphasizes good tasting, all natural foods. Each product should have a unique set of features that are desired by consumers.

They think **packaging** is extremely important because more and more decisions are being made in the store. An example is the canister they recently introduced to package rice cakes. It is stackable, so retailers like it. It enables Hain to tell more of a product story, commands attention, has a stay-fresh lid so that product lasts longer. All of which gives it a competitive advantage with retailers, consumers and Hain itself.

Through their wide and deep **product mix**, Hain has great **distribution** strength as they can provide 6 brands of products that sell well in many product categories. As the president says in the video, they can fill 50 feet of shelf space with their large number of skus (stockkeeping units) and few other producers can do that. This supports the new concept of category management in which retailers try to maximize their business in a product category regardless of brands. Hain helps retailers by having a mix of products that sell well.

They manage products throughout the **product life cycle** by looking for ways to re-invent mature products through new flavors, sizes, etc. An example is their mini rice cakes. To attract new consumers, younger consumers, and consumers who want something sweet, they introduced mini-munchies—an extension of mini rice cakes with sweet flavorings.

Through research (secondary and primary), they generate many **new product** ideas which flow to a new product committee. That committee is composed of the brand management team, operations and sales teams. The committee decides which new product ideas best fit with the current product mix, which they can produce most cost effectively and which they can bring to market at a competitive price. This is not a low price as Hain sells on quality.

Their vision is to become the premier specialty food company in the U.S. by pursuing high growth opportunities. To do this, they will expand brands while keeping in mind that taste, nutrition, innovation and quality are the basic elements of their **brand equity**.

Description of Video: This video has interviews with Irwin D. Simon, President and CEO and Ellen B. Deutsch, Sr. VP of Global Marketing. It has scenes of shoppers in grocery stores and still of Hain brands and labels and scenes of management meetings.

Teaching Tips: This video can be used to illustrate the Objectives and Strategies for Individual Products, Product Life Cycle, Branding and Packaging sections of Chapter 10. The first part of the video addresses individual product issues through asking questions such as why does it exist?, etc.

The idea of product mix can be explored by considering the synergies possible by having three lines of products: natural, diabetic and kosher. Emphasis should be placed on realizing that these types of products all have special requirements in production and that a firm set up to make any one of these can make the others more easily and cost effectively than a regular food processor. Second the concepts of depth and width are linked to distribution effectiveness. Ask students to think from the retailer's point of view how much easier it is to deal with one manufacturer than with five or ten in filling shelves for these specialized goods. There are all sorts of cost efficiencies in ordering, processing, inventory and display.

Finally talk about branding. Bring out the elements of the Hain brand equity. Ask why these matter to consumers? Why would these lead consumers to pay higher prices? At this point introduce the issue of packaging. The example of the canister for rice cakes is a good one because it adds value to the product and supports the higher price. It is an obvious win-win-win for everyone. What about the mini-munchies? Are these a good idea? Will they attract new customers? Do they offer something unique to the consumer?

You can close with the mini-munchies discussion because this leads to the concept of new products and their importance as the life blood in the product life cycle. If the mini-munchies don't make it, what impact will that have for mini rice cakes? For Hain?

Nivea: Managing an Umbrella Brand (Parts 1 and 2)

Should Accompany Chapter 10 of Solomon/Stuart

Summary:

Content of Video: This video comes in two parts which are discussed separately below. Part I sets the stage for understanding the history and values of the Nivea brand. Part II introduces marketing updates for the brand in the decade of the 1990s and discusses that Nivea is not well known in the US.

Part I: Nivea is produced by Beiersdorf of Hamburg, Germany. It is an old brand based on a successful water and oil emulsion and introduced to the market in 1911. Traditionally Nivea has been positioned as honest, down-to-earth and for everybody at an affordable price. At the end of WWII, the brand was given by the Allies to companies in other countries. Since then, Beiersdorf has bought the brand back.

Beiersdorf is strongly committed to constant, on-going research to perpetually upgrade and update their products. This commitment to R & D and quality is at the heart of the Nivea brand.

A study in the 1960s indicated that Nivea was perceived as reliable, good quality and confident, but that these characteristics were not thought of as modern or exciting. So, Beiersdorf developed a two pronged strategy of stabilizing the leading market position of Nivea and transferring that brand equity to various line extensions. They introduced the "Only Me" campaign which ran for 15 years and highlighted a different aspect of the product's performance. This positioned Nivea as a skin care brand rather than just a cream. In the universe of Nivea brands, the original Nivea Crème was the sun and the other sub-brands (for men, hair care, baby products, sun products, etc.) were the planets around the umbrella brand. This led Nivea to enter new product categories such as color cosmetics. The challenges in doing so is: (1) does the product fulfill a need? And (2) how should the specific category requirements be balanced with the values of Nivea?

Part II: This segment begins by noting that the decade of the 1980s was one of success for Nivea. New market research in 1990 found that the values of Nivea (down-to-earth, etc.) were the same as those of the 90s consumer. This led Nivea to develop a brand philosophy that described the core values of the Nivea personality, discussed the role of sub-brands and strengthened Nivea's number one position. This was necessary because so many people worked on this brand that their actions needed to be coordinated to produce the famous consistency Nivea strives for in quality, products and marketing. Next Nivea initiated a new campaign called the Blue Manifesto to show normal people doing normal everyday kinds of things.

Because Nivea is not well known in the U.S., it ran the "Face the Day" campaign to emphasize the key benefits of all Nivea products and to reinforce the Nivea core values. This and other Nivea international advertising is based on the similarities of skin care around the globe. Nivea personnel argue that skin is similar and so are the expectations of the consumer. They believe that by adhering to the brand's core values of good quality at an affordable price, they build consumer trust. They point out that the brand must grow in a constant way and not be overburdened or deviate. They look to balance continuity with innovation.

Description of Video: The video contains shots of Nivea production, lots of Nivea ads (both print and television) over the last century and interviews with Norbert Krapp, VP of Global Marketing, Dr. Peter Wittern, Director of

Research, Ms. Franziska Schiedebach, VP Marketing, Womens' Products and Antonio Liberatore, Head of Manufacturing.

Advice to Students: Norbert Krapp tells students to be open, to visit other countries and learn about them. Franziska Schiedebach tells students to stay close to the market and to consumers and always think "what does the consumer want? Need?"

Teaching Tips: To use the Nivea video in class, prepare students by discussing branding first and then showing the video because the video assumes a basic level of knowledge about branding and introduces the concepts of umbrella and sub-brands. After showing the video, ask students to evaluate the Nivea name (Creating Product Identity section of Chapter). Before seeing the video or coming into contact with the Nivea brand, did the term Nivea mean anything to them? Is it desirable or undesirable for a name to have no meaning? What values has Nivea tried to build into the brand? How does their advertising support those values?

If you asked students to visit drug and grocery stores to the Nivea brands, now is a good time to ask them to report on the packaging, pricing, product variety, etc. of Nivea compared to similar brands on the shelf. Students who found ads for Nivea should report on how well the ads support the brand's values.

Ask the students if they think Nivea will be successful in penetrating the U.S. market with the advertising and merchandising described above. Why or why not? What would Nivea have to do to increase its visibility and popularity in the U.S.?

Student Assignment: Assign students to visit drug and grocery stores to evaluate Nivea's merchandising in the U.S.. They should check prices, product variety, shelf positioning, labeling, packaging and in-store promotion of Nivea and a similar product. Assign other students to hunt through magazines to find examples of Nivea advertising and to analyze the content of the ads? What do they communicate? What impression of Nivea do they create? Perhaps students could ask their friends to examine the ads and interpret them.

Computer Friendly Stuff, Case 3: Maybe You Can Judge a Bug by Its Cover

Should Accompany Chapter 10 of Solomon/Stuart

Summary:

Content of Video: This video covers three topics: product line, packaging and naming/branding of products.

Product Line: Chris begins by stating that they needed to expand their product line for several reasons. First, what's new one Christmas is old by the next in the toy industry, so their customers were screaming for new products. Second, retailers want to deal with companies that have multiple products. For them to bring in a new product requires a lot of paperwork, so they like to spread this over multiple products. Further, the retailers take one more seriously if you have multiple products because it looks like you will be around for awhile. They came up with a product called Monitor Morphs.

Names/Branding: They think names are important. They should connote something about the product. In this case, that's fun, so CFS tries to use fun names as that helps to move products and because if it's fun to say, it's fun to describe to prospects. This element of fun runs through all of their products from the company name, Computer Friendly Stuff, to products, Computer Bug and Monitor Morph to their new division, Corporate Friendly Stuff, to their latest product, Stubby Chubbies which are chubby stuffed animals with stubby legs.

Packaging: He describes the three packages the company used in their first year of operation. The first was a lab beaker with the bug inside and the CD-Rom under the lid of the beaker. It was a bad package as took up too much shelf space, didn't stack, buyers couldn't see the CD-Rom and the bug wouldn't stay in place. The second package was a box with a clear window. The box was designed to look like a computer and the bug could be seen through the window. The CD-Rom was behind the bug. This was a good package, but buyers still couldn't see the CD-Rom behind the bug and it was an ugly grey for computers.

The third package was a great package. It was a blister pack that was bright yellow and the CD-Rom could be easily seen on the package. When they used this package for Christmas of 1998, orders increased. The lesson they learned from this is that one doesn't always need to reinvent the wheel. Initially, they wanted a unique package, but they learned that sometimes, things are done a certain way because they work.

Description of Video: This video is again an interview with Chris Cole, founder and president of Computer Friendly Stuff. The packages are demonstrated by Adrianne who holds all packages up and makes facial and physical gestures to go with the commentary. Because she has on a white hat and is surrounded by stars, this has a slightly Christmas-y feel to it. There are also a few scenes of them dealing with customers.

Teaching Tips: To deal with the idea of product lines, before class have students investigate what monitor morphs and corporate friendly stuff are by going to the web site. After showing the video, begin with a discussion of how the various products in the line are related to each other. Ask whether they help the company deepen their penetration in the main product line or add new markets for CFS. The bug, morphs and stuffed animals may all be aimed at the same market, so this is a penetration strategy. The animals, however, might also appeal to the non-computer user and could add new users. The corporate friendly stuff is sold to a different market segment and therefore adds to the market for CFS. Emphasize the importance of market penetration or market development in expanding the market and sales for a company such as CFS. This, in addition, to the reasons that Chris gives in the video are why firms broaden or deepen their product lines.

Next move to the name issue. Ask if the name creates some consistency among the product lines. One could argue that it does because it has the same humorous element. This helps to reinforce the brand image in the consumer's mind because each product/brand is similar to the others in terms of humor. They just naturally go together and are likely to be stored in long term memory together.

Finally, discuss the importance of packaging. Ask the students what are the important characteristics that a good package should have. They should be able to move from the elements of a good design for the computer bug to a list of attributes for all products. For example, the product needs to be visible. In the case of the computer bug, the first two packages hid the product. The package needs to be attention getting. The third package is a bright yellow whereas the other two packages were rather dull. You might ask how the package used by CFS fulfills the functions of packaging described in the text. (How does it protect the product? Make it easy to handle and store the product?, communicate about the package?

Lands' End: Perceptual Recipe for Success

Should Accompany Chapter 11 of Solomon/Stuart

Summary:

Content of Video: This video describes four ingredients that make Lands' End a success in the catalog business. These are: People, Products, Services and Company Policies.

People—It's not just people that are important, but the type of people. Lands' End employees are chosen for their natural friendliness, good communication skills, willingness to work and cooperativeness. From the telephone operators to management, everyone is motivated to do a good job and employees are empowered to do what it takes to get the job done.

Products—Quality products from the days of sailing gear through the introduction of clothing and luggage have dominated the offerings at Lands' End. Recently, they have introduced three new catalogs: Coming Home with soft household goods, Land's End Kids and Beyond Buttondowns, featuring menswear. The introduction of Coming Home illustrates Lands' End's commitment to filling consumer needs. Their catalog featured a sheet with a 12" pocket that was an instant success because mattress makers were making mattresses thicker, but the sheet makers were unaware of this. So, folks couldn't get their sheets to stay on the bed.

Services—Whether its hemming, monogramming, friendly, fast, reliable service or fast shipment, consumers have come to expect wonderful service from Lands' End, made possible because of the high caliber of people employed there.

Company Policies—published and posted everywhere are the 8 principles of business:

1. Make quality products a priority.
2. Price products honestly.
3. Accept any return for any reason.
4. Ship product faster than anyone else.
5. What's best for the customer is best for the company.
6. Eliminate the middleman and markup.
7. Keep prices down by operating efficiently.
8. Don't operate fancy and expensive stores.

All of these ingredients are mixed together in only two places: the Lands' End catalog and the Lands' End facilities in Wisconsin.

Description of Video: Many shots of people at work at Lands' End, shots of the exterior of the building and a Lands' End outlet plus interviews with Joan Conlin, Director Customer Services, Phil Schaecher, Sr. VP of Operations and Rob Hayes, Merchandise Manager.

Teaching Tips: Use this video with Chapter 11 to get at the necessary mix of products and services in a business such as the catalog industry. Ask "Which is most/more important to consumers?" Which could be sacrificed? Where does

Land's End fall on the goods-service continuum? Towards the good-dominated or people-dominated ends of the continuum?

Ask students to apply each of the characteristics of services to Lands' End. (You might have listed these on the blackboard before showing the video.) Ask how the concepts of core and augmented services apply at Lands' End.

How would you evaluate Lands' End service quality? Could or does Lands' End use the critical incident method to evaluate service? (It does through the collection and analysis of customer comments from telephone calls, letters and internet.)

Discuss how the 8 principles help to improve Lands' End's service operations. What's the value in posting them everywhere? To continually remind employees.

Bojangles with
Randy Poindexter

Should Accompany Chapter 12 of Solomon/Stuart

Summary:

Content of Video: This video touches on all four of the elements in the marketing mix, but the most attention is given to the element of pricing. Both the concept of demand and the price elasticity of demand are defined and applied to the Bojangles situation. Although price is the only element in the marketing mix that contributes to profits, it is often the least appreciated.

The elements of the Bojangles experience are a unique, Cajun-style product, that's made from scratch and served in a fun, festive restaurant. It is backed by strong promotion and distribution has increased to more than 242 restaurants in 8 states.

To set price, one has to factor into the pricing equation, the quality of the product, services provided, cleanliness of restaurant, advertising, merchandising and promotions to reach the price point desired. The result must be a price consistent with the consumer's perception of value.

Bojangles is in a situation of price elasticity, so when the issue of combo pricing arose, it took it slow and carefully factored in the major elements of pricing. The idea behind combo pricing is to trade a consumer who might otherwise have only purchased one or two items into buying a package that contains an entrée, a side and a drink because the packaged price is lower than the total of the individual items priced separately. The risk you run, according to Randy Poindexter, is that you trade some consumers down.

Bojangles went with the combo pricing and experienced double digit growth. Most of the combo growth comes at lunchtime when consumers are presumably buying a full meal. Today, it's a sandwich and a fixin' and a drink rather than just a sandwich and that's good for Bojangles' bottom line.

Description of Video: Only Randy Poindexter is interviewed in the video, but there are lots of shots of Bojangles' restaurants, the chicken, employees at work and people eating in the restaurant.

Teaching Tips: This video lends itself to a discussion of the relationship between price and the other elements of the marketing mix (section 1 of chapter 12). It can also be used to discuss demand and price elasticity of demand as illustrated in the video. But it is most useful for discussing pricing objectives—especially the relationship between image and pricing, customer satisfaction and pricing. Ask students to think about the image of Bojangles. Does it lend itself to higher or lower prices than other quick-food establishments. Does the uniqueness of its product justify a higher price?

Combo pricing is basically a form of price reduction; buy the larger package because it's cheaper than all the individual items priced separately. Does instituting combo pricing lower consumers' perceptions like a straightforward price reduction would?

If competing restaurants have combo pricing and Bojangles doesn't, how would that affect consumers' perceptions of price at Bojangles? Is combo pricing necessary to meet the competition? Are consumers trained to look for combos when they visit quick food establishments?

Student Assignment: If you live in a state where there are Bojangles, you could ask students to visit Bojangles and other quick food establishments to check the prices and combos available. The goal would be to determine if it costs more or less to eat a meal at Bojangles. Knowing this will help to answer the questions above as to whether or not Bojangles is perceived as higher or lower priced than other similar restaurants. Also, students should check the cost of a combo against the total price of ordering the items individually to determine how much they would save. We know that the just noticeable difference that usually stimulates purchase is at least 10%. How does that affect this situation? Are all of the combos at least 10% less expensive?

Computer Friendly Stuff, Case 4:
What Does that Have to Do
with the Price of Bugs in China?

Should Accompany Chapter 13 of Solomon/Stuart

Summary:

Content of Video: This video focuses on pricing. It begins with Bill Martens, co-founder of CFS, discussing the relationship between pricing and profits. He outlines three strategies: (1) tight profits (narrow margins), (2) reasonable profits and (3) very good profits (wide margins). Tight profits, he says, were liked by Chris Cole because they helped to attract customers and sales. Bill favored reasonable profits because that would help them stay in business. Very good profits, he says, are a strategy of charging as much as you can for as long as you can until imitators move in or sales drop.

Once they had decided on a strategy between tight and reasonable, they had to calculate costs in order to actually set prices. Costs were more difficult than they had expected because they had to determine the costs of things such as molds and replacement of molds. After establishing costs, they had a wholesale price of $7.50 and a suggested retail price of $14.99 using the tight-to-reasonable profits strategy. They compared this with other prices in the industry and found that a few dollars either way made little difference. They had been able to test their pricing at the various trade shows and flea markets they sold at during the year.

As they tried to sell to large retailers, however, they found that their pricing strategy didn't work because it did not allow for costs such as commissions to reps and distributors (as much as 10%) or the cost of advertising coops and promotions.

They went back to the "pricing board" and decided on a strategy of reasonable to very good. Their new prices were $8.99 wholesale and $17.99 retail. When they introduced monitor morphs, the new product benefited from the revised pricing strategy.

What did they learn? That everything is negotiable. Although they do not negotiate with individuals and small stores, they must negotiate with large retailers who have the most pricing leverage because of their large volume of sales. These deals are complex and must include discounts and allowances for promotion.

They also found that they must plan for fluctuating currency rates. When rates change, this affects everyone's profits. For example, rates dipped so low during the Asian crisis that the New Zealand couple that gave CFS its first initial sales boost was forced out of business.

Description of Video: This video is an interview with Bill Martens, co-founder of CFS, while he is playing a game of pool or billiards with Chris Rubeo of CFS. There are scenes of selling and negotiating to reinforce Bill's comments and screens that list the types of pricing strategies and reasons why they negotiate.

Teaching Tips: Because this video is about pricing, you might ask students to visit computer and toy stores to check the "price" of the computer bug. The result may be a variety of prices. (Keep in mind that the computer bug can be ordered directly for $17.99—yet another price!)

After showing the video, ask students to describe the three pricing strategies outlined by Bill (tight, reasonable and very good strategies). Ask what are the benefits and drawbacks of each.

Next, relate the strategies described in the video to those in the text. Ask students if CFS is using a cost-based, demand-based or competition-based strategy. They are using a cost based strategy. Did they attempt any demand-based pricing? One might argue that looking through the catalogs and testing pricing at the trade shows and flea markets was a form of demand-based strategy.

In the video, Bill comments that they found that changing the price a few dollars either way would not change demand. When they discovered this, what should they have done? What does this comment suggest about the nature of demand? (That it's inelastic within that price range and they should/could have raised their price.)

As the video makes clear, this strategy didn't work because it didn't cover the cost of reps and coop advertising. Ask the students if the new pricing structure ($8.99 and $17.99) are the result of a new pricing strategy. The answer is no; they are still using a cost-based strategy. The difference is that they didn't include all of their costs to start with.

Stress that pricing is not static. It's constantly changing depending on who they are selling to. "The price" is almost an abstract concept as perhaps only a few small stores or individuals actually pay that. Discuss why this negotiation is necessary (greater power on the part of large retailers and to accommodate fluctuating market situations in the case of the New Zealand firm).

If one orders a computer bug from the web site, one pays the $17.99. What has happened to CFS's margins when one orders from them directly. Should they sell over the web site more cheaply (because they don't have the coop and rep expense)? The answer is probably not as that would hurt sales of their retailers. End by summarizing the factors uncovered in the discussion that affect pricing.

DHL

Should Accompany Chapter 14 of Solomon/Stuart

Summary:

Content of Video: This video profiles DHL, the leader in international express mail service for fast, reliable service as shown by a recent study. The keys to DHL's leadership are: (a) use of information technology, (b) understanding the customer's business (c) anticipating new markets and market needs and (d) constantly improving customer service.

A. Information Technology—There are several scenes of employees using scanners and computers in the shipping and tracking of packages.

B. Understanding the customers business—To stress understanding the customer's business, Brian Billings of DHL says that they find business customers to be constantly demanding and vocal and that competition in these markets is intense—all of which leads to the development of new products and services.

C. Anticipating needs—DHL's efforts to constantly seek out new markets and needs is underscored in Brian's comments about DHL's expansion over time. It is also reinforced in examples of new services introduced by DHL. One is pre-clearance of packages for customs so that goods are not held up at customs points. Another example is logistics services in which goods move goods from origin to destination without stopping at intermediate holding points. This meets the needs of industries when fashion or technology can outdate goods in a short period of time. As corporations reduce the costs of holding inventory and warehousing, this opens new possibilities to DHL.

D. Customer service—Finally, DHL's greatest strength is its focus on customer service. They constantly strive to improve service by hiring their own employees and not turning packages over to agents and through extensive training of employees. DHL employees are known for their caring, can-do attitude. Brian recounts the example of a DHL courier who recently took a package from an individual in a car in heavy traffic.

Description of Video: This video shows numerous still shots of DHL airplanes, employees at work and lots of shots of DHL vehicles against identifiable foreign backgrounds such as Rome and Russia. It also includes an interview with Brian Billings, Sr. VP of Marketing and Planning.

Teaching Tips: This video can be used with the physical distribution section of Chapter 14. Discuss concepts such as order processing, warehousing, materials handling and transportation and inventory control in class before showing the video. List these on the blackboard.

After showing the video, ask students how DHL can help reduce the expense and effort of each of the concepts listed on the blackboard. Stress that DHL might be able to take over some of these for the company. Recently, DHL has taken warehousing of parts for Kubota. When customers call the Kubota number, they are actually calling DHL which then ships the parts and notifies Kubota. Another example is DHL's agreement with Roche Logistics to store, pick and pack, distribute and manage inventory for diagnostic analytical systems for F. Hoffman-LaRoche Ltd. Discuss in class why it is cheaper and easier for DHL to do this than for the manufacturing firms.

At the end of the video, students are asked which environmental factors (economic, political and cultural) would affect their selection of an international express mail service for their company's perishable foodstuffs from the U.S.

to Asia. If you don't want to use this, you can avoid it by cutting the video off after Brian's comments about using local people to manage local business as there are a few seconds where the screen is blank.

If you do want to use it, you might want to hold this discussion before getting into detailed discussion of order processing, warehousing, etc. as this is much more general than physical distribution. For perishable goods, the fastest route to market is the best. So, DHL's pre-clearance services would be useful to speed delivery as would their logistics service as the goods would never sit still. Unfortunately, these services may cost more (economic factor). Making sure that goods are handled properly could be a function of understanding the local market (cultural factor) and DHL's use of local people would facilitate this. Finally, DHL is perceived as a global company, not a U.S. one (as it has the largest share of international rather than U.S. delivery business) which might help it politically in markets where the U.S. is not popular.

Hain Food Group Part II

Should Accompany Chapter 14 of Solomon/Stuart

Summary:

Content of Video: This video discusses the distribution of Hain Foods through four channels: supermarkets, natural food stores, specialty grocery stores and warehouse clubs. There are both specialty and discount stores in this distribution mix. One reason is that natural foods are experiencing double digit growth that makes them attractive to grocery chains and warehouse clubs as well as their traditional niche in the specialty market. This growth should continue. As the population ages, more will become diabetic and therefore potential consumers of Hain's Estee brand of foods.

To serve these markets, Hain has 9 regional sales directors who work with 50 food brokers. The brokers, in turn, work with 500 food distributors so that Hain products wind up in over 20,000 outlets nation-wide. In different channels, Hain markets products differently. In the warehouse channel, they are looking for volume with lower prices and demo foods so consumers can sample them. They are utilizing vending machines because they are also a good way to introduce Hain to the final consumer. They are suppliers to the military and are looking into selling to prison systems and abroad to international markets.

They find that distribution varies depending on the consumer. Their psychographic profiles of consumers indicate that customers on the West Coast are more likely to buy natural foods. Consequently, more of their warehouse inventory and promotion is aimed at the West Coast consumer.

Hain relies on electronic data interchange, EDI, to exchange data with retailers, food brokers and food distributors. These rapid data exchange enables them to speed the flow of data and product so that all parties can maximize revenues, reduce markdowns, and lower inventory carrying costs.

Hain can grow in five ways: new products, new distribution, strategic alliances, acquisitions and international. The company has chosen international and plans to sell to the U.K. first because of the synergies there with the U.S. market. This is part of Hain's vision of being the premier specialty food group.

Description of Video: This video contains interviews with Ellen B. Deutsch, Sr. VP of Global Marketing, Michael N. Miller, VP Sales and Irwin D. Simon, President and CEO. It has shots of consumers shopping in grocery stores, stills of Hain products and brands and is accompanied by music from Hain promotions.

Teaching Tips: Because Hain distributive channels are described in the video, begin the discussion with the type of channels that Hain has. Discuss the different types of intermediaries—the food brokers and distributors and what each of those do. Discuss the advantage to Hain of having multiple channels of distribution. Talk about why each of these channels is necessary.

Hain accesses different consumers with each channel. How does that affect the nature of the channel making it shorter or longer?

What is the function of information flows in the channel? How does the flow of information facilitate inventory control to maximize revenues and reduce markdowns as the case claims?

Finally, ask if Hain has intensive, selective or exclusive distribution. In the past, their distribution may have been selective (in specialty stores), but now they appear to be using intensive distribution. Thus, to increase sales, they have to find new distributive channels and outlets. Ask the students about the prospects abroad. Will the U.K. be a good market for all of the Hain foods? What about the natural foods? Diabetic foods? Kosher foods? Might these lines have differing probabilities of success? If so, which ones would students recommend selling into the English market and why?

Forum Shops:
Entertainment Retailing

Should Accompany Chapter 15 of Solomon/Stuart

Summary:

Content of Video: This video shows and describes a new phenomena in retailing, entertainment retailing which is built around a central theme. Because it adjoins Caesar's Palace in Las Vegas, this shopping center took its theme from ancient Rome. It's the Forum Shops with a very authentic Roman decor and architecture. Unlike its suburban cousins, the Forum Shops is not laid out in a rectangle or long bar. It's Y-shaped and consumers enter the base of the Y from Caesar's which means that they walk a little ways before they must branch left or right. At that intersection, there is a Roman fountain that is pictured behind Maureen in the video. If they go to the right, they will come to the fountain where Bacchus hourly invites the closeby Gods and shoppers to a party. If they go to the left, they will wind up at the fountain where hourly, Gadrius and Alia do battle with fire and water to see who will rule Atlantis. Thus, each arm of the shopping center leads to a major attraction which gives consumers a reason to stroll to the end of the arm. On the way, they will pass a wonderful mix of shops.

While many of the shops at the Forum are expensive, designer shops—Gucci, Ferragamo, Bulgari, Karan, others are very ordinary stores—The Disney Store and the Gap. So, there is something here for everyone.

The architecture and attractions create a sort of fantasy extension to the rest of Las Vegas in which consumers may be likely to spend more than they would otherwise. After all they are on vacation and they may have been lucky in the casinos. This is explained by Maureen and reinforced by some consumers interviewed in the video.

But all of this fun is carefully structured. The Forum Shops are open longer hours to accommodate those in the casinos and those that work strange hours in Las Vegas. Because of the attractions and many benches and sidewalk cafes, you will find as many men there as women. The Forum Shops has cleverly created an environment that intrigues men as well as women. The Forum Shops also focus on training shop people to treat customers well—especially foreign customers who may have a language problem or be unfamiliar with shopping in the U.S.. After all, they usually bring more money to spend. Finally, the Forum Shops give longer leases, but don't give any retailer exclusivity. They are, however, careful to make sure that each retailer they add brings something new to the Forum.

To attract customers, the Forum Shops advertise extensively on billboards, in-flight magazines and Las Vegas entertainment guides. They use a lighthearted approach to reduce the possible intimidation that some shoppers might feel at the Forum. They also run fam (familiarization tours) with travel agents as people nowadays are going to shopping destinations on vacation.

Description of the Video: The video features many shots of stores at the Forum, the fountains of Bacchus and Atlantis and some of the action at Atlantis along with interviews with Maureen Crampton (Director of Marketing, The Forum Shops), and Robert Wynn (Atlantis Show Tour).

Teaching Tips: Show the video and elicit general student reactions. What did they think? Would they like to shop there? Did it look like fun? What did they like? Was there anything that they disliked? What's the purpose of the entertainment? (To get people to walk to the end of the Y and to keep them there longer.) How important is the design?

Shopping centers are usually classified as regional, local or neighborhood. Does a concept like The Forum Shops add another category? Remember that this is a destination for some consumers. There are now more people coming to Las Vegas to shop than to gamble. Why would consumers want to spend their vacation shopping? (They don't have time the rest of the year? Well, it is entertaining and it doesn't coast a thing to stroll around. There may also be an urge to see what those really high toned stores are like. Note that the average shopper has an income between $50 to $60,000. They may not have many opportunities to shop at designer stores, but they are welcome here. So, this experience is out of the ordinary for them and there's always the urge to take something back—just to show that you've been.)

Unlike most shopping centers, The Forum Shops have no anchors—no major department stores. It consists of specialty stores. Ask students why they think there are no department stores—not even exclusive ones like Neiman Marcus.

Discuss the image of The Forum Shops. What are the elements of their image? How does their promotion and the message of their advertising enhance that image?

Starbucks: Brewing a
Brand Concept

Should Accompany Chapter 15 of Solomon/Stuart

Summary:

Content of Video: According to *Fortune* magazine, Starbucks has affected a fundamental change in U.S. life. How? By focusing not on the product, but on the coffee house experience. By following their unique premise, that "everything matters" they have created an experience that elevates coffee drinking to an art form and coffee houses to the place where Americans choose to relax and socialize.

To keep their uniqueness, they shunned mass marketing. They wanted to build the brand through resonance and relevance (the emotional side of coffee drinking) rather than through breadth and depth of taking the product to market. (Breadth is more stores and depth is geographic expansion.)

To create a unique environment, they hired an architect from Disney who put together a creative team that designed standardized coffeehouse interiors that can be built affordably under a number of real estate limitations. The story of Starbucks is built around the siren in their logo. She's mischievous and she mesmerizes the coffee and lures one to the cup. To tie everything together, the team created logos for each coffee which are seen beside the coffee's name on the menu board. These same logos or stamps appear in color on the packages of the coffee. They are designed to capture the spirit of the coffee.

Another unique emphasis of Starbucks is its emphasis on its people. Employees get stock shares and are made to feel like part of the company. Starbucks expands this focus on people in each community they locate in by sharing their values and showing compassion for its citizens by making the community a better place to live, not just work. The company has traditionally been linked to causes such as AIDS, Hospice and food banks. It has recently initiated the Starbucks Foundation that centers on children in need.

In expanding abroad, Starbucks sought partners who share the same values. As the president says, they can not share the same cultures, but they can share such values as treating employees with respect and dignity and caring for the product they sell. Starbucks first entered Japan because of the caliber of the partner they found there.

Their current challenge is to retain their uniqueness, their intimacy with the customer? Their founder and CEO says that they must retain the ability to constantly entertain customers, provide them with special moments and even surprise them. Not easy when they have over a 1,000 stores some of which are licensees and some of which are joint ventures.

Advice to Students: The president says that you should find what you love and do that. Not to worry about money—you'll never have enough. Focus on people. The founder says believe in your dream, yourself and the American dream.

Description of video: This video is full of many shots of customers inside Starbucks stores, store exteriors, shots of Seattle and Japan. The interviews are with: (in order) Jerome Conlon (VP of Consumer Insights and Brand Planning), Scott Bedbury (VP of Marketing), Wright Massey (VP of Design), Howard Behar (President) and Howard Schultz (Founder and CEO).

Teaching Tips: This video lends itself nicely to the sections in Chapter 15 about store image, the actors (personnel) and the theater (locations). A good starting point is discussing how to classify Starbucks. In the video it is described as a retailer, but its function is seen as entertaining customers—Massey talks about storytelling and entertainment. How is Starbucks a form of entertainment? How important is the coffee to Starbucks? What elements of its design (store layout, packaging, logo, etc.) could be lost without changing the experience? How important are the people to the Starbucks experience? What is their role? How is it different from other coffeehouses?

For this case, one could ask students to visit a Starbucks. If they do so before seeing the video, give them a list of criteria upon which the Starbucks store should be evaluated. This might include layout, product line, packaging, employees, lighting, etc. Ask them to notice what most customers are doing? Are they just drinking a cup of coffee, reading a book, talking to other? How long do they stay? (This is a good lesson in market research by observation.) How do their findings compare with the content of the video? Has Starbucks retained its intimacy or does it seem more like a mass-market outlet? If they have, what accounts for this?

If you show the video without sending students to a Starbucks, ask the same questions but you will have to rely on student recall.

If students find it difficult to think of Starbucks as intimate, you might ask students what they would change to improve. Answers to this might depend heavily on the contrast between Starbucks and other coffeehouses that the students have visited and liked.

Mountain Travel Sobek

Could Accompany either Chapter 15 or 17 of Solomon/Stuart

Summary:

Content of Video: This video introduces us to the category of adventure Travel—trips to out of the way places. These trips attempt to provide travelers with experiences that capitalize on spontaneity and serendipity. They are for people who seek the unusual—adventure. Because the market consists of people who do not normally want to travel in groups, the groups are small (15 or fewer) and generally longer so that one can be intimate with the place they are visiting and the trips are led by highly knowledgeable guides.

MTS is the combined companies of Mountain Travel that specialized in trekking and Sobek that specialized in river rafting. This merger enables them to better serve the market that is important because competition in adventure travel has increased greatly. These two firms are not unique any more and they are responding to the competition.

In the late 1990s, the average age of adventure travelers is expected to rise as people are living longer, staying fit longer and have higher incomes. Therefore MTS is adding softer and shorter trips to their offerings.

To reach their market, MTS is supplementing their catalog with higher technology promotional devices—an interactive CD-ROM and a web site that gives complete trip details among other information. The question raised in the video is the fit between their market and the high technology promotions. In the video, Richard Weiss says that their market will be computer literate faster than anyone expects and that when the market reaches that literacy, MTS will be ready—that right now the company is just practicing.

Description of Video: This video has shots of action shots of people on adventure trips as well as still photos taken on trips. There are interviews with Richard Bangs, Founding Partner, and Richard Weiss, President of MTS.

Teaching Tips: As indicated below the title, this case could be used with either the retailing chapter because MTS sells its trips directly (mail order section) or the advertising chapter because they are it is using new technology (choose the media section) in its promotional mix.

Although not mentioned in the video, the MTS web site has won several awards. Ask students to check out the web site (mtsobek.com) or show it in class. By visiting the web site and trying to find a trip, the students can better answer the question of what are the advantages and disadvantages of this form of promotion and selling? Ask students to evaluate the web site on a number of criteria such as ease of use, graphics, completeness of information, speed of response and availability of the information they need. They should try the custom search to see it finds a trip for them and take their adventure IQ to test their knowledge of adventure sites. They can try searching for a trip or read travel journals about other people's trips. The questions to ask in class are whether they found the site exciting? Did it make adventure travel attractive to them? Did they have trouble finding the information they needed? (If you want to make sure they visited the web site, have them send you a travel postcard!)

Compare this with catalogs. What are the differences in buying from each? In what ways are catalogs superior? There are comments in the video about the wonderful graphics and color of the catalog. Most consumers will not be able to print wonderful, colorful pictures off the web site. The catalogs last longer than impressions from the web.

They may lie around the house for months or years enticing consumers. MTS also has tried mailing videos to potential purchasers. The videos are better for color than most home printers and they provide motion which catalogs do not. They are longer than the videos on the web and easier to view and review. How do all of these forms of technical promotion be used together? How can they be used to complement each other in selling adventure travel? Stress that it is not really a decision of using catalogs or the net, but how to use each in the most effective manner—how to make all the older and newer media work together.

Lands' End: The Internet

Should Accompany Chapter 15 of Solomon/Stuart

Summary:

Content of Video: This video introduces us to landsend.com. The company finds that new customers who don't normally use catalogs may shop at Lands' End on line and which current customers also use Lands' End on line. As one customer said, "I can't always find my catalog, but I can always find my computer."

Before putting up a web site, Lands' End spent five months of research and development. They concluded that there were two types of web sites: (a) flashy, bells and whistles sites with videos and (b) non-flashy, text-oriented, non-video sites. L.E. opted for the latter because they realize that videos take a long time to download and that their customers are too time pressured to wait.

What does the web site look like? Like the catalog, of course. There are many sections such as Dateline Dodgeville (news from Lands' End), services, gifts, swimwear, let's talk which is questions and answers, the company and its policies and the library which is all the stories, articles and testimonials about Lands' End. Putting all of that on the web site illustrates one of the features of the web—unlimited space for information.

The most popular section is the order section, but to reassure customers concerned about security, L.E. developed an electronic order blank that is encrypted when sent and decrypted at L.E.. So, it's a very safe way to order.

The internet has also proven to be effective in reaching international customers. They are much more likely to contact the firm through e-mail than through expensive telephone lines!

The video ends by posing the question: "Why would a company that prides itself on friendly sales representatives want anyone to order without those friendly voices?"

Description of Video: This video is a few shots of people at Lands' End, an interview with Mike Atkins, VP of Marketing, and many shots of the Lands' End web site. The swimwear site is explored in the video.

Teaching Tips: This video can be used with the catalog, direct selling and electronic selling sections of the textbook. The internet is taking off and this video illustrates some of the features of successful internet sites. It is easy to use; not intimidating; looks familiar because it looks like the catalog; it's safe and it provides more information that most people would ever want to know.

Have students visit the Lands' End site before class so that they can talk about their experiences with it. Discuss how shopping on the internet is different from using catalogs—what are the advantages and disadvantages? (These are the barriers and maybe the positives of shopping electronically.) How does shopping on other sites compare with the Lands' End site? Which is more convenient, easy to use, informative, easy to navigate?

End with the question in the case: There are times when the internet is faster, more and more convenient such as the case of the Indonesian man in the video. There are times when one has very simple orders that can be handled faster over the internet; telephone calls might be more useful if one has questions about sizing, or special problems. You may find it easier to shop on the internet at work than through catalogs and the telephone at work (Don't let the boss know). Obviously there are times when anyone might use the net as opposed to the telephone and vice-versa. The internet simply gives customers one more way to access Lands' End and as is said at the beginning of the video, it brings them more customers as well.

Computer Friendly Stuff, Case 5: Caught Up in the Web

Should Accompany Chapter 15 of Solomon/Stuart

Summary:

Content of Video: This video focuses on selling over the world wide web. One would normally think that a company selling computer paraphernalia would naturally want to sell over the web, but as the video illustrates, on-line selling, even for a computer-related company, isn't as easy as one would think.

There are advantages of selling over the internet such as anyone on-line is a likely customer, people could sample the product off CFS' web site and the margins for direct sales are much better. These are outweighed, however, by the disadvantages. First of all, CFS chose the domain name computerbug.com which makes sense, but if one types computer bug, there are over 50,000 matches which means that finding the company and its products is very difficult. Second, just enough orders came in to take up their time, but not enough to be profitable or to hire someone else to handle the orders. They found that working with the web in terms of creating and maintaining the web site and filling orders took too much time away from what they do best—creating innovative, new products.

In developing a sales strategy, they thought of three strategies: (1) we sell it, we ship it; (2) they sell it, we ship it and (3) they sell it, they ship it. Because they were using strategy (1) and it wasn't working, they opted for #2. They began to sell product through GiftTree.com. Each day, the folks at CFS collected the orders and shipped the goods which saved them effort and the expense of creating a selling web site. They also learned that when the computer bug was featured on the front page of this site, they sold more.

Eventually, they added selling to 911Gifts.com which exemplifies the third strategy. CFS sells to 911Gifts which warehouses the product, sells it and ships it.

Now, CFS finds its web site is better as an on-line catalog or press kit than a selling site. At the end of the video, Chris Rubeo's puppet (of the computer bug) reinforces the main point of the video by screaming that they need a selling strategy.

Description of the Video: This video is almost exclusively an interview with Chris Rubeo of Creative Development sitting at his computer terminal. There are shots of the home page of GiftTree.com and 911Gifts.com as well.

Teaching Tips: This video relates to the section in the text about on-line retailing. Before showing the video in class, ask students to visit the computerbug.com web site (if they have not for an earlier video). They should take note of the features at the web site. Does it encourage purchase over the web site? What are the features of the site? How does it attempt to answer any questions that consumers might have such as "What is computer bug?" "How does it work?"

In class, ask students if they think that computerbug should sell through their own web site and why or why not? Probably, most students will think that CFS should sell off their web site. After getting some class reaction, then show the video. Then, discuss what the video teaches about web site selling. As the text notes, there are many barriers to selling over the web. What were the barriers for CFS? How does selling through GiftTree and 911Gifts help to reduce barriers to consumers? Why does the computer bug sell better when it is on the home page? What does that tell us about browsing activity of on-line shoppers? Would selling CFS products over the web anger their retailers? (Why or why not?) Is comparison shopping on price a problem for CFS? Ask students whether they would rather buy the computer bug in a retail store or over the net? Elicit reasons for their response and discuss how web sites might overcome any objections that students would have about purchasing the computer bug over the internet.

Lands' End: Teaching Consumers About Lands' End

Should Accompany Chapter 16 of Solomon/Stuart

Summary:

Content of Video: This video describes how Lands' End's communicates with its customers through personal selling and advertising. The first part of the tape discusses how Lands' End reaches current customers through personal selling in the form of customer service representatives. They are chosen because they are easy-going, friendly and treat customers like friends. Liking to talk is the number one requirement for the customer representative job. We get to listen in on a telephone call handled by Sally Kunkel.

Customer representatives get extensive training in terms of the job and computers and are taught to reassure customers that their needs will be met.

For those calls that cannot be handled by the regular customer reps, there is the Special Customer Service Center which will shop for customers. They may help customers with special size problems, design a whole wardrobe or match old Lands' End merchandise with new products. Joan Conlon tells of the time that the shoppers tried to outfit a Dalmatian in Lands' End polartec children's pajamas.

To reach potential customers, Lands' End uses advertising. Because their customers are relatively well-heeled, they advertise in such media as the Smithsonian, the New Yorker, and the New York Times. When they introduced their new mesh shirt, they bought a lot of advertising in print, radio and television. They developed a new ad which was a split message commercial. The ad cut off in the middle was followed by an ad from another advertiser and then the second half of the Lands' End ad was shown. Lands' End thought this type of ad would cut through the clutter, but they found that customers were upset because they thought the TV stations were cutting off the Lands' End ad. This taught Lands' End not be casual in their communications with their customers.

Customer reps keep track of all customer comments and those are collected into a report once a month and looked at in each department. Letters from customers are also posted around the Lands' End facility.

At the end, viewers are asked if it is really necessary to log all of the customer comments.

Description of Video: This video shows many scenes of customer representative at work, in training and examples of the TV ad for the mesh knit shirt. There are interviews with Joan Conlin, Director Customer Relations, Sally Kunkel, Telephone Operator, and Mike Atkins, VP of Marketing.

Teaching Tips: This Lands' End video fits well with chapter 16. You can begin by asking how Lands' End uses personal and mass appeals in its communications with consumers. The telephone calls are personal and the ads are mass appeals. Next ask how these interact effectively. How do they complement each other? What are the goals of each communication and how can these be measured?

Discuss the example of the TV ad in terms of source, medium, message, noise, feedback and decoding. What problems were there? What did Lands' End learn from this. If you used the student assignment (below), now is the time to discuss the ads that students found.

This leads up to answering the question of whether or not Lands' End should collect and process all of the customer comments. This is important because it is a form of feedback. They should collect all of the comments in order to determine how common a problem is and to make sure that no problem goes undetected. Also bring out that these comments are also a basis for rewarding representatives who have done a good job.

Student Assignment: Ask students to look for Lands' End ads to bring to class to analyze in terms of source, message, medium, possible problems in decoding, noise and feedback.

FD & B Part II

Should Accompany Chapter 16 of Solomon/Stuart

Summary:

Content of Video: In the beginning of this video, there are several screens that the define the role of the ad agency today according to FD & B. They are as follows:

To make a difference today's marketers need the capabilities of an advertising agency that has the experience, talent and desire to deliver targeted, creative solutions to marketing problems, quickly and efficiently.

To make a difference, the agency must create and execute effective advertising as well as strategically integrated promotion, public relations and direct marketing.

To make a difference the agency must understand the multiplicity of media available, discern their efficiency, synergistically plan for the media and maintain the know-how to negotiate and purchase media, time or space economically.

To make a difference, the agency must base all efforts on a deeply defined strategy. At F D & B, this process is called STRATEGICS.

STRATEGICS stands for synergistic thinking rigorously applied to effectively generate integrated creative solutions. In short, strategy is all.

To serve a client, FD & B believes that you must know who the customer is, what the distribution is, what the budget is and what the appeals of the product are. With this information, they can use STRATEGICS to provide direction, creativity and thoroughness for the programs they develop for clients.

In positioning, they believe that you should focus on the one key point that you want the consumer to take away. What is it about the product that will make it attractive to the consumer, given their lifestyle? For Hain Foods, it's that Hain makes better for you, all natural, delicious alternatives than the higher-fat foods you've been eating.

In using STRATEGICS for MasterCard, they developed a For a Clean Bill of Health promotion. The objectives were to increase credit card usage by consumers and to encourage non-accepting health care providers to use MC not only because it might help their business, but also because they could provide their customers with the Clean Bill of Health promotion. They developed this campaign by beginning with what they needed to accomplish before they decided on the vehicle. This reinforces the importance of objectives.

Some of the challenges facing advertisers today is how to cut through clutter? To determine how shopping will change with the growth of direct mail ordering, selling over the internet and the use of debit cards?

FD & B's approach is a buyer-seller dyad that focuses on the needs and resources of the client, not the other way around. When they have smaller clients, they start smaller—maybe with a test market.

They follow a process that asks what resources do we have? What are the key objectives that they need to build the client's business and profitability? They are engaged in integrated marketing communications and find that the promotional mix is constantly changing. Today it includes more public relations, direct mail and the internet. When many of the technology media merge such as telephone, cable and computer, promotions will be more targeted, more measurable and need a wider mix to get the message across.

Description of Video: This video contains ads from F D & B's clients, scenes of people at work at F D & B and interviews with partners Philip Franznick (President), Kevin P. Franznick (Exec. VP), Todd Brenard (Sr. VP) and Jennifer Friebely, Account Supervisor.

Teaching Tips: This video can be used to discuss the changes taking place among advertising agencies. The manifestos that are seen on screen at the beginning of the video state a number of new ways that ad agencies must operate. The main changes are that ad agencies must be problem solvers, have a strategic focus, generate creative, integrated solutions and have the ability to use the new media effectively. This should relate to the section in chapter 16 about the promotion mix.

Before showing the video talk about the importance of promotional objectives, finding the right message and thinking about how the message is affected by different media. After the video, ask students to discuss the examples in the video. For Hain Foods, what was the positioning? How would that affect promotions aimed at current users? Non-users? Would it be equally effective for both groups? How would changes in media such as internet access on the home television affect promotion for Hain or MasterCard?

For the Clean Bill of Health campaign, who were the targets? What were the objectives? How would those affect choice of media?

You could also hold a general discussion of how the internet is changing the face of advertising and consumer shopping. What effects does this have on the promotional mix?

Got Milk Part I

Should Accompany Chapter 17 of Solomon/Stuart

Summary:

Content of Video: This video recounts the impetus, research, message selection, moment of creation and media selection that led to the successful Got Milk? campaign.

Impetus: The California Milk Processors board was created in 1993 to deal with the decline in milk consumption. By the mid 1990s, there were far more competitors to milk including new age beverages, more brands of sodas and even bottled and flavored waters.

Research: Jeff Manning of the Board hired Goodby, Silverstein and Partners to create a new campaign for milk. First, they collected milk advertising from around the world and found that advertising message continually stated, we're not boring; we're drunk by healthy adults. Their strategy was to tell people "Milk is good for you." The problem with that is that people already knew that. So, this advertising was boring.

Next they set out to discover consumer perceptions toward milk. In the process, they asked some focus groups to go without milk for a week. The result was very enlightening. People felt they had been tricked or tortured. They recounted stories of awful experiences where they had suffered because they couldn't have milk and their day was ruined.

Message selection: By digging deeper in these stories, they found that they always began with a food situation which developed into a food with nothing situation. They termed this "milk deprivation" and they decided to use this as the message. They chose a humorous approach because humorous ads are the ones most likely to be remembered.

Moment of creation: When putting together their presentation for the Milk Processors' Board, an agency person asked Jeffery Goodby, "what should I write on this board?" Offhandedly, he remarked "Got Milk?" Upon reflection, they decided that asked the important question "Do you have enough milk to avoid milk deprivation?" in a non-boring fashion.

Media selection: They used television because it is the most visible medium. One of their most popular ads was entitled "heaven." It shows a jerk walking down the street and happily firing someone. Then, he is killed by a truck and winds up in 'heaven' where there's a large plate of cookies. He takes a few bites and opens the fridge only to find empty bottle of milk. The letters Got Milk? pop up in flames. Obviously he's not in heaven! This exemplifies the style of the campaign in which little dramas are told but with a missing element that turns out to milk.

The campaign was a success. Consumers loved it. The video ends with Jon Steel commenting: "That's what advertising does. It creates relationships between brands and consumers."

Description of Video: This video consists of interviews with Jeff Manning, Executive Director of the California Milk Processors' Board, Jon Steel, Director of Account Planning of Gooby, Silverstein and Partners and Jeffery Goodby of Goodby, Silverstein & Partners. There are also shots of people pouring milk and Got Milk? commercials.

Teaching Tips: This video lends itself to several sections in Chapter 15. First it shows that institutions (non-profits) as well as corporations do advertising (Who advertises section); it discusses message creation and media selection and it emphasizes the research that companies need to do in order to develop relevant advertising campaigns.

The primary value of this video is to illustrate how a successful ad campaign can be developed if (as Jon Steel in the video says) you ask the right questions. What would have happened if they had not asked people to go without milk for a week? Probably a whole different campaign.

To extend the discussion, you might ask students whether or not the campaign should be changed or dropped in favor of a new one? After all, it's been around awhile and consumers may be getting tired of it. While you can't definitively answer that question in class, it would be instructive to talk about how Jeff and the folks Goodby, Silverstein would know when to drop the campaign. What market research information would they need to make this decision?

Intel: The Power Behind the PC Part II

Should Accompany Chapter 17 of Solomon/Stuart

Summary:

Content of Video: This video describes the advertising campaign by Intel to introduce the Pentium II chip. This campaign was especially important because of the furor caused by the flaw in the original Pentium chip. Research on consumer reaction to the flaw indicated that consumers were more concerned about Intel's reaction to the situation than they were about the flaw: they realized that the flaw would affect only a minute number of users. This made Intel's advertising job easier in 1996 when they introduced the Pentium II.

Because Intel's previous ads had necessarily had a strong educational element to explain the microprocessor, this educational element was used in the new ads. The campaign was built around bunny people – so called because they wore the suits used by technicians. Because the suits are called bunny suits, the people are called bunny people. These technicians represent the scientific side of chip manufacturing, but the bunny people were shown in situations all around the world helping people to unleash the power of PCs. Thus, they gave Intel a softer, more human side.

To be successful, the campaign would have to be highly consistent because consistency is important in building brand images. In addition, brand images should be kept simple and focused. This is particularly true of an ingredient brand like Intel. Consistency also lends itself to successful global standardized advertising.

What should Intel do in the future? Their long range strategy will demand lot of information and understanding about the consumer and the marketplace.

Advice to Students: Dennis Carter offers two pieces of advice to students: (1) take **informed** risks and (2) learn everything you can. You never know what knowledge or skill set will be demanded in the future.

Description of the Video: This video contains interviews with Dennis Carter, VP and Director of Sales and Marketing and Anne Lewnes, Director of Worldwide Advertising. Between interview segments are scenes of chip manufacture, shots of the exterior of the Intel facility and several Intel ads.

Teaching Tips: This video fits with the message section of chapter 17. After showing this video, ask students what the basic message of Intel's advertising is. Is it product or institutional advertising? How does the message enhance the Intel brand? Why are factors like consistency, simplicity and focus important? Why do these factors work well in global advertising?

Because the only ads shown in the video are television ads, ask students how the campaign could be adapted to other media such as print? Ask if it would work in radio? (Probably not because the bunny people couldn't be seen.) Students might be given time in class to do layouts for print ads using the bunny people. The ads should be judged on their ability to enhance the Intel name, to be meaningful to people of various cultures and their consistency with the Intel ads shown in the video.

Mad Dogs and Englishmen
Part IV: Creating Advertising

Should Accompany Chapter 17 of Solomon/Stuart

Summary:

Content of Video: This video covers some of the elements in putting together an advertising campaign. These are: the brief, the creative team, focus on the consumer, print ads, television ads, radio, and direct response. These are illustrated with examples of an anti-fur campaign, Yoohoo and Moviefone ads.

The **brief:** A one page document summarizing the key messages including why consumers would like the product.

Creative team: Creates the creative concept from the brief. While this is usually the copywriters and art people, Mad Dog believes that it can be done differently. In the video they describe a creative team which they put together of everyone in the firm who was interested in fashion whether they were a receptionist, artist or technical person. This team made their pitch in a conference room turned into a mountain meadow with ideas on picnic plates—certainly a creative pitch. As Nick Cohen, the founder, says it taught people a lot of skills, to really listen to others and to respect that creativity could come from anywhere, not just the creative department. .

Focus on the consumer: In advertising think like yourself. It's just communication. What would cause you to pay attention to an ad? Or not to throw it away in the garbage? This is illustrated in the anti-fur campaign which was designed so that consumers would watch it without shutting down. Past ads had been disturbing and talked of animal death, but this campaign used humor and asked consumer to evolve, i.e. appealed to their better nature.

Print: Colors and photos capture attention, but are expensive. Thanks to the internet and books and technology, artists can put scenes together from different pictures and re-touch them to look real. Avoids expensive photographic shoots.

Television: Must shoot TV ads. The creative team comes up with storyboards that outline the ad. Then the production people hire a director and production crew that signs up a casting director who gets actors. After shooting, the ad is edited. All of this makes TV much more expensive. TV ads are illustrated with an ad for Yoohoo.

Radio: Is much less expensive and because its longer (60 seconds as opposed to 30 second TV ads), you can give more information. It can be combined with TV. Might run image ads on television and support that with radio commercials that explain promotions.

Direct Response: Can be advertising, mail internet, infomercials, print ads—most any advertising media. This consists of one-on-one communication with the audience. Used for special offers and to build a database through response. Direct response mail is used with discrete, targeted audiences. You would never use direct response for image advertising.

The video ends with comments from the CEO of Moviefone, that their firm judges an ad agency by its ability to be funny, engaging, a little bit weird and memorable. That's why they picked Mad Dogs and Englishmen.

Description of Ad: This ad has shots from Yoohoo and Moviefone ads, stills of the anti-fur ad, scenes of people working at Mad Dogs and interviews with Nick Cohen, Chairman and Founder, Dave Cook, Creative Director, Trixie Ferguson, Account Supervisor, Gisela Poley, Account Planner, Mikal Reich, Creative Group Director, Robin Danielson, President, Valerie Hope, Production Director, Sandi Bachom, Director of Broadcast Production, Paul Levine, General Manager and Andrew Jarecki, CEO of Moviefone.

Teaching Tips: This video meshes with the message and media sections of Chapter 17. To discuss messages, use the anti-fur ad campaign to discuss why this works. Is Robin right that this ad will be more effective than previous anti-fur ads? Why is the idea of evolving less threatening? Why does it appeal to people's better nature? Will this ad work better?

For the media section, discuss the pros and cons of each type of media and how they can be used in combination. How could the anti-fur ad campaign be extended to television, radio, direct response? Why would a firm want to use direct response for this campaign? (Because they want to build a database of individuals who might support the cause behind the campaign.)

Divide the class into groups and assign each group to come up with an ad for the anti-fur campaign for different media. Then discuss the results and talk about how the ads could be used to support each other.

NASCAR: Racing
for Sponsorships

Should Accompany Chapter 18 of Solomon/Stuart

Summary:

Content of Video: This video describes NASCAR's activities in the sponsorship and licensing arenas. As the early part of the video makes clear, NASCAR is intimately ties to several hundred well known corporations and their brands. Because stockcar racing is an expensive sport, the NASCAR association, racing/driving teams, race tracks and race circuits have traditionally sought corporate funding. A look at any stockcar shows that it may be covered with as many as 100 corporate logos.

Sponsorship occurs when a firm backs a driving team (Jeff Gordon is sponsored/backed by DuPont); whereas licensing occurs when a firm produces its product but puts the NASCAR logo on it. So, if an apparel firm makes tee-shirts and prints Jeff Gordon's face and his car on it, that's a licensing situation. Through sponsorships (set amounts of money) and licensing (royalties on the use of the name and logo) NASCAR, teams, races and racetracks make both product and promotion decisions. The two are inextricably intertwined.

Through sponsorships and licensing, NASCAR tries to leverage the associations of its brand, expand its market and promote NASCAR to users, markets or mediums with which it is not normally associated. NASCAR selects very few (about 50) of the 2000 firms that annually apply for NASCAR licensing and sponsorships. So, NASCAR selects firms with which to partner based on the quality of the firm's products, the soundness of the firm, whether it has national distribution and promotion and how much effort it will put behind the NASCAR affiliation. Coca-Cola has long been a NASCAR sponsor. It is typical of what NASCAR wants in a sponsor: coupling of the NASCAR name with a respected quality product and lots of enthusiastic, innovative marketing effort to promote both brands. Another example is the NASCAR Barbie. This doll reaches a market (young women) that NASCAR would not normally reach in a setting (home and play) where it would not normally be found. All of these efforts accelerate NASCAR toward being the number one sport in the U.S. and make it the fastest growing sport.

Why are firms willing to put all this money into NASCAR? The answer is brand loyalty. NASCAR fans are very, very brand loyal and studies show that 40% of them will switch brands to support a NASCAR brand. 85% to 90% of NASCAR fans buy brands because they are associated with the sport. When Coca-Cola brought out a NASCAR Coke bottle, it was the biggest promotion in Coca-Cola's history. There are over 120 million NASCAR fans who will buy NASCAR-affiliated merchandise. Studies show that these fans are mostly middle to upper middle class so they have considerable purchasing power.

Through outlets such as NASCAR GARAGE TELEVISON, NASCAR promotes its own brand. The association maintains tight control over drivers, events and the level of competition. In doing so, they maintain a good image of drivers, races and NASCAR itself. It has cleaned up the NASCAR image from the early days and today is a sophisticated marketing group.

At present, NASCAR is looking for a hotel chain to partner with as the Official Hotel of NASCAR. George Pyne discusses this at the end of the video. Thus, the video has a decision-oriented ending.

Description of Video: The video has many scenes of cars on the track, still shots of licensed merchandise, shots of Big Bill France (founder of NASCAR) and early racing, shots of fans and interviews with Steve Parks (NASCAR driver), George Pyne (VP of Marketing), Dee Scott, Liz Schlosser and Steve Boguski (NASCAR licensing), Tom Deery (VP Winston Racing Series) and Paul Brooks (VP, Office of the President).

Teaching Tips: This video can be used with chapter 18 in the promotions section. The Coca-Cola bottle described by George Pyne in the video is a sales promotion item put out by Coca-Cola with NASCAR approval. Because the motivation for sponsorships and licensing for NASCAR is to promote the sport, the video might be best used in the promotion section. NASCAR evaluates ALL of its sponsorship and licensing opportunities in terms of how they will promote NASCAR—that is the critical criterion that would-be sponsors or licensees have to meet.

The questions to ask students after showing the video are: How do sponsorships promote the manufacturer's products? Use DuPont as an example. It spends a lot of money sponsoring Jeff Gordon and DuPont doesn't sell consumers goods. So, how does this sponsorship pay off for Jeff Gordon? The key is to emphasize that many products in which DuPont is an ingredient brand are bought by NASCAR fans. (Remember this is a more upscale group than in the past). Ask students to think about whether the following products would make good sponsors for NASCAR and discuss why? Candy such as Skittles (is a NASCAR sponsor), Prestone (is a NASCAR sponsor), Lee Dungarees (not a NASCAR sponsor), Rolex or Elgin (not NASCAR sponsors), Honda (not a sponsor). Discuss the Barbie doll? Does this make sense for NASCAR? What's the goal of Mattel who makes the Barbie doll or NASCAR is having such a product?

This is all a lead-up to the question of a hotel chain that NASCAR can affiliate with. There are many possibilities. Maybe the hotel question could be assigned as a paper to be reported on at the next class after the rest of the licensing/sponsorship questions above have been discussed in class. The hotel chain must have positive brand associations, be able to meet a variety of needs and market segments and most importantly, it must be one of the top hotels in the industry and have a plan for marketing NASCAR through the hotel. The last (marketing plan) is crucial.

Computer Friendly Stuff, Case 6:
No Title Given on Video

Should Accompany Chapter 18 of Solomon/Stuart

Summary:

Content of Video: This video focuses on the use of personal selling for Computer Friendly Stuff. Three topics are covered. The first is why sales reps are needed; how to obtain reps; how to pay reps; the benefits/disadvantages of reps; how to motivate them and the need for reps during difficult negotiations.

Why are reps needed? Chris explains that although they had been somewhat successful, what really accelerated their sales was the hiring of sales reps. He gives an example of a rep who was able to obtain a $21,000 order from a retail chain that CFS had unsuccessfully courted. The reason? The rep already had a relationship. One hires reps to get *access* to their accounts.

How to obtain reps? Initially, CFS tried to obtain the services of sales reps by sending samples to reps who advertised in the back pages of trade show magazines, but they were unsuccessful. Finally, they were able to obtain the services of Joel Wildman, a veteran toy buyer and rep when Joel and his son discovered Computer Bugs at a trade show. CFS immediately hired Joel who brought three reps with him. Through him as their sales manager, they have expanded their sales network to 32 reps who sell to the toys, gift and computer markets.

How to pay reps? For a small, start-up firm like CFS without many funds, the choice of how to pay reps is simple. One uses commissions of, in this case, 5 to 10% to pay for this access to customers. But larger, well-established firms use their sales force to service their accounts and pays them a salary with smaller commissions of 1 to 2%. These larger firms expect their marketing department to promote their new products and they use the sales force in a facilitating role.

Benefits/Disadvantages of using reps? Benefit: Because reps spread their costs over multiple lines, a firm such as CFS has lower selling costs. Disadvantage: Because reps carry multiple lines, CFS product does not get as much push from the salesman as it would if the rep only carried CFS products.

How to motivate reps? Generally, commissions help to motivate reps, but Joel also sends them press kits and samples along with a constant flow of information that includes such things as success stories, special offers and general updates.

Chris poses the situation of when motivation doesn't work—a free lance rep who is not selling. The solution? Fire him because this is an unpleasant situation for everyone.

Need for reps during difficult negotiations? Chris illustrates the need for reps to handle negotiations by posing a situation in which the buyer asks for a better wholesale price, but offers to advertise the product in their catalogue mailed to 2,000,000 households. But they want to split the advertising costs by $3,000. They also offer CFS the option of ideal placement such as end-of-aisle or by-the-cash register for two weeks during Christmas for a mere $2,000. The chain also wants to pay in 60 days which means CFS must incur production costs, but wait 60 days for payment. AND they want the order on consignment which means that they return any unsold merchandise. Last they do not want to pay any shipping charges. As Chris asks, "Confusing?" "Unfair?" Absolutely, and that is why reps who are accustomed to this kind of negotiating are necessary to close the deal in CFS best interests.

Description of Video: This video features Chris Cole, CEO of CFS, sitting with a display of CFS plush toys and talking about selling. There are film clips of Joel Wildman and his son and one of their New York sales reps inserted to reinforce specific points.

Teaching Tips: This video relates to the section on personal selling in chapter 18. It is especially good for discussing the concepts of push and pull. In the video, Chris contrasts the situation of small and large firms and how they use their sales force. After showing the video, the discussion might begin with why and how CFS and large firms use their sales forces. Ask the students what is the relationship between this and push and pull. They should easily be able to relate the CFS uses a push strategy and larger firms a pull strategy. The impact of these different strategies (push vs. pull) can then be discussed in terms of the need for reps (large firms are well-known and have easier access) and how the reps are used (for access and selling by CFS and for servicing by large firms). Because the sales effort is greater for reps from small firms, they need higher pay (commissions) and more motivation. Because large firms have greater power vis-à-vis the buyer, they can demand better terms; whereas CFS needs to have a skillful rep to negotiate for them.

Personal Selling with Kathleen Carroll Mullen of General Electric

Should Accompany Chapter 18 of Solomon/Stuart

Summary:

Content of Video: This video focuses on one salesperson in GE's electrical products division. It gives her background (degree in mechanical engineering), probes why she likes her job (the variety), what she thinks is important (knowing the customer very well and anticipating their next requests) and the importance of building a relationship with the customer.

Through on-screen statement, the video defines personal selling, places it in the promotional mix, and defines two types of selling (transactional and relationship). It also describes the Request for Quote (RFQ) process and why a good sales person works with customers to anticipate RFQs. It also stresses that it takes a team to put together proposals for big bids. The salesperson must meet with the customers' technical people to understand the technical specs of the project, with their own production people to understand what it will require to meet the bid and with the marketing people to determine pricing.

The video describes a situation when Carroll Mullen was a trainee and received a RFQ from an unknown company. At the end of the RFQ, the purchaser asked to learn more about GE and what it could do for them. Because of the effort involved in putting together a large bid and because the company was not one of the Fortune 100 firms that GE was targeting, management did not encourage Carroll, but she pursued it anyway. The result was an initial sale of $50,000, but through the relationship established, over $130 million has been sold to the firm and the account is still growing. This illustrates the importance of relationships.

Finally, it specifies that making a proposal or presentation and supplying a bid does not close the sale. Closing the sale requires that you know when the customer is ready to close. If you close before they are ready, you may get the initial sale, but you won't get repeat sales which is the basis of relationship selling.

At the end, Carroll describes the joy of getting a sale. She says "you win really, really big or you can lose really, really big."

Description of Video: This video consists of shots of Carroll Mullen in plants, in her office, outside GE facilities, driving her car, talking to company personnel and making a presentation as well as interviews with her.

Teaching Tips: This video fits with the personal selling section of Chapter 18. It illustrates the types of selling and the selling process very well. It acquaints students with what a sales person does and it may help to eliminate or change negative impressions that students may have of selling.

Discuss personal selling before showing the video and afterwards ask students if the video changed their perception of selling. Did it deepen their understanding of selling? The emphasis on a team to put together a bid may be intriguing to them as they may have thought of this as a lonely occupation.

Watson Pharmaceuticals Part II

Should Accompany Chapter 12 of Solomon/Stuart

Summary:

Content of Video: In this video, Watson Pharmaceuticals personnel discuss pricing of their generic products. Pricing of generics depends on speed to market, the level of competition from other generics, the use of non-price marketing weapons, the efforts of the pharmacist, the actions of consumers and the setting of pricing objectives by the firm.

Pricing depends on whether the generic is the first, second or third to market. When the branded drug goes off patent, the first generic to the market will usually capture 40 to 50% of sales and be priced at 60 to 70% of the branded drug's price. The second generic can only compete on price so its price is usually 10% less than the first generic. Distributors, however, are likely to stick with the first generic because they have had it approved and it's in their pipelines. It's too difficult to switch.

When the second generic comes along, pharmacists will usually ask the manufacturer of the first generic for a similar price decrease. Most often the first will reduce their price because otherwise the second generic manufacturer will continue to reduce price until profits are destroyed.

The price of the branded product is not reduced because the manufacturer can count on 15 to 20% of the market remaining loyal to the brand.

Generics usually compete on price because there are relatively few other ways for them to compete. They may offer extra services, give a discount if the distributor pays more quickly or they may focus on a special area. Watson focuses on pain management by making 6 to 7 analgesic products. Frequently distributors want to buy all products in a certain area from one distributor. This enables Watson to bundle their products.

The pharmacist is key in moving generics. Even if a physician has written a prescription for a branded drug, the pharmacist can call him/her and ask to use the generic. Usually because of the price reduction to the consumer, the physician agrees. This is a win-win-win situation as the customer gets a lower price, the pharmacist gets a higher markup and Watson gets increased sales.

Before engaging in any project, Watson carefully examines the expected return on investment and sets clear pricing objectives. These have to be reviewed over time because of new product introductions, revisions of existing products, competitive changes, changes in the PLC, competitor price changes, and rising or falling costs.

Description of the Video: This video is a set of interviews with Brian J. Smith, VP of marketing and Edward F. Tykot, Product Manager. There are many scenes of pharmaceutical production and factory personnel between and over interviews.

Teaching Tips: The pharmaceutical industry is a good one to discuss the differences between price and non-price competition. Discuss these two concepts in class and point out that most manufacturers would like to be in a non-price competitive situation.

Show the video and afterwards ask students when non-price and price competition occur in this industry. Obviously non-price competition occurs when branded drugs are protected by the legal environment (patents). When these expire, one would expect price competition to occur, but it may not—at least no to the extent one would expect.

Ask students whether they think the industry becomes price competitive when patents expire. Ask why or why not? Price competition is not so severe because a firm can speed the product to market. If they are the first to market, they have a hold on the market. After that, their actions really determine how much price competition occurs in the industry.

To draw out the factors that help to reduce price competition in this industry ask students a series of questions taken from Chapter 12.

1. How the elements of place and product affect price?
2. How do profit objectives affect pricing in this industry?
3. How do competitive actions affect pricing?
4. How flexible are pricing objectives and why?
5. Is demand ever inelastic? Due to what marketing mix element?
6. How might inflation or recession affect the demand for generics?